KU-268-833

Modern Economics
An Introduction for Business and
Professional Students

MODERN ECONOMICS

An Introduction for Business and
Professional Students

FIFTH EDITION

Jack Harvey
B.Sc. (Econ.), Dip. Ed. (Oxford)

MACMILLAN
EDUCATION

Jack Harvey 1969, 1974, 1977, 1983, 1988

All rights reserved. No reproduction, copy or transmission
of this publication may be made without written permission.

No paragraph of this publication may be reproduced, copied
or transmitted save with written permission or in accordance
with the provisions of the Copyright Act 1956 (as amended),
or under the terms of any licence permitting limited copying
issued by the Copyright Licensing Agency, 33–4 Alfred Place,
London WC1E 7DP.

Any person who does any unauthorised act in relation to
this publication may be liable to criminal prosecution and
civil claims for damages.

First edition 1969
Reprinted 1970 (twice), 1971 (twice), 1972, 1973 (twice), 1974
Second edition 1974
Reprinted 1975, 1976
This edition 1977
Reprinted 1978 (twice), 1979, 1982
Fourth edition 1983
Reprinted 1985, 1986, 1987
Fifth edition 1988

Published by
MACMILLAN EDUCATION LTD
Houndmills, Basingstoke, Hampshire RG21 2XS
and London
Companies and representatives
throughout the world

Printed in Hong Kong

British Library Cataloguing in Publication Data
Harvey, Jack
Modern economics : an introduction for
business and professional students.—
5th ed.
1. Economics
I. Title
330 DN HB171
ISBN 0–333–46665–9 (hardcover)
ISBN 0–333–46666–7 (paperback)

Contents

III   HOW TO PRODUCE – THE THEORY OF PRODUCTION

IV   FOR WHOM? HOW THE FACTORS OF
PRODUCTION ARE REWARDED –
THE THEORY OF DISTRIBUTION

V MONEY AND FINANCIAL INSTITUTIONS

Preface to the First Edition

The primary aim of this textbook is to meet the needs of students taking economics as part of their professional examinations in banking, company-secretaryship, accountancy, insurance, surveying, transport, hospital administration, business studies and commerce. It provides, too, a useful groundwork in economics for GCE 'A' Level and degree and CNAA courses.

But its starting-point is not economics as an examination subject. The author's experience as an examiner has convinced him that the standard of attainment will improve only if the student's approach is on the right lines. Unfortunately, many students still seem to think that their Examining Board includes economics as part of the course only out of sheer cussedness. Hence preparation consists mostly of dull memorisation of facts in the hope that this will scrape the necessary pass.

This book can claim to deal with 'modern economics' in two senses. First, it presents economics as a method of thought, not a mere body of knowledge. It explains simple economic analysis and shows how it can be applied both to the problems of everyday life and to the particular decisions of the professional man. Instead of being merely a dull grind, economics is shown to be as relevant vocationally as other course subjects. In this way it is hoped to change the motivation of the student, for only by such an approach will he gain any value from his study.

Second, the book recognises that modern economics is increasingly concerned with the difficulties of maintaining full employment, a stable level of prices, a steady rate of growth, balance-of-payments equilibrium, etc. It is therefore divided almost equally between a study of the determination of prices in individual markets and of the factors which govern the level of activity as a whole.

In deciding what to include, the author has had two basic considerations – the requirements of the examination syllabus and the level of difficulty with which a student, often studying part-time and without the help of a tutor, can be expected to cope. The first presents few problems, for the syllabuses of the various Examining Boards are fairly similar in their requirements. Thus elementary analysis is supplemented by some description of the economy and its institutions. The second lies far more within the discretion of the author. Here the basis of selection has been 'when in doubt, leave out'. The dominant aim is that the student should understand, and be able to apply competently, simple basic concepts rather than be confused with half-digested advanced refinements.

Numerous diagrams have been included. Not only do these aid learning by the impact of the visual impression, but they are a neat form of expressing relationships. Moreover, in order to assist reading and note-taking, the text is, wherever possible, enumerated under headings and sub-headings.

Although the book is complete in itself, there is a *Study Guide and Workbook* to accompany it. This consists of notes on the salient points of the text, simple exercises in the use of diagrams and in the application of principles, and quiz and multiple-choice questions to concentrate the student's attention on the essential groundwork. There is also a selection of questions taken from past examination papers of the various examining bodies.

Some apology may be due to students who are already familiar with my *Elementary Economics* or *Intermediate Economics*. This books tends to come half-way between, but borrows from each where it is felt that little improvement in exposition could be achieved by rewriting.

I would like to place on record my indebtedness to Mr. M. K. Johnson, Lecturer in Economics, Hatfield Polytechnic. Not only has he suggested many of the diagrams, but he has also been kind enough to read the typescript and to make many valuable comments.

1969   J.H.

Preface to the Fifth Edition

Facts have been brought up to date and the text revised to cover recent changes in institutions, the development of economic theory and the evolution of government policy over the last ten years. Thus topics dealt with more fully include: new sources of finance for small firms, privatisation, the Stock Exchange, stagflation, monetarism, supply-side economics, the EEC and the current economic problems of the UK and the government's approach to them.

However, theory is still kept as simple as possible. Thus the basic elements of Keynes's analysis of cyclical unemployment are retained, though reference is made to its weaknesses as revealed by experience.

The student's attention is drawn to the fact that there is an up-dated accompanying *Workbook* to consolidate understanding of basic principles.

J.H.

Guidance to the Student

The saying that 'a little practice is worth a lot of theory' is a dangerous half-truth. There is nothing so practical as sound theory. That is why this book is concerned mainly with simple economic theory. By applying it, the professional person can find the answer to many of the problems with which he or she is continually being confronted. 'Would it be wise to lend so large a sum to Farmer Giles in view of current government policy as regard subsidies to agriculture?' asks the bank manager. 'What effect will the construction of a motorway have on the value of different types of property in the vicinity?' asks the surveyor, valuer and estate agent. 'Is the government likely to increase the rate of income tax or capital gains tax in the next budget?' asks the accountant. 'How best can the liquid assets of the company be invested?' asks the company secretary. And so on.

You are urged to study economics, therefore, not merely to pass an examination, but because it will make you a better professional person. Indeed, if you approach it in this way, the examination will take care of itself.

But you must study systematically and thoroughly. To this end you are advised to proceed as follows:
1. Read through the whole book quickly.
2. Read the *Study Guide* to the particular chapter.
3. Study each chapter carefully in the textbook. Underline important points, and try to find illustrations of these points from your own particular professional experience. Be sure that you *understand* each stage in the argument before proceeding to the next. At times progress may appear slow, but there are no short cuts. Theory cannot be memorised.
4. Write notes covering the chapter material, tabulating points and linking them in diagrams wherever possible. Here the *Student's Notebook for Modern Economics* should save time. Such notes will give precision to

your ideas, consolidate your understanding, and prove invaluable for examination revision.

5. Answer the questions in the *Workbook*. Check your answers with those given. Add to your notes where necessary.

6. Obtain practice in answering the type of question set by the appropriate examining body. Remember that even the simplest-looking question usually requires the statement and application of a fundamental principle.

Part I

Introduction

1 What Economics is about

1.1 The Economic Problem

Wants and Limited Means

'You must cut your coat according to your cloth.' 'You can't get a quart out of a pint pot.' 'You can't make a silk purse out of a sow's ear.' How many of our everyday sayings draw attention to the fact that, in comparison with all the things we want, our means of satisfying those wants are quite inadequate! Just think of the extra things we could buy if our incomes were larger – new clothes, new furniture, a better car, a video-recorder, a cine-camera. The list has no end, for, even if these wants were satisfied, new wants would arise.

This, then, is the 'economic problem' – unlimited wants, very limited means. And we can never completely overcome the difficulty. But what we can do is to make the most of what we have. In other words, we *economise*.

In order to see more clearly what is meant by 'economising', we can study the spending decisions of a housewife. Indeed, this illustration is more appropriate than it may seem at first sight, for 'economics' is derived from a Greek word meaning 'the management of a household'.

Our housewife's task is to make her fixed housekeeping allowance 'go as far as possible'; in other words, from limited resources she seeks to obtain the maximum satisfaction for the family. Certain goods – those she regards as necessities, such as bread, milk, tea and butter – are purchased in regular quantities almost by habit; but this does not mean that she would not vary her spending on them were there to be any significant change in their prices. Nevertheless, what really lies behind her spending decisions can best be seen if we concentrate on those goods to which she gives frequent consideration. As our housewife walks past the shop windows in the High Street, a hundred and one different goods compete for the money in her purse. Should she buy beef or chicken for the Sunday dinner? Peas

3

would be nice – but they are still so dear that cabbage will have to do for one more week. But how everybody would love new potatoes! And they've gone down 2p a pound since last week! Yes, she will buy new potatoes instead of old. And so our capable housewife goes on, comparing the prices of different goods and asking herself whether the pleasure her family will obtain from them will be worth their cost – the inroads they make on her limited housekeeping allowance.

But it is not only the housewife who has to economise. How the schoolboy schemes to get the most out of his pocket-money! And the businessman faces the same problems in running his factory. Should he produce this good or that, or some of both? How many of each good? Should he employ extra labourers or would it be better to install a machine to do the work? Would it be more profitable to hire transport or to buy his own lorry? And so on.

Turn to the newspaper any morning, and it soon becomes obvious how often the government, too, is forced to choose as it plans the broad lines upon which the economy shall develop. More offices, new roads, and better hospitals – all are competing for the materials and capital used by the construction industry. Extra houses, new factory sites, and conservation areas – all are claiming a share of the limited land available. In these and many other instances, the government has the task of making the most of the nation's resources.

Opportunity Cost

Thus we see that economics is really concerned with the problem of choice – the decisions forced upon us by the smallness of our resources compared with our wants (Figure 1.1). And, as we choose, so we have to sacrifice. If the newspaper boy spends his Christmas tips on a bicycle, then it is likely that he will have to go without the air rifle that he also wanted. In deciding to work overtime on a Saturday afternoon, a worker forgoes leisure time and the football match he would otherwise have watched. When the farmer sows a field with wheat, he accepts that he loses the barley it could have grown. And so with the nation. If extra materials and capital are required to accelerate the building of houses, roads and hospitals, then there will be less left for producing offices, power stations, sport centres, and so on. In all walks of life, having 'this' means going without 'that'. We therefore speak of 'opportunity cost' – the cost of something in terms of alternatives forgone (more accurately, in terms of the *best* alternative sacrificed).

In practice, economising is not so much a complete rejection of one good in favour of another, but rather deciding whether to have a little bit more

FIGURE 1.1
The Economic Problem

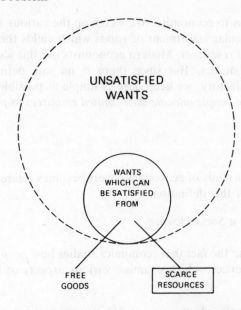

of one and not quite so much of another. It is principally, as we shall see in Chapter 5, an adjustment at the margin.

'Free' and 'Scarce' Goods

Few goods are so plentiful that nobody will give anything for them. Air, perhaps, is one of the few exceptions. Occasionally, too, there is such an abundant apple harvest that a farmer says 'help yourself'. Such goods are termed 'free' goods. Usually, goods are 'scarce' – they can be obtained only by going without something else. With such goods we have to economise, and so they are often referred to as 'economic goods'. It is worth noting, however, that over time there is no hard-and-fast dividing-line between economic and non-economic goods. Desert wastes can be transformed into rich agricultural land by irrigation; coal-mines are left derelict as new fuels are developed. Scarcity is relative to demand.

In future when we speak of 'goods' we shall be referring to economic goods, including, without further distinction, both commodities and services.

1.2 The Scope of Economics

Definition of Economics

Scarcity forces us to economise. We weigh up the various alternatives and select that particular assortment of goods which yields the highest return from our limited resources. Modern economists use this idea to define the scope of their studies. But since there is no one definition which is completely satisfactory, we keep ours as simple as possible. *Economics is the study of how people allocate their limited resources to provide for their wants.*

Amplification

The field which a study of economics covers becomes clearer if we examine certain points of this definition.

1. Economics is a Social Science

This follows from the fact that economics studies how *people act* (compare the physical sciences, which examine various aspects of man's environment).

2. Economics is Closely Concerned with the Findings of Other Sciences

Because economics studies human behaviour, it must, in reaching conclusions, refer to other branches of study. The alternative, advocated by some economists, of restricting economics to pure scientific analysis, curtails its usefulness. Thus most people would consider that the economist should have something to say on the question 'Should income tax be made more progressive?' But the reply would have to be along the following lines: 'The tax yield would almost certainly increase; but higher-income groups might not work so hard. While I can suggest theoretical reasons for this, you should also consider what the psychologist has to say. Furthermore, the pattern of consumption may change as the rich have less income to spend. For possible social effects, consult the sociologist. Finally, it will also help in making incomes more equal. That concerns me in that it may increase the proportion of total income spent – but ethics and politics have most weight in deciding whether greater equality of incomes is desirable.'

3. Economics Selects a Particular Aspect of Human Behaviour

But, although economics is closely connected with such social sciences as ethics, politics, sociology, psychology and anthropology, it is distinguished from them by its concentration on one particular aspect of human behaviour – choosing between alternatives in order to obtain the maximum satisfaction from limited resources. This modern, narrower approach is an improvement on Professor Alfred Marshall's definition – 'a study of mankind in the ordinary business of life' – because this, as it stands, would embrace all forms of human activity.

In effect, the economist limits the study by selecting four fundamental characteristics of human existence and investigating what happens when they are all found together, as they usually are. First, the ends of human beings are without limit. Second, those ends are of varying importance. Third, the means available for achieving those ends – human time and energy and material resources – are limited. Fourth, the means can be used in many different ways: that is, they can produce many different goods.

But no one characteristic *by itself* is necessarily of interest to the economist. If, for instance, you have two wants and you cannot choose between them, you are between the devil and the deep blue sea, and you will never get as far as the problem of allocating resources between them. Similarly, 'free' goods are of no interest to the economist since resources do not have to be allocated to obtain them. Nor is the mere scarcity of means necessarily of significance. Where resources can be used only in one way, e.g. lichen-bearing volcanic land in Iceland for rearing sheep, they do not, although scarce, have to be 'economised'. Using such land for sheep does not mean that the owner has less of other things. Its use therefore gives rise to no problems, and the economist is interested only in the relatively minor point of determining the earnings of such land. Only when all four characteristics are found together does an economic problem arise.

4. Economics Accepts Ends as Given

The economist is not concerned with the ends as such – why, for instance, people prefer milk to wine or beef to lamb. Nor must he or she pass judgement on those ends on *moral* grounds. That is the task of ethics rather than of economics. Ends must be accepted as they are.

But although wants are given, the economist must point out the full cost of achieving them. Individual ends have economic implications for the ends of society as a whole. A man, for instance, may decide that he wants to get drunk every day. Here the economist must point out the full cost of this end – the cost to the man of getting drunk, plus the cost to society if he cannot work the next morning or eventually becomes a charge on the National Health Service as an alcoholic.

5. Economics Concentrates in Practice on Market Phenomena

The scope of economics covers all circumstances in which man is forced to choose because of limited means. It includes, therefore, both the decisions made by Robinson Crusoe on his desert island and those of consumers and producers in a modern society where choice involves exchange.

In practice, however, the economist prefers to limit investigation to those goods and services which are exchanged against money. Since all these have a 'price' it is possible to make use of exact measurement and total dissimilar goods in terms of the common standard.

Nevertheless, as pointed out above, the economist must be careful to include any social costs or social benefits which are not allowed for by an individual in making a decision. Or, if the project is so large that it is likely to have external effects elsewhere, for example the proposed third London airport, a cost–benefit analysis may have to be used to cover these full effects. Moreover, since the economist can only quantify in terms of money, some costs and benefits which are not exchanged directly in a market, e.g. environmental costs and benefits, have to be given 'shadow prices'.

6. Economics Covers the Distribution of Goods as well as their Consumption and Production

Since the economist is concerned with how people provide for their wants, the investigation of the production of goods must be followed by an examination of how those goods are distributed among the various members of society. The economic effects of any redistribution of goods by the government, e.g. on incentives to produce, must also be studied.

To sum up, the economist is not interested in ends. Nor is the economist concerned directly about the physical aspects of the limited means – the mechanical principles of the plough, the chemical properties of the soil or the biological characteristics of the seed. Both ends and resources are accepted as given. The subject of study is how men mobilise these resources to achieve their ends and how efficient are the methods which they choose.

1.3 The Methods of the Economist

The Object of Study

It is possible to study economics for the pleasure it yields as an intellectual discipline; people solve mathematical problems for this reason. But the great economists have pursued their study chiefly because it can benefit mankind. The investigation of an economic system is necessary to see how and where it can be improved – how more wants can be satisfied with the given resources. Hence the economist endeavours to solve problems as scientifically as possible and then applies the results to secure increased welfare in the real world. For example, by studying how the price system works in theoretical conditions, it is possible to suggest how it can be made to work better in real life.

The Difficulties

But, in pursuing such studies, economists face three major difficulties:

1. Economists Cannot Experiment

The task of a science is to formulate laws describing what will happen when there is a change in a given set of circumstances. The physicist and chemist can conduct their investigations by experimenting under controlled conditions in a laboratory. But because economists are dealing with human behaviour rather than with physical properties, these means are denied them:

(*a*) Since facts concerning people are difficult to ascertain, they can never be quite sure of the initial position.

(*b*) It is impossible to isolate a group of consumers or business people in a test-tube to see how they would react to a given change. The most the economist can usually do as regards consumers' behaviour, for instance, is to take a sample survey.

(*c*) The economy is subject to continuous change, and so conditions cannot be held constant while the effect of one particular measure is observed.

(*d*) Because the economy is so complex, no body of economists could follow through all the results of any given change.

(*e*) Any measurements are only approximate, and even so take time to collect.

Because of these difficulties, economists can only be approximate in their investigations in real life. Nevertheless, the information available is increasing and becoming more precise, e.g. through market research and government statistical enquiries. Thus economists' predictions are likely to gain in accuracy.

2. Economic Studies are Rarely Distinct From Those of Other Sciences

Even though the economist may derive propositions which could have a bearing on policy, their usefulness may be restricted until they are combined with the findings of other sciences (see. p.6). Moreover, when state planning of the economy increases, the area over which economics overlaps with politics also increases.

3. Economists Cannot Directly Measure Welfare

The economist who is concerned with social welfare must recognise that in the last resort people do not want the goods themselves but simply the satisfaction they obtain when consuming those goods. But while goods can be measured either in quantity or money value, it is quite impossible to measure satisfaction. It is probable, for instance, that a low-income worker derives more enjoyment from £50 spent on a holiday at Brighton than a millionaire does from £50 spent on a dinner. But we can never be sure – simply because satisfaction, like pain, is a personal feeling which cannot be measured objectively.

So the economist, using the best approximation, works on the principle that, because two loaves are better than one, an increase in goods represents an increase in welfare. Even so, he cannot measure all goods. If he gives a value to the vegetables grown in gardens or to do-it-yourself repairs to cars, should he not logically include also something for house-wives' cleaning and cooking services? Because it is impossible to know where to draw the line, the economist simplifies matters by confining attention to those goods which are exchanged against money (see p.297).

The Scientific Approach

In spite of the above difficulties, economics can still claim to be a science. It is not the facts of a subject but how it is studied that makes a science. Economics, although it studies a particular aspect of human behaviour, adopts scientific methods.

In the first place, it does not attempt to set out criteria for determining what is good or bad, what ought or what ought not to be – any more than physics attempts to say that liquids are 'better' than solids. It is concerned only with objective or positive statements – those which can be tested by an appeal to facts, even though those facts have not yet been col-lected – and with the consequences of certain actions. As soon as econom-ists say what ought or ought not to be, they introduce subjective views or, as they are more usually described, 'normative statements' or 'value judgements'. That is why, for instance, the economist must accept ends as given, expressing no opinion as to whether those ends are 'good' or 'bad'.

Second, the study of economics has a particular object in view – the establishment of principles, propositions, theories or generalisations expressing fundamental relationships within the subject-matter. In this it goes beyond *descriptive economics*, which concentrates on a mere description of an economy – its institutions (firms, banks, government organisations, etc.), its population, its system of taxation, and so on. But studies ended there could hardly be termed 'scientific'. While descriptive economics is desirable, indeed necessary, it merely describes the mechanism. What we really want to know is how the mechanism operates.

That is the task of *analytical economics*, which sets out to establish general principles about the way in which an economic system works. In discovering these principles, economics makes use of the methods of other sciences. These methods are: (1) induction, (2) deduction.

1. Induction

In the inductive approach, the economist observes facts, classifies those facts, and then tries to observe any causal relationship between them. For instance, the economist may discover that the price of eggs falls in the spring. This would be connected with the increase in the supply of eggs at that time of the year, and from this a generalisation can be established that an increase in supply, other things being equal, leads to a fall in price.

The weakness of the inductive approach is that the scientist can never be sure that the principles established are 100 per cent foolproof. Hence, whenever possible, he or she will endeavour to substantiate by deduction what has been discovered by induction.

2. Deduction

In economics, it is the deductive method of establishing a theory which is used the most. The economist builds a 'model', selecting what he considers are the most relevant variables in the situation being studied, and assumes that other variables will be constant in their behaviour. Indeed, he often goes further, assuming that all variables are constant except one. The economist can now concentrate on what is likely to happen when this variable changes. Then, by a process of logical reasoning, propositions are derived. In more detail, the sequence is:

(*a*) The economic phenomenon to be explained is selected. Of course, if the analysis is to be useful, the problem must be of practical significance.

(*b*) The initial assumptions (frequently referred to as 'postulates') are made. These should be as close to reality as possible, and this is where descriptive economics can be very helpful. But, although we are concerned with human behaviour, realistic assumptions are not impossible. In the main we are interested in market, not individual, reactions. Dealing in large numbers means that patterns of behaviour emerge, and we can thus think in terms of an 'average economic individual'. Thus it is quite reasonable to assume that, in disposing of personal income, this average consumer will act rationally, seeking to obtain maximum satisfaction from it.

Of course, we have to simplify initially, confining ourselves to broad assumptions, from which we can obtain only broad generalisations. Later the assumptions can be changed according to particular circumstances, and the conclusions modified accordingly.

(c) Logical reasoning establishes propositions or hypotheses from the assumptions of the model. Let us take a simple example. We wish to discover what price will prevail in a market. We make three assumptions: (i) a high degree of competition, on the basis of price, among buyers and among sellers, and between buyers and sellers; (ii) more will be demanded the lower the price; (iii) more will be supplied the higher the price.

Demand and supply thus move in opposite directions for a given change in price. The conclusion we come to is that the price of the good will settle where the amount supplied equals the amount demanded. Any other price will not be a settled price. If it is above, there will be more offered for sale than is demanded. Stocks will pile up, and some suppliers will lower their prices. As the price falls, so more will be demanded, and this will go on until demand equals supply. Similarly, when the price is below that where demand equals supply, shortages lead buyers to offer higher prices. As the price rises, so more will be supplied, and this goes on until demand equals supply (see p.41). We have thus built up a model showing how price is determined in a market – a very useful piece of economic theory.

By modifying the assumptions we can make the model closer to real life or show how changes in the economic system work. For instance, let us make the assumption that, as a result of an advertising campaign, people's tastes change, so that they want more of the good at the market price than formerly. The economist describes this by saying that the conditions of demand have changed, and that demand has increased (see p.36). At the original price, demand now exceeds supply. As before, this will cause the price to rise and supply to expand until a new price is arrived at where once more demand and supply are equal.

(d) Propositions derived by deduction are tested by observed data. If actual events conform to the predictions made, our hypothesis can be termed a theory. But theories are never proved once and for all. Out of hundreds of accurate predictions, one or two cases may occur which appear to refute the theory. The theory may then have to be qualified, perhaps being reformulated at a lower level of generality. The aim must be to try to refute a theory by finding cases which disagree with it, rather than to look for facts which 'fit the theory'. If the theory is refuted by the facts again and again, then it should be discarded altogether and another constructed. The process of deduction may have been wrong, or the wrong assumptions may have been made. The continual construction, testing, refutation and reformulation of theories gradually improves their generality.

If the principles established are not disproved by such testing, they can be used to predict what will happen in particular instances, for they show how the different parts of a system are related to one another. It should be noted, however, that such forecasts are not unconditional statements of what *will* occur. The nature of an economic proposition is simply of the form '*if* this occurs, *then* such and such will result'. For example, *if* demand increases, *then* other things being equal, price will rise (see p.42). When we apply general principles to particular cases, we are in the realm of what is often called *applied economics*.

It is this power to predict which enables firms (including professional people) and governments to plan with a reasonable degree of accuracy. The theory of price, for instance, would enable a building firm to make some forecast of the effect of an increase in the demand for houses on bricklayers' wages. Or, if there were widespread unemployment in the economy, a knowledge of the principles determining the level of activity could suggest appropriate measures to reduce it.

1.4 Economic Theory and Policy

But why, it might be asked, if propositions have been arrived at scientifically, should economists appear to disagree so often? Take the statement, 'Britain must remain in the European Economic Community (EEC) because it will lead to a faster rate of economic growth.' Why might economists disagree on this?

1. They May Not Agree on the Facts

Can we be certain that Britain's rate of economic growth has accelerated since she joined the EEC? Facts are deficient, for example, calculations of Gross National Product (GNP) over time are not unambiguous (see pp.305–7).

2. They Disagree on the Causal Connection

Even if a faster rate of economic growth has been achieved since joining the EEC, can we be sure that membership is the cause of this increase? There may be more than one explanation, e.g. the discovery of North Sea oil or increased capital investment in agriculture and industry. It may be difficult to decide which explanation fits the facts best.

3. The Statement Really Rests on a Value Judgement – That Economic Growth is a Good Thing

Some economists might consider that other objectives – more leisure, less worry, the avoidance of friction through competition, and so on – are in a fairly affluent society more desirable.

4. They May Unconsciously Let Individual Bias Creep into their Analysis and Interpretation of the Facts

While, as scientists, economists try to be as objective as possible, they are often examining subjects upon which they have strong personal feelings. Thus an economist who is an ardent supporter of Anglo-American relationships may unconsciously fail to give full weight to evidence supporting an increase in the growth rate of the EEC countries.

But this does not mean that the economist is without value. If, for instance, he is employed in a business enterprise, the scope of his work is fairly well defined – to promote the success of the business in terms of profits.

As regards government policy, however, the advice the economist can give may be less definite. In any case, the final decision will usually rest on the judgement of the politician. For one thing, a government is seldom faced with a simple choice, since ends are usually a compromise between alternatives. The first task of the economist is to point out any inconsistency between aims. For instance, in certain circumstances, the aim of economic expansion may conflict with the aim of balance-of-payments equilibrium.

Second, the economist can show the full implications of a particular policy. For instance, if a very high level of employment is the aim, then he should point out that this could make it more difficult to maintain a steady price level.

Third, he may be able to recommend more economic ways of achieving a given end. This is possible because, although ends may be given, there are economic and non-economic means of achieving those ends. Is it better, for instance, to obtain food supplies by importing from abroad or by home production?

2 Methods of Allocating Resources

2.1 The Questions that have to be Answered

How We 'Economise'

As we have seen, we respond to the economic problem by 'economising'.

(*a*) Wants are placed in some order of importance, and the more important are satisfied first. Of course, some wants can be satisfied more easily than others because some goods take less of the scarce means of production than other goods. Allowance must be made for this. For example, if a person wants a car only twice as much as he wants a motor-cycle, but its real cost (that is, in terms of the resources used) is eight times as much, then probably he will have to be content with the motor-cycle and his want for the car must go unsatisfied.

(b) Resources are used as effectively as possible, without waste.

Waste occurs when resources stand idle. If, for instance, workers are unemployed, we are not making full use of scarce labour. The same applies when land and machinery stand idle, unless the cost of using them is greater than the value of what they can produce.

Second, waste occurs if resources are employed to make things which are not really wanted. Relating production to wants has become more dificult in the modern, complex economic organisation. The peasant farmer of the Middle Ages produced to satisfy the wants of his family, and he could allocate his resources between wheat, rye, barley, meat, etc., according to their needs. But today people specialise in the work they do. Each day, the bank manager, the bus conductor, the tinker, the tailor, the soldier and sailor all go about their respective tasks. Other people are baking bread, growing potatoes, bringing milk to town. Thus our system must now provide answers to a multitude of questions. How many suits shall the tailor make? Have we got the right number of bank managers? How much bread shall the baker bake? How much milk shall the farmer send to town?

15

If too much bread is baked, it will go stale; if too much milk is sent to town, the surplus will go sour, and it would have been better if the farmer had turned it into cheese. Over-production involves waste, and waste means that the resources could have been used to satisfy some of our other 'wants'. Clearly, then, any organisation of production requires a method of estimating the size of wants.

Third, waste occurs if the organisation of production is faulty. This takes place, for instance, when many small firms are producing goods which could be made by a few large firms using fewer resources. It happens, too, when the layout of the factory is such that workers have to spend unnecessary time in passing from one particular machine to another. Likewise the organisation may be defective because processes are not fully integrated – as occurs when steel ingots are allowed to cool before being rolled into steel sheets. Or it may be that the centre of production was badly chosen. If a blast furnace, for instance, were situated without regard to its accessibility to supplies of iron ore, coke and limestone, waste would result, because extra resources are needed to transport those materials. Finally, for full efficiency, the organisation of production must be continually revised to allow for new techniques, new processes and new power supplies.

It follows, therefore, that any system which is adopted for solving the economic problem must answer the following questions:

1. What assortment of goods will yield the greatest possible satisfaction?
2. How, out of the various alternatives, do we employ our limited resources to produce this assortment as efficiently as possible?
3. Who are to enjoy the goods which are produced?

In short, the questions are: What? How? For whom? These are the divisions of consumption, production and distribution of the old classical economists.

Alternative Economic Systems

Broadly speaking, there are two distinct methods by which these questions are answered. Either the decisions can be made by an overriding authority, such as the state, in what is usually referred to as a 'command economy'; or they can follow automatically from the free operation of the price system motivated by private enterprise in a 'market economy'. Communist countries lean towards the first, and the Western world towards the second. But neither method by itself is completely satisfactory, and so all economies contain a mixture of both.

2.2 A Central Planning Authority: The Command Economy

Where there is an all-powerful planning authority, it estimates the assortment of goods which it considers people want and directs the means of production accordingly. It decides, too, the basis upon which the goods produced are distributed. Economic efficiency depends largely, therefore, on how accurately wants are estimated and resources allocated. Here we may mention four criticisms of the system.

First, ascertaining the satisfaction which individuals derive from consuming different goods is impossible. But a modified price system can be introduced to help, changes in prices signalling possible changes in wants.

Second, many officials are required to estimate wants and to direct resources to produce for them. In as much as such officials are avoidable in a private enterprise economy, they represent wasted resources, for they could be employed to satisfy more wants. Moreover, the use of officials may give rise to bureaucracy – excessive form-filling, an addiction to 'red tape', slowness in coming to a decision and an impersonal approach to consumers. At times, too, officialdom has been accompanied by corruption.

Third, even when wants have been decided upon, difficulties of co-ordination arise. On the one hand, wants have to be dovetailed and awarded priorities. On the other, resources have to be combined in the best proportions. Usually plans are co-ordinated through numerous committees, directed at the top by a central planning committee. Yet members of this committee would be primarily politicians with little experience of administration. And, even if they were able, they would still have to face the difficulties of managing a large organisation (see p.109).

Fourth, it is argued that state ownership of the factors of production, by lessening incentives, diminishes effort and initiative. Direction of labour may mean that persons are dissatisfied with their allotted jobs. Officials may follow cautious policies because they find it easier to earn 'brickbats' than 'bouquets' (see p.91). Thus it is possible that production would be lower than under private enterprise.

2.3 Private Enterprise: The Market Economy

Under private enterprise, the emphasis is laid on the freedom of the individual, both as a consumer and as the owner of a factor of production (usually labour).

As a consumer, wants are expressed through the price system. As the owner of a factor of production, he seeks to obtain as large a reward as possible. Where a good is relatively scarce, consumers 'bid' up its price.

This increases the earnings of factors and the profits of firms producing that good. As a result, factors are attracted into the industry, and supply increases in accordance with consumers' wishes. On the other hand, if consumers do not want a particular good, its price falls, producers make a loss, and factors leave the industry.

The price system therefore indicates the wishes of consumers (subject to the existing distribution of income) and allocates the community's productive resources accordingly (see Figure 2.1). There is no direction of labour; people are free to work wherever they choose. Efficiency is achieved simply through its effect on the size of private 'profit'. Furthermore, the rewards which the factors earn decide who shall obtain the goods produced, for such earnings are spent by their owners in the market.

In this way the price system acts, as it were, like a marvellous computer, registering people's preferences for different goods, transmitting these preferences to those responsible for producing the goods, and moving the factors to produce them. What is more, all this occurs without employing a host of officials.

FIGURE 2.1
The Price Mechanism under Private Enterprise

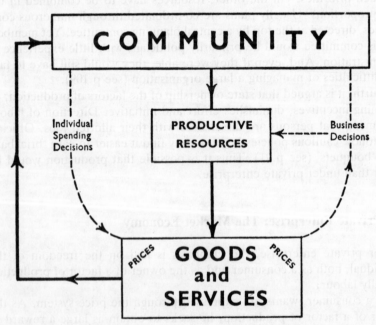

Unfortunately, in practice the price system does not produce entirely satisfactory results, nor does it work quite so smoothly as indicated above.

First, it is those consumers with the most money who exercise the greatest weight in spending. Thus resources may be devoted to producing luxuries for the rich to the exclusion of necessities for the poor. While this results from the unequal distribution of wealth rather than from the private enterprise system, it must be remembered that the latter tends to produce, and even to increase, such inequality.

Second, some vital services which are not marketable, e.g. defence, police and justice, would not be produced adequately by private enterprise. Indeed, in most advanced countries, the state now provides for what are considered to be basic needs – education, medical care, insurance against sickness, industrial accident, unemployment, etc.

Third, competition itself may sometimes lead to inefficiency. Small units may persist when co-ordination is vital to securing the advantages of large-scale production. Competitive advertising may waste resources. Uncertainty as to rivals' plans may hold back investment.

All the above defects can be avoided where the state decides what to produce. More working-class flats and fewer large mansions are built, nuclear weapons are produced as well as bowling-alleys, the wastes of competition do not arise.

Fourth, in practice, the competition upon which the efficiency of the capitalist system depends is liable to break down. An employer may be the *only* buyer of a certain type of labour in a locality. If so, he is in a strong position when fixing wage-rates with a number of independent and unorganised workers. Similarly, on the selling side, there may be only one seller because competitors can be excluded. This weakens the position of consumers because they cannot take their custom elsewhere. Later we shall discuss monopolies in more detail. Here we need only note that where they result in inefficiency and the restriction of supplies, as (for instance) when fish are dumped back into the sea, they are harmful to the community. Of course, in a command economy, the state represents one big monopoly, but the supposition is that it would not act contrary to the interests of the people.

Fifth, in practice the mechanism of the price system may not work smoothly because there are obstacles to the movement of factors of production in response to price changes (see pp.209–11). As a result, supply is not adjusted easily and quickly to changes in demand.

Sixth, the private profit motive does not always ensure that *public* wealth (as distinct from the sum total of *private* wealth) will be maximised. A manufacturer building a factory does not consider the soot which falls from his factory chimney on the nearby washing-lines. It is not a cost to him, but it is a cost to the community who live in the neighbourhood. On the other hand, there may exist certain 'social benefits' which are not allowed for by the individual producer when calculating the return to his outlay. Thus, when considering whether to build a civil airbus, he merely estimates whether the receipts from fares will cover the costs. The fact that in the process he gains 'know-how' for the development of military aircraft does not enter his calculations. Under central planning, the state can allow for such social costs and social benefits when planning production.

Last, in a market economy, where individuals decide what to produce, there occur periods when factors of production are allowed to stand idle because producers as a whole consider that the prospects of making a profit are poor. On the other hand, under central planning, the people who decide which wants shall be satisfied are also the people who direct factors into the production of the necessary goods and services. All factors, therefore, are fully employed.

The advantages of the private enterprise system correspond closely to the defects of the central planning system, and vice versa. But one big defect of the central planning system has remained unstated. Once individuals have given power to the state to prescribe what is good for them, to own all the factors of production and to direct labour, it may not be long before the state has usurped absolute political power in addition to its economic power and the people are at the mercy of a dictatorship. Individuals then exist for the state, and not the state for the individual. Thus the ultimate decision as to whether a market economy is to be preferred to a command economy (in their extreme forms) really hinges on the question whether you are prepared to run the risk of being ruled by a dictator or whether you would rather be left free to choose your own job accepting such defects of the private enterprise system as unemployment, inadequate provision for future production, and the existence of wide variations in wealth.

2.4 Britain's Mixed Economy

Second thoughts over the desirability of private enterprise have arisen largely because in the twentieth century the above defects, particularly unemployment, have become more pronounced. Fortunately today we know a lot more about how the government can take remedial action (see Chapter 26).

Thus we are not faced with a straight choice between complete private enterprise and full central planning. Instead we can use the state, not so much as a dictator, but rather as a wise father who allows his children a large measure of personal freedom, who looks ahead and lays plans in order to avoid many of the dangers into which they might stumble.

Britain therefore has a mixed economy, her economic system making use of both methods in an attempt, as it were, to get the best of both worlds. In the main, however, production is still carried on under private enterprise, for the public sector (central and local government and the nationalised industries) accounts for only 30 per cent of total production. Nevertheless, even in the private sector, there is regulation to varying degrees.

Thus the economic activities of the government of the UK can be said to have one or more of the following objects:

1. To produce those goods and services which would either not be provided by private enterprise, or might be produced very indifferently (see Chapter 29).
2. To take over the production of certain goods and services because they can be produced more efficiently by the resources of the state than by the resources of private enterprise. Under this heading we are thinking principally of the nationalised industries, but it also applies to roads, libraries and other goods provided by local authorities.
3. To protect the individual, both as a consumer and a worker, from the operations of powerful interests, such as monopolies.
4. To overcome frictions, e.g. to the movement of labour, which hamper the efficient operation of the price system.
5. To modify the price mechanism when shortages, e.g. in housing, would entail hardship.
6. To control the entrepreneur in order to allow for the public costs or public benefits of his own plans.
7. To regulate the economy in order to secure full employment.
8. To obtain a balanced regional development.
9. To maintain a stable level of prices.
10. To improve the balance of payments in order that:
    (*a*) foreign currency reserves may be strengthened;
    (*b*) aid may be given to less developed countries.
11. To ensure a steady growth of the national product.
12. To overcome great inequalities in the distribution of wealth and to ensure:
    (*a*) a minimum standard of life for all;
    (*b*) equality of opportunity for all.

Some of these objectives may be complementary. Thus a strengthening of the foreign currency reserves may be a prerequisite for steady growth, for they provide the cushion against balance-of-payments deficits which are liable to occur from time to time when the level of activity is high. On the other hand, some objectives may be competitive. Thus the nearer the economy moves to full employment, the greater is the danger of inflation.

Politically some people would like more government control, and others less. This book tries to avoid taking sides. It simply explains how the price mechanism operates, where the defects occur, and what the government can do to avoid or to mitigate the results of such defects. Often, as we go along, we shall direct attention to government action in the particular sphere under discussion. At other times, we shall discuss government policy specifically and in more detail, as with interference in the price system, nationalisation, the localisation of industry, the control of monopoly, the regulation of international trade, the promotion of employment and the maintenance of a stable currency.

2.5 Micro- and Macroeconomics

An Economic System

Broadly speaking, any economic system consists of two parts:

1. *Firms* – business units from the sole proprietor to the government, deciding what to produce and employing the productive resources (Figure 2.2).
2. *Households* – the consumers of the goods and services produced and the suppliers of the productive resources.

FIGURE 2.2
The Flow of Goods and Productive Resources in an Economic System

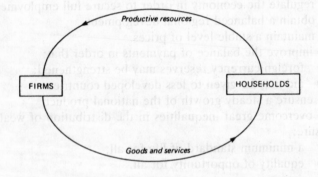

Microeconomics

A study of the price system, therefore, is largely concerned with:

1. How the supply of a particular good or service is related to the demand for it.
2. How the demand for a particular factor of production is related to its supply.

As we shall see, this relationship of demand to supply is based upon prices established in the different product and factor markets. Furthermore, all prices are relative to one another. A change in any one price in the economic system establishes a ripple which touches all markets, both product and factor, sometimes directly (as in the case of substitutes) but usually indirectly and even remotely.

This allocation of the different goods and factors through markets is shown in Figure 2.3, which is an extension of Figure 2.2. A development of Figure 2.3, through demand and supply analysis, is the concern of the first part of this book. Since it is largely a study of individual markets – small parts of the economy – it is usually referred to as *microeconomics* (from the Greek word *micro* meaning 'small').

FIGURE 2.3
The Allocation of Products and Resources through Prices in the Market

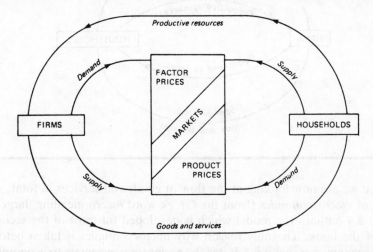

Macroeconomics

So far, so good. And, if we had been studying economics sixty years ago, this would have been the scope of our investigations – the allocation of goods and services between different uses through the mechanism of the price system. But is it possible that the price system could give rise to another problem – that some productive resources might remain unemployed?

The classical economists thought not. They held that, if there were unemployed factors of production, competition between them would lead to a fall in their price, and this would make it profitable to employ them.

Experience of unemployment towards the end of the nineteenth century, and particularly in the 1930s, however, convinced economists that this need not happen. In 1936 Professor J. M. Keynes highlighted a major cause: the breakdown in the flow of money income. To analyse the level of activity, we need a diagram showing the money payments in total which result from the exchange of goods and resources (Figure 2.4).

FIGURE 2.4
Real and Money Flows in an Economic System

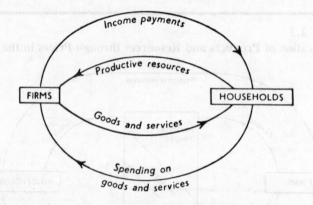

Since we are now looking at the flow of goods and services in total, we speak of *macroeconomics* (from the Greek word *macro* meaning 'large'). Figure 2.4 outlines the model which is developed for most of the second part of the book. The only reason why microeconomics is taken before macroeconomics is that it is felt it is the easier for newcomers to economics to understand.

Part II

What to Produce

3 How Price is Formed in the Free Market

3.1 Value and Price

As soon as we wish to know what to produce, there immediately arises the question: 'How can people indicate what they want?' A mere statement of want is meaningless, for, as we showed in Chapter 1, people always *want* something. A want is significant in economics only when a person is prepared to give up something in order to satisfy it. As the strength of the different wants varies, so will the amounts which people are willing to give up. In other words, different goods have a different *value* to them. Value is measured in terms of 'opportunity cost'. For example, if Ms A is willing to work five hours for the money which will buy a hat, we say that the value of the hat to her is greater than the value of the five hours' leisure forgone. Value therefore means the rate at which a particular good or service will exchange for other goods. It is important to note, however, that, while to have value a good must be capable of satisfying a want, a good which satisfies a want need not necessarily have value. For example, air satisfies a want; but, in normal circumstances, the supply is so great that nobody will give anything in exchange for it. Because it has no power to command other goods in exchange, it has, in economics, no value.

In modern economic systems we rarely exchange goods directly against other goods. We make use of a 'go-between', or, as it is usually said, a medium of exchange. This medium of exchange is money and the values of goods are expressed in terms of money. In other words, we *price* the goods and services. Price can be defined, therefore, as the value of a commodity or service measured in terms of the standard monetary unit. By comparing prices, we can compare the *rates* at which different goods can be exchanged.

Changes in *relative* prices, if supply conditions have not changed, indicate a relative shift in the importance of those goods. Thus price changes can signal a change in what people want. We must therefore

27

examine the mechanism by which the signals are flashed up. We begin by looking at the 'market' – where values are established by exchange.

3.2 Markets

Definition

'I'm offered £550 for this heifer. Surely, gentlemen, you're going to offer more than that for such a fine animal. No more offers? Going at £550. For the last time of asking, any advance on £550? Going at £550, going, gone.' Down comes the hammer. 'Sold at £550 to Mr Giles on my right.'

This is the local cattle market. On his stand above the auction ring is the auctioneer. Inside the ring, a black-and-white heifer paces round and round. Appraising the animal are the farmers from the neighbouring countryside. Some are buyers, some sellers. The market fixes the price at which those who want a good can obtain it from those who have it to sell.

Note that to the economist only exchange value is of significance. The farmer selling the heifer may have considered that it ought to have made more than £550. Or, as it was the first calf reared by his son, it may have had great 'sentimental value' to him. Such niceties, however, mean little to the economist.

Of course, prices are not always fixed by auction as in the local cattle market. Auction is the method usually employed where there are many potential buyers but the seller only comes to the market infrequently or wishes to dispose of his goods quickly. If there are few buyers and sellers, e.g. in the purchase of a house or a second-hand car, the final price may be arrived at by 'higgling', the seller meeting and arguing with the prospective buyer personally.

But where goods are in frequent and regular demand, to dispose of them by auction or higgling would take far too long. Hence goods such as foodstuffs, clothing, household utensils and new cars are given a definite price by the shopkeeper. However, this does not mean that buyers have not influenced this price. If it is too high, the good will not be sold. If it is too low, the shopkeeper will be left without stocks. The price asked will have taken account of this.

Nor should it be assumed that a market must be held in a particular place. Second-hand cars are often bought and sold through newspaper advertisements. Second-hand furniture may be disposed of by a card in a local shop window. Above all, developments in transport, communications and methods of selling (e.g. by grade or sample) may mean that the area of the market is extended.

Therefore, we can no longer speak of a market as being that particular place where the goods are bought and sold, for the whole business might be conducted by telephone. The arrangement by which buyers and sellers are brought together may be formal or informal. Moreover, the economist is chiefly interested in the market from the point of view of its function – the fixing of the price, i.e. the exchange value, of the particular commodity – and the actual organisation is studied chiefly from this aspect. Thus we can define a market simply as *all those buyers and sellers of a good who influence its price*. The result is that there is a tendency for the same price, allowing for costs of transport, to be established for the same commodity within the market.

World Markets

Today modern transport is so extensive and so rapid that many commodities have a 'world' market: that is, a change in the price of the commodity in one part of the world affects the price in the rest of the world. Such commodities are wheat, coffee, oils, and the basic raw materials such as wool, cotton, mineral oil, rubber, tin, lead, zinc and uranium. What are the necessary requirements for a commodity to have such a wide market?

First, there must be a wide demand. The basic necessities of life (e.g. wheat, vegetable oils, wool, cotton) answer this requirement. In contrast, such goods as national costumes, books translated into little-used languages, souvenirs, postcards of local views and foods which satisfy local tastes have only a local demand.

Second, commodities must be physically capable of being transported. Land and buildings are almost impossible to transport. A customer may require a personal service from the producer, but the distance he can travel is usually limited. Labour, too, is particularly immobile, workers being loath, in spite of the attraction of a higher wage, to move to a different country or even to a different locality (see Chapter 16). Closely connected with this is the action of governments, which, by a tariff policy or import quotas, may effectively prevent certain commodities from entering the country.

Third, the costs of transport must not be prohibitive – they must be small in relation to the value of the commodity. Thus the market for bricks is small, while that for diamonds is world-wide. Similarly, wheat and oil are cheap to transport compared with coal because they are more easily handled, though as sea transport is the cheapest form of transport coal mined near the coast can be sent long distances.

Last, the commodity must be durable. Goods which perish quickly, such as milk, bread, fresh cream and strawberries, cannot be sent long distances. Nevertheless, modern developments, such as refrigeration, canning and air freight transport, are extending the market even for these goods.

Perfect and Imperfect Markets

In a market the price of a commodity ruling in one part affects the price paid in another part. Hence the same price tends to be established. Where any price differences are eliminated quickly, we say the market is a 'perfect' market (*note*: this is not quite the same as 'perfect competition'; see Chapter 11).

For a market to be perfect, certain conditions have to be fulfilled. First, buyers and sellers must have exact knowledge of the prices which are being paid elsewhere in the market. The development of communications, particularly the telephone and electronic system, has facilitated this. Second, both buyers and sellers must base their actions solely on price. Neither buyers nor sellers have a preference to deal with one particular person because of loyalty or mere unreasonableness. If, for instance, one seller suddenly puts up the price of his good, then customers immediately go to a cheaper seller. Similarly, if he were to lower his price, customers would so flock to him that he would sell out quickly unless he raised his price to that asked elsewhere.

Examples of perfect markets are the precious-stones market of Hatton Garden and, above all, the organised produce markets and the Stock Exchange, both of which are described later. In these markets the two essential conditions are fulfilled. Buyers and sellers are usually professional dealers who make their income by watching prices carefully and buying accordingly. It is essential, therefore, for them to be acquainted with any fluctuations in price in any part of the market, and the result of their operations is that variations in price are quickly eliminated.

But these conditions are not usually satisfied in other markets. Buyers and sellers neither have perfect knowledge nor act solely on the basis of price. The ordinary housewife, for instance, cannot always afford the time to go from one shop to another in order to compare the prices of everyday purchases, though it is noticeable that she is usually much more careful when spending on the more expensive goods bought at infrequent intervals. In the same way, shopkeepers do not always know what other shopkeepers are charging for similar goods. Moreover, purchasers are influenced by considerations other than price. Thus they may continue to deal with one particular trader even though he is charging a slightly higher price simply because they are loyal to someone who has given them good service in the past. It is this personal relationship which is the basis of the 'goodwill' built up by a business. Moreover, although two goods may be virtually the same physically, in the mind of the purchaser they may be entirely different. This process of making the good slightly different from that of other producers is known as 'product differentiation', and over one-half of present-day advertising is directed to convincing people of the superiority of each particular brand. Such advertising therefore renders the market less perfect and should be contrasted with the other type of advertising where the aim is to inform the public. This latter type tends to widen the market and to render it more perfect.

The result is that only where the market is composed of many professional dealers is it likely to be fully perfect. In other markets, price differences persist and such markets are said to be 'imperfect'. As we have already hinted, imperfect markets are often found in retailing.

Organised Produce Markets

As we have shown above, the market for certain commodities is a very wide one, largely because they have a high value relative to their cost of transport and are non-perishable over a fairly long period. Moreover, many of these commodities are in general and constant demand, either because they form a basic raw material for a widely used finished good or because they constitute one of the main foodstuffs or beverages for a large section of the world's people. Such commodities therefore figure prominently in international trade and it is these with which we are concerned in the following discussion.

England's foreign trade commenced with the export of raw wool in the thirteenth century, and it was extended by the subsequent development of the chartered companies. These were based on London, and it was here that merchants gathered to buy and sell the produce which the companies' ships brought from abroad. This commerce conducted by London not only grew larger as trade extended but became more continuous as supplies of commodities came forward at different times of the year from different parts of the world. It was natural, therefore, that in London the same buyers and sellers would meet regularly to conduct business.

The big change, however, came about with the expansion of international trade following the Industrial Revolution. Britain became the greatest importing and exporting nation of the world. London, her chief port and commercial city, not only imported goods for home use but, assisted by the fact that British ships were the great carriers of the world's trade, built up an entrepôt business, acting as a 'go-between' in the distribution of such commodities as tea, sugar, hides, skins and wool, to many other countries, particularly those of Western Europe.

Hence formal 'organised produce markets' developed. These markets are distinguished from other sorts of market in that buying and selling takes place in a recognised building, business is governed by agreed rules and conventions, and often only special persons are allowed to engage in transactions. Generally the public are excluded, even from watching. They are thus a highly developed form of market, and today London has exchanges or auction centres for buying and selling such commodities as rubber, wool, tea, coffee, furs, metals (tin, copper, lead and zinc), grain and shipping freights (the Baltic Exchange). It must not be thought, however, that such organised produce markets exist only in London. Liverpool has exchanges for cotton and grain, while most of the large trading countries such as the USA (wheat, maize and cotton) and Australia and New Zealand (wool) have their own exchanges. In fact, with the development of shipping services by other countries, the tendency has been for trade which formerly passed through London to be sent direct from the producing countries to markets nearer the consuming populations. Even so, much buying and selling of such commodities as sugar, metals and grain is still conducted in London. Payment to merchants for the business they transact forms a part of Britain's 'invisible exports' (see p.415).

Broadly speaking, organised markets fulfil three main functions. First, they enable manufacturers and wholesalers to obtain supplies of the commodities they require easily, quickly and at the competitive market price. This is because such markets provide a centre where expert buyers and sellers, each having very complete knowledge of the particular commodity, can meet for the purpose of dealing. In them, price is very sensitive to any change in demand and supply; thus they are 'perfect markets'.

Second, for those commodities which can be graded very accurately, these markets allow persons who would be adversely affected by a change in their prices to protect themselves from heavy loss. Thus producers of cotton, rubber or tin like to know in advance what price they will receive for their output. On the other hand, a cotton spinner has to protect himself from a rise in the price of raw materials between the time of quoting a price for his yarn and the time of manufacture. All can achieve their objectives by 'hedging' on the 'futures' market.

Where a good is bought for delivery the same day, the deal is known as a 'spot' transaction and the price as the 'spot price'. With many goods, however, it is possible to buy today for delivery some time in the future. The good may not actually be in stock, but the seller contracts to obtain and deliver the good at the agreed time. Such a deal is known as a 'futures' transaction, and the price agreed upon as the 'future' or 'forward' price. For a commodity to be dealt in on a 'futures' market, it is necessary that (*a*) the commodity is durable, thereby enabling stocks to be carried; (*b*) the commodity can be easily graded and its quality determined by tests which yield almost identical results without the aid of samples when applied by different experts; (*c*) dealings are sufficiently frequent to occupy professional dealers; and (*d*) the commodity is one which is subject to price fluctuations.

In future dealings the dealer uses his expert knowledge to make a profit on the future price of the commodity in which he or she specialises. If he thinks that the price is likely to rise, he is known as a 'bull', and he will buy and accumulate stocks now in order to sell at a profit later. On the other hand, if he thinks the price is going to fall, he is known as a 'bear', and he will sell stocks, even if he does not have them, hoping to buy at a lower price when delivery is due. At any time a dealer will quote a price (according to the view he takes of the future) at which he is prepared to buy or sell at some future date. Thus a cotton grower can cover himself against a fall in price by selling his produce forward at a price which will cover his cost of production and yield a reasonable profit, while a cotton spinner can quote a weaver a price for yarn and guard himself against loss by buying the raw cotton forward. Both are covered against adverse price changes, the risk being accepted by the dealer.

In doing this, the dealer usually performs the third main function of organised markets – the evening out of price fluctuations due to changes in demand and supply. At a time when an increase in supply would cause the price to fall considerably, he adds his demand to the normal demand in order to build up stocks, and thereby keeps the price up. On the other hand, when the good is in short supply, he releases stocks, and so prevents a violent rise in price. In this respect the dealer performs a parallel function to the wholesaler (see Chapter 8). The difficulty is that speculation on the future price may dominate the real forces which influence it, causing violent price fluctuations in response to changes in optimism and pessimism.

3.3 Forces Determining Price

Demand and Supply

'That animal was cheap,' remarks Phil Archer as the auctioneer's hammer falls. 'And no wonder,' replies Brian Aldridge, 'this has been a long winter. We're now in the middle of April, and the grass is hardly growing. Hay and silage are getting pretty short, I can tell you. It's mostly breeders who are bringing their cattle into the market today – they're being forced to sell quicker than they expected. Old Giles is about the only farmer who will take the risk of buying extra cattle to feed. When you come to think about it, Phil, it's many a year since you saw so many fine-looking animals knocked down at around £550.'

What can we learn from Brian Aldridge's observations? Simply that the £550 at which the heifer was sold was not really determined by the final bid. The real factors producing the relatively low price were the reluctance of farmers to buy and the number of young animals being offered for sale. In short, the price was determined by the interaction of the forces of demand and supply. We shall examine each in turn.

Preliminary Assumptions

Our first task must be to analyse how these forces work in an imaginary market – for eggs. To simplify our investigation, we shall assume:

(a) a single grade of eggs – all eggs are exactly the same in size and quality;
(b) no transport costs within the market;
(c) the market consists of so many relatively small buyers and sellers that there is keen competition;
(d) a *perfect market* in the sense that price differences are quickly eliminated, because buyers and sellers (i) have complete knowledge of prices and conditions in other parts of the market, and (ii) act solely on the basis of price;
(e) no interference by the government in the free operation of market forces, e.g. by price control, regulating supply, etc.

3.4 Demand

Demand in economics is the desire to possess something and the willingness and the ability to pay a certain price in order to possess it. In other words, it is not merely a wish or a desire but an effective demand, i.e. desire backed by money. It refers specifically to how much of a good persons would actually be willing to buy at a given price over a period of time.

For the purposes of exposition, it is helpful if we separate the factors affecting demand into: (1) price; (2) the conditions of demand.

1. Price, the Conditions of Demand Remaining Unchanged

Normally a person will demand more of a good the lower its price. Why this is so will be shown later (Chapter 5). For the present it can be accepted because it conforms to our everyday observation. 'Winter sale, prices slashed' announce the shops when they wish to clear their stocks of winter clothing – and people queue to secure luxury items which have been marked down in price.

If we take a single commodity, say eggs, we can draw up a table showing how many eggs a person would be willing to buy at different prices. If they are very expensive, other foodstuffs will, as far as possible, be substituted; if they are cheap, people may even pickle them. By adding up the demand of all buyers of eggs in the market at different prices for a given period of time it is possible to obtain a table for the whole market which we call a *market-demand schedule*. Let us assume that this is as shown in Table 3.1.

Table 3.1
Demand Schedule for Nonsuch Market for the Week ending 24 May 1987

Price (pence per egg)	Eggs demanded (thousands)*
12	3
10	9
8	15
6	20
4	25
2	35

*What buyers would take at each price.

Note that this schedule does not tell us anything about the actual market price or how much is in fact sold. All it says is: '*If* the price is so much, then this quantity will be demanded.' It is an 'if' schedule.

This schedule can be plotted on a graph (Figure 3.1). If we assume that demand can be plotted for all intermediary prices we obtain a demand curve *D*. It is now conventional for price to be measured up the *y*-axis and the quantity along the *x*-axis.

FIGURE 3.1
Quantity Demanded and Price

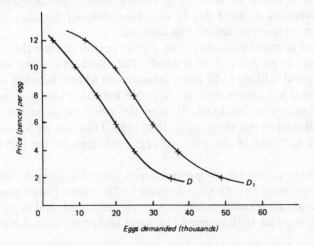

2. The Conditions of Demand

It may well happen that something occurs to cause housewives to demand more or less eggs at each given price. In other words, the demand schedule is revised. Suppose, for instance, that farmers join together to run an advertising campaign describing new egg dishes. More eggs are now likely to be demanded at all prices. This gives us a revised demand schedule as follows:

Price (pence per egg)	Eggs demanded (thousands)
12	12
10	20
8	25
6	30
4	37
2	49

When we plot this revised demand schedule, we have a new curve, D_1, to the right of the old one. Had conditions so changed that demand decreased at all prices, the new demand curve would have been to the left of the old one.

The influence of both (a) price, and (b) the conditions of demand on the quantity demanded is thus shown on Figure 3.1. The former determines the shape of the demand curve – its slope downwards from left to right; the latter determines its position within the axes – an increase in demand shifting the curve to the right, a decrease to the left. To assist clarity of exposition, a change in demand resulting from a change in price of the commodity will in future be referred to as an *extension* or *contraction* of demand; a change in demand due to new conditions of demand will be described as an *increase* or *decrease* in demand.

Conditions of demand may change in a short period of time through:

(a) *A change in the price of other goods*. The effect on the demand for the particular good is likely to be more pronounced where the good whose price has changed is a *close substitute*. Suppose that fried tomatoes are an alternative to eggs for breakfast. If now the price of tomatoes falls, housewives will tend to buy them rather than eggs. Thus although there has been no initial increase in the price of eggs, the demand for them has decreased.

Similarly, where goods are *complementary*, a change in the price of one good has a pronounced effect on the demand for the other. For example, a fall in the price of cars results in more cars being purchased, and eventually this leads to an increase in the demand for tyres and petrol (see also p.50).

(*b*) *A change in tastes and fashion*. An advertising campaign on behalf of eggs would increase demand; a scare that eggs were the source of an infection would decrease it.

(*c*) *Expectations of future price changes or shortages*. The fear that the price of eggs may rise considerably the following week will induce people to increase their demand now in order to have eggs in stock.

(*d*) *Government policy*. A selective tax on eggs paid by the consumer, by increasing the price, would decrease demand; a rebate paid to the consumer would increase it (see Chapter 29).

In the longer period, a change in the conditions of demand can result from:

(*e*) *A change in real income*. If there were an all-round increase in real income (that is, money income adjusted for any change in the price level over the period), people could afford more eggs, and demand would probably increase. On the other hand, it might now be possible to afford mushrooms for breakfast, and these would take the place of eggs (see p.58).

(*f*) *Greater equality in the distribution of wealth*. The wealth of a country may be so distributed that there are a few exceptionally rich persons whereas the remainder are exceedingly poor. If many poor persons felt they could not afford eggs, greater equality of wealth would be likely to increase the demand for eggs.

(*g*) *A change in the size or composition of the population*. Additional people coming into the market increase demand, expecially if eggs figure prominently in their diet.

3.5 Supply

Supply in economics refers to how much of a good will be offered for sale at a given price over a given period of time. As with demand, this quantity depends on (1) the price of the good, and (2) the conditions of supply.

1. Price, the Conditions of Supply Remaining Unchanged

Normally more of a good will be supplied the higher its price. The real reason for this is explained in Chapter 12. But even a brief consideration of how the individual farmer reacts to a change in price will show that it is likely to be true. If the price of eggs is high, the farmer will probably consume fewer eggs in order to send as many as possible to market. Moreover, the higher price would allow the farmer to give chickens more food so that they would lay a few extra eggs. When we extend our analysis to the market supply, it is obvious that a higher price for eggs would enable other farmers – the less efficient – to produce eggs.

Hence we are able to draw up a *market-supply schedule* for eggs. This consists of the total amounts supplied at different prices by all the sellers in the market for a given period of time. Let us assume that this is as shown in Table 3.2.

Table 3.2
Supply Schedule for Nonsuch Market for the Week Ending 24 May 1987

Price (pence per egg)	Eggs supplied (thousands)*
12	40
10	32
8	25
6	20
4	13
2	7

*What sellers would offer at each price.

Once again it must be noted that this is an 'if' schedule, for all it says is: '*If* the price is so much, then this quantity will be offered for sale.'

We can plot this schedule (Figure 3.2), and, assuming supply can be plotted for all intermediate prices, obtain a supply curve *S*.

There is a fundamental difference between demand and supply. Whereas demand can respond almost immediately to a change in price, a period of time must usually elapse before supply can be fully adjusted. For the first day or two the only way in which the farmer can send more eggs to market because their price has risen is by eating fewer himself. By the end of the week output may have been increased by giving the hens more food or by leaving on the light in the hen-house all night; the higher price covers the extra cost. But, to obtain any sizeable increase, the farmer must add to his hens; if all farmers are following the same policy, this will take about five months, the period required to rear laying hens from chicks.

These different periods of time are dealt with more fully in Chapter 11. Put simply, each period of time produces a supply curve of a different slope.

2. *The Conditions of Supply*

The number of eggs supplied may change even though there has been no alteration in the price. In the spring, for instance, chickens lay more eggs,

FIGURE 3.2
Quantity Supplied and Price

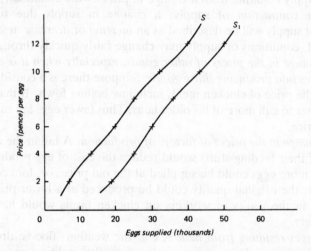

and in the autumn less. Thus more eggs will be supplied at all prices in the spring, and fewer in the autumn. In other words, the supply schedule changes from time to time. A new supply schedule for the spring could read as follows:

Price (pence per egg)	Eggs supplied (thousands)
12	50
10	43
8	36
6	30
4	25
1	19

This new schedule shows that, whereas in winter only 25 000 eggs were supplied at 8p each, during the spring 36 000 could be supplied at that price. Or, looked at in another way, 25 000 eggs can be supplied in the spring at 4p each compared with 8p each in the winter. When plotted, the revised supply schedule gives a new supply curve, S_1, to the right of the old one. Had supply decreased, the new supply curve would have been to the left.

Like demand, therefore, supply is influenced by both (1) price, and (2) the conditions of supply. The former determines the shape of the curve – its upward slope from left to right. The latter determines its position within the axes – an increase in supply shifts the curve to the right, a decrease to the left. To distinguish between the two, we shall refer to a change in supply resulting from a change in price of the commodity as an *extension* or *contraction* of supply; a change in supply due to new conditions of supply will be described as an *increase* or *decrease* in supply.

In general, conditions of supply may change fairly quickly through:

(*a*) *A change in the prices of other goods, especially when it is easy to shift resources into producing those goods.* Suppose there is a considerable increase in the price of chicken meat, including boiling fowls. It may now pay the farmer to cull more of his older hens. Thus fewer eggs are supplied at the old price.

(*b*) *A change in the prices of factors of production.* A fall in the cost of pullets or of their feeding-stuffs would reduce the cost of egg production. As a result, more eggs could be supplied at the old price, or, looked at in another way, the original quality could be produced at a lower price per egg. A rise in the wages of workers on chicken farms would have the opposite effect.

(*c*) *Changes resulting from nature*, e.g. the weather, floods, drought, pest, or from *abnormal circumstances*, e.g. war, fire, political events.

(*d*) *Government policy.* A tax on the output of eggs or an increase in the employer's national insurance contribution would result in fewer eggs being offered for sale at the old price. That is, the supply curve moves to the left. A subsidy, on the other hand, by decreasing costs, would move the supply curve to the right (see Chapter 29).

Other changes in supply take a longer period of time. Such changes can occur through:

(*e*) *Improved techniques.* Technical improvements reduce costs of production, shifting the supply curve to the right. Thus improved automatic feeding appliances might be developed, or selective breeding may produce hens which lay more eggs over a given period.

(*f*) *The discovery of new or the exhaustion of old supplies of raw materials.*

(*g*) *The entry of new firms into the industry.*

3.6 The Determination of Price

The demand and supply curves can be combined in a single diagram (Figure 3.3).

Now let us show how the economist builds a simple model to establish economic principles (see also pp.11–13). Remember our original assumptions:

FIGURE 3.3
The Determination of Equilibrium Price

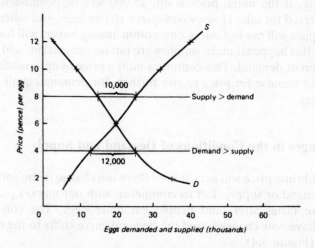

1. Many relatively small buyers and sellers.
2. Keen competition between buyers, between sellers, and between buyers and sellers.

We must add to these our two assumptions (we shall put them on a firmer footing later) regarding demand and supply:

3. More will be demanded at a lower price than at a higher price.
4. Less will be supplied at a lower price than at a higher price.

These two assumptions are illustrated by the slope of the demand and supply curves in Figure 3.3.

Given assumptions (3) and (4), the two curves slope in opposite directions. Thus they cut at a single point – in our example where the price is 6p. The economist predicts that in our hypothetical 'nonsuch market', where these conditions of demand and supply exist, the price of eggs will move towards and eventually settle at 6p. This price is called *the equilibrium or market price.*

This proposition can be proved as follows. Suppose that initially the price of eggs is fixed at 8p. Here 15 000 will be demanded but 25 000 supplied. There is thus an excess supply of 10 000. This means that sellers are left with surplus supplies. Competition between sellers means that some are willing to sell their supplies at less than 8p. Thus the price falls. As this happens, some supplies are withdrawn from the market, and there is an extension of demand. This continues until a price of 6p is reached, when there is no excess of supply over demand, 20 000 eggs being both demanded and offered for sale. Thus 6p is the only price at which there is harmony between buyers and sellers.

Similarly, if the initial price is 4p, 25 000 will be demanded but only 13 000 offered for sale. Housewives queue to buy eggs, and sellers see that their supplies will not last out. Competition among buyers will force up the price. As this happens, more supplies are put on the market, and there is a contraction of demand. This continues until a price of 6p is reached. Then there is no impulse for price to rise further, for demand equals supply at 20 000 eggs.

3.7 Changes in the Conditions of Demand and Supply

The equilibrium price will persist until there is a change in the conditions of either demand or supply. Let us commence with our market price of 6p.

Suppose tastes alter, and people eat more eggs. The conditions of demand have now changed, and the demand curve shifts to the right from D to D_1 (Figure 3.4).

At the original price of 6p we now have an excess of demand over supply – 30 000 eggs are demanded, but only 20 000 supplied. As explained in the previous section, competition among buyers will now force the price up – to 8p – where 25 000 eggs are both demanded and supplied.

FIGURE 3.4
The Effect on Price of a Change in the Conditions of Demand

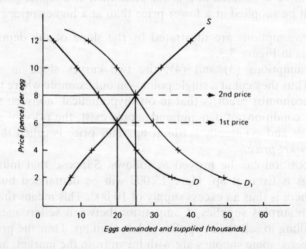

Similarly a decrease in demand, resulting, for instance, from a significant fall in the price of tomatoes, would cause the curve to shift to the left and the price of eggs to fall (see pp.36–7).

Likewise, a change may occur in the conditions of supply. At any given price, more eggs can be produced during the spring than at other periods of the year, and so the supply curve shifts to the right from S to S_1 (Figure 3.5).

At the original price of 6p we now have an excess supply over demand – 30 000 eggs are supplied, but only 20 000 are demanded. Here competition among sellers will mean that the price falls to 4p, where 25 000 eggs are both demanded and supplied.

FIGURE 3.5
The Effect on Price of a Change in the Conditions of Supply

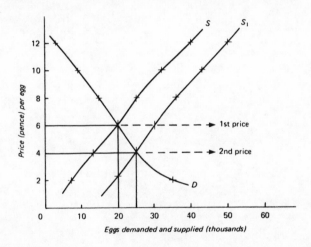

3.8 The 'Laws' of Price

Our analysis above has been based on three main assumptions:

1. The demand curve slopes downwards from left to right.
2. The supply curve slopes upwards from left to right.
3. Market conditions are such that an excess of demand over supply causes price to rise; an excess of supply over demand causes price to fall.

The conclusions which we can derive are of such general application that they can be termed 'laws'. They can be stated as follows:

1. Price tends to make equal the amount which buyers wish to buy and the amount which sellers are prepared to offer for sale.
2. Price will settle at one point – where the quantity offered for sale equals the quantity demanded.
3. An increase in demand (that is, a shift of the demand curve to the right) will lead to a rise in price and in the quantity bought and sold.
4. A decrease in demand (that is, a shift of the demand curve to the left) will lead to a fall in price and in the quantity bought and sold.
5. An increase in supply (that is, a shift in the supply curve to the right) will lead to a fall in price and a rise in the quantity bought and sold.
6. A decrease in supply (that is, a shift in the supply curve to the left) will lead to a rise in price and a fall in the quantity bought and sold.

4 Applications of Demand and Supply Analysis

We have shown how price is determined in the free market, illustrating the explanation with demand and supply curves. Our task now is to show how this analysis can be applied to practical problems, especially those relating to government policy. First, we consider questions concerned with the role of price in the free market economy; second, we look at other problems and examine how demand and supply analysis can help.

4.1 The Functions of Price in the Free Market

In a free market, price both indicates and motivates.

1. It 'Rations out' Scarce Goods

At any one time the supply of a good is relatively fixed. It therefore has to be apportioned among the many people wanting it. This is done by adjusting price. As price rises, demand contracts; as it falls, demand expands. At the equilibrium price, demand just equals the supply. Should supply increase, the total quantity can still be disposed of by lowering the price; should supply decrease, price would have to be raised.

We can illustrate how price works by considering two current problems:

(a) *Who shall be allowed to park in a congested area?* There is traffic congestion in the centre of Barthem City because of the many cars parked at the kerbside. The city council decides that this is because parking is a free good – it costs motorists nothing to park their cars. It is decided to limit car-parking to one side of the road and to 800 places, each with a parking meter. The demand schedule for one-hour parking is estimated to be as follows:

Price (Pence)	Demand
30	450
20	800
10	1200
0	1800

The council therefore fixes a charge of 20p. The 1000 motorists who will not pay this price do not therefore bring their cars into the city centre.

(b) *Why do 'touts' obtain such high prices for Cup Final tickets?* To ensure that the regular football supporter who watches his team from the terraces each Saturday shall be able to afford a Cup Final ticket, prices are fixed by the Football Association. Let us simplify the argument by assuming that the Football Association has one price, £10, for 100 000 tickets, but that a free market price would be £30. In Figure 4.1, when the price is £30 demand equals the available supply of 100 000 but at the controlled price of £10 demand exceeds supply by 150 000.

FIGURE 4.1
Excess Demand for Cup Final Tickets

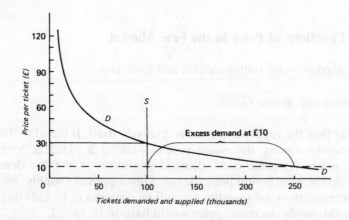

But some tickets are obtained by 'touts', buyers who wish merely to resell at a profit. These tickets are sold in a free market, where demand and supply determine price. The demand comes from those keen club supporters not lucky enough to be allocated a ticket but willing to pay more than £10. As the price rises, some persons possessing tickets may be induced to sell them to the touts. Thus the demand and supply curves are roughly as shown in Figure 4.2, giving a 'spiv-market' price of £100.

FIGURE 4.2
The 'Tout' Price of Cup Final Tickets

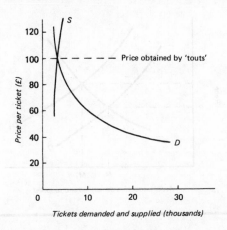

An important conclusion can be drawn from this example: where price is controlled below the market price, only some form of rationing can ensure that everybody gets a share of the limited supply. Normally this is achieved by the Football Association, which, after allocating so many tickets to each finalist, limits each affiliated club to approximately two. The alternative would simply be a 'first come, first served' method of distribution, penalising those who could not queue and increasing the scope for tout activity.

2. It Indicates Changes in Wants

Even if a planning authority organised production, it would still find it advantageous to introduce a modified form of price system. This is because prices are the signals by which the community indicates the extent to which different goods are wanted and any changes in those wants.

Consider how the demand for housing accommodation in London has increased over the last thirty years, partly through the pressure of population and partly through the rise in real income. As a result, rents have risen from OP to OP_1 (Figure 4.3).

3. It Induces Supply to Respond to Changes in Demand

When demand increases, price rises and supply expands; when demand decreases, price falls and supply contracts. Thus in Figure 4.3, the increase

---

FIGURE 4.3
The Effect on Rents of an Increase in the Demand for Accommodation

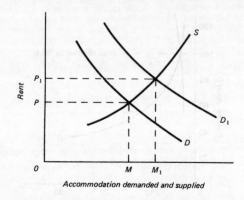

Accommodation demanded and supplied

---

in price has made it profitable for extra housing accommodation, equivalent to MM_1, to be supplied. This may be achieved by converting existing houses into flats and by building a number of small houses on a site formerly occupied by one large house.

In Chapters 11 and 12 we explain in more detail how supply responds to changes in demand.

4. It Indicates Changes in the Conditions upon which Goods can be Supplied

Where resources are limited and fully employed, more of one good can be produced only at the expense of producing fewer other goods. If the cost of producing a given commodity rises, this should be signalled to consumers who can then decide to what extent they are prepared to pay these higher costs by forgoing other goods. Again this is achieved through price. Assume in Figure 4.4 that the cost of producing good x has increased because the raw materials have risen in price. Where demand is depicted by D, most consumers meet the higher costs (price rises by PP_1) rather than do without the good. Where demand is depicted by D_1, many consumers do without the good when its price rises (demand falls by MM_1), substituting other goods for it.

5. It Rewards the Factors of Production

When the price of a good rises, producers can afford to offer a higher reward to the factors they use in order to attract them from other uses.

FIGURE 4.4
The Effect of a Change in the Conditions of Supply on Price and Quantity Traded

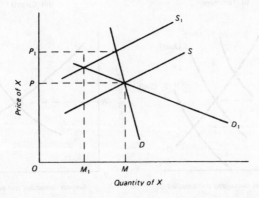

Quantity of X

Such rewards give the owners of the factors of production spending power. In this way the division (or, as it is more usually termed, the 'distribution') of the cake which has been produced is determined. (Chapter 15 will consider in more detail the rewards to factors of production.)

4.2 Further Applications

1. Why do the Prices of Agricultural Products Fluctuate More than the Prices of Manufactured Goods?

Price changes occur because of changes in the conditions of demand and supply. Generally speaking, the conditions of demand for both agricultural products and manufactured goods are, over not too long a period, fairly stable. But the supply of agricultural products, unlike that of manufactured goods, varies from season to season, and, because of weather, plant disease and farmers' decisions, from year to year. Nor is storage easy, particularly in the case of foodstuffs. Thus the amount of agricultural products coming on the market fluctuates considerably, and so prices also fluctuate. The difference between the two can be seen by comparing tomatoes and carpets (Figure 4.5). Whereas the price of tomatoes varies between OP_1 and OP_2, that of carpets remains steady at OR.

FIGURE 4.5
Fluctuations in the Prices of Tomatoes and Carpets

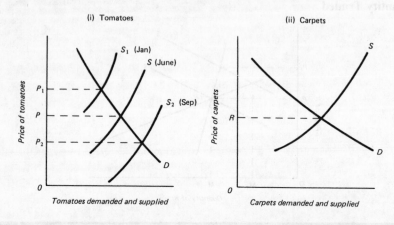

Tomatoes demanded and supplied   *Carpets demanded and supplied*

2. How Would an Increase in the Demand for Cars Affect the Price of Tyres?

Cars and tyres are 'jointly demanded'. In Figure 4.6 the increased demand for cars leads to an increased demand for tyres, and the prices of both rise. Later it will be shown how slight modifications could be made to the supply

FIGURE 4.6
Joint Demand

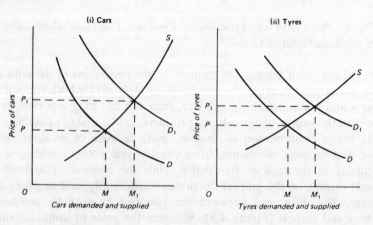

Cars demanded and supplied   *Tyres demanded and supplied*

curve for tyres to allow for differences in the length of time under consideration (see pp.156–7).

3. How Would an Increase in the Price of Petrol Affect the Price of Paraffin?

Petrol and paraffin are 'jointly supplied'; an increased production of one automatically increases the production of the other. Suppose that demand for petrol increases, but that there is no change in the demand for paraffin. The price of petrol rises from OP to OP_1, and supply expands from OM to OM_1 (Figure 4.7). But this means that the supply of paraffin is automatically increased, though there has been no change in price. Thus the supply curve for paraffin moves from S to S_1, and the price of paraffin falls from OR to OR_1. In practice, it is probable that the oil companies would try to increase the demand for paraffin, e.g. by advertising oil-fired central heating. If this proved successful, the price of paraffin would recover.

FIGURE 4.7
Joint Supply

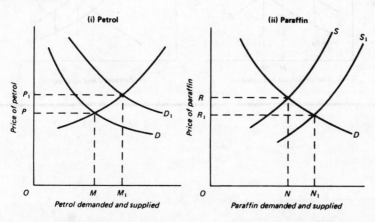

4. How Could the Government Secure the use of Solid Fuel rather than Oil for Central Heating?

Here the government must endeavour to reduce the price of coal and to increase the price of oil by operating on the supply sides. To aid coal, it could give producers a subsidy or reduce railway-transport charges. On the other hand, oil could be penalised by the imposition of a tax, either when it is imported or sold. The position is shown in Figure 4.8. Subsidies allow more coal to be supplied at all prices, and the supply curve moves to the right. Price falls, and demand expands. The tax on oil decreases the amount which can be sold at the old prices, and the supply curve moves to the left. Price rises, and demand contracts.

Of course, if the government does not wish to interfere with supply in these ways, it will have to try to influence demand, e.g. by advertising central heating using solid fuel.

FIGURE 4.8
The Effect on Quantity Bought of a Subsidy and a Tax

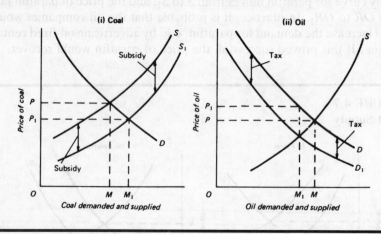

5 A Further Look at Demand

5.1 Why the Demand Curve Normally Slopes Downwards

Our conclusion in Chapter 3 – that more of a good will be demanded the lower its price – was based solely on our everyday observations of how buyers act in a market. Can we, by explaining *why* people demand more of a good as its price falls, put this conclusion on firmer ground?

The answer is 'yes'; and we shall use what is known as the 'marginal utility theory'. Other theories, such as the indifference curve analysis or revealed preference, may from the point of view of method be more satisfying, but the marginal utility theory is shorter to explain and often more useful in simple analysis.

Our method of approach will be as follows. Our main interest is in the market demand curve. But the market demand is made up of the demand of all the individuals who comprise the market. If, therefore, we study the behaviour of the individual buyer as he spends his income, and it can be said that other buyers act similarly, we can conclude that the market and individual patterns of behaviour are similar.

Maximising Satisfaction

We assume that every individual has limited resources – represented by a limited money income – and that each acts 'rationally'. 'Rational' must not be interpreted in a value sense as being 'sensible'. It might not be sensible for someone to spend a large part of his income on cigarettes, but that is up to him. All the economist means by 'rational' is that the individual is consistent in his behaviour in the sense that he tries to get the most out of his limited resources. This is a reasonable assumption. There may be the odd consumer who acts frivolously, but since we are dealing with a relatively large number of consumers in the market we can think of a typical consumer who does act 'rationally'.

Because resources are limited, buying one good involves going without something else. In disposing of incomes, therefore, people weigh up the various 'opportunity costs', and try to obtain the maximum satisfaction from their expenditure. Normally their choice does not necessitate making an absolute decision between one good and another, but rather presents itself as whether to have a little more of this by sacrificing a little bit of that.

Here again it might be questioned whether the consumer really does follow this careful procedure. How many people when purchasing a good weigh up its pros and cons and compare it, according to its price, with other goods? Surely, most expenditure is purely automatic? Admittedly, much expenditure is habitual – but this does not mean that people give no thought to it. Our immediate reaction to a selective increase in tax on petrol or cigarettes, for instance, is to ask whether we cannot make do with less. In any case, following a routine for minor matters (including everyday purchases) allows more time for thinking about those things which are outside the usual run of events. Thus while we may not consciously consider the satisfactions to be obtained from other goods every time we buy a packet of tea, we are careful when furnishing a home to weigh up the merits and price of a refrigerator as opposed to a washing-machine.

Questions to be Answered

There are three basic questions we have to answer:

1. What conditions will hold when the consumer has obtained the maximum satisfaction from limited resources? In other words, what are the equilibrium conditions?
2. How does the consumer achieve this equilibrium?
3. What happens when the equilibrium is disturbed by a price change?

Let us deal with each in turn.

Preliminary Assumptions

(a) Our consumer is a housewife.
(b) She has a limited housekeeping allowance per week.
(c) She acts rationally to maximise satisfaction from this limited income.
(d) During the period of time under consideration, income and tastes do not change.
(e) She knows how much satisfaction each unit of a good will give.
(f) She is one of a large number of buyers; as a result her demand does not directly affect the price of the good.

1. The Equilibrium Condition

Our housewife will be in equilibrium when she would not switch a single penny of her expenditure on one good to spending on another.

We can be more explicit by introducing the term 'utility'. In economics, this simply means that a good has the power to satisfy a want, with no attempt being made to say whether it is useful or commendable. Utility merely implies that the good is wanted by somebody. Note, too, that we cannot measure utility; like love, pain or fear, it is purely subjective to the individual.

Our housewife, it has been assumed, knows in her own mind how much satisfaction each good affords her. Her objective is to obtain the greatest possible utility from her income. In other words, she seems to maximise total utility (Figure 5.1).

FIGURE 5.1
Factors Affecting the Equilibrium of the Housewife

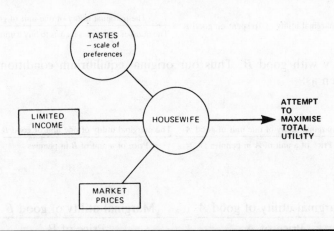

She does this by a careful allocation of her limited income as she purchases a variety of goods. All the time she is asking: 'If I spend a penny more on cheese, will I obtain more or less utility than if I spent the penny on margarine?' She will not be in equilibrium until the utility from the last penny spent on good A (in the sense of the penny she only just decided to spend) is equal to the last penny spent on good B, and so on. Her spending adjustments are borderline ones – they take place at the *margin*.

Note that we did *not* say that she obtained the same utility from the last pound of cheese as she obtained from the last pound of margarine. If, for instance, cheese were four times as expensive as margarine, that would obviously be unreasonable. We should expect four times the amount of utility if we were spending four times on one good what we were spending on another.

Sometimes, however, we cannot buy goods in 'pennyworths' – the good is 'lumpy' and we have to take a whole 'lump' of it or nothing at all. Can we restate our equilibrium condition to allow for this? We can do so if we first define more carefully this concept of the margin and what we mean by 'marginal utility'.

Each small addition to a given supply of a good is called the *marginal increment*, and the utility derived from this increment is known as the *marginal utility*. Our original condition of equilibrium can therefore be stated as:

The marginal utility of 1p spent on good A = The marginal utility of 1p spent on good B, etc.

But the marginal utility of 1p spent on good A depends on how much of a unit of good A you get for 1p. Thus:

$$\text{The marginal utility of 1p spent on good } A = \frac{\text{The marginal utility of one unit of good } A}{\text{The number of pennies it costs to buy a unit of good } A}$$

Similarly with good B. Thus our original equilibrium condition can be rewritten as:

$$\frac{\text{The marginal utility of one unit of good } A}{\text{Price of a unit of } A \text{ in pennies}} = \frac{\text{The marginal utility of one unit of good } B}{\text{Price of a unit of } B \text{ in pennies}}$$

That is:

$$\frac{\text{Marginal utility of good } A}{\text{Price of A}} = \frac{\text{Marginal utility of good } B}{\text{Price of B}}$$

2. How Does the Consumer Achieve this Equilibrium?

The question must now be asked: 'How can our housewife arrange that the utility of the last penny spent on different goods shall be the same?' The answer is to be found in the so-called *law of diminishing marginal utility*. Although wants vary considerably in their nature, they all possess the underlying characteristic that in a given period they can be satisfied fairly quickly. Thus, if someone drinks lemonade to quench his thirst, the first glass will yield a great amount of satisfaction. Indeed, the second glass may be equally satisfying. But it is doubtful where he will relish the third glass to the same extent, since his thirst has now been partially quenched. If he continues to drink the lemonade, there will come a time when a glass gives him no additional satisfaction whatsoever and, in fact, it might be that he would be better off without it – there is a *disutility*. We can therefore state a general rule that the utility derived from any given addition to a consumer's stock of a good will eventually decline as the supply increases.

This means that our housewife, who knows how much utility she will derive from an additional unit of a good compared with another unit of any other good, can arrange that equal utility is derived from the last penny spent on each good by varying the quantity she buys. If she buys more of a good, the stock of other goods remaining fixed, its marginal utility relative to other goods falls. Similarly, if she reduces the quantity she buys, the marginal utility of the good relative to other goods rises. She goes on making these marginal adjustments until she is in equilibrium.

3. What Happens when the Equilibrium is Disturbed by a Price Change?

Provided that there is no change in her income or in the relative importance of her various wants and that the prices of goods remain constant, our housewife's pattern of expenditure will remain unaltered.

But what happens if the price of a good changes? In the language of economics, it disturbs her equilibrium position. Suppose, for instance, that the price of cheese falls from 120p to 95p per lb, the prices of other goods remaining unchanged. How will this affect her demand for cheese? We can proceed in either of two ways:

(*a*) The fall in the price of cheese will enable her to obtain more cheese than before for every penny, including the last, which she was spending on it. More cheese usually implies greater total satisfaction. The last penny she was spending on cheese therefore now yields a greater satisfaction than the last penny being spent on other goods. Thus to reduce the utility obtained from the last penny spent on cheese, she buys more cheese.

(*b*) The alternative form of the equilibrium condition is:

$$\frac{\text{The marginal utility of last lb of cheese}}{\text{Price of lb cheese}} = \frac{\text{The marginal utility of } B, \text{ etc.}}{\text{Price of } B}$$

A fall in the price of cheese destroys this relationship; the marginal utility of cheese to its price is now higher than with goods *B*, *C*, etc. To restore the equilibrium relationship, the marginal utility of cheese must be decreased. Hence our housewife buys more cheese.

The reasons for this expansion in the demand for cheese can be analysed more closely. The fall in price means that our housewife is now able to purchase as much cheese as before and still have money left over. This is an *income* effect of a price fall – she can now buy more of all goods, not only of cheese. But in addition to this 'income effect', more cheese will tend to be bought because of a *substitution* effect. At the margin it means that a penny spent on cheese will now yield more satisfaction than a penny spent on margarine, etc. Thus cheese is substituted for other goods. If cheese is a good substitute, its marginal utility will diminish comparatively slowly as the consumption of it increases. A given price fall will therefore lead to a considerable increase in the quantity of cheese demanded.

5.2 Exceptional Demand Curves

Normally the demand curve slopes downwards from left to right, showing that demand extends as price falls. It is possible, however, to envisage circumstances in which the reverse occurs – a fall in price bringing about a contraction of demand, and a rise in price an extension.

1. Inferior Goods

Certain goods can be termed 'inferior' in that less is spent on them as income increases, people preferring other goods as incomes rise. Bread, cheap cuts of meat and low-quality floor-coverings are examples.

Now with most goods, e.g. strawberries, demand is likely to increase with a rise in income. The income effect on demand of a price fall will therefore be positive, reinforcing the substitution effect which is always in a positive direction. But with inferior goods the income effect on demand is negative, working in the opposite direction to the substitution effect. Take the case of cheap meat. A fall in its price would result in a tendency to substitute it for better cuts, such as steak, but the income effect would work in the opposite direction, people tending to replace cheaper meat with steak. If the income effect were greater than the substitution effect, the net result would be that less cheaper meat would be demanded at the lower price.

The income effect of a price fall will be more significant the greater the proportion of one's income which is spent on the good. And, if a large part of one's income is spent on an 'inferior' good (as may happen when income is low), the income effect may be so considerable as to outweigh the positive substitution effect. Suppose, for instance, that a person is so poor that 40 per cent of income has to be spent on bread in order to obtain the necessary calories to live. Now suppose that a loaf of bread falls in price from 40p to 20p per lb. The same amount of bread can now be obtained for only 20 per cent of money income, the other 20 per cent being available for spending on different goods. In other words, there has been a substantial increase in real income. As the person is now better off, it is quite likely that a more varied diet will be sought. Foods, other than bread, will be bought but, since they will yield calories formerly provided by bread, they will tend to replace bread, the demand for which will thus contract even though its price has fallen.

The above is really an extreme case. What is an 'inferior' good depends largely upon one's level of income. Take a cheap joint of meat, for instance. To a particular person this may be an 'inferior' good, the negative income effect of a price fall outweighing the substitution effect. But there would also be poor people who could not have afforded this joint at the old price. For them both the income effect and the substitution effect of a price fall would be positive. Thus, when we look at the *market* demand curve (as opposed to an individual's demand curve), we could easily find that it follows the normal shape, showing that more is demanded as price falls.

2. Price Movements are Linked with Expectations

With certain goods, expectations are an integral part of demand. The best example is securities bought and sold on the Stock Exchange, where a person's current demand is largely determined by what he thinks will be the price of the security in the future. In this case, a rise or fall in the price of a security may well be associated with a larger or smaller quantity respectively being demanded if people think that the rise or fall will continue.

3. Goods Having 'Snob Appeal'

Certain goods, e.g. diamonds, model gowns and mink coats, may be wanted chiefly for ostentation – the desire to impress others. Should the price of such a good fall so much that it comes within the reach of many more people, original purchasers may no longer want it. Hence total demand could be less. Here again, however, we must distinguish between the individual and market demand curves. Although 'snob' buyers may leave the market when the price of the good falls, it is likely that large numbers of new buyers would enter, thereby adding to demand at these lower prices.

In each of the above types of situation, we have analysed the abnormality of the demand curve as a direct link between price and demand. With all three, however, we cannot ignore the fact that there is a close connection with changes in the conditions of demand. The first has a change in income, the second a change in expectations, and the third a change in tastes. Our theory explaining consumers' behaviour should be able to cope at one and the same time with a change in conditions of demand which are implicit in a change of price. It is a weakness of the marginal-utility approach that it fails to do so.

5.3 Elasticity of Demand

Consider Figure 5.2. At price OP, demand for both commodities A and B is OM. But when the price of both falls by PP_1, demand for A expands by only MM_1, whereas that for B expands by MM_2. In other words, there are differences in the responsiveness of demand to a change in price. We measure the degree of responsiveness by what is known as the 'elasticity of demand'.

FIGURE 5.2
Elasticity of Demand

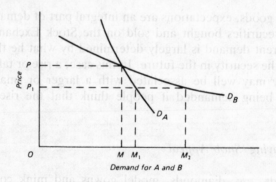

Demand for A and B

Measurement of Elasticity of Demand

Elasticity of demand always refers to the elasticity at a particular price, and in what follows when we talk about 'elasticity' it will be assumed that there is some price in mind.

Elasticity of demand is defined by comparing the *rate* at which demand expands with the *rate* at which price falls. If the former is greater than the latter, we say that demand is elastic; if it is smaller, we say that demand is inelastic. When they are equal, elasticity of demand is said to be equal to unity. Using this definition, elasticity of demand can be measured in two ways. One is direct, showing the degree of elasticity; the other is indirect, merely indicating whether the demand for the good is elastic or inelastic.

1. A Direct Comparison of the Rate at which Demand Changes with the Rate at which Price Changes

When we wish to compare *rates* of change, we have to work in terms of proportionate (or percentage) changes. We can therefore define elasticity of demand as the proportionate change in the amount demanded in response to a small change in price divided by the proportionate change in price. That is,

$$\text{Elasticity of demand} = \frac{\text{Proportionate change in demand}}{\text{Proportionate change in price}}$$

$$= \frac{\dfrac{\text{Change in quantity demanded}}{\text{Original quantity demanded}}}{\dfrac{\text{Change in price}}{\text{-Original price}}}$$

$$= \frac{\dfrac{\text{New quantity} - \text{Old quantity}}{\text{Old quantity}}}{\dfrac{\text{New price} - \text{Old price}}{\text{Old price}}}$$

We can illustrate by an example from the demand schedule on page 35. When price falls from 10p to 8p, demand for eggs expands from 9000 to 15 000. Elasticity of demand is thus equal to:

$$\frac{6000/9000}{2/10} = \frac{2/3}{1/5} = 3\tfrac{1}{3}$$

Similarly, for a fall in price from 4p to 2p, elasticity of demand equals $\tfrac{4}{5}$.

It will be noted that there is a different in elasticity when we measure for a price rise or a price fall. Thus when price fell from 10p to 8p, elasticity was $3\tfrac{1}{3}$; but when it rises from 8p to 10p, elasticity is $1\tfrac{3}{5}$. The difference occurs because we were measuring the price change from different prices and for a relatively large change. Were the price change only $\tfrac{1}{2}$p instead of 2p, the two results would be more nearly equal. Where the price change is infinitely small, measurement of elasticity of demand is at the same point, and there is only one elasticity.

2. A Comparison of Total Outlay as Price Changes

For the purpose of economic analysis, it is usually sufficient to refer to elasticity of demand in broad terms. Where elasticity is greater than 1 (the change in the quantity demanded is more than proportionate to the change in price), we say demand is elastic. Where it is less than 1 (the change in the quantity demanded is less than proportionate to the change in price), we say demand is inelastic. If it is 1 (the change in the quantity demanded being proportionate to the change in price), elasticity is described as being equal to unity.

This broad approach can be used to measure elasticity in a slightly different way. If the proportionate expansion in demand is greater than the proportionate change in price, the total amount spent on the good will increase. In other words, demand is elastic when, in response to a fall in price, total outlay increases; or, in response to a rise in price, total outlay decreases. Similarly, demand is inelastic when, in response to a fall in price, total outlay decreases; or, in response to a rise in price, total outlay increases. Demand is equal to unity when as price changes, total outlay remains the same.

The rule can be remembered as follows:

price change, then total outlay changes in *opposite* direction – demand elastic;
price change, then total outlay changes in *same* direction – demand inelastic.

Thus, with the demand schedule on p.35, we have:

Price of eggs (pence)	Demand (thousands)	Total outlay (thousand pence)	
10	9	90	
8	5	120	Elastic demand
6	20	120	
4	25	100	Inelastic demand

Between 8p and 6p, elasticity of demand equals unity.

Important Points Regarding Elasticity of Demand

(1) *Demand curves are unlikely to have the same elasticity throughout their length*. Thus for the demand schedule on page 35, we have seen that demand is elastic at prices above 8p and inelastic at prices below 6p.

(2) *The important exceptions to the above*, when elasticity of demand is the same throughout the whole length of the curve, are:

(a) *Demand absolutely inelastic*, people buying exactly the same amount of a commodity whatever its price (Figure 5.3*a*).

FIGURE 5.3
Constant Elasticities of Demand

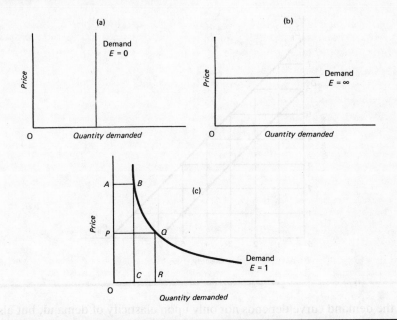

(b) *Demand perfectly elastic*, people ceasing to buy the commodity at all if its price rises slightly (Figure 5.3*b*). This is the demand curve for his good which faces an individual seller under conditions of perfect competition (see p.139).

(c) *Elasticity of demand equal to unity*, where total outlay is constant at all prices. The curve here is known as a 'rectangular hyperbola', and all rectangles representing outlay (price x quantity demanded) are equal. For example, rectangle *OABC* equals rectangle *OPQR*.

(3)   *Any other straight-line demand curve has a different elasticity of demand for each different price*. Take the demand curve D_A (Figure 5.4), for example. For a price fall of a penny: (*a*) at 5p, elasticity of demand is 5; (*b*) at 2p, elasticity of demand is $\frac{1}{2}$.

The reason for this is that although a straight-sloping line means that demand changes by a constant amount for a given price change, the *rate* at which price itself is falling depends on the price and quantity from which we start. This rate will therefore be higher for a given price change the lower the price under consideration.

(4)   *Usually we cannot compare the elasticities of demand of different goods by comparing the slopes of the respective demand curves*. The slope

FIGURE 5.4
Elasticity of a Straight-line Demand Curve

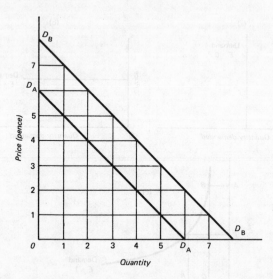

of the demand curve depends not only upon elasticity of demand, but also on the vertical and horizontal scales chosen. Furthermore, even if the same scales are chosen for different commodities, we cannot safely say that, where the demand curve for one commodity slopes more steeply than another, the demand for the first commodity is less elastic. Compare, for example, the parallel demand curves D_A and D_B above. At the same price of 4p, elasticity of demand for commodity A is equal to 2, while for commodity B it is equal to 1.

The reason for the difference is that, although we have taken the same price, we have started measuring proportionate changes in quantity demanded from different quantities. Only at the position where two demand curves with different slopes cut can we be *certain* that the difference in their slopes will reflect a difference in the elasticity of demand.

Factors Determining Elasticity of Demand

1. The Availability of Substitutes at the Ruling Market Price

As a good falls in price, so it becomes cheaper relative to other goods. People are induced to buy more of it to replace goods which are now relatively dearer. How far they can carry out this replacement will depend upon the extent to which the good in question is, in their own minds, a substitute for the other goods. Goods within a particular class are easily substituted for one another. Beef is a substitute for lamb, bloaters are a substitute for kippers, and so on. Thus if the price of beef falls, people will buy more beef and less lamb. Between one class and another, however, substitution is more difficult. If the price of meat in general falls, there will be a slight tendency to buy more meat and less fish, but this tendency will be very limited, because meat is not nearly so perfect a substitute for fish as beef is for lamb.

We must be careful, however, over labelling the demand for the accepted necessities of life as 'inelastic' and the demand for luxuries as 'elastic'. With both, the substitution factor may be more important. Thus, although bread is a necessity, at a high enough price demand for it might be elastic because it has to compete with potatoes or cake. Similarly, a Rolls-Royce is a luxury, but demand for it will be inelastic if no substitute gives a similar prestige. In any case it is difficult to state categorically which goods are necessities and which luxuries. But we can use the concept of elasticity of demand to help, saying that where the demand for a good is very inelastic over a wide price range, that good can be regarded as a necessity, and vice versa.

2. The Number of Possible Substitute Uses

Where a good can be substituted for another good, its demand tends to be elastic. And the more goods it can be substituted for, so the more will demand for it extend as its price falls. Thus reductions in the price of plastics have led to large extensions of demand as they have been substituted for materials used in such articles as enamel bowls, galvanised buckets, paper wrappings, glass garden cloches, wooden toys and tin containers.

3. The Proportion of Income Spent on the Good

When only a very small proportion of a person's income is spent on a good, as (for example) with pepper, salt, shoe polish, newspapers, matches and toothpaste, no great effort is made to look for substitutes when its price rises. Demand for such goods is therefore relatively inelastic. On the other hand, when the expenditure on a good is fairly large, as (for example) with most groceries, a rise in price would provide considerable incentive to find substitutes. Thus supermarkets have succeeded because, when they cut prices, large numbers of customers are attracted from other retailers who are selling the same good at a higher price.

4. The Period of Time

Since it takes time to find substitutes or to change spending habits, elasticity may be greater the longer the period of time under review. In practice, many firms try to overcome the ignorance or conservatism of consumers by advertising, giving free samples, or making special offers.

5. The Possibility of New Purchasers

In discussing the possibility of substitution above, we have looked at elasticity of demand from the point of view of the individual consumer. But when we are considering the market demand curve, we must allow for the fact that, as price falls, new consumers will be induced to buy the good. In fact with many goods, such as cars, video-recorders, washing machines, etc., of which people require only one, it is the fall in price bringing the good within the range of the demand of new consumers which leads to the increase in demand. Hence a fall in price which induces people in a numerous income-group to buy will result in a considerable elasticity of demand. A fall in price which affects only the higher and smaller income-groups, however, will not produce many new customers and hence the market demand schedule tends to be inelastic in this price range.

Uses of the Concept of Elasticity of Demand

The concept of elasticity of demand must be fully understood, for it figures prominently in both the theoretical analysis of the economist and the practical decisions of the businessman and government. The following are a few examples.

1. Theoretical Economics

(a) *To define 'perfect competition' in selling a good*. The economist, in order to explain the working of the economy, usually begins by constructing a model of how it works under theoretical conditions known as 'perfect competition' (see pp.138–42). On the selling side, an essential criterion of perfect competition is that everybody in the market produces so small a quantity of the total supply that no one seller can influence the price of the good by the amount he puts on the market. He has to accept market price as given for any output he might produce. That is, he sees the demand for his good as perfectly elastic (see p.139). (Similarly, on the buying side, no one purchaser must be able to influence the price by the size of his demand – see pp.140–1.)

(b) *As a helpful tool in analysing problems connected with changes in the conditions of supply*. Many problems analysed by the economist can be tackled adequately only by making use of the concept of elasticity of demand. Consider, for example, the question 'What effect will a rise in wages have on numbers employed in the car industry?' The answer hinges largely on the elasticity of demand for the product made by that labour. An increase in wages will move the supply curve of the product to the left. Output will contract – but how much it contracts depends upon the elasticity of demand. In Figure 5.5 demand is elastic, it will contract to OM_1; if inelastic, to OM_2 (see also pp.220–1).

FIGURE 5.5
Elasticity of Demand and a Change in the Conditions of Supply

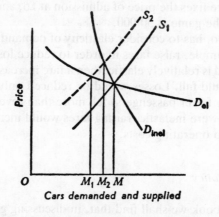

---

2. Business Decisions

(a) *The supermarket.* The policy of the supermarket rests largely on the high elasticity of demand for its products. When it cuts the price of a good, the supermarket expects a considerable expansion in demand by winning customers from retailers selling at a higher price. Thus it is most successful in selling standardised goods, such as branded groceries, but less successful where customers form a personal attachment to the shopkeeper, as with butchers, tailors, etc.

(b) *The monopolist.* A monopolist is not faced with a horizontal, i.e. a perfectly elastic, demand curve when selling his product, for the price of the good is affected by the quantity he puts on the market (see Chapter 13). Therefore, he looks at the demand schedule for his good and fixes the amount, and thus the price, at which he makes the highest profit.

Let us imagine a football club which is staging a European Cup match. Let us further imagine that there is no comparable attraction within fifty miles and that the price of admission is fixed by the club, which pursues the policy of making as big a profit as possible. Expenses of the club will be roughly the same whether few or many watch the game. The relevant portion of the demand schedule is as follows:

Price of admission (£)	Number of spectators willing to pay that price	Total outlay by spectators (£)
2	60 000	120 000
4	56 000	224 000
6	50 000	300 500
8	32 000	256 000

The club therefore fixes the price of admission at £6, and the total number of spectators at the game is 50 000.

British Rail, too, has to consider elasticity of demand when fixing fares. Should it, for example, raise fares in order to reduce losses? If, at existing fares, the demand is relatively elastic, then a fare increase would mean that total revenue would fall. Losses would be reduced only if operating costs (through carrying fewer passengers) fell more than revenue. On the other hand, if demand were inelastic, raising fares would increase total revenue without adding to operating costs.

3. Government Policy

Throughout this book we shall find that, in discussing government economic policy, elasticity of demand looms large. For instance, the Chancellor of the Exchequer must always take account of it when considering the effect of imposing a selective tax on a particular good. The demand may be so elastic that the increase in price might cause such a falling-off in the demand for the good that the total tax received was less than formerly. Suppose, for instance, the demand schedule for a commodity is as follows:

Price (pence)	Quantity demanded (000s)
20	1000
30	600
40	200

Assume also that supply is at constant cost per unit and that the market price is 20p at which 1 million units are being sold. The Chancellor of the Exchequer now decides to tax the good, imposing a tax of 10p on each unit. The result is that sales drop to 600 000 and his total tax receipts amount to £60 000. Later he goes further, increasing the tax to 20p per unit. This raises the total price of the good from 30p to 40p. Between these two prices, demand is very elastic. Only 200 000 are now sold, and the Chancellor's tax receipts are reduced to £40 000. Thus if the Chancellor wishes to raise revenue without increasing VAT generally, he selects a good which has an inelastic demand. This is one reason why tobacco and alcohol bear selective rates of tax. Since they are regarded as luxuries, the higher price which results is not considered to be too serious a burden on the consumer.

Other examples of the application of elasticity of demand to government policy are: (*a*) How is the burden of a selective indirect tax shared between the consumer and the producer? (See pp.392–4.) (*b*) How will a selective tax or subsidy on its products affect the size of an industry? (See pp.390–1.) (*c*) Would devaluation or depreciation of the currency on foreign exchange markets improve the balance of payments? (See pp.443–4.) (*d*) Will an improvement in the terms of trade improve the balance of payments? (See pp.405–6.)

5.4 Other Elasticities of Demand

When we refer to 'elasticity of demand' without qualification, we are speaking, as above, of what is more precisely '*price* elasticity of demand'. But the concept has other applications.

Income Elasticity of Demand

An increase in real income usually increases the demand for goods to a varying degree. Thus it is possible to speak of *income elasticity of demand* – the proportionate change in demand divided by the proportionate change in real income which has brought it about. If demand increases 20 per cent, for instance as a result of a 10 per cent increase in real income, income elasticity of demand equals 2. Which goods have a high income elasticity of demand depends upon current living standards. In Western Europe today, it is the demand for such goods as cars, washing-machines, dish-washers, central-heating, video-recorders, new houses and personal services which expands the most as income increases. In contrast, necessities, such as potatoes, salt, eggs and soap, have a low income elasticity of demand.

Cross-Elasticity of Demand

Where two goods are related, e.g. as substitutes or complements, a change in the price of one will lead to a change in demand for the other. Thus a rise in the price of oil leads to an increase in the demand for coal, while a fall in the price of video-recorders leads to an increased demand for video-tapes.

The extent to which the demand for a good changes in response to a price change of another good is known as *cross-elasticity of demand*:

$$\text{Cross-elasticity of demand} = \frac{\text{Percentage change in the quantity demanded of good } X}{\text{Percentage change in the price of good } Y}$$

With substitutes, cross-elasticity is positive. For example, an increase in the price of Y would lead to an increase in the demand for X (as with oil and coal in the example above). With complements, cross-elasticity is negative, since a fall in the price of Y leads to a rise in the demand for X (as with video-recorders and tapes above). The closer the substitutes or complements, the larger will be the figure for cross-elasticity. A cross-elasticity near zero signifies that there is little relationship between the two goods (Figure 5.6).

FIGURE 5.6
Cross-elasticity of Demand

Cross-elasticity

Complementarity ←————————————————————→ Substitutability
                            —   ○   +

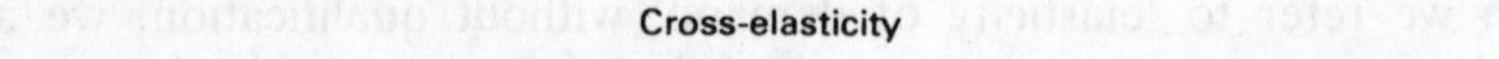

Part III

How to Produce – the Theory of Production

Part III

How to Produce – the Theory of Production

6 The Firm

So far we have given only a very approximate explanation of how supply responds to a change in price. For the next nine chapters our task will be to examine the supply curve a little more closely. As with demand, we have to study the actions of individuals (in this case the firms producing goods). By considering the decisions a firm has to make, we try to establish general principles governing its behaviour.

6.1 The Role of the Firm

Definition of the Firm

In Chapter 2 we showed that an economic system consists of two main parts: (1) *households*, the units which provide productive resources and consume the goods produced; (2) *firms*, the units which hire productive resources in order to produce goods and services. As we shall see, this definition of a firm is very wide, including all forms of organisation from the sole trader to government departments. In the chapters which follow, however, we shall be concentrating on the decisions of firms which produce goods for sale in the market. Chapters 6 to 10 will be concerned mainly with the decisions on hiring and combining the factors of production. Chapters 13 and 14 will look at problems connected with the size of output. First, however, we must consider what economists are really referring to when they talk about the different 'factors of production' and 'production'.

The Factors of Production

The classical economists divided the factors of production into four groups – land, labour, capital and organisation. The rewards going to these factor groups were called rent, wages, interest and profit, respectively.

But their narrow classification, based on physical characteristics, has serious weaknesses:

(1) It is over-simplifying the problem to think that all factors can be separated and put into one of the four distinct compartments, land, labour, capital and organisation. These compartments themselves overlap. Land, used in its popular sense, can be improved and increased by capital spending on fertilisers, drainage and irrigation, while much of the acquired skill of a worker can be regarded as a return to the capital investment incurred in training him. Nor can labour free itself entirely from risk-bearing. A steel-worker may find that he has to accept a job at a lower wage should the demand for steel fall.

(2) Within each compartment there are wide divergences. An architect is a far different sort of worker from the bricklayer's mate, and the hotel manager to the hotel porter, but the classification lumps them all together under the heading of 'labour' and thereby is inclined to imply that they are all the same. From an economic point of view, one factor is only the same as another in so far as it is a perfect substitute for it or, in other words, if a firm were indifferent as to which one it used.

(3) The differences between units of a factor in the same group may be greater than the differences between the groups. Thus a bricklayer's labourer is, from an economic point of view, as closely akin to a concrete-mixer as he is to a book-keeper.

Any form of classification of the factors of production is bound to run into difficulties. Thus present-day economists conduct much of their analysis by talking about factors of production generally – resources which co-operate in the production of goods and services wanted by the community. But they also recognise that certain factors do have some common, broad and important characteristics which permit a general classification useful for purposes of analysis. Unfortunately, some obscurity has resulted because the old classical economists' terminology has been retained.

Land now refers solely to the resources provided by nature, e.g. space, rain and minerals. In practice, it is treated as a separate factor of production in order to examine the nature of the earnings of any factor which is fixed in supply. Such earnings are termed 'economic rent'.

Labour refers to the actual effort, both physical and mental, made by human beings in production. It is this 'human' element which distinguishes it from other factors, for it gives rise to special problems regarding mobility, unemployment and psychological attitudes.

Capital, as opposed to land, is man-made. Goods can be classified as:

(*a*) *Consumer goods*. Those goods which directly satisfy consumers' wants and are in the hands of the consumer, e.g. a loaf, a bicycle, a table.

(*b*) *Producer goods*. Those goods which are not wanted directly for their own sake, but for the contribution they make to the production of consumer goods, e.g. buildings, machines, tools, raw materials. Sometimes the same good may be either a consumer good or a producer good, depending on its use. A car, for instance, may be used simply for pleasure, or by a sales representative for business.

Capital, as a factor of production, consists of producer goods and stocks of consumer goods not yet in the hands of the consumer. It is treated as a separate factor of production in order to emphasise (*a*) the sacrifice of present enjoyment which is necessary to obtain it, and (*b*) the fluctuations in economic activity which occur because its use extends over a period of time (see Chapters 17 and 26).

Enterprise refers to the acceptance of the risks of production which arise through uncertainty. This is a somewhat narrower meaning than that given by the classical economists to the *entrepreneur* – the person or persons who decided what goods to produce and brought the factors of production together to produce them.

Today the role of organising the factors of production is regarded as a managerial function which can be performed by a paid manager, i.e. by a highly skilled form of labour. What really distinguishes enterprise from other factors is that it has to carry all the risks of production. How these risks arise will be examined in more detail later. Briefly, they occur because production takes time. The entrepreneur engages labour and buys raw materials and machinery now in order to produce a good which will not be sold until some time in the future. Whether costs are recovered will depend upon the demand for the good when it comes to be sold. There may be a change in tastes in the meantime; or a rival may, through a better process, be putting the good on the market at a lower price. In such ways, an expected profit may turn out to be a loss.

Profit or loss is the reward of uncertainty-bearing. Whoever accepts this ultimate risk is the true entrepreneur – the farmer working on his own account, the doctor who starts his own practice, the persons who buy shares (the 'risk' capital) in a company, or the citizens of a state (who gain should a nationalised industry achieve a profit, but ultimately bear any losses made).

Production

Early economists, such as the French Physiocrats of the eighteenth century, considered that only work in the extractive industries (agriculture, mining and fishing) was productive. Adam Smith, however, went one stage further for he included manufacturing in the term 'productive labour', though he was careful to deny that persons who merely rendered services were productive. In a much-quoted passage he states: 'The labour of the menial servant does not fix or realise itself in any particular subject or vendible commodity . . . Like the declamation of the actor, the harangue of the orator, or the tune of the musician, the work of all of them perishes in the very instant of its production.' Nevertheless, the inadequacy of this definition can be easily appreciated, for, according to it, the persons who make the dresses for the actresses and the scenery for the stage would be productive, while the actors and actresses themselves are not, and the farmer who grows the food is productive while the cook is not!

To arrive at a more satisfactory definition we have to ask: 'Why do people work? What is the reason for production?' The answer is simple – to satisfy wants. Consequently people who render services must be regarded as being productive. The actor, the nurse, the musician and the dress-maker are all satisfying wants. Similarly in a factory, the clerk who calculates the wages and the boy who sweeps the floor are as productive as the machine-tool operator making the nuts and bolts. All are helping to produce the final product – the good which will satisfy wants.

Human wants can take different forms. Most people like a paper to read at the breakfast-table. Thus the newspaper boy who takes the paper from the shop to the customer's letter-box is productive. Most people, too, prefer to buy their potatoes weekly rather than store the whole of their winter supply from when the crop is lifted in the autumn. Thus the farmer who keeps them in clamps or the merchant who puts them in a shed is satisfying the wants of consumers, and is similarly productive. Utility is created not only by changing the *form* of our scarce resources, but also their *place* and *time*. All these forms of activity are therefore productive.

6.2 The Objectives of the Firm

Where production is based on the free enterprise system, a firm has to cover its costs if it is to stay in business. Thus regard must be paid to 'profitability', and it is usual to assume that the firm seeks to maximise profit.

But it has to be asked whether firms in practice are always single-minded in seeking to *maximise money* profits? The answer is no; there is a range of possible objectives.

Personal motives may be important, especially where the manager is also the owner of the firm. Thus emphasis may be placed on good labour relations, the welfare of the workers, the desire for power, political influence, public esteem or simply 'a quiet life'. To cover such objectives profit would have to be interpreted in a wider sense than 'money profit'.

With major companies there is in practice a gap between the ownership and its administration. The business is run by professional managers, and is too complex for shareholders to be able to exert effective control. This applies even to the institutional shareholders, who avoid being directly involved in the running of the business. Thus the motives of the full-time executive managers tend to override the shareholders' desire for maximum return on capital invested. Managers may be anxious for the security of their own jobs and, instead of taking the calculated risks necessary to earn maximum profits, tend to play for safety. More likely, they will be motivated by personal desires for status. Provided they achieve a level of profit which is satisfactory in the sense that it keeps shareholders content, their positions and salaries can be enhanced by expanding the firm to where it *maximises sales* rather than profits. Alternatively, the *rate of growth* may be maximised. Either objective becomes a possibility when competition is imperfect.

Even when there is an emphasis on money profit, a firm may stress its *long-term position* rather than immediate maximum profit. Security of future profits may be the dominating motive for mergers and takeovers as an alternative to developing new products and techniques. Moreover, where there is an element of monopoly, a firm can follow its own pricing policy rather than have it determined by competitive market conditions. In such circumstances it may not adjust prices to short-term changes in demand and supply conditions. For one thing, there are the administrative costs of printing and distributing new price lists. For another, frequent changes in price tend to offend retailers and customers.

Again, a firm enjoying a degree of *monopoly* has always to assess what effect the pursuit of maximum profit may have on its overall position in the long term. Will a high price attract new entrants or encourage the development of a rival product? Will it lead to adverse publicity and eventually to government intervention by a reference to the Office of Fair Trading?

Finally, a firm has often to modify its objectives in deference to *government policy*. Thus it may be expected to follow government guidelines regarding wage increases, to have regard to the environment in the disposal of its waste products and even to retain surplus workers for a time rather than add to an already high level of unemployment.

Yet, while we must take account of these other objectives, our analysis cannot proceed far if any are seen as the main motive force of the firm. In any case they merely supplement the profit objective, for profits have to be made if the firm is to survive. Thus it is useful to start with the broad assumption that firms seek to maximise profits. We can then establish principles concerning how resources should be combined and what output should be produced.

6.3 The Decisions of the Firm

To maximise its profits, a firm will have to produce an output which will achieve the largest possible difference between total receipts and total costs. Thus it will always have an incentive to keep the cost of producing a given output to a minimum. This entails a number of decisions:

1. What legal form shall the business take?
2. What techniques shall be adopted, and what shall be the scale and scope of operation?
3. Where shall production be located?
4. How shall the factors of production be combined?

Such decisions are concerned largely with the factors of production, and will be discussed more fully in Chapters 7 to 10.

But the firm has also to consider how costs and receipts change as output varies, choosing that level of output which will maximise its profits. Thus it has a further decision:

5. What output shall be produced?

This is the question which is discussed in Chapters 11 and 13.

6.4 The Legal Form of the Firm under Private Enterprise

After deciding what to produce, the entrepreneur must consider what legal form the business shall take and how to raise the initial capital. It may be that the two decisions are closely linked from the beginning. But it must be remembered that, unless the business starts as an offshoot of a parent company, it has to be fairly successful before it can induce outsiders to subscribe capital on a large scale for its development

Capital is often classified as (a) fixed capital, and (b) working capital. Fixed capital covers factors which are used many times – factories, machines, land, lorries, etc. Working capital is for purchasing single-use factors – labour, raw materials, fertiliser, petrol, etc. – more or less the factors which are referred to later in this chapter as *variable* factors.

Finance for *working capital* can be obtained from a variety of sources – the bank, trade credit, advance deposits from customers (e.g. for building a house), hire-purchase companies, factor houses, tax reserves, inter-company finance and the government (e.g. through the Enterprise Allowance Scheme which on conditions provides an allowance of £40 per week for a year when starting a new business). Alternatively, fixed capital may be converted into working capital by hiring or leasing plant and vehicles or renting buildings.

Fixed capital finance is more difficult to raise – people recognise that if they lend for this purpose they have to part with their money for a longer period and accept a greater risk. Thus, as we shall see, it is only when the firm has grown to a certain size that its legal form has much bearing on the ease (and therefore the cost) with which it can borrow capital. Initially, therefore, it is likely that the legal form of the business will rest primarily on the degree of control which the entrepreneur wishes to exercise personally and the various legal advantages which different types afford. The position is summarised in Figure 6.1.

The Sole Proprietor

The sole proprietor is the oldest form of entrepreneurial organisation. Even today, from the point of view of numbers, small firms predominate, but in their total productive capacity, they are far less important than joint-stock companies. Such one-person firms range from the chimney-sweep and window-cleaner working on his or her own account to the farmer, shopkeeper and small factory-owner who employ other workers and may even own many separate units. Nevertheless, these businesses all have the same characteristic of being owned and controlled by a single person. It is this person's task to make all decisions regarding the policy of the firm, and it is he or she alone who takes the profits and bears the brunt of any losses which are made. This makes for energy, efficiency and a careful attention to detail.

As a form of entrepreneurial organisation, however, the sole proprietor suffers from three main disadvantages. First, the development of such a firm must proceed slowly because the sources of capital are limited. The success of the venture, especially in its early stages, depends very largely on the person in charge, and nobody is likely to provide capital for the business unless there is that confidence in the proprietor which comes from personal contact. Hence the main source of capital is the personal savings of the owner himself together with such additional sums as can be borrowed from relatives, close friends, a bank or perhaps the Council for Small Industries in Rural Areas. In time, development and expansion may take place by 'ploughing back' profits, but this will probably be an extremely slow process, and such firms generally remain comparatively small.

The second disadvantage is that, in the event of failure, not only the assets of the business but also the private assets and property of the proprietor can be claimed against by creditors. In short, there is no limited liability.

FIGURE 6.1
The Forms of Enterprise and the Raising of Capital

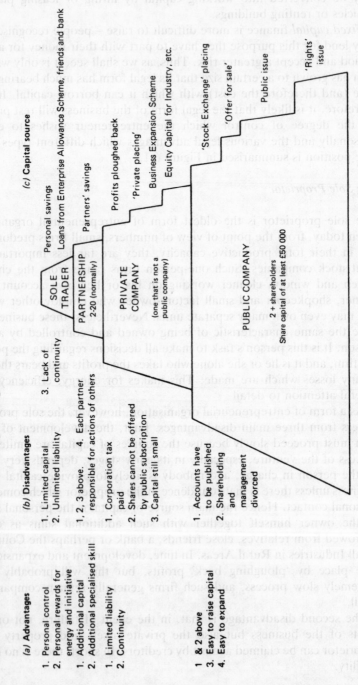

(a) Advantages

1. Personal control
2. Personal rewards for energy and initiative
1. Additional capital
2. Additional specialised skill
1. Limited liability
2. Continuity
1 & 2 above
3. Easy to raise capital
4. Easy to expand

(b) Disadvantages

1. Limited capital
2. Unlimited liability
1, 2, 3 above. 4. Each partner responsible for actions of others
1. Corporation tax paid
2. Shares cannot be offered by public subscription
3. Capital still small
1. Accounts have to be published
2. Shareholding and management divorced
3. Lack of continuity

(c) Capital source

Personal savings
Loans from Enterprise Allowance Scheme, friends and bank
Partners' savings
Profits ploughed back
'Private placing'
Business Expansion Scheme
Equity Capital for Industry, etc.
'Stock Exchange' placing
'Offer for sale'
Public issue
'Rights' issue

SOLE TRADER

PARTNERSHIP
2–20 (normally)

PRIVATE COMPANY
(one that is not a public company)

PUBLIC COMPANY
2 + shareholders
Share capital of at least £50 000

Third, there is lack of continuity; on the retirement or death of the owner, a one-person firm may cease to function.

Because of these disadvantages, the sole-proprietor form of organisation is, in the main, confined to those businesses which are just starting up, or to certain industries, such as agriculture and retailing, where requirements of management make the small technical unit desirable.

The Partnership

A larger amount of capital is available when persons combine together in a 'partnership'. Normally not more than twenty (ten in the case of a banking concern) may so join, but exceptions can be authorised by the Department of Trade. Each partner provides a part of the capital required and shares the profits on an agreed basis. Yet the amount of capital which can be raised in this way is still inadequate for modern large-scale organisations. The result is that partnerships remain relatively small, being particularly suitable to that type of business, such as retailing and the professions (doctors, dentists, consulting engineers and lawyers), where the capital provided is not so much in the form of money as in professional skill and experience, each partner probably specialising in a particular branch.

Moreover, in securing capital through partners, disadvantages are incurred. The risk inherent in unlimited liability is increased because all partners are liable for the firm's debts irrespective of the amount of capital which each has individually invested, and private fortunes may be called upon to meet the demands of creditors. Only if a partner takes no share in the management of the firm, and there is at least one ordinary partner, can the privilege of limited liability be enjoyed. Second, any action taken by one partner is legally binding on all the other partners. From this it follows that not only must each partner have complete confidence in the others but that, as the number of partners increases, so does the risk inherent in unlimited liability. Finally, by giving notice to the others, one partner may terminate the partnership at any time, while it is automatically dissolved upon the death or bankruptcy of any one partner. This means that surviving partners have either to buy his share or find a purchaser who is acceptable to everyone. In such circumstances, therefore, the continuation of the business often involves great trouble and expense.

The Joint-Stock Company

The joint-stock company first developed in Tudor times when England's foreign trade began to expand. Instead of a trading ship being owned by one person, it was financed by a number of people who bought 'shares' in a company formed for the purpose. Yet, until the middle of the nineteenth century, people were reluctant to take shares in such companies since they enjoyed no limited liability. By purchasing only one share a person risked not merely the money invested but, should the company be forced into liquidation, the whole of his or her private fortune. Moreover, this unlimited liability made it virtually impossible to adopt the technique of spreading risks by investing in different companies.

The Industrial Revolution made it essential that more capital should be available to industry. Hence, in order to induce small savers to invest, the privilege of limited liability was bestowed by Act of Parliament in 1855.

Today the joint-stock company is the most important form of business organisation. The advantages it enjoys over the partnership are limited liability, continuity, the availability of capital (since investors can spread their risks and sell their shares easily), and, should the need arise, ease of expansion. Indeed, some kinds of business could not be conducted on a small scale, and these have to start as joint-stock companies, either being sponsored by important interests, or else developed as subsidiaries of existing large firms.

Against these advantages, however, certain disadvantages, which could add to costs, have to be considered. Even small companies have to file with the Registrar of Companies an audited balance sheet and an Annual Return giving the names of the directors, while large companies have to give more detailed information. Furthermore, any assets of the company which have been built up over the years will increase the value of the original shares (usually owned by the family). When the time comes to wind up the company, e.g. owing to retirement, any increase in the value of the shares may be subject to capital gains tax.

The *long-term finance* of a company is obtained in four main ways: (a) selling 'shares' in the company; (b) borrowing; (c) obtaining a government grant or loan; (d) retaining profits.

Shares

A 'share' is exactly what the name implies – a participation in the provision of the capital of a company. Shares may be issued in various units, usually from 5p upwards, and people can vary the degree to which they participate by the number of units purchased. The investment of money in a company does involve certain risks, of which two are paramount. The first is that the return on the capital invested may be less than expected because profits are disappointing. The second is that share prices in general may have fallen at the moment when the owner wishes to sell his or her holdings. To minimise these risks, investors usually spread their holdings over different companies and vary the magnitude of the risks undertaken by having a portfolio of shares, debentures and government bonds.

(i) *Ordinary shares.* The dividend paid to the ordinary shareholder depends mainly on the prosperity of the company. If profits are high, the dividend is usually correspondingly high; if there are no profits, then there may be no dividend. Moreover, the payment of a dividend to an ordinary shareholder ranks last in the order of priority, while if the company should be forced into liquidation the ordinary shareholder is repaid only after other creditors have been paid in full. Thus the 'ordinary share' is termed 'risk capital' (and often referred to as an 'equity'). In return for bearing the risks of the business venture each ordinary shareholder has a say in the running of the company, voting according to the number of shares held. At the general meeting, directors are appointed or removed, changes made in the company's method of raising capital and conducting business, and auditors appointed. Thus the ordinary shareholders, because they take the major risks and decisions regarding the policy of the company, are the real 'entrepreneurs'. In practice, however, their rights are rarely exercised. Providing the company appears to be doing reasonably well, few share-holders trouble to attend meetings. Moreover, unless the company is very large, the directors are often in a strong position in that they will probably hold or control a large proportion of the ordinary shares. Indeed, at times voting rights are specifically excluded (usually signified by 'A' shares).

(ii) *Preference shares*. If investors wish to undertake a slightly reduced risk, they can buy preference shares. Such a shareholder is entitled to a dividend payment before the ordinary shareholder, but only at a fixed per cent no matter how high the company's profits. In addition, only in exceptional circumstances, such as when it is proposed to alter their rights or to wind up the company, or when their dividends are in arrears, can these shareholders vote at ordinary meetings. Should, however, the company be forced into liquidation, the preference shareholder ranks above the ordinary shareholder in the redemption of capital.

Preference shares may also be 'cumulative'. If the company cannot pay a dividend one year, arrears may be made up in succeeding years before the ordinary shareholders receive any dividend. Since 1965 preference shares have lost popularity through their unfavourable tax treatment (see p.84).

Borrowing

The long-term loans of a company are usually obtained by issuing 'debentures'. These bear a fixed rate of interest irrespective of the profit made by the company. Since this interest payment is a first charge on the income of the company, the risk to the investor's income is not so high. Moreover, should the company fail, debenture-holders are paid out first. In fact, 'mortgage debentures' are secured on definite assets of the company. One other advantage of debentures is that they are redeemable after a specified period. Should the company be unable to meet its interest charges or to redeem the loan when due, the debenture-holders can force it into liquidation.

Unlike the ordinary shareholder whose investment is bound up with the fortunes of the company, the purchaser of a debenture eliminates risk as far as possible. In essence, such a person is merely lending the company money. Hence he or she enjoys no ownership rights of voting on management and policy. But a company whose profits are subject to frequent and violent fluctuations is not in a position to raise much of its capital by debentures. Such a method is really suitable only to a company making a fairly stable profit (sufficiently adequate to cover the interest payments), and possessing assets (such as land and buildings), the value of which would not depreciate a great deal were the company to go into liquidation.

A company having a large proportion of fixed-interest loans to ordinary shares is said to be 'highly geared'. Such a company will be able to pay high dividends when profits are good, but unable to make a distribution when profits are low. Where profits are expected to rise in the future, therefore, a company may prefer to raise capital for expansion by issuing debentures if the cost of doing so is not too high.

But it is the present-day corporation tax which is the main impulse in this direction. Debenture interest (but not preference-share interest) is included in the costs of a company for the purposes of calculating tax. Thus it reduces taxable profits. On the other hand, if finance is raised by shares, there is no prior interest charge and profits (which are subject to tax) are that amount higher. This tax situation has, since the introduction of corporation tax in 1965, led companies to finance capital expansion as far as possible by fixed-interest loans rather than by the sale of shares. Preference shares are now hardly ever issued.

Government Grants and Loans

Grants and loans are available to firms setting up in Development Areas (see pp.373–4), and also to farmers on a percentage basis for expenditure on certain improvements, e.g. roads, hedge-planting.

Retained Profits

Not all profits are distributed to shareholders. In addition to providing for depreciation and for a contingency fund, profits will be regarded by a successful company as its major source of capital for future expansions.

Private and Public Companies

Joint-stock companies are of two main kinds, private and public.

The Private Company

A private company is simply a company that is not a public company and the formalities involved in its formation are few. But under the Companies Act, 1948, it has to satisfy the following conditions:
(i)   neither shareholders nor debenture-holders exceed fifty in number;
(ii) shares are not offered for sale by public issue;
(iii) directors have the power to disapprove any proposed transfer of shares;
(iv) none of its shares is held by another company, unless the aggregate shareholding of the two companies is fifty or less;
(v)   no corporate body acts as a director;
(vi) nobody other than the registered holder has any interest in the company's shares;
(vii) no person or body outside the company is in a position to control its policy.

The private company, while conferring limited liability, allows the business to be privately owned and managed. It is thus particularly suitable for either a medium-sized commercial or industrial organisation not requiring finance from the public, or for a speculative venture where a small group of people wishes to try out an idea and is prepared to back it financially to a definite limit before floating a public company. While private companies are considerably more numerous than public companies, their average capital is much smaller.

Until 1980 funds for expansion were severely limited since shares cannot be offered for sale by public advertisement. But as part of the government's desire to encourage growth of the economy through the development of small businesses, new sources of 'venture capital' have arisen. Banks and other institutions have been more willing to provide medium-term loans especially as, under the Loan Guarantee Scheme, the Department of Industry guarantees 80 per cent of loans up to £75 000. More important is the Business Expansion Scheme by which individuals enjoy tax relief on up to £40 000 share capital each year provided it is held for five years, and if shares are subsequently sold they are excused capital gains tax.

This growth in venture capital has been helped by the unofficial 'Over the Counter' market for unquoted shares which has been organised by a few licensed dealers.

Because the shares of a private company are illiquid in that they cannot be offered for sale by public advertisement, a difficult stage in its growth may be reached when its capital is in the region of £250 000, for it is still too small to make a public issue. The gap can be bridged in four main ways.

First, a stockbroker may effect a 'private placing' of shares or debentures with a life insurance company or an investment trust, who are usually in a position to ignore the disadvantages of holding securities of private companies. Second, help might be obtained from the new issue market, where both issuing houses and merchant bankers assist firms to raise capital even providing some themselves. Third, there are a number of specialised finance corporations. Thus for agriculture there is the Agricultural Mortgage Corporation, which will lend on the security of land and buildings. For other firms, Charterhouse Development, Equity Capital for Industry and the Industrial and Commercial Finance Corporation (a branch of Finance for Industry) are among those who will help with long-term finance. Fourth, the commercial banks have now entered the medium-term loan field, particularly through their merchant bank branches.

The Public Company

When a large amount of capital is required, the first step is usually to form a public company. This must have at least two shareholders, an authorised minimum capital of £50 000 and carry the designation 'public limited company' – abbreviated to Plc – after its name. But it is the second step which is really important – getting its shares 'quoted' on one of the Stock Exchange markets – the Unlisted Securities Market or the Stock Exchange (see pp.273–5). This entails an exhaustive examination of the company's affairs which have to be advertised very fully in at least two leading London newspapers, while if no new issue is being made, a supply of shares has to be made available by existing shareholders sufficient to make dealing and the price fixed realistic.

The capital required can be raised by a 'placing', an 'offer for sale' or a 'public issue by prospectus'. The first is the usual method when only about £1 million is required, for the costs of underwriting and administration are less. An issuing house, licensed dealer or investment company agrees to sell blocks of the shares privately to persons who it knows are likely to be interested in them.

For larger amounts of up to £5 million an offer for sale is a likely method. The shares are sold *en bloc* to an issuing house, which then offers them for sale to the public by advertisement similar to a public issue. The above two methods are the only ones available to companies whose shares are dealt in on the Unlisted Securities Market.

For more than £10 million, a public issue by prospectus is the method usually employed. Here the company's object is to obtain from the public in a single day the capital it requires. Hence it must advertise well and price its shares a little on the cheap side. The advertisement is in the form of a prospectus which sets out the business, history and prospects of the company together with its financial standing and the security offered. It must be issued at least three days before the allotment of the securities, so that the prospectus can be adequately examined and reviewed in the financial papers. Attached to the prospectus there is usually an application form which the would-be subscriber completes and sends with the application money (which may be required in full or in part).

In practice, the sale is usually conducted through an issuing house, which advises on the terms of the issue. It will also arrange to have the issue underwritten: that is, it will find a number of institutions, such as merchant bankers, which, in return for a small commission, will take whatever part of the issue is left unsold. However, such underwriters do not have to rely entirely on permanent investors to buy the securities on the day of issue, for speculators, known as 'stags', are usually operating, and they buy the shares hoping to resell them quickly at a small profit. Furthermore, where a company is raising additional capital, existing shareholders are now usually given the right to purchase new shares through a 'rights issue' in proportion to shares already held and usually at a favourable price.

Co-operative Societies

Although there were many co-operative societies in operation before the Rochdale Pioneers, 1844, it was these twenty-eight artisans, mostly cotton weavers, who started the modern co-operative movement. By subscribing a few pence per week, they accumulated an initial capital of £28, with which they rented a small store and started trading with small stocks of flour, oatmeal, sugar, butter and candles. Profits were distributed to members in proportion to their purchases. Today (1985) there are 103 retail co-operative societies in the UK with an aggregate membership of some 8 million. Turnover is £3450 million per annum, accounting for 5.3 per cent of Britain's retail trade. In addition, these retail societies largely provide the capital and control the operation of the Co-operative Wholesale Society.

The minimum shareholding in a retail co-operative society is usually £1. Only if a full share is held does a member enjoy voting rights, but not more than one vote per member is allowed irrespective of the number of shares held. Until fairly recently, societies distributed profits as a dividend in proportion to the value of a member's purchases over the period. Today, however, most societies make use of the National Dividend Stamp scheme operated by the Co-operative Wholesale Society. Stamps are given to customers in proportion to their purchases, and a book of stamps can be redeemed for cash, goods or a deposit in a share account, in which case a bonus is usually added. Not only has this system allowed co-operative shops to compete with supermarkets and stores, but it is much cheaper to operate than the old 'divi' method. Nor does the member have to wait at least six months before receiving the dividend, while the national stamp can be given by other traders, e.g. petrol stations.

Co-operative societies described above are organised directly by consumers and are therefore called 'consumer co-operative societies'. Producers have also formed 'producer co-operative societies' to market their members' produce. They are chiefly important in the marketing of agricultural produce, particularly where production is carried on by small farmers, as in Denmark, New Zealand and Spain. Nevertheless, they have been slow to develop in the UK. Instead, marketing difficulties have been dealt with by the government setting up Marketing Boards.

6.5 State Enterprise

We considered in Chapter 2 the various reasons why the state should interfere in the operation of a market economy. Such intervention takes various forms. Sometimes it merely involves modifying the operation of the price system, as when subsidies are granted, import duties imposed or prices controlled. At other times, however, the state supervises, or actually undertakes, the production of goods and services. Thus we have producing units ('firms') in the public sector of the economy – government departments, public corporations and local authorities.

With certain goods and services, e.g. defence, the maintenance of law and order, and certain social and welfare benefits (such as health, education, and insurance against unemployment, sickness and retirement) there is little disagreement with state provision. But where, for various reasons, the state has taken over industries formerly organised under private enterprise, there has been considerable controversy and opposition. There are arguments for and against in every case. The final decision regarding nationalisation is therefore largely a political one.

In this section we take no sides in the political argument. Instead we simply glance at the possible economic arguments for nationalising certain industries and then consider some of the problems of organisation and operation which have arisen.

Economic Arguments for Nationalisation

Nationalisation still covers a wide range of industries – the Bank of England, water supply, atomic energy, electricity supply, coal, rail, canal and some road transport, iron and steel, ship-building but some of them, e.g. aerospace, cable and wireless, oil exploration, telecommunications, gas, civil aviation and road transport, have been returned to private enterprise. Since these industries differ in such matters as their importance, size and type of product, not all the economic arguments for and against nationalisation apply equally to each. The following are therefore merely generalised arguments which could, but need not, apply to an individual industry.

(1) *Single control over all the firms in the industry enables the full advantages of large-scale production to be achieved.* Competition between firms may result in their working at less than the optimum size (see pp.147, 187) because uncertainty as regards rivals' plans may inhibit investment through fear of over-investment by the industry as a whole. It may also give rise to duplication of research, unnecessary differences in design of tools and product, and inefficiency of operation. The National Coal Board, for instance, has developed a standard pattern of miners' safety helmet, while it has been able to reduce underground haulage on some coal fields by using a nearer shaft (Figure 6.2).

FIGURE 6.2
An Advantage of Common Ownership in Coal-mining

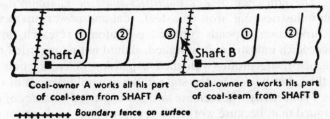

Coal-owner A works all his part of coal-seam from SHAFT A

Coal-owner B works his part of coal-seam from SHAFT B

Boundary fence on surface

Before nationalisation separate owners meant separate workings and long haulages when workings had reached 3. Under nationalisation, this sector of coal-mine A can be more economically worked from shaft B, in the direction of the arrow.

Similarly, nationalisation secures commercial and financial economies. Thus competitive advertising costs between firms are eliminated, while, in borrowing, a state-owned industry can usually obtain finance more cheaply than a private firm.

(2) *State ownership is essential for the necessary capital investment.* Private owners may not have the resources or be willing to commit themselves to long-term capital outlays. Thus the development of atomic energy has been undertaken by the state for both security and technical reasons, while the railway modernisation programme would have been too risky for private ownership. Moreover, some losses may be justified by

external benefits, e.g. relief of unemployment, less congestion on the roads.

(3)   *State ownership is a means of controlling monopoly.* Some industries must inevitably be organised as monopolies, either because this power is legally conferred (e.g. public utilities, where otherwise chaos might result) or because the economies of large-scale production are so large (e.g. atomic energy, electricity generation). It is argued that the best way of controlling such monopolies is state ownership, for there is then the assurance that they will work in the public interest and not merely for high profits.

(4)   *A pricing policy can be adopted which allows a highly capitalised industry to break even on all costs.* Where initial fixed costs are very high – e.g. in electricity supply – it is impossible to charge a single price which will generate sufficient revenue to cover total costs (see p.182). However, by creating a monopoly which can discriminate between customers and charge different prices to each according to what they are willing to pay, total revenue can be increased. On the other hand, since such monopolies are essential public utilities, it is held that they should be under direct state control.

(5)   *The efficiency of key industries must be guaranteed.* There are certain industries, e.g. iron and steel, coal and power, upon which most other production depends. Others, e.g. atomic research, are vital for defence. Such industries, it is argued, should not be regarded merely as a source of private profit (with their expansion or contraction dependent upon this), but be run by the state in the general interests of the nation.

(6)   *Productivity will increase through improved attitudes of employees.* It is argued that, because workers will enjoy better working conditions and be motivated by being employed by the state and not a company striving for its own profit, increased worker productivity will result.

Problems of Organisation

Even after it has been agreed that the state should either supervise or undertake the production of goods and services, it still has to be decided how the management shall be organised. Two fundamental principles, each pulling in opposite directions, need due consideration.

The first principle arises because where the state is granted powers, the citizen requires some assurance that the powers granted to the state to produce goods are not being abused by authoritarianism, inefficiency or monopolistic exploitation. This is known as the principle of 'public accountability'.

The most efficient form of accountability is achieved when a government department produces the goods or services. The department usually has a minister at its head who accepts full responsibility for the work of his department. This minister is subject to examination in Parliament, and it is his or her task to explain general policy in debate and to answer questions on even minor details of administration. In finance, too, there is also strict control, for the Treasury is careful to see that money is spent economically and within the limit authorised by Parliament.

Nevertheless, the government department method of organisation cannot be used in providing all goods and services. Not only would Parliament be overworked if it tried to exercise detailed control, but the industries would also be the subject of continual political conflict. Above all, while the government department organisation ensures maximum accountability, it has certain weaknesses in providing economic goods and services, weaknesses which become more apparent where it has been or is possible to organise the production through private enterprise. Apart from the inherent deficiencies of the Civil Service (such as lack of initiative, addiction to red tape and the rigid Treasury control of finance and staffing), public accountability itself entails some conflict with the second principle, that of 'economic efficiency'.

This principle was discussed in Chapter 2, and it was shown how private enterprise was very effective in solving the two main aspects of efficiency, the estimate of consumers' demand and efficiency in supply. Firms decide what and how to produce. If their decisions are correct, a profit is their reward; if they are wrong, and production is misdirected, then they, and only they, are the losers.

But what happens when the department is the producer and its civil servants are accountable to Parliament for day-to-day details of administration? The result is the 'play-for-safety' attitude already commented on. Moreover, accountability through Parliament has additional defects. It might lead to difficulties in pursuing long-term industrial and commercial objectives because the minister in charge is frequently changed through either reorganisation of the government or a swing of the political pendulum. Furthermore, much of the parliamentary questioning in day-to-day matters could be irrelevant and ill-informed in that it covers technical matters beyond the understanding of the average MP, or it may be even positively harmful, being used solely as an instrument of political opposition.

The result of this conflict between the two principles of public accountability and economic efficiency has been the development of special governmental (sometimes called 'quasi-government') bodies, variously termed commissions, boards, authorities and corporations. Though they differ in the nature and importance of the functions performed, as well as in the degree of independence enjoyed, all are subject to some measure of government control. Figure 6.3 gives an indication of the nature of their functions.

FIGURE 6.3
Forms of Public Organisation for the Supervision or Provision of Goods and Services

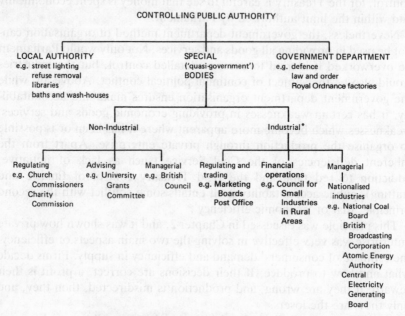

* 'Industrial' in this context means the bodies are connected with a particular industry or serve industry in general.

The Organisation of the Nationalised Industries

Within the principles outlined above, the organisation of the nationalised industries presents some common features.

(1) The boards are 'bodies corporate'. This means that they have a legal identity and therefore, like a company, have a life of their own, can own property, and sue and be sued in the courts.

(2) The assets of the industry are vested in the board and the nationalising Act usually gives the board instructions as to its general responsibilities. Thus the National Coal Board is charged with:

(a) working and getting the coal in Great Britain;
(b) securing the efficiency development of the coal-mining industry;
(c) making supplies of coal available, of such qualities and sizes, in such quantities and at such prices, as may seem best calculated to further the public interest.

(3) A minister is given an overall control of the board. He exercises, as it were, the shareholders' rights in a company, the 'shareholders' of a board being the community. It is the minister, therefore, who appoints the board's members, though the nationalising Act usually specifies their general qualifications. In addition, the minister may give the board directions of a general character as to how they shall exercise and perform the functions with regard to matters which appear to affect the national interest. This usually includes authorising capital development, supervising borrowing and appointing auditors. The aim, therefore, is to give the board freedom in its day-to-day administration but with some subordination in its general policy. Boards are not subject to parliamentary questioning on detailed matters of administration, but they are required to submit annual reports to Parliament, for which the government usually sets aside a day to debate.

(4) In financial and staffing matters, the boards are free from Treasury control. They are required to pay their way, taking one year with another, free from state subsidy. They engage their own staff, arranging directly, through employees' trade unions or associations, pay and conditions of service.

(5) In order to avoid parliamentary questioning on matters of detail, and to ensure a degree of direct representation by customers, consumers' councils have been established for the coal, electricity and transport industries. They consist of twenty to thirty unpaid members appointed by the minister. Nominations for members are put forward by bodies whom the minister selects as being representative of consumers, e.g. local authorities, women's organisations, professional associations, trade unions, and trade associations. The coal industry has two national councils, one for industrial and one for domestic users, but the 'consultative councils' of the other industries are organised on a regional basis. The functions of these councils are:

(a) to deal with complaints and suggestions from consumers, although they are also expected to act on their own initiative in such matters;
(b) to advise both the boards and the minister of the general views of consumers.

Unfortunately, either through ignorance, the remoteness of the offices, or general lack of confidence, little use has so far been made of these councils by consumers.

In short, therefore, the new public corporation tries, as it were, to get the best of both worlds: on the one hand, the world of energetic industrial enterprise found in the private enterprise system; on the other, the world of accountability to the public, to whom it belongs and whom it serves.

The detailed internal organisation of the corporations has varied. Two illustrations will serve to demonstrate this point. The Coal Industry

Nationalisation Act, 1946, set up a National Coal Board (NCB) with the responsibilities already mentioned. But the rest of the organisation of the coal industry was such as this board should determine. In practice, collieries are grouped in areas, each under an Area Director who is directly and personally responsible to the NCB. The day-to-day work of running the collieries is under the direction of colliery managers.

It seems, however, that originally the problem of size was under-estimated, for subsequent nationalising Acts brought an increasing tendency to decentralisation. Thus the Electricity Council which was established in 1948, is really only a central representative body for the industry as a whole, being composed mainly of the chairmen of the twelve Area Boards, with an independent chairman or vice-chairman appointed by the minister. The nationalising Acts established the twelve Area Boards, and the assets of the industry were vested in them. The Area Boards were also given the *statutory* responsibility for the distribution of electricity. Each board adopted its own pattern of organisation and arrangements for fulfilling its statutory obligations.

Economic Problems of Nationalisation

Apart from problems of a constitutional nature – internal organisation, the exact responsibility of the minister, the extent of, and opportunities for, parliamentary review – economic problems arise.

These problems stem chiefly from the fact that often the nationalised industries are monopolies. On the demand side there is therefore some loss of consumers' sovereignty. Initially, for instance, a person can choose between gas, electricity, coal and oil when deciding on central heating; but thereafter he or she is more or less committed. Should the consumer be dissatisfied with subsequent prices rises, the ultimate sanction – taking custom elsewhere – is not available. On the supply side, too, there are grounds for concern. Prices are fixed with the object of covering costs, but since prices are fixed on a cost basis, what guarantee is there that costs are kept to a minimum by efficient operation? It is felt that periodic independent efficiency investigations should be made. Moreover, in the past, governments have restricted price rises as part of their anti-inflation measures. This does mean, however, that the corporations cannot fulfil their obligation of paying their way unless they are given subsidies from central government funds.

Problems of scale, e.g. of co-ordination, also arise in managing these vast industries. Yet these same problems exist in the private sector, and there seems little reason why state industry should be inferior in its ability to solve them.

Some criticis argue that investment decisions in many of the nationalised industries have not been altogether wise. While some error is bound to occur in a dynamic economy (the discovery of North Sea natural gas, for instance, upset the Coal Board's projections of future demand for coal), there is more than a strong suspicion that the nationalised industries came off favourably in the allocation of capital soon after they were created because the government had a vested interest in their success.

Finally, the nationalised industries have not yet really discovered how and when to award wage increases, especially when losses are being made! Threats of strike in these basic industries, e.g. railways, have led to government intervention and the aggravation of the wage-cost inflationary spiral.

6.6 Privatisation

Nature of Privatisation

'Privatisation' implies more than the movement of assets from the public to the private sector. Rather it embraces all the different means by which the disciplines of the free market in the provision of goods and services can be applied to the public sector. Thus this 'pushing back the frontiers of the state' covers:

(a) the transfer of the nationalised industries to private ownership, e.g. British Telecom, British Gas, British Airways, British Airports Authority;
(b) selling other state assets, either completely (e.g. Britoil, Rolls-Royce, motorway service areas) or partially (e.g. woodlands owned by the Forestry Commission, British Petroleum shares, council housing);
(c) opening-up State monopolies to outside competition, e.g. relaxing licensing restrictions to allow private bus firms to compete with publicly-owned services;
(d) 'contracting-out' to the private sector services paid for out of public funds, e.g. refuse collection, street cleaning, hospital ancillary services;
(e) charging beneficiaries for publicly-provided goods and services, e.g. museums, medical prescriptions, school meals, council housing.

Reasons for privatisation

Although the Labour government initiated a form of privatisation when in 1977 it sold a part of the state's British Petroleum shares in order to be less dependent on borrowing to cover its PSBR, privatisation is really based on the market economy philosophy of the Conservative party. Thus while Mrs Thatcher's first term of office still concentrated on the PSBR objective, privatisation was extended by returning to the private sector firms which had been recently acquired (e.g. British Aerospace and Cable and Wireless) and by encouraging contracting-out of services. But during her second term beginning in 1983 privatisation measures were extended and integrated in line with her private enterprise views and supply-side policies (see pp.263–4). It is in this context, therefore, that the advantages claimed for privatisation have to be analysed.

1. Reduced Burden on the Public Purse

As a one-off, short-term measure the proceeds from state asset sales have helped to cover a worrying PSBR. Indeed, where state industries have had recurrent deficits (with debts eventually having to be written off, e.g. coal, railways, airways), there is a long-term relief to the public purse. On the other hand, it can be argued that such 'write-offs' can be regarded as subsidies for external benefits, e.g. the relief of unemployment.

2. Freedom from Detailed Political Control

Some political control over general policy and the scale of borrowing is necessary to achieve a degree of accountability. But some governments have seen public enterprises as legitimate instruments of macroeconomic policy, e.g. countenancing over-manning to preserve jobs in periods of unemployment, holding prices to combat inflation, and restricting investment spending to reduce the PSBR.

Thus managers of the nationalised industries have felt frustrated at not being able to pursue pricing and long-time investment strategies unencumbered by government interference, preferring to reap the rewards for success and carry the consequences of failure.

3. Improved Efficiency Through Competition in the Market

Economic efficiency must be considered from both the demand and supply sides. The market indicates consumer preferences (e.g. for ownership of council housing as opposed to renting), while competition promotes efficiency in supplying consumer goods and services.

As monopolies, however, the nationalised industries have tended to take some profits in the form of a 'quiet life' since competition does not force Boards to push the industry to the highest possible efficiency. Even at the lower levels, managers may seek to maximise their own empires and budgets.

4. Greater Resistance to Trade Union Power

Where the state is the ultimate provider of funds, wage demands can more easily be pressed by trade unions and conceded even though not justified by profits. Moreover, especially in the basic industries such as coal, rail and steel, wage rises have been granted on a *national* basis. It is suggested that privatisation undermines the ability of militant public sector trade unions to secure high wages and protection of employment through such subsidies from the taxpayer.

5. Creation of a Property-Owning Democracy

The sale of shares has been so arranged that they have as broad an appeal as possible both as regards price and allocation. Special encouragement has been given to employees to buy shares. Although many purchasers have subsequently sold, a much wider public has been introduced to share ownership.

It is claimed that those who have retained their shares reflect the current movement towards private ownership (e.g. in the success of the sale of council houses), and the private provision of services (e.g. medical and pension schemes).

Difficulties of Privatisation

In section 6.5 we discussed possible reasons for nationalising certain industries. It must be recorded, however, that few of those industries have, in practice, justified the claims of those who advocated nationalisation. Some such as coal and steel, have been over-capitalised, largely because funds were available at relatively low rates of interest or because the industries were given priority for political reasons. This has led to 'crowding-out' of investment in the private sector. Moreover, profit targets have been missed with persistent regularity and, even after the government has written off debts, the sequence of losses is repeated. Nor have the energy industries in particular shown a high sensitivity to such external considerations as air pollution or the protection of the rural environment. Estimates of future demand, e.g. for coal, ships and steel, have been widely optimistic, while monopoly powers have enabled them to base prices on costs with consequent lack of efficiency.

Even so privatisation is no guarantee that these problems will be eliminated, but steps have been taken to introduce some form of competition wherever possible or to introduce devices to ensure that regard is paid to the 'public interest'.

The major difficulty is that while privatisation eliminates direct government involvement in decision-making and responsibility for particular industries, many, especially the 'natural monopolies' (chiefly public utilities) have retained their monopolist and monopsonist positions. This can result in exploitation of consumers by monopoly pricing and inefficiency through lack of competition.

Consequently, where possible, indirect competition has been fostered. For example, gas still has to compete with coal, oil and electricity, while Mercury has been granted a licence to compete in telecommunications with British Telecom. Similarly, Racal's Vodafone is a major competitor in car telephones with British Telecom's Cellnet. The most striking progress has been in the rapid growth of express coach services with reduced fares after competition with the National Bus Company was allowed.

An alternative arrangement has been to grant independence to firms on a franchise basis for a limited period, e.g. regional television companies. Provision is made to prevent mergers and, in reviewing the franchise, consideration can be given to past conduct as regards quality of service and sensitivity to the wishes of the public as well as to the price tendered. The difficulty with this method is that investment may be inhibited by lack of certainty of long-term future operations.

Where some form of competition is difficult to devise, the responsibility for protecting the public interest may rest with a regulatory body. Thus the Office for Telecommunications (OFTEL) acts as a watchdog for unfair practices, though doubt has been expressed as to whether it has sufficient powers to be really effective. Furthermore, price rises are limited to 3 per cent *less* than the rate of inflation. This ensures that the consumer receives some benefit of technical improvements, but encourages efficiency in that the company is allowed to retain any additional cost savings.

Another problem in deciding on privatisation is that it is not always easy to separate regulatory, strategically vital or welfare functions from those appropriate to provision through the market. Thus privatisation has been carried out on a pragmatic basis, selecting industries which are making profits but which are not natural monopolies, e.g. British Telecom, British Airways. In contrast, the decision on privatising the Water Authorities is less clear-cut.

Difficulty has also been experienced in fixing a satisfactory price at which the industry's shares are offered to the public. If the offer is over-subscribed, the government is accused of not realising the full potential of public assets; if shares are left with the underwriters, the object of achieving a wide ownership is defeated for eventually they are bought by the institutions. The latest method (British Airports Authority) was to offer a proportion of the shares at a fixed price, and the rest by tender. The device of offering a bonus royalty share for every ten shares held for the first three years has not been so successful as hoped for, since many small purchasers have taken their profits by selling.

Conclusion

Until 1979 the mixed economy, where public bodies were responsible for producing nearly one-half of the national product, appeared to be generally accepted. The privatisation policy of the Thatcher government has reopened the debate on the proper role of the state in the economy, for reducing the size of the public sector has become an end in itself.

Yet not all government activities can be satisfactorily privatised, e.g. education and medical treatment for the majority of people. For these there must be a continuing process of improving their management and accountability by efficiency scrutinies and by monitoring their progress within the financial limits imposed.

7 The Organisation and Scale of Production

When assembling its plant, organising its factors of production and deciding how to get the finished product to the customer, the firm will consider the pros and cons of producing on a large scale and the advantages to be obtained from specialisation.

Because specialisation is the fundamental principle upon which modern production is organised, we begin this chapter by examining it. We do so with particular reference to labour under the traditional heading of 'the division of labour' but, as we shall see, it is equally applicable to machines, localities and even countries.

7.1 The Division of Labour

Increased production results when the labour force is so organised that each person specialises on a particular job. Thus in the simple task of making a table, one worker will be sawing the wood, another planing it, a third cutting the joints, a fourth gluing together the various parts, and the last polishing the finished article. This increased production is achieved because:

(1) *Each worker is employed in the job in which his or her superiority is most marked*. Suppose that, in one day, Smith can plane the parts for 20 tables *or* cut the joints for 10, whereas Brown can either plane 10 tables *or* cut the joints for 20. If each do both jobs, their combined production in a day will be 15 tables planed *and* 15 table joints cut. But Smith is better at planing, while Brown is better at cutting joints. If they specialise on what they can do best, their combined production will be 20 tables planed *and* 20 table-joints cut – an increase in output of a third. Later, when we consider international trade, we shall develop this argument to show that specialisation can still be advantageous even if one person or country is superior in both lines of production.

Even if initially every worker were equally proficient at the different jobs it would, for the following reasons, still pay to organise them so that they specialised.

(2) *Practice makes perfect, and so particular skills are developed through repetition of the same job.*

(3) *Economy in tools makes possible the use of specialised machinery.* Consider Figure 7.1. In (*a*) every man has a saw, a plane, a chisel and mallet, a gluepot and brush, and a polishing cloth. In (*b*) the principle of division of labour has been introduced. One man works a circular saw, another a mechanical plane, a third cuts joints with a special tool (a mortiser), a fourth glues and clamps the tables, and the last uses a sander and polisher electrically powered. These specialised tools are economic because they are in constant use, and output from them is much greater. Thus, not only does the division of labour set free talented men for research and invention, but it encourages both because the fruits can be used profitably.

(4) *Time is saved through not having to switch from one operation to another.* In the above example, if one man were making the table himself, he would have to put away each different tool after using it. When he specialises, he keeps to the same tool all the time.

FIGURE 7.1
Specialisation and Economy in Tools

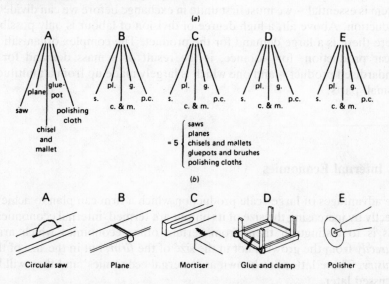

(5) *Less time is taken in learning a particular job.* In the making of a table, only one tool and one operation have to be mastered. This makes it easier for labour to move from one industry to another.

(6) *The employer can estimate costs of production and output more accurately.*

But while it benefits the manufacturer and eventually the consumer, the division of labour has disadvantages both to the worker and to society. The worker may feel that his job is monotonous, while with some occupations, such as paint-spraying, there is increased risk of occupational disease. Moreover, the skilled specialist may become redundant when demand falls, and the interdependence involved in our complex organisation of the economy can lead to widespread unemployment when a small group of workers goes on strike or a source of raw materials dries up. Finally, standardised products tend to replace the individual work of the old craftsman. Nevertheless, it must be emphasised that these drawbacks are but a small price to pay when compared with the great benefits resulting from the division of labour.

Naturally, the degree of division of labour which can be introduced varies from one industry to another. In small or sparsely populated countries, there are insufficient workers to allow a minute division in a number of industries. Hence countries like Switzerland concentrate on a narrow range of manufactured products. Again, in some industries, such as agriculture and building, where the same operations are not taking place each day, many 'Jacks of all trades' are required. Moreover, an exchange system is essential – we must first unite in exchange before we can divide in production. Above all, a high degree of division of labour is only possible where there is a large demand for the product. The complex organisation of car production, for instance, is the result of a mass demand for a standardised product – and one which is largely made up from a multitude of small parts.

7.2 Internal Economies

The advantages of large-scale production which a firm can plan to achieve directly by increasing the size of its output are termed 'internal economies'. This is to distinguish them from certain other economies which arise *indirectly* from the growth, not in the size of the *firm*, but in the size of the *industry*. These latter are known as 'external economies' and they will be discussed later.

Internal economies can be conveniently classified under five headings: technical, managerial, commercial, financial and risk-bearing.

1. Technical Economies

In the actual making of the good, as distinct from its distribution, economies result when production is on a large scale.

First, production can be broken down into many separate tasks because workers can be employed full time on each. At once all the advantages of the division of labour are achieved. In the production of lower-priced coats, for instance, the multiple tailor employs in his factory a 'flow' method of production. One worker specialises in the actual cutting of the cloth, another tacks the various parts together. Later in the process a girl might concentrate on the making of the button-holes, while another sews the buttons on. The larger the scale of production, the further can the degree of specialisation usually be carried, especially when, as with the motor-car, the product largely consists of a multitude of tiny parts.

Second, the larger producer is also able to employ specialised machinery because he can keep it fully occupied. Moreover, only the large firm can afford to carry out research or to provide canteen and welfare facilities for its employees.

Third, the initial outlay and operating costs of a large machine may be lower than when two or more machines do the same work. For instance, a double-decker bus can carry twice as many passengers, but the initial cost is not twice as much, nor are the running costs doubled. It may even be that there is a mechanical advantage in working on a large scale. In farming, for instance, the tendency with modern machinery is for fields to become larger, for less time is wasted in turning the bulkier machines.

Last, economies are achieved through linking processes. For instance, in steel-making the large mills can save fuel by rolling the ingots into sheets before they cool.

Generally technical economies fix the size of the unit actually producing, rather than the size of the firm, which may consist of many units. Where technical economies of scale are large, the size of the typical unit will tend to be correspondingly great, as (for example) in the production of cars, sheet steel, gas and electricity. Where, however, increased output merely means duplicating and reduplicating machines, then the unit tends to remain small. For instance, in farming at least one combine-harvester is necessary for about 500 acres. Thus the size of the individual farm still remains relatively small, for as yet no decisive technical economies can be derived from large machines. Where technical economies are few and yet the firm is large, consisting, as with chain stores, of many operating units, its size is usually because other types of economy are possible, as follows.

2. Managerial Economies

Increased output allows specialists to be fully employed. Thus the division of labour can be introduced into the task of management. In a shop, for instance, owned and run by one person, the owner, while having the ability to order supplies, manage the books, and sell the goods, has yet to do such trivial jobs as sweeping the floor, weighing articles and packing parcels, jobs which could be done by a youngster straight from school. The owner's sales, however, may not warrant employing someone else. The large business overcomes this difficulty. A brilliant organiser can devote all of his or her time wholly to the work of organising, while the routine jobs can be left to a lower-paid worker.

The function of management can itself be divided, expert administrators taking charge of production, sales, transport and personnel departments. Such departments may even be sub-divided, the sales department, for instance, having sections for advertisement, exports, and customers' welfare.

3. Commercial Economies

Economies are achieved by the large firm both in buying raw materials and in selling the finished product. Favourable terms may be granted to the large firm placing a bulk order for materials because such an order is of more value to the producer of those materials. It may mean, for instance, that its plant can be worked to capacity or without delays for re-setting machines and tools. This principle of lower charges for a bulk order applies in various stages of production. The price of photographs advertising a product, for instance, would be quoted by the photographic firm according to the size of the order, while, for the transport of the finished goods, special rates would probably be obtained by the large firm because costs of transport, especially rail transport, do not increase in the same proportion as the volume of the goods to be transported.

Economies can be achieved, too, in the selling of the product. Often the sales staff are not being worked to capacity, and so more goods can be sold at little extra cost. In any case much less work is involved proportionately in packaging and invoicing a large order than when the same amount of goods is split up into many orders. Moreover, the large firm often manufactures many products and then one commodity acts as an advertisement for another. Thus Wall's ice-cream is also an advertisement for the company's pork pies and sausages, while Hoover vacuum cleaners help to sell Hoover washing-machines. In addition, a large firm may be able to sell its by-products, though to a small firm this might be unprofitable. Indeed, one large cinema group claimed that its box-office takings failed to cover expenses, the overall profit only being due to its ice-cream sales!

Finally, when the business is sufficiently large, the principle of the division of labour can be introduced on the commercial side, expert buyers and sellers being employed.

Such commercial economies represent real advantages to the community, for they help to lower prices through better use of scarce resources. On the other hand, where a large firm is merely using its muscle to *force* suppliers into granting it favourable prices, it will simply result in higher prices to other buyers.

4. Financial Economies

In raising finance for expansion, the large firm has nearly all the advantages. It can, for instance, offer better security to bankers and, because it is large and well known, will be able to raise new capital at a lower cost than a small firm. There are two reasons for this. Not only do investors have more confidence in the large, well-known firm, but they prefer shares which are regularly traded on the Stock Exchange, for then it is comparatively easy to dispose of them should the need arise.

5. Risk-bearing Economies

Here we can distinguish three sorts of risk. First, there are risks which can be insured against. With these the small firm is not at so great a disadvantage, for insurance enables such firms to pool risks.

Second, certain businesses usually bear some risk themselves, saving some of the profits made by the insurance company. Here the large firm has a definite advantage. London Transport, for instance, can cover its own risks, while a large bank can call in funds from other branches when there is a run on the reserves in a particular locality and thus, by meeting all the demands on it, restore the confidence of the public.

The third kind of risk is one that cannot be reduced to a mathematical probability and thus cannot be insured against – risk arising from changes in demand for the product or in the supply of raw materials; this is usually referred to as risk arising from 'uncertainty'. To meet fluctuations in demand the large firm can diversify output (like the Rank Organisation) or develop export markets. On the supply side, materials may be obtained from different sources to guard against crop failures, strikes, etc.

7.3 The Combination of Firms

Horizontal, Vertical and Lateral Combination

The advantages of large-scale production provide a strong impetus for firms to combine. (A further reason – to establish monopoly power – will be discussed later.)

Horizontal integration occurs where firms producing the same product combine under the same management. Thus Guinness took over Distillers.

Vertical integration consists of the amalgamation of firms engaged in the different stages of the production of a good. Thus Dalgety own both Ross Produce — potato suppliers — and Golden Wonder Crisps. Vertical integration may be 'backward', i.e. towards the production of the raw material, or 'forward', i.e. towards the finished product. In practice, horizontal integration, as opposed to vertical integration, has little relevance to technical economies of scale and is more closely associated with securing monopoly power (Figure 7.2).

FIGURE 7.2
Horizontal and Vertical Integration

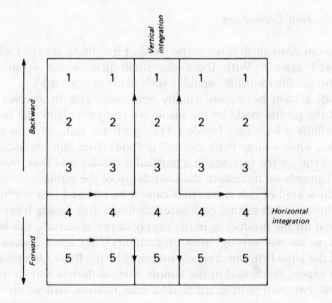

Lateral integration occurs where a firm increases the range of its products. Concentration on one product may make a firm vulnerable to a change in fashion, a switch in government policy or a recession. Thus the firm diversifies, often by taking over other firms producing completely different products. P&O for instance, includes among its interests shipping, road transport and construction.

The Holding Company

Combination may be secured by a complete takeover, with the parent company buying all the shares of a smaller firm and absorbing it completely, or by the formation of a holding company in which the parent company owns over 50 per cent of the shares (giving it a 'controlling interest'), with the smaller company preserving its identity as a separate trading unit and enjoying considerable independence of action. (Unilever and Great Universal Stores are examples of holding companies.)

The latter method, however, is open to misuse. Companies have been formed for monopoly purposes, while by 'pyramiding' a whole group of firms may be concentrated in the hands of a few people owning comparatively little capital. Suppose, for instance, that this capital is £100 000. This can be used to control the affairs of a company which has a total capital of £400 000 if only half of this is in the form of ordinary shares. Indeed, the process can be continued. The snag is that where the interests of the subsidiary firms are sacrificed to those of the group as a whole, minority shareholders who do not happen to be members of the controlling group may suffer. Consequently the Companies Act 1947 made it easier for the public to be aware of the controlling power of a holding company over its various subsidiaries.

7.4 The Predominance of the Small Firm

In spite of the advantages possessed by the large firm, small firms still predominate in the UK. In farming two-thirds of the total holdings are less than fifty acres in size, while in retailing nearly three-quarters of all firms consist of only one shop.

But the same applies even in manufacturing, where, one would imagine, technical economies of scale would be all-important. Table 7.1 illustrates this fact.

Table 7.1 shows the size of the technical unit, the factory or workshop, in *manufacturing* only. If we ignore the fact that a firm can consist of more than one establishment, the table reveals two important features: (i) the small establishment is typical of manufacturing in the UK, over nine-tenths employing less than 100 persons; (ii) these small firms employ less than one-third of the labour force.

Any explanation of the predominance of the small firm, therefore, has to cover two essential facts: (i) small firms are especially important in particular industries, such as agriculture, retailing, building and personal and professional services; (ii) variations in the size of firms exist even within the same industry. Both can be covered by a consideration of particular conditions which can exist in demand and supply.

Table 7.1
Size of Manufacturing Units in the UK, 1985

Employees	Number of firms	Percentage of total firms	Number of employees (000)	Percentage of total employed
1–9	98 923	65.9	328.4	6.6
10–99	41 712	27.8	1233.8	25.0
100–999	8 897	5.9	2313.8	46.9
Over 1000	511	0.4	1060.8	21.5
Total	150 043	100	4936.8	100

Demand

The advantages of large-scale production are concerned with *technical* efficiency. But *economic* efficiency relates the conditions of supply to demand. Thus methods of large-scale production are not economically efficient unless justified by the size of the demand.

Some firms may therefore remain small simply because the market they supply is relatively small for the following reasons:

1. The market is limited to local demand for certain goods, e.g. groceries, personal services.
2. Physical difficulties make the cost of transporting goods long distances excessive, e.g. perishable goods (small market gardeners), bulky goods of comparatively low value (bricks), or where natural difficulties have to be surmounted (water, gas).
3. Demand is limited to a few articles of one pattern, e.g. highly specialised machine-tools, which are often individually designed.
4. Product differentiation may split up the market artificially (see p.185).

Supply

Where demand is small, firms are forced to remain small. But even when demand is comparatively large, factors on the supply side may result in that demand being satisfied by a number of small firms, instead of by a few large firms enjoying the advantages of large-scale production. These factors may be classified as follows:

(1) *Institutional*. Friction may prevent growth. Thus, as we have already noted, firms may find it difficult to raise capital at a crucial size. On

the other hand, with some industries, e.g. retailing and personal services, it is possible to start with little capital.

Taxation, too, may reduce the size of a firm which is personally owned. Thus inheritance tax and capital gains tax may mean that an estate or property holding has to be sold in fragments in order to pay the tax.

(2) *Vertical disintegration*. It may be possible to break down the technical process so that different firms can each perform a small part of the whole task. Thus separate firms may produce a single component, carry out research, advertise, sell by-products, etc.

(3) *Managerial attitudes*. The small owner-manager may not have the ability to supervise a large firm, or may simply not want the extra worry. Or, as in farming and retailing, the owner may be willing to work long hours (that is, he or she accepts a lower rate of profit) because a value is put on being one's own boss.

(4) *Diseconomies of scale occur fairly early in the firm's growth*. Such diseconomies can occur because of the lack of adaptability of highly specialised machines to fluctuations in demand.

But the main diseconomies occur in management. As the size of the firm increases, the task of management cannot be given to a number of men without creating difficulties. Co-ordination problems arise, and rivalries develop. This means that one person must be in overall command – yet such persons are in very limited supply. In certain industries these difficulties arise earlier than in others. Rapid decisions are required where demand changes quickly (e.g. in the fashion trades), or supply conditions alter (e.g. through the weather in agriculture). Or care may have to be given to personal requirements of customers (e.g. in retailing and services), or to detail (e.g. in agriculture). This may necessitate the close supervision of management, and thus the firm has to be small (Figure 7.3).

7.5 External Economies

Apart from *internal economies* – the advantages which a firm can obtain for itself by operating on a large scale – economies may result as the *industry* grows in size. The latter are known as *external economies*.

The concentration of similar firms in an area often results in mutual benefits. A skilled labour force is developed; common services, such as marketing organisations, can be set up; roads and social amenities are provided; technical colleges run courses catering particularly for the local industry; a reputation for its products may be founded; and ancillary firms may move to the district to supply specialised machinery, collect by-products, etc. While economies of concentration do not influence the firm when planning the scale of production they must be taken into account when deciding where production shall take place, for the saving in costs

FIGURE 7.3
Factors Influencing the Size of the Firm

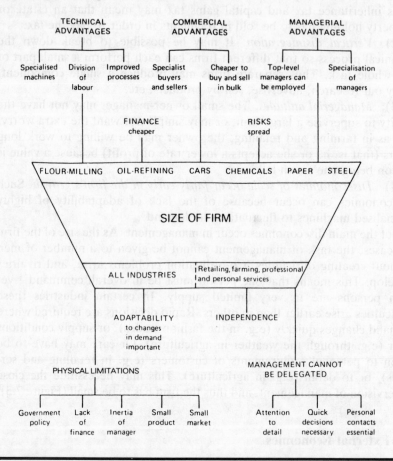

which can result may outweigh any diseconomies which arise through traffic congestion, smoke, etc. Indeed, they may be so important that firms continue to go to particular localities long after the original reasons why the industry was established there (e.g. abundance of raw materials or power) have passed away.

External economies can also take the form of common information services provided either by associations of firms or even by the government itself.

Finally, as the industry grows in size, specialised firms may be established to provide components for all producers. Since such firms can achieve longer runs, these components are supplied more cheaply than if each main producer had to manufacture its own requirements.

8 The Distribution of Goods to the Consumer

8.1 The Scope of Production

A manufacturer will have to decide whether to produce one good, or many variations of the same good, or a number of different goods. Whatever his plans, he will still have to decide on how to get his finished goods to the consumer.

He himself may undertake the task. But if he does so, he must be willing to employ sales representatives, run delivery transport, carry stocks, organise exports, advertise his product, advise customers, give credit and establish servicing centres. Many of these are highly specialised functions, and full-time experts can only be employed on them if output is large enough. Furthermore, the manufacturer's main ability lies in organising the production of the good rather than the selling of it.

The result is that the principle of the division of labour is often applied to the task of getting the good to the consumer. This is achieved by forward vertical disintegration. Just as the manufacturer buys raw materials and components from other producers, so specialists will accept the task of getting the goods to the consumer – the final stage of the whole productive process.

These specialists can perform many different tasks themselves, or each separate task may itself be put in the hands of a specialist. We simplify, however, and group them together under the headings of 'wholesalers' and 'retailers'. Figure 8.1 shows how they fit in to the various stages in the production of chocolate.

8.2 The Wholesaler

The wholesaler buys goods in bulk from producers and sells them in small quantities to retailers according to their requirements. But, to promote this main task, he helps the process of production in a number of ways.

FIGURE 8.1
The Parts Played by the Wholesaler and Retailer in the 'Production' of Chocolate

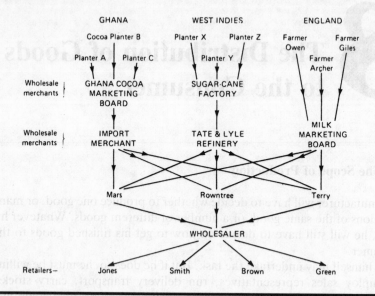

1. Economising in Distribution

Since many shops, especially those stocking a large variety of goods, order their supplies only in small quantities, it is not economical for each producer to sell directly to them. Such a practice would mean employing many sales representatives, packing many separate parcels and making numerous transport journeys. Figure 8.2a shows that sixteen contacts and van journeys are necessary when four chocolate firms deliver directly to four retailers.

Figure 8.2b, on the other hand, shows that, when the goods are delivered in bulk to a wholesaler, the number of contacts and journeys is reduced to eight.

In agriculture particularly, where the goods are perishable, it simplifies matters considerably if the farmer, instead of trying to contact retailers himself, can deliver his produce to a wholesaler or commission salesman, for example at New Covent Garden, and leave the actual selling to him.

Similarly, in the construction industry, where there are numerous small builders, it is easier for manufacturers to deliver through builders' merchants.

FIGURE 8.2
The Role of the Wholesaler

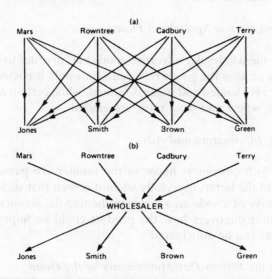

2. Keeping Stocks

Consumers like the convenience of being able to obtain a good at a shop just when they require it. This means that stocks have to be held. Often, however, neither the producer nor the retailer has the necessary storage facilities or capital for this, and so it is left to the wholesaler.

In other ways, too, the costs of storage are removed from the producer or retailer. While loss through fire, flood or rats can be insured against, no insurance can be taken out to cover a loss through a fall in demand. Thus a wholesaler, who holds stocks of a good which is liable to go out of fashion, relieves the manufacturers and the retailers of that risk.

The holding of stocks is, in itself, a valuable economic function. Stocks help to even out fluctuations in price resulting from sudden but temporary fluctuations in demand and supply. Thus brick stocks in the hands of merchants are replenished during the winter and run down during the remainder of the year.

3. Arranging Imports from Abroad

Manufacturers abroad could rarely be bothered to ship small parcels to individual retailers or undertake the foreign currency transactions involved. These tasks are left to a wholesaler, the import merchant, who is known and trusted. Often the import merchant goes abroad to establish and develop trade connections.

4. Carrying Out Certain Specialised Functions

Not only does the wholesaler advertise goods but, in order to make selling easier, he may process the goods received. Thus milk is pasteurised, hams are cooked, tea is blended and sugar is refined, while certain commodities, such as cotton, wheat and wool tops, are graded.

5. Channelling Information and Advice

Suggestions which customers make to the retailer are passed on to the wholesaler, and the latter, especially when it is seen that such suggestions are representative of a wide area, conveys them to the manufacturer. Thus the manufacturer discovers how the product could be improved or how fashion changes can be anticipated.

6. Assisting in the Day-to-Day Maintenance of the Good

With many products, particularly vehicles and machinery, an efficient maintenance service is essential. The manufacturer can be relieved of this task by the wholesaler, who can provide a local and quick maintenance, repair and spare-part service.

8.3 The Retailer

Functions of the Retailer

The retailer performs the last stage of the productive process, for it is he who puts the goods in the hands of the actual consumer. His work has been summarised thus: 'to have the right goods in the right place at the right time'. His functions, as set out below, are chiefly an enlargement on this. It must be appreciated, however, that, in actual practice, there is not always a clear distinction between the wholesaler and the retailer, and thus it will be found that, in some cases, their functions overlap.

1. Stocking Small Quantities of a Variety of Goods

What is the 'right good' depends on the customer, for different people have different tastes, and what suits one may be undesirable to another. Thus having the 'right good' depends largely on stocking different varieties of the good so that each customer can make his or her individual choice, pay for it, and take delivery there and then. In part, a shop is a showroom where the customers can examine and compare the different goods one with the other and make their own selection. This is particularly helpful when customers are choosing goods which are only bought infrequently.

The size of the stocks the retailer carries will depend on many factors. Some manufacturers even stipulate that a certain minimum stock shall be carried before they will allow a retailer to sell their goods. Usually, however, it is left to the retailer. He will consider the popularity of the product, the possibility of obtaining further supplies quickly, the perishability of the good or the likelihood of it going out of fashion, the season (especially if it is approaching Christmas or if there is a seasonal demand for the good) and the possibility of a future change in its price. Above all, he must allow for the cost, in the form of interest on bank advances, of carrying stocks.

2. Taking the Goods to Where it is Most Convenient for the Customer

Taking the goods to where it is most convenient for the customer may merely mean that the retailer sets up his shop within easy reach. It is for this reason that we see retailers congregated together in the centre of most towns, though, with goods such as groceries, which are in everyday use, small shops are often dotted around residential districts. Where customers are very dispersed (as in country districts) the retailer may have a 'travelling shop' of some form or another.

While, with the majority of goods, customers take their purchases with them, the retailer may arrange delivery. This occurs with goods such as coal and furniture where transport is essential, but it also applies where the customer requires the extra convenience of having goods delivered, as (for example) with milk, the early-morning newspaper, laundry, and groceries supplied by high-class stores.

3. Performing Special Services for Customers

In the course of running the main business, the retailer performs many services for the convenience of his or her customers, all of which help to build up goodwill. Where the good is not in stock, it will be ordered, and, in other matters where contact with the manufacturer is necessary the retailer often acts for the customer. Thus goods are returned to the manufacturer for repair, though, in order to effect such repairs more quickly, a repair service may be maintained, e.g. cycle, radio and television retailers.

With many goods, too, such as fishing tackle, photographic equipment, musical instruments, machinery and sports gear, special advice can be provided. Indeed, some manufacturers insist on their retailers having technical competence.

Finally, for the greater convenience of customers, goods may be sent on approval or credit facilities arranged through hire purchase, special credit accounts, etc.

4. Advising the Wholesaler and Manufacturer

A retailer maintains close contact with customers. From them he discovers, either through a chance remark in the course of conversation or by direct suggestion, how a good could be improved or the type of good people would like. This information finds its way to the manufacturer, who will probably act upon it, and eventually the modification or the new good will be produced.

Types of Retail Outlet

Retailing might be widely defined to include all shops, mail-order firms, garages, bus companies, launderettes, betting shops or indeed any organisation which sells products or services to the consumer. It is usual, however, to take a narrower view and to confine retailing to shops and mail-order outlets, as follows.

1. Independents

These are mainly small shops with no other branches, and they account for about two-fifths of retail trade turnover. Yet, in spite of their advantages of individual attention to customers, 'handy' locations for quick shopping trips, and the willingness of owners to accept a lower return for the benefits of being their own boss, these independents are steadily losing ground to the larger stores.

A major bid to avert the decline has come through the voluntary chains, such as Spar, Mace and Wavy Line, of which about a third of the independents are members. While retaining their independence, members buy in bulk from the wholesaler and use common advertising and display techniques.

2. Multiples

These can be defined arbitrarily as organisations of ten or more shops. Some, such as Mothercare and Dorothy Perkins, sell a particular type of good. Others, such as Marks & Spencer, Boots, F. W. Woolworth and British Home Stores, have a fairly extensive range of products. Together they comprise some 50 per cent of the market.

Their chief advantages are that they can obtain the economies of bulk buying and centralised control, eliminate the wholesaler, invite instant recognition through their standardised shop fronts, and establish a reputation through brand names.

3. Supermarkets

These may be defined as self-service shops with a minimum selling area of 200 sq. metres, but the trend in recent years, especially among the multiple grocery companies, has been towards super-stores (of at least 2000 sq. metres) and hypermarkets (see below). While organisationally they would count as multiples, their share of the food trade warrants separate attention. In 1978 they accounted for half the grocery trade and a third of total retail food sales.

The field is led by the five major retail grocery chains: Tesco, Sainsbury, Associated Dairies (ASDA), Argyll Stores and Dee Corporation. Their strength lies in economies of scale, low labour costs, a clear and attractive display of merchandise, bulk buying and selling under their own label (e.g. Sainsbury cornflakes, Tesco coffee). As a result they have highly competitive prices and have gained ground rapidly.

Indeed, many of these self-service organisations have extended their activities beyond groceries to self-service of goods showing higher profit margins, e.g. clothing, do-it-yourself supplies and hardware.

4. Hypermarkets

Urban congestion, inadequate parking space and rising rents have made High Street sites increasingly expensive. To an increasing extent the answer to these problems has been the very large 'out-of-town' shopping centre or 'hypermarket' to cater for the car-borne weekly shopper.

However, in the UK this development has been retarded by planning considerations of the environmental cost in downtown decay or intrusion on the countryside. In 1985, however, local planning authorities were urged to take account of the benefits of this trend in that they extended the public's range of shopping facilities.

5. Department Stores

Competition from multiples has forced department stores to alter somewhat their traditional pattern of having separate departments under the control of a responsible buyer, often described as 'many stores under one roof', in favour of bulk-buying by central office, more self-service, and extended credit facilities. As a result they have managed to retain nearly 5 per cent of the market.

The main groups are House of Fraser, Debenham, the John Lewis Partnership and Great Universal Stores.

6. Co-operatives (see pp.87–8).

7. Mail Order

Mail-order business, which accounts for just over 3 per cent of the retail market, is particularly susceptible to higher postal charges.

The major companies, Great Universal Stores, Littlewoods Mail Order, Freemans and Empire Stores, sell by agency and illustrated catalogues, purchases usually being arranged through weekly interest-free payments. Over one-half of all sales are accounted for by women's clothing and household goods.

Factors Affecting the Type of Retail Outlet

Over the last twenty years, the pattern of retailing has moved away from the small, independent shop towards the larger organisation, notably the multiples, supermarket chains and mail-order firms. This trend reflects a greater emphasis on competition through lower price rather than by better service.

The larger firms are in a strong position to cut prices. Not only do they obtain the advantages of large-scale production (particularly those of selling a whole range of goods and of buying in bulk), but they can use their bargaining strength to secure further price discounts from manufacturers. Indeed, the largest may force the manufacturer to supply goods under the retailer's 'own-brand' label at a price below that at which other retailers can buy the manufacturer's national brand. Moreover, since large retailers cater for a whole range of shopping, e.g. food, they can attract customers into stores by 'loss-leaders'.

Economic factors influencing this trend have been:

1. *Increased income*, which has led to a swing in expenditure towards the more expensive processed foods and consumer durable goods.
2. *An increase in car ownership*, which has enabled people to move from the city centre to the outer suburbs. Shops have followed, not only to be near their customers, but also to obtain larger sites with parking facilities, lower rents and less congestion. The car has also made customers more mobile, enabling them to travel to good shopping centres where they can purchase all their requirements at a single stop.
3. *An increase in the number of married women going to work*, which has promoted the demand for convenience foods and labour-saving devices. It has also led to the reduction of the number of shopping

expeditions, a trend helped by the wider ownership of refrigerators and freezers.

These factors are likely to remain important in the future. It seems probable, therefore, that new supermarkets will take the form of discount stores or hypermarkets selling a wider range of products having higher profit margins than those on groceries. Moreover, the more favourable response to recent planning applications is enabling new stores to be developed outside towns, while cash-and-carry warehouses are now available to consumers who can buy in quantity.

Such changes are likely to be at the expense of the medium-sized business, for the smaller local retailers offer 'convenience' services.

8.4 The Future of the Middleman

Criticisms of Middlemen

Wholesalers and dealers who come between the manufacturer and the retailer or the consumer are often referred to as 'middlemen'. They are frequently criticised on the ground that they take too large a share of the selling price. It is argued that, if the manufacturer sold direct to consumers, prices could be reduced.

But, as we have seen, wholesalers relieve producers of essential functions, allowing them to obtain the advantages of specialisation in marketing products. Such forward vertical disintegration is usually the cheapest way of getting the good to the consumer.

However, this does not mean that all criticism of middlemen is unjustified. Sometimes their profit margins are too high. This may occur through continuing with antiquated methods or by a single middleman playing off one small producer, such as a farmer, against another (hence the formation of producers' co-operatives).

The Elimination of the Wholesaler

In recent years a tendency for the wholesaler to be eliminated has been due to: (i) the growth of large stores, which can order in bulk; (ii) the development of road transport, which reduces the necessity of holding large stocks; (iii) the desire of manufacturers to retain some control over retailing outlets in order to ensure that their products are pushed or that a high standard of service, freshness, etc., is maintained; (iv) the practice of branding many products, which eliminates many specialised functions. In other cases, however, the elimination of the wholesaler has been confined to sales of high value goods such as furniture and television sets; to circumstances where the producer and retailer are close together, as with the market gardener who supplies the local shop; and to cases where the manufacturer does his own retailing.

To some extent the wholesaler has responded to this challenge by developing in two main directions: (*a*) by establishing the cash-and-carry warehouse, sometimes called the 'the retailers' supermarket'; (*b*) by becoming the organiser of a voluntary chain of retailers, who are supplied, and to some extent controlled, by him, e.g. Spar.

Direct Selling by Manufacturers

Selling direct to consumers by the manufacturer occurs chiefly where: (*a*) the manufacturer wishes to push the product (e.g. beer and footwear) or to ensure a standard of advice and service (e.g. sewing-machines); (*b*) the personal service element is important (e.g. made-to-measure clothing); (*c*) the manufacturer is a small-scale producer-retailer, often selling a perishable good (e.g. cakes and pastries), or serving a local area (e.g. printing); (*d*) so wide a range of goods is produced that a whole chain of shops can be fully stocked (e.g. Maynard sweets, Manfield shoes); or (*e*) the good is highly technical or made to individual specifications (e.g. machinery).

9 The Location of Production

A firm has to decide where to produce. It will reach its decision by considering: (*a*) the advantages of producing in different areas; (*b*) the level of rents in these different areas. Thus, although the rent of sites in an area may be high, it can pay a firm to go there if the advantages of that particular area mean that other factors cost less.

9.1 The Advantages of Different Localities

These can be classified as: (1) natural, (2) acquired, (3) government-sponsored.

1. Natural Advantages

Costs are incurred both in assembling the raw materials and in distributing the finished product to the consumer. In manufacturing some products, the weight of the initial raw materials is far greater than that of the final product. This is particularly true where coal is used as the source of heat and power, e.g. in iron and steel production (Figure 9.1). Here transport costs are saved by producing where raw materials are found (e.g. on coal and iron-ore fields), or are easily accessible (e.g. near a port).

On the other hand, with some industries the costs of transporting the finished product are greater than those of assembling the raw materials, e.g. ice-cream, furniture, beer, mineral waters, metal cans, and glass containers. With these, it is cheaper for a firm to produce near the market for its goods. Thus, Wall has ice-cream factories close by most large concentrations of population, and Metal Box tin and plastic container factories are scattered throughout Britain.

What is really important as regards transport costs is their ratio to the

FIGURE 9.1
The Production of Pig-iron – a 'Weight-losing' Industry

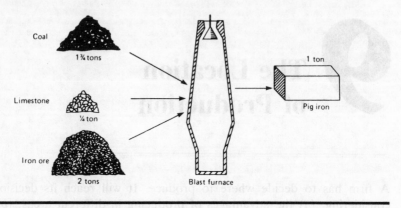

Coal
1¾ tons

Limestone
¼ ton

Iron ore
2 tons

Blast furnace

1 ton
Pig iron

value of the product. Thus sand and gravel are excavated locally, whereas special types of brick are transported long distances.

Generally speaking, transport improvements and new developments (e.g. electrical power) have helped firms to move away from their sources of raw materials. The tendency now is, therefore, for firms to concentrate, not on the coalfields, but on the outskirts of areas of high population which provide both a supply of labour and a market for the finished good.

A river, estuary or coastal location may be essential when huge quantities of water are required by an industry (e.g. chemicals, atomic power), and this may also be important for waste disposal.

Besides accessibility to raw materials and nearness of markets, suitability of climate is a further natural advantage which may have to be considered when locating production. Indeed, in agriculture, it is usually decisive, provided soil conditions are not adverse.

Under 'natural advantages' we can also include an adequate supply of the type of labour required. Thus high technology industries have been attracted to the south-east of England by the skilled labour available, while the abundance of cheap labour has been important for the development of mass-production in Taiwan and Hong Kong.

2. Acquired Advantages

Improved methods of production, the development of transport, inventions and new sources of power may alter the relative importance of natural advantages and so change location. Thus, as high-grade iron-ore fields became exhausted and improved techniques reduced coal consumption, it became cheaper to transport the coal than the iron ore to produce pig iron, the production centres for which shifted to near the ports importing iron ore and the low-grade iron-ore fields of Lincolnshire. Similarly, improved transport may upset the relative pulls. Finally, new inventions, such as 'humidifiers' for producing a damp atmosphere, and water-softeners, can make an industry less dependent upon a particular locality.

Yet we must not overstress the importance of the above changes. Even when natural factors have disappeared, an industry often remains in the same region. Thus the steel industry persists in most of its older centres and cotton production is still concentrated in Lancashire. Indeed, it has been said that the ability of a locality to hold an industry greatly exceeds its original ability to attract it. This is due to the acquired or 'man-made' advantages which arise as the industry expands. Such advantages were mentioned in Chapter 7 when we studied external economies of concentration. A skilled labour force, communications, marketing and commercial organisations, nearby ancillary industries (either to achieve economies of scale or to market by-products), training schools, etc., in the locality, and a widespread reputation for the products of the region, all help to lower costs of production, thereby making the locality attractive to new firms.

3. Government-sponsored Advantages

The heavy concentration of firms in certain districts can have harmful social effects – traffic congestion, smoke pollution, a lack of open spaces, strain on the public transport system during peak hours, etc. Above all, when an industry becomes localised in a particular area, a serious unemployment situation can arise if there is a fall in demand for its products. Thus, over the last fifty years, some of Britain's older industries (e.g. cotton, shipbuilding and jute) have declined, and coal has been replaced by oil as a source of power. This has led to relatively heavy unemployment in Lancashire, the north-east coast, Northern Ireland, Central Scotland, South Wales and a number of other districts, for newer industries have preferred to go to the Midlands and particularly to south-east England.

The government, therefore, has had to interfere in the decisions of firms when siting their plants. So far it has not resorted to compulsion, though it used to refuse to give Industrial Development Certificates (now discontinued) in areas enjoying a high level of employment. Instead it has offered financial inducements – investment grants and tax concessions – to attract firms to those areas where unemployment is most severe, the 'Assisted Areas' (see Chapter 28).

Such financial advantages would have to be considered by a firm when deciding where to site its factory.

9.2 The Level of Rents in Different Areas

In addition to the advantages of being in a particular locality, a firm will also have to consider the cost of land there relative to the cost of land elsewhere.

The cost of the land will be decided by the price system. Other firms, possibly from other industries, may be looking for the same site advantages. Thus the cost (that is, the price) of the land will be fixed by competition among the various firms wanting to go there, and it will settle at the highest price which the keenest firm has to pay – its opportunity cost.

Now the firm that can pay the most will be the one which values its advantages the highest compared with the advantages of land elsewhere. Thus, early in its history, it seemed that the cotton industry might settle on the Clyde, for the locality had all the natural advantages of south-east Lancashire. But the Clyde had advantages for producing iron and steel and for building ships, and in these her superiority was most marked. Thus shipbuilding firms were prepared to pay extra for this advantage. For cotton manufacturers this extra cost of a site on the Clyde exceeded any disadvantage of being in Lancashire. Hence ship-building firms settled along the Clyde, and cotton firms in Lancashire.

In the final analysis, therefore, it is not the absolute advantages of a district which decide where a firm locates but the advantages relative to those of every other district. Thus an industry whose outlay on unskilled labour forms a high proportion of its production costs would, other things being equal, be able to bid more for land in an area of cheap labour than one whose spending on such labour was minimal. And, in any town centre, we see the same principle at work – shops oust other businesses, and houses are converted into offices.

9.3 Conclusions

A firm will normally choose a site where the benefits are greatest compared with its costs. Where it is producing in a comparatively new industry, natural advantages will play an important part.

Even so, we cannot assume that, outside the heavy industries, they will be decisive. Thus the Barlow Report on the Distribution of the Industrial Population of 1940 quotes a Board of Trade statement which emphasises the important part which even historical accident may play. This statement even goes as far as to assert that the cotton industry first settled in Lancashire for no particular reason, except perhaps that the woollen industry was already there, the foreigners were kindly received and that Manchester had no corporation (thereby being free from restrictive practices). Similarly, the Rover Motor car assembly plant was established at Cowley chiefly because William Morris, the founder, had a cycle business in Oxford.

Moreover, electricity has now practically eliminated dependence on a coalfield site. Yet firms may still go to the original areas, largely because of the advantages acquired over time. Others may choose to be nearer their markets. Some 'footloose' firms have even located in certain districts, particularly south-east England, largely because the managing directors (or their wives) have preferred living there!

The various factors influencing location are summarised in Figure 9.2.

FIGURE 9.2
Factors Influencing the Siting of a Business

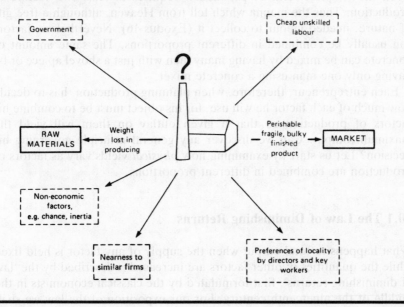

10 Combining the Factors of Production

Even the simplest form of production requires at least two factors of production. Thus the manna which fell from Heaven, although a free gift of nature, needed labour to collect it (Exodus 16). Nevertheless, factors can usually be combined in different proportions. The same amount of concrete can be mixed by having many men with just a shovel apiece or by having only one man using a concrete mixer.

Each entrepreneur, therefore, when planning production, has to decide how much of each factor he will use, for his object must be to combine his factors of production so that a given outlay on them will yield the maximum output. Can we discover any general principle governing his decision? Let us start by examining how *physical* yields vary as factors of production are combined in different proportions.

10.1 The Law of Diminishing Returns

What happens to total output when the supply of any factor is held fixed while the quantities of other factors are increased is described by the 'law of diminishing returns', first formulated by the classical economists in the middle of the nineteenth century. For our exposition of the law we shall assume:

1. Production is by two factors only.
2. All units of the variable factor have the same efficiency – one unit is a perfect substitute for another.
3. There is no accompanying change in techniques or organisation.

Given these assumptions, the law can be stated as follows: if one factor is held fixed, but additional units of the varying factor are added to it, eventually the extra output resulting from an additional unit of the varying factor will become successively smaller. Since the additional output

Table 10.1
Variations in Output of Potatoes Per Week Resulting from a Change in Labour Employed

Number of workers employed on the fixed unit of land	Output (50 kg bags)		
	Total	Average	Marginal
1	2	2	2
2	16	8	14
3	54	18	38
4	80	20	26
5	95	19	15
6	108	18	13
7	120	17.1	12
8	130	16.2	10
9	138	15.3	8
10	142	14.2	4
11	142	12.9	0
12	132	11	−10

NOTES

(a) *Total output* is the total yield (50 kg bags) from all factors employed.

(b) *Average output* refers to the average yield per worker. It therefore equals

$$\frac{\text{Total output}}{\text{Number of workers employed}}$$

(c) *Marginal output* refers to the marginal yield (50 kg bags) to labour, and equals the addition to total output which is obtained by increasing the labour force by one worker. That is, marginal output equals total output of $(n + 1)$ workers − total output of n workers.

(d) There is a fundamental relationship between average output and marginal output. Marginal output equals average output when the latter is at a maximum (Figure 10.1). This relationship is bound to occur. So long as the marginal output is greater than average output, the return to an additional labourer will raise the average output of all labourers employed. On the other hand, as soon as the marginal output falls below average output, the additional labourer will lower the average output. Hence when average product is neither rising nor falling, i.e. is at its maximum, it is because marginal product equals average product.

This relationship can be made clearer by a simple example. Suppose Botham has played twenty innings and that his batting average is 60 runs. Now if in his next innings he scores more than 60, say 102, his average will increase − to 62. If, on the other hand, he scores less than 60, say 18, his average will fall − to 58. If he scores exactly 60 in his twenty-first innings, his average will remain unchanged at 60.

resulting from an extra unit of the varying factor is known as the 'marginal product', the law refers to eventual diminishing marginal productivity.

The law can be illustrated by following the classical economists' assumptions that land is the fixed factor and that the number of labourers employed on this fixed amount of land is varied. Suppose potatoes are being produced. Table 10.1 shows a purely hypothetical yield.

Our example shows that the physical productivity of a factor can be varied by combining it in different proportions with another factor. Thus when 4 labourers are employed on the fixed piece of land, the marginal output is 26 bags; when there are 8 labourers, the marginal output is only 10 bags. The maximum return per labourer is achieved when there are 4 labourers to the given plot of land. Diminishing returns occur because labour is an imperfect substitute for land. The result is that when we increase the number of labourers, total output increases, but at a diminishing rate. We could only maintain the maximum return per labourer by increasing the amount of land. Otherwise – after 3 labourers, the extra return resulting from an additional labourer becomes progressively smaller. When 11 labourers are employed, they start to get in one another's way. Marginal product is nil, and thereafter becomes negative. Total output is then declining absolutely.

Some Important Points Regarding the Law of Diminishing Returns

In order to avoid any misconceptions, it is helpful to call attention to certain fundamental points regarding the law of diminishing returns.

1. The units of the variable factor are homogeneous. The marginal product of labour does not fall because less efficient labourers are being employed. Diminishing returns occur because more labourers are being employed on a fixed amount of land – and, through physical considerations, labour is an imperfect substitute for land. (If it were otherwise, all the world's food supplies could be grown on a garden plot: extra land would not be necessary, since output could be increased merely by adding labourers.)

2. The law applies only if one factor is held fixed. (If both factors can be varied, we have a change of 'scale'.)

3. The law is not applicable if the factors can only be combined in fixed proportions. If, for instance, you must have one labourer to one shovel to obtain any output, then merely increasing the number of labourers by one will add nothing to output; the marginal product is nil. For the law to hold, the proportions in which the factors can be combined must be variable. For this reason, the law is often referred to as the law of variable proportions.

4. The law does not formulate any *economic* hypothesis or theory. It is merely technical, stating physical relationships. While the physical productivity of an extra labourer is important to a farmer in deciding how many to

FIGURE 10.1
The Relationship Between the Number of Labourers Employed, Average Output and Marginal Output

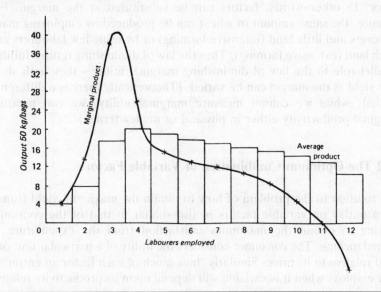

employ, it will not *determine* the decision. We also have to know the cost of an extra labourer relative to the cost of an alternative factor. That is, we have to consider economic data as well as technical relationships.

5. There are no changes in techniques.

The Practical Applications of the Law of Diminishing Returns

The law is significant both in our everyday lives and in the theoretical analysis of the economist.

First, it helps to explain the low standard of living in many parts of the world, particularly the Far East. Increasing population is cultivating a fixed amount of land. Marginal product, and thus average product, are falling – and so, therefore, is the average standard of living.

Second, it shows how an entrepreneur can arrive at an equilibrium position in purchasing factors of production. So far we have assumed that we have just two factors, land and labour, and that land is fixed. But suppose that there is another variable factor, say capital. Now the farmer will have to decide how labour can be combined with capital.

He will want to ensure that a given outlay on them will yield maximum output. This is essentially the same problem that faced the consumer when allocating his expenditure. And, in the same way that a consumer could adjust his marginal utility by adding to or subtracting from the amount of a commodity possessed, so the entrepreneur can adjust the marginal productivity of a factor by varying the amount of it which he uses with another factor. In other words, factors can be substituted at the margin. For instance, the same amount of wheat can be produced by employing many labourers and little land (intensive farming) or by using few labourers and much land (extensive farming). Thus the law of diminishing returns fulfils a parallel role to the law of diminishing marginal utility – they both show how yield at the margin can be varied. (Theoretically there is a difference in that, while we cannot measure marginal utility, we can measure marginal productivity either in physical or money terms.)

10.2 The Optimum Combination of Variable Factors

The solution to the problem of how to obtain the maximum yield from a given outlay on variable factors is also similar to that of the consumer seeking to obtain the maximum satisfaction from the expenditure of limited income. The consumer considers the utility of a particular unit of a good relative to its price. Similarly, how much of each factor an entrepreneur employs when it is variable will depend upon its productivity relative to its cost.

Let us go back to our example of labour and capital, which are being used to produce a given product – potatoes. The farmer will be in equilibrium, i.e. he will cease to rearrange the combination of labour and capital, when, for the last pound spent on both, he obtains the same amount of product. Suppose, for instance, the last pound's worth of labour is yielding a greater physical quantity of potatoes than the last pound spent on capital. It will obviously pay the farmer to transfer the last pound from capital to buying more labour, for this will increase total physical yield.

But labour and capital are obtained in different units, the units being of different prices. Thus we cannot compare directly the productivity of one labourer with that of one unit of capital, say a mechanical hoe; we must allow for their respective prices. If the cost of one labourer is only a third of the cost of a mechanical hoe, then the marginal product of a worker need only be one-third of the hoe's to give the same yield for a given expenditure. Thus the entrepreneur will be in equilibrium in combining factors which can be varied when the following fundamental relationship has been established:

$$\frac{\text{Marginal product of factor } A}{\text{Price of factor } A} = \frac{\text{Marginal product of factor } Z}{\text{Price of factor } Z}$$

A corollary of this is that, like the housewife in purchasing her goods, the entrepreneur will tend to buy more of a factor as its price falls, and less as it rises. Suppose the wage rate rises, but the marginal product of labour remains unchanged. The fundamental relationship stated above has now been destroyed. To restore the position it is necessary to raise the marginal product of labour and to lower that of capital. The law of diminishing returns shows how we can do this – by combining less labour with more capital. In short, a rise in wages without a corresponding increase in the productivity of labour will tend towards the substitution of machinery for labour.

The above argument helps to explain why in Britain more capital is combined with a given amount of labour in agriculture compared with Ireland; relative prices are different. Similarly, if land is variable as well as labour, agriculture will be extensive where land is relatively cheap (as in Canada) and intensive where it is relatively dear (as in Britain).

A third application of the law of diminishing returns is to show how costs vary with changes in output when one or more factors are fixed. It is to this problem that we now turn.

11

Deciding on the Most Profitable Output

11.1 The Costs of Production

Costs as Alternatives Forgone

Suppose a man sets himself up as a shopkeeper selling sweets. Suppose, too, that he invests £2000-worth of his savings in the business, and that over a year his receipts are £40 000 and his outgoings £22 000. It is probable that he would say that his profits over the year were £18 000. But are they really? The economist would answer 'no'.

The reason for this is that the economist is not so much concerned with money costs as with opportunity costs – what a factor could earn in its best alternative line of production. This concept of costs has a bearing on: (*a*) the economist's concept of 'profits'; (*b*) the extent to which production should be carried on in the short period when certain factors cannot be transferred to an alternative use.

Opportunity Costs and Profit

The £22 000 money outgoings of the shopkeeper above can be regarded as 'explicit costs'. But, when we look at costs as alternatives forgone, we see immediately that the shopkeeper has certain 'implicit costs'. This is because, although he uses his own capital and labour, both could earn a reward in alternative lines of production. Say, for instance, his capital could be invested elsewhere at 12 per cent. There is thus an implicit cost of £240 a year. Similarly with his own labour. His next most profitable line, we assume, is as a shop-manager earning £11 760 a year. There are thus £12 000 implicit costs in addition to the explicit costs to be taken from his revenue.

Normal Profit

But we have not finished yet. The shopkeeper knows that even in running a sweet business there is a certain amount of 'hazard' through uncertainty – a hazard which he avoids if he merely works for somebody else. The shopkeeper must therefore anticipate at least a certain minimum profit, say £2000 a year, before he will be prepared to set up business on his own, i.e. before he will become an entrepreneur. If he does not make this minimum level of profit, he feels he might just as well go into some other line of business or become a paid shop-manager. Thus another type of cost (which we call 'normal profit') has to be allowed for – the minimum return which keeps an entrepreneur in a particular industry after all other factors have been paid their opportunity cost. Normal profit is a cost because if it is not met the supply of entrepreneurship to that particular line of business dries up.

We therefore have the following costs: explicit costs, implicit costs, normal profit. Anything left over after all these costs have been met is 'super-normal', 'abnormal' or 'pure' profit. In terms of our example, we have:

	£	£
Total revenue		40 000
Total costs: explicit	22 000	
implicit	12 000	
normal profit	2 000	
		36 000
Super-normal profit		4 000

Fixed Costs and Variable Costs

For the purposes of our analysis, we shall classify costs as either *fixed* or *variable*.

Fixed costs are those costs which do not vary in direct proportion to the firm's output. They are the costs of indivisible factors, e.g. buildings, machinery, vehicles. They arise because, for technical or other reasons, such factors have to be engaged in a certain size or quantity but, once engaged, they can be used over a period of time at no further cost. Even if there is no output, fixed costs must be incurred, and for a time, as output expands, they remain the same.

Variable costs, on the other hand, are those costs which vary directly with output. They are the costs of the variable factors, e.g. operative labour, raw materials, fuel for running the machines, wear and tear on equipment. Where there is no output, variable costs are nil; as output increases, so variable costs increase.

In practice it is difficult to draw an absolute line between fixed and variable costs; the difference really depends on the length of time in mind, as follows. When current output is not profitable, the entrepreneur will have to contract production. At first, overtime work will cease; if necessary, workers will be paid off at the end of the week. In time, more factors become variable – administrative staff, sales representatives, research workers – and if receipts still do not justify expenditure on them, they too can be dismissed. A factor becomes variable as soon as a decision has to be taken as to whether or not it shall be replaced, for then alternative uses of the factor have to be considered. Eventually, machines have to be replaced; even they have become a variable cost. A decision may now have to be taken as to whether it will be profitable to remain in business.

The distinction between fixed and variable factors and costs is useful in two ways. First, in economic analysis, it is a means of distinguishing between differences in the conditions of supply which arise as we vary the period of time under consideration. The economist divides time into the *short period* and the *long period*. The short period is defined as a period when there is at least one fixed factor. While, therefore, supply can be adjusted by labour working overtime and more raw materials being used, the time is too short for altering fixed plant and organisation. Thus in the short period, because some factors are fixed, the firm cannot achieve the best possible combination for a given output. The long period, however, is sufficiently long for supply to be adjusted, not only by altering the variable factors, but also the fixed factors; here, therefore, supply can respond fully to a change in demand. Factors can once more be combined in the best possible way and, as we shall see, at a given price more can be supplied.

Second, as we shall see later, the distinction between fixed and variable costs is fundamental when the firm is considering whether or not to continue producing in the short period. In the long period all costs of production, fixed and variable, must be covered. But in the short period fixed costs still remain even if there is no production. They have been paid once and for all simply because it was necessary to have some 'lumpy' factors even before production could start. Only variable costs are saved by ceasing to produce; and so, provided these are recovered by receipts, the firm will continue to produce. Anything that it makes above such costs will help to recoup its fixed costs.

11.2 How Do Costs Behave as Output Expands?

The Relationship Between the Costs of Production and a Diminishing Marginal Product

In our discussion of the law of diminishing returns, we referred to quantities of factors and their yield in physical terms only. This was necessary to show how the return to a factor varies when it is combined in different proportions with other factors.

However, in its endeavour to make as large a profit as possible, the firm is concerned not so much with physical quantities of factors and their yield, but with those quantities translated into money terms. It can then see directly the relationship between costs and receipts at different outputs and is thus able to decide what output will give the maximum profit. Our first task, therefore, is to find out how costs are likely to change as output increases. We shall assume perfect competition in buying factors of production – the demand of each firm is so small in relation to total supply that any change in demand will not directly affect the price of those factors.

In the short period there are, by definition, bound to be fixed factors. And, in the law of diminishing returns, we found that, when a variable factor was applied to a fixed factor in increasing quantities, for a time the marginal product might increase but eventually would diminish.

How will this affect costs as output expands? Let us assume that just two factors are being used, one of them fixed. If each additional unit of the variable factor costs the same, but the output from each additional factor is increasing, the firm is obtaining an increasing amount of output for any given additional expenditure on the variable factor. In other words, the cost of each additional unit of output is falling as output expands. When the marginal product of the variable factor is diminishing, the cost of an additional unit of output is rising. (The reader can test this for himself by giving the fixed factor a price, say £10, each unit of the variable factor a price, say £4, and each unit of output a price, say £1, for converting the total product at different amounts of the variable factor into total revenue. Table 10.1 for diminishing returns can be used.) The cost of producing an additional unit of output is known as *marginal cost* (MC).

The above conclusions can be represented diagrammatically (Figure 11.1).

Cost Schedules

Table 11.1 illustrates this relationship between output and costs. The figures, which have been kept as simple as possible, are for an imaginary firm, Rollermowers, maker of lawnmowers. Fixed costs (FC) amount to

Table 11.1
Costs of Rollermowers Ltd (in £)

Output per week (units)	Fixed cost (FC)	Total variable cost (TVC)	Total cost (TC)	Marginal cost (MC)	Average fixed cost (AFC)	Average variable cost (AVC)	Average total cost (ATC)
0	10 000	—	—	—	—	—	—
10	10 000	2 000	12 000	200	1 000	200	1 200
20	10 000	3 400	13 400	140	500	170	670
30	10 000	4 400	14 400	100	330	146.7	480
40	10 000	5 400	15 400	100	250	135	385
50	10 000	6 750	16 750	130	200	135	335
60	10 000	8 600	18 600	180	166	143.3	310
70	10 000	11 000	21 000	240	142.9	157.1	300
80	10 000	14 000	24 000	300	125	175	300
90	10 000	17 900	27 900	390	111.1	198.9	310
100	10 000	23 000	33 000	510	100	230	330
110	10 000	29 600	39 600	660	90.9	269.1	360
120	10 000	38 000	48 000	840	83.3	316.7	400

NOTES
(a)   TC of *n* units = FC + VC of *n* units.
(b)   MC is the extra cost involved in producing an additional unit of output. That is, MC of the *n*th units = TC of *n*–1 units. Here output is shown in units of 10, so that this difference in total cost has to be divided by 10.
(c)   AFC of *n* units = $\dfrac{FC}{n}$
(d)   AVC of *n* units = $\dfrac{\text{TVC of } n \text{ units}}{n}$
(e)   ATC = $\dfrac{\text{TC of } n \text{ units}}{n}$
(f)   MC bears the same relationship to ATC and AVC as marginal product does to average product: that is, MC cuts both ATC and AVC when these two are at a minimum. The same reason applies as in our earlier example of marginal product and average product.

FIGURE 11.1
The Relationship Between Returns and Costs

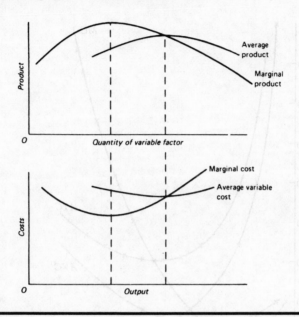

£10 000 and, as variable factors are added, output expands. At first there is an increasing marginal product; as a result MC is falling. This has its effect on average total cost (ATC) until approximately 75 units are being produced. From then onwards, as the fixed factors are being worked more intensively, diminishing returns cause the ATC curve to rise.

These curves can be plotted on a graph (Figure 11.2).

The following relationships between the curves should be noted:

1. AFC and AVC added vertically give ATC.
2. AFC is a rectangular hyperbola, since AFC × units of output = K (a constant).
3. The MC curve cuts both the AVC and the ATC curves when they are at a minimum.
4. Minimum AVC occurs at a smaller output than minimum ATC.

   AVC is at a minimum when the return to the *variable* factor only is at a maximum. But when we are considering ATC the cost of the fixed factor also has to be taken into account, and AFC continues to fall even after AVC begins to rise. While AFC is falling at a greater rate than AVC is rising, ATC will continue to fall.

FIGURE 11.2
Cost Curves

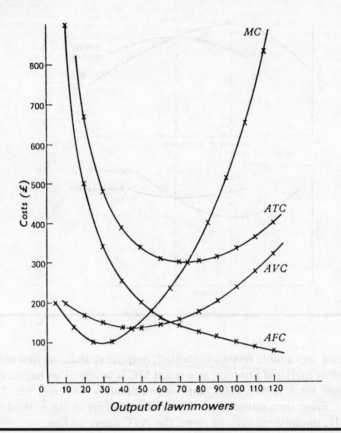

11.3 Perfect Competition

In order to assess whether a firm is maximising its profits we have to know:

(a) the price at which it can sell different outputs and the price at which it can buy different quantities of factors of production;

(b) whether it is free to enter another industry where it can make higher profits.

Both considerations involve us in a study of the degree of competition which exists.

The degree of competition can vary. But we have to start our analysis somewhere, and so, to begin with, we make the simplifying assumption that there is 'perfect competition' – the highest degree of competition possible. For the rest of this chapter and the next, therefore, we shall be building up a model under the assumptions of perfect competition. Later these assumptions can be modified to bring the model closer to real life by allowing for forms of 'imperfect competition'.

The Conditions Necessary for Perfect Competition

For perfect competition to exist, certain conditions must hold.

1. A Large Number of Relatively Small Sellers and Buyers

There must be a large number of sellers relative to demand and a large number of buyers relative to supply.

If there are a large number of sellers relative to demand in the market, any one seller will know that, because he supplies so small a quantity of the total output, he can increase or decrease his output without it having any significant effect on the total supply, and therefore on the price of the good in the market. In other words, he has to take the market price as given and can sell any quantity at the ruling market price. In short, he is a *price-taker*. Here any change in market conditions is reflected in price and, as we shall see, the firm responds by adjusting its output.

This is illustrated in Figure 11.3, where (*a*) shows market price *OP* determined by the demand for and supply of the goods of the industry as a whole. But the industry supply is made up of a thousand producers, each,

---

FIGURE 11.3
The Firm's Demand Curve Under Perfect Competition

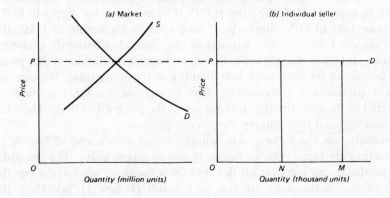

we will assume, of about the same size. Each individual producer, therefore, sells such a small proportion of the total market supply that he can double his output from *ON* to *OM* or halve it from *OM* to *ON* without affecting the price at which he sells his units (Figure 11.3*b*).

In other words, in perfect competition, a seller is faced with an infinitely elastic demand curve for his product. If, in our example, he charges a higher price than *OP*, nobody will buy from him; if he charges less than *OP*, he will gain no advantage and will not be maximising his revenue, for he could have sold all his output at the higher price, *OP*.

The difference between perfect and imperfect competition on the selling side can be seen in Figure 11.4.

FIGURE 11.4
The Firm's Demand Curve Under Perfect and Imperfect Competition

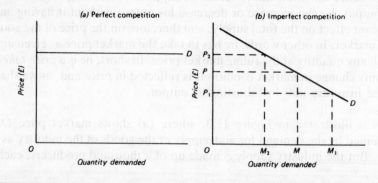

The producer in (*b*) sells such a large proportion of the market supply that a change in his output affects the price he receives for his product. When he supplies *OM*, the price is *OP*. If he increases his supply to *OM*₁, the price falls to *OP*₁. Similarly, if he decreases his supply to *OM*₂, the price rises to *OP*₂. Or, such a producer can, instead of fixing the quantity, fix price and leave the market to decide how much it will take at that price. But he cannot fix both price and quantity at the same time. We can call such a producer a *price-maker*. Any change in market conditions is reflected in the quantity the firm can sell at the price it has fixed. Here the firm can respond by changing the price it charges.

Similarly, on the buying side, purchasers of goods and of factors of production are faced with an infinitely elastic supply curve. For example, one producer can increase his demand for a factor of production but the price of the factor does not rise as a result (Figure 11.5*a*). Here the producer's demand is so small relative to the market supply that he can buy

FIGURE 11.5
The Supply of a Factor Under Perfect and Imperfect Competition

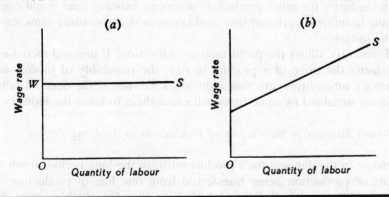

all the labour he requires at the prevailing market wage rate *OW*. On the other hand, in (*b*) the producer employs such a large proportion of the market supply of labour that when he takes on more workers the wage rate rises.

2. *Homogeneous Product*

Buyers must regard the product of one producer as being a perfect substitute for that of another, and purchase solely on the basis of price. This means that if one producer raises his price, all consumers immediately buy from his competitors. Where goods are graded, e.g. wheat and cotton, there is identity of product in the same grade.

But such identity of product does not exist where there is a real or imaginary difference (e.g. a special wrapping or brand name) or where reasons other than price (e.g. goodwill) influence buyers. Here an individual producer can raise his price without necessarily losing all his customers. To some extent, therefore, there is a downward-sloping demand curve for his product.

3. *Perfect Knowledge*

There are two aspects of perfect knowledge:
(*a*) sellers and buyers must know the prices being asked in other parts of the market so that they can act accordingly;
(*b*) In order to make free entry effective, a would-be producer must also know what profits are being made by other producers and the profit he could reasonably expect to make.

4. Free Entry

(*a*) If the number of sellers is to remain large, there must be free entry to the industry for other producers, otherwise existing firms could combine to influence price or they could grow in size as existing firms leave the industry.

(*b*) Free entry allows the profit motive to function. If demand increases, causing the price of a product to rise, the possibility of profits will attract other firms into that industry. Likewise, if the demand falls, losses sustained by some firms will cause them to leave the industry.

5. Perfect Mobility of the Factors of Production in the Long Period

A change in the demand for a product must, in the long period, result in factors of production being transferred from one line of production to another. Moreover, all factors, including entrepreneurship, must be equally available to all firms. As we shall see, however, in real life this does not occur. Entrepreneurs do not possess perfect knowledge. Therefore they have to estimate, and in this some are better than others.

6. No Transport Costs

This is not an essential condition, but it will simplify our analysis.

In real life all these conditions never exist simultaneously, though for those agricultural products where grading is possible, e.g. wheat, the conditions of perfect competition apply very closely. It must therefore be re-emphasised that the assumption of perfect competition must be regarded as an analytical device which enables us to arrive at some fundamental conclusions.

11.4 The Short-period Equilibrium Output of the Firm Under Perfect Competition

Since the firm is seeking to maximise its profits, its equilibrium output will be that amount where the difference between total revenue and total costs is greatest. At this output, the firm will have no incentive to increase or decrease production.

The firm will therefore be concerned with two broad questions:

1.   How much will it obtain by selling various quantities of its product?
2.   How much will it cost to produce these different quantities?

At first sight it may seem that maximum profit will occur at that output where average cost is at a minimum. But this is unlikely to be so. The real question which the entrepreneur will be continually asking is: 'If I produce a further unit of output, will it cost me less or more than the extra revenue I shall receive from the sale of it?' In other words, attention is concentrated at the margin. If an extra unit of output is to be profitable, then the extra revenue obtained for it must be greater, or at least equal to, the extra cost of producing it. That is, *marginal revenue* (the addition to total revenue received from the last unit of output) must at least equal *marginal cost* (the cost of producing the last unit of output).

Under perfect competition, the producer will obtain the market price for his good, whatever his output. In other words, marginal revenue (MR) = price; thus the price line is also his MR curve (see Figure 11.6).

FIGURE 11.6
The Equilibrium Output of the Firm under Perfect Competition

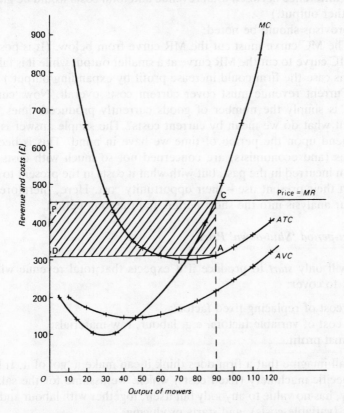

Furthermore, although under perfect competition the prices of factors of production do not rise to the firm as it demands more, MC eventually rises because, in the short period, there are fixed factors, and so diminishing returns set in.

The Equilibrium Output of Rollermowers

Let us return to our imaginary firm. Assume that the market price of mowers is £450. We can impose this MR curve on the cost curve diagram (Figure 11.6).

Now at any output where MR (price) is above MC, Rollermowers can increase profits by expanding output. Where MC is above MR (price), it can increase profits by contracting output. Its equilibrium output, therefore, is where MR (price) equals MC: that is, at an output of 90 units. Here ATC is £310. Thus super-normal profit equals total receipts (£40 500) – total costs (£27 900) = £12 600 = shaded area PDAC (Figure 11.6). (The reader can check this by seeing whether, from the total costs given in Table 11.1, the difference between total revenue and total costs would be greater at any other output.)

Two provisos should be noted:

(1)   The MC curve must cut the MR curve from below. (It is possible for the MC curve to cut the MR curve at a smaller output while it is falling, but in this case the firm could increase profit by expanding output.)

(2)   Current revenue must cover current costs overall. Now 'current revenue' is simply the number of goods currently produced times their price. But what do we mean by current costs? The simple answer is that they depend upon the period of time we have in mind. This is because businesses (and economists) are concerned not so much with costs that have been incurred in the past, but with what it costs in the present to hold factors in their present use – their opportunity cost. Here, therefore, we divide our analysis into the short period and the long period.

The Short-period 'Shut-down' Price

A firm will only *start* to produce if it expects that total revenue will be sufficient to cover:

(*a*)   the cost of replacing fixed factors;
(*b*)   the cost of variable factors, e.g. labour, raw materials;
(*c*)   normal profit.

We shall imagine that a firm does think it can make a 'go' of it. It buys highly specific machinery (fixed costs) which, we assume for the sake of simplicity, has no value to anybody but itself, together with labour and raw materials (variable costs), and starts producing.

But, as time goes by, it finds that its original expectations are not being fulfilled. The price at which it can sell its good is lower than estimated. Although it is covering the cost of variable factors (those which vary directly with the size of output), it sees that the margin above this cost will be insufficient to cover fully the replacement cost of machines by the time they wear out. In other words, the business as a whole will prove unprofitable.

This is where the idea of opportunity costs must once more be introduced. Suppose our firm stops production. What will it save? Obviously it will save the cost of those factors, the variable costs, which vary proportionately to output. But will it save anything on its machines by not using them? The answer is 'no' – because they have no alternative use, they cannot be transferred elsewhere. Their opportunity cost is zero; in other words, there is no cost of using them! There is nothing which can be done now about past expenditure on those machines. In economics, as in other walks of life, 'bygones are forever bygones'. Not using the machines now cannot recoup past expenditure. It is stuck with them, for better or worse.

Consequently our firm takes a philosophic view of the situation. It has some perfectly good machines which, if used, will add nothing to costs. So, provided the cost of labour, raw materials, etc. – the variable factors – is being covered, it goes on producing. Anything earned above the cost of these factors will help to recoup the cost of the fixed factors.

How can we tell if variable costs are being covered? Simply by looking at the AVC curve. If we take Rollermowers as an example, a price of £135 for a mower would just enable the firm to produce in the short period. Here MC would equal MR, and, with an output of 45 units, TVC would just be covered. Any price lower than this, however, would mean that at an output where MC = MR, total receipts (price x output) would be less than TVC (AVC x output). Rollermowers could not make a 'go' of it even in the short period; and so we can call £135 the 'shut-down' price. At any price above £135 an output where MC = MR will give a surplus above TVC, and this will help towards paying off the firm's FC.

11.5 The Long-period Equilibrium of the Firm and Industry

In the long period, all factors are variable. This has two effects:

1. The *firm* can vary the size of its plant in order to obtain a given output at the lowest possible cost.
2. New firms can obtain plant in order to enter the *industry*; or alternatively firms need not renew plant and can leave the industry.

We shall develop each of these effects in turn.

Returns to Scale

The firm must have started off with some plant, and, in deciding on its size, have taken into account the advantages of producing on a large scale. But it may have misjudged its future sales. They may be larger than originally expected; as a result, plant capacity is too small. On the other hand, sales may have been overestimated; as a result, plant capacity is too large.

Let us assume that Rollermowers has underestimated what it can sell. As a result of starting with too small a plant for its output, it has had to work it more intensively by increasing its variable factors – labour, etc. That is, it is working under conditions of diminishing returns.

But in the long period it can remedy this situation. It decides to enlarge its *capacity* to combine more capital with labour. This gives it the chance to acquire more specialised machines, for these are justified by the larger output. Probably, too, it will be able to introduce more division of labour and even secure commercial and other economies.

Thus, as we saw in Chapter 7, as the *scale* of output increases, costs per unit fall. In other words, up to a certain point (an output of *OM* in Figure 11.7), additions to plant produce new short-run cost curves for any given capacity, each lower than the other. Here there are increasing returns to *scale*.

FIGURE 11.7
Increasing and Decreasing Returns to Scale

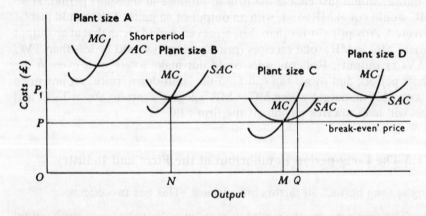

Beyond output *OM*, decreasing returns to scale set in. This could arise through the increased difficulties of making decisions, or, in other words, through the fixed nature of entrepreneurship. And, from *OM* onwards, these diseconomies resulting from the fixed nature of management out-weigh any economies still being achieved of a technical, commercial, financial or risk-bearing nature. Thus, although plant is adjusted to cope with a larger output, the minimum average cost per unit possible is still higher, even in the long period, than at a smaller output.

The Optimum Size of the Firm

In the above example, the firm's long-period costs of production per unit are at a minimum when output is OM. This is known as the optimum size of the firm; it is its *most efficient* size.

As we have seen, this 'most efficient' size varies from one industry to another. When technical economies of scale are important, as (for instance) in the production of steel and cars, decreasing costs occur over a large output. On the other hand, in some industries, such as farming and retailing, reductions in average cost which may be obtained by working with large machines are exhausted at a relatively small output. From then onwards, only economies of a commercial, financial, risk-bearing, or managerial nature can be secured. But as output increases, management problems are more likely to arise. Personal attention to detail is im-possible, quick decisions are more difficult, and flexibility is lost. As a result, diseconomies occur, and eventually these diseconomies outweigh the economies of increased size, thereby producing increasing costs. The optimum size is thus a compromise of forces pulling in opposite directions.

In practice, the optimum size of a firm is not a fixed one. Not only do the relative prices of different factors of production change (resulting in changes in the shape of the cost curves), but techniques are improved (again changing the position of the curves). Hence the concept of an optimum size of firm is theoretical; it is, as we shall see, the size to which firms *tend* to conform in the long period as, in their efforts to survive, they compete with other firms.

The Industry

We now consider the effects of competition between firms. In the long period not only can existing firms alter the size of their plant to secure greater efficiency, but new firms, observing the super-normal profits being earned by firms already producing, will be able to obtain plant to enter the industry. Output will increase.

But this increased supply by the industry will cause the market price to fall. That is, the horizontal price line facing the individual firm will fall in the long period, e.g. from OP_1 (Figure 11.7). Furthermore, this adjust-ment will continue until no super-normal profits are being made, for only then will there be no incentive for firms to enter the industry.

If one firm is more efficient than the others, it will be making super-normal profits. This could occur, for instance, because it was producing OQ with plant size C, when other firms were each only producing ON with plant size B. In the long period, some of these firms would increase their size of plant towards plant size C. As a result of the increased supply, price would fall. Firms failing to adjust towards the more efficient size would be forced out of business.

Thus competition forces existing or new firms towards plant size C, and increased output forces price down to OP. If there were a higher price, some firms could be making super-normal profits, and new firms entering would increase supply and force down the price. On the other hand, if price were less than OP, no firm could break even in the long period when all factors had to be paid their current price. OP is therefore referred to as the 'break-even price'.

To summarise: in the long period and assuming conditions of perfect competition, each firm will be producing at the 'optimum' size OM and the price of the product will be OP. Each firm, too, will be in equilibrium at output OM because price equals marginal cost. The industry is in equilibrium because: (*a*) each firm is in equilibrium; (*b*) there is no incentive for firms to enter or leave the industry, because no super-normal profits or losses are being made.

We can illustrate the above from Rollermowers' cost curves (Figure 11.2). Let us assume that it chose the optimum size of plant in the first place – all firms have to conform to its cost curves in the long period or go out of business.

In the long period, all costs must be covered – but with no super-normal profits if the industry is to be in equilibrium. This will occur when Rollermowers' output is 75 units and the market price of mowers is £300. Here total revenue (£300 x 75) equals total cost (average cost x output, £300 x 75). £300 is thus the 'break-even' price.

12 The Supply Curve of the Industry Under Perfect Competition

12.1 Introduction

So far we have concentrated our attention on the behaviour of the firm. But the individual firm is only one of a large number comprising the industry. To obtain the supply curve of the industry, therefore, we have to add together the supply curves of these firms. This will give us the market supply curve, the one which interacts with the demand curve to fix price.

In practice, the term 'industry' presents difficulties. In everyday speech 'industry' includes firms producing goods which differ slightly, e.g. cars, washing-machines, furniture, etc. But the reader is reminded that, when we defined perfect competition, we assumed a homogeneous product. Our definition of an industry must therefore be the group of firms producing the total amount of an identical good supplied to the market. Variations in this definition can be allowed for later (see Chapter 14).

We total the output of the individual firms at different prices to obtain the market supply schedule. Generally speaking, more is supplied the higher the price. But why this is so differs in principle according to whether we are considering the short or the long periods. Each must therefore be examined separately.

12.2 The Short Period

In the short period firms can adjust their output by varying the amount of the variable factors (raw materials, operative labour, etc.) which they combine with their fixed factors. But no new firms can enter the industry, because they cannot obtain plant. Thus the short-period supply curve is explained simply by the way firms' outputs respond to a change in the price of the good produced.

Consider, for example, Rollermowers' cost schedules, Table 11.1. Any price below £135 per mower will stop production, because TVC are not covered. At higher prices, however, it will produce an output where price = MC. The part of the MC curve above the AVC curve (see Figure 11.6), therefore, is its short-period supply curve as follows:

Price (£)	Outputs (units)
135	45
185	55
240	65
300	75
390	85

Suppose, for the sake of simplicity, that the industry consists of three other firms each less efficient than Rollermowers. Their outputs (starting from minimum AVC) are given under A, *B* and *C* in the following schedule:

Price (£)	Firm A	Firm B	Firm C	Rollermowers	Total
135	—	—	—	45	45
185	—	—	45	55	100
240	—	45	55	65	165
300	50	55	65	75	245
390	55	65	75	85	280

This is shown graphically in Figure 12.1. The MC curves of the four firms are summed horizontally to obtain the short-period supply curve of the industry.

FIGURE 12.1
The Short-period Supply Curve of the Industry

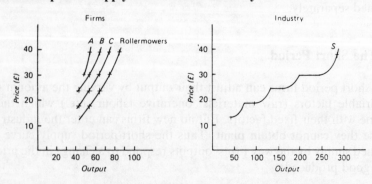

It will be observed that the supply curve derived above is not smooth, but stepped. This is because we have taken only four firms. If there had been very many firms each differing only slightly in efficiency, we should have had a much smoother curve.

Since all firms under perfect competition must produce where MC is rising, their output will be greater the higher the price. Thus the short-period market supply curve rises from left to right, showing that more is supplied the higher the price.

12.3 The Long Period

The Long-Period Equilibrium of the Firm

Our discussion of the firm showed that, in the long period, each existing firm (including any attracted into the industry) will be producing at its optimum size *OM* and at a price *OP* where total costs are just covered (Figure 11.7). Now since new firms can come into the industry on identical terms, there would be a long-period supply curve for the industry which will be perfectly elastic at price *OP*. In other words, the supply curve would be horizontal.

But such a conclusion can be arrived at only on the very theoretical assumptions of perfect competition. In particular, this assumed that:

(*a*) each firm is so small that its demand for a factor does not affect the price of that factor;
(*b*) there is perfectly free entry into the industry.

A rigid acceptance of these conditions, however, is impossible. First, it creates a theoretical difficulty – if all firms are at the peak of efficiency since they are operating at a minimum average cost, which goes out of business if the price of the goods falls slightly? Second, it leads to a conclusion – that supply can be increased indefinitely at constant cost – which is most unlikely. We can overcome both objections by making either of the above assumptions more realistic.

The Price of Factors of Production and the Size of the Industry

While an individual firm may be so small that its demand will not affect the price it has to pay for factors of production, the collective action of all firms in the industry will have repercussions. In the past, we have referred to these 'industry results' as *external* economies and diseconomies of scale.

Now it could happen that, as the industry expands, there are external economies of scale – growing reputation, skilled labour availability, transport improvements, etc. These will tend to lower the cost curves for individual firms as the output of the industry expands. On the other hand, there may be diseconomies which will raise costs. One such likely result of the expansion of the industry will be an increasing price of the factors of production. Given full employment, as the size of the industry's output expands, higher rewards will have to be paid to attract factors from other industries.

In practice, therefore, at the same time as the increased supply resulting from the entry of new firms tends to lower the price of the product, the cost curves of the firm are tending to be pushed down by external economies and pushed up by external diseconomies of scale. In other words, external economies will make for increased supply at a lower cost – there are decreasing costs to the industry; external diseconomies will make for increased supply at a higher cost. The actual slope of the long-period supply curve – downwards or upwards – will depend upon the balance between the two.

Suppose, for instance, that the entry of a fourth firm, D, to the industry in Figure 12.2 drives up the prices of the factors of production without giving any external economies. As a result the cost curves of all firms moves from (a) to (b), each firm in (b) having a higher minimum average total cost. This gives a new supply for the industry, M_4, at a higher price OP_1, as compared with the previous supply, M_3 at a price OP (Figure 12.2c). That is, there is an upward-sloping industry supply curve.

Perfectly Free Entry

Even if there were no institutional barriers to entry into an industry (e.g. through cartel or other agreements or through conditions imposed by the government), the condition of free entry is effective only if:

(a) there is perfect knowledge;
(b) factors of production are perfectly mobile and equally available to all firms.

As soon as either of these conditions is relaxed, firms of differing degrees of efficiency will result.

Is it likely that these conditions will apply as regards entrepreneurship? The answer is 'no'. Our assumption of 'perfect knowledge' means that entrepreneurs outside the industry are aware of any super-normal profits being earned by existing firms, of the prices of all factors of production, and of all the different ways in which the good can be produced.

Obviously, the extent of such knowledge is so vast that entrepreneurs must differ in the degree to which they possess this knowledge. And this disparity becomes even more marked when we introduce dynamic considerations. Fluctuations in demand, improvements in techniques and changes in the relative prices of factors of production are continually giving free to changes in the conditions of demand and supply. Entrepreneurs therefore have to plan ahead according to their estimates. Some entrepreneurs will make more accurate estimates than others.

What this means is that equally efficient entrepreneurs are not available to all firms. At any one time, therefore, some firms are making supernormal profits of varying degrees, while others are marginal in that they are just making normal profits. This situation is shown diagrammatically in Figure 12.3.

FIGURE 12.3
Differences in Efficiency of Entrepreneurs

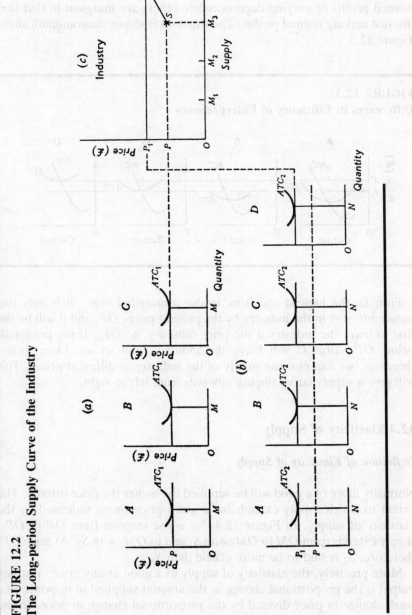

FIGURE 12.2
The Long-period Supply Curve of the Industry

Firm D is the lowest-cost firm, in the sense that... it is only just induced to stay in the industry by the present price, OP, and it will be the first to leave the industry if the price falls... to OP. If the price falls below OP, firm C will have the... to go on. Once again, therefore, we can plot the supply of the industry at different prices. This will give a supply curve, sloping upwards from left to right.

12.4 Elasticity of Supply

Definition of Elasticity of Supply

Normally, more of a good will be supplied the higher the price offered. The extent to which supply expands when the price rises is indicated by the elasticity of supply. In Figure 12.4, for a rise in price from OP to OP_1, supply expands from PM to OM, and to OM, with S_1. At price... therefore, S_1 is said to be more elastic than...

More precisely, the elasticity of supply, of a good at any price or any output is the proportional change in the amount supplied in response to a small change in price divided by the proportional change in price... supply schedule on p. 38, for instance, when the price of eggs rises from 10p...

rise to changes in the conditions of demand and supply. Entrepreneurs therefore have to plan ahead according to their estimates. Some entrepreneurs will make more accurate estimates than others.

What this means is that equally efficient entrepreneurs are not available to all firms. At any one time, therefore, some firms are making supernormal profits of varying degrees, while others are marginal in that they are just making normal profits. The situation is shown diagrammatically in Figure 12.3.

FIGURE 12.3
Differences in Efficiency of Entrepreneurs

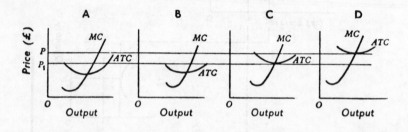

Firm *D*, the highest-cost firm, is also a marginal firm – it is only just induced to stay in the industry by the present price, *OP*, and it will be the first to leave the industry if the price falls, e.g. to *OP*$_1$. If the price falls below *OP*$_1$, firm *C* will leave the industry, and so on. Once again, therefore, we can plot the supply of the industry at different prices. This will give a supply curve sloping upwards from left to right.

12.4 Elasticity of Supply

Definition of Elasticity of Supply

Normally more of a good will be supplied the higher the price offered. The extent to which supply extends for a given price rise is indicated by the elasticity of supply. In Figure 12.4, for a rise in price from *OP* to *OP*$_1$, supply extends from *OM* to *OM*$_1$ with *S*$_1$ and to *OM*$_2$ with *S*$_2$. At price *OP*, therefore, *S*$_2$ is said to be more elastic than *S*$_1$.

More precisely, the elasticity of supply of a good at any price or at any output is the proportional change in the amount supplied in response to a small change in price divided by the proportional change in price. In the supply schedule on p.38, for instance, when the price of eggs rises from 10p

FIGURE 12.4
Elasticity of Supply

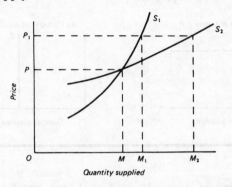

Quantity supplied

to 12p, supply extends from 32 000 to 40 000. Elasticity of supply is therefore equal to:

$$\frac{8/32}{2/10} = \frac{5}{4}$$

As with elasticity of demand, we say that supply at a given price is elastic if elasticity is greater than 1, and that it is inelastic if elasticity is less than 1.

Limiting Cases

There are two limiting cases of elasticity of supply which are of economic significance:

1. Elasticity of Supply Equal to Infinity

The main uses of this concept are: (*a*) where a single firm demands so small a proportion of a factor of production that it can obtain an infinite amount at a given price – that is, there is perfect competition in buying factors of production; (*b*) where production takes place at constant cost. In both cases, the supply curve is horizontal (Figure 12.5*a*).

2. Supply Absolutely Inelastic

Here a good is fixed in supply whatever the price offered (Figure 12.5*b*). It applies to rare first editions and Old Masters, and, by definition, to fixed factors in the short period.

FIGURE 12.5
Extremes of Elasticity of Supply

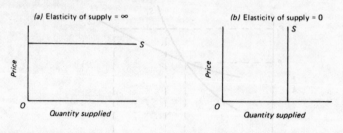

Whereas elasticity of demand equal to 1 was significant because it described the case where total expenditure on the good remained constant at all prices, unitary elasticity of supply has no such significance. (Any straight line passing through the origin will give a supply curve with a constant elasticity of 1, for such a line describes a situation where supply always changes in the same proportion to a given price change.)

Factors Determining Elasticity of Supply

Elasticity of supply is determined by: (1) the period of time under consideration; (2) the relationship between the individual firms' minimum supply points; (3) the cost of attracting factors from alternative uses. We shall consider each in turn.

1. Time

Supply is usually analysed under three periods:

(*a*) *Momentary equilibrium.* Here the supply is fixed, and elasticity of supply = 0. An example is cut Christmas trees on Christmas Eve. With many goods, some increase in supply can take place by (i) drawing on stocks, or (ii) switching factors of production from one product to another (where a firm makes two or more different products).

(*b*) *Short-period equilibrium.* Usually a variation in supply means that there must be some change in the factors of production employed. But this takes time – and the period differs between one factor of production and another. In the short period, as we have seen, it is possible to adjust supply only by altering the variable factors (raw materials, labour, etc.).

(*c*) *Long-period equilibrium.* Other factors, the fixed factors (e.g. land already sown, capital equipment, etc.), can be altered in the long period.

Only in the long period, therefore, can a full adjustment of supply to a change in price take place. Elasticity is greater in the long period.

This is because the difference between the short and the long periods has an important effect on costs. Since, in the short period, supply can be expanded only by adding to the variable factors, it means that, unless there is surplus capacity, the best possible combination of the factors of production cannot be achieved. Too many of the variable factors are being applied to the fixed factors, and the law of diminishing returns operates. Increased production, in other words, is obtained only by decreased efficiency, and we have increasing marginal cost.

In the long period, because all factors can be varied, the optimum combination can be achieved. Increased efficiency produces a smaller rise in costs per unit as output expands. But it may take a long time before this position is reached. Expanding rubber production, for instance, takes seven years while new trees mature.

It follows that, because the supply curve of an industry consists of the MC curves of the firms in it, a given rise in price will produce a smaller expansion of supply in the short period than in the long period. The longer the period of time under consideration, the greater elasticity of supply will tend to be. If we refer to Figure 12.4, S_1 could well represent the short-period supply curve, and S_2 the long.

2. The Relationship Between Firms' Minimum Supply Points

The supply curve is obtained by aggregating the supply of the individual firms. If these firms each offer a supply to the market at more or less the same minimum price, then supply will tend to be elastic at that price. Similarly at higher prices – the greater the number of firms coming in, the greater the elasticity of supply.

If, on the other hand, the entry of firms is spread over a wide range, supply will tend to be less elastic.

3. The Cost of Attracting Factors of Production

In order to expand production, additional factors have to be attracted from other industries. For an industry as a whole, this means that, even in the long period, higher rewards will have to be paid. What we have to ask, therefore, is: How much of a factor will be forthcoming in response to a given price rise? In other words, what is the elasticity of supply of factors of production? And, more significant, what are the influences determining this elasticity?

In answering this question, we can first consider what happens when one particular industry, e.g. office-building, wishes to expand. Let us concentrate on one factor of production, labour. As the demand for building labour increases, so the wages of building labourers rise. But they rise, not only to the office-building industry, but to all other industries using it – house-building, road construction, public works, etc. How will it affect these industries?

First, they will try to substitute other factors (e.g. cement-mixers, bulldozers, etc.) for the labour which now costs more. Is such substitution physically possible? If so, how elastic is the supply of these alternative factors? Will their price rise sharply as the demand increases? If physical substitution is fairly easy, and the supply of alternative factors is elastic, it will mean that a small rise in wages will release much labour for the office-building industry.

Second, higher wages will lead to increased costs in building houses, constructing roads, etc. The supply curve of these products therefore moves to the left, and, the higher the proportion of wages to total costs, the further will it move. The extent to which it leads to a reduced production of these alternative goods will depend upon the elasticity of demand for them. If elasticity is high, the small rise in the price of the good will cause a considerable contraction of demand, and labour will be released for office-building. If, on the other hand, demand is inelastic, even a considerable rise in wages will have little effect on the output of houses, etc., and the increase in the supply of labour to office-building will be correspondingly small.

We see, therefore, that the two main influences affecting the elasticity of supply of a factor to a particular industry are: (*a*) the degree of substitution by other factors; (*b*) the elasticity of demand for the alternative goods it produces.

Practical Uses of the Concept of Elasticity of Supply

1. The Elasticity of Supply of a Good is a Major Factor in Determining How Much its Price will Alter when there is a Change in the Conditions of Demand

This is apparent in the following examples:

(a) *Why does a crisis in the Middle East lead to a sharp increase in the price of gold?* The threat of war in the Middle East leads holders of assets, particularly the local oil-rich rulers, to seek a store of wealth which will hold its value. Because of its general acceptability, such an asset is gold. There is thus an increased demand for gold, D_1, and, since supply is almost inelastic, the price rises from OP to OP_1 (Figure 12.6).

(b) *Given free markets how would the price of cane sugar be affected in the short period and the long period if the demand for sugar increased?* Once again we can assume a fairly inelastic demand curve for sugar. The

FIGURE 12.6
The Effect of a Middle East Crisis on the Price of Gold

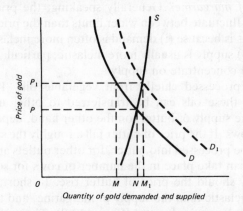

Quantity of gold demanded and supplied

original price is *OP* (Figure 12.7). Demand then increases from *D* to D_1. The supply of cane sugar in the short run is inelastic, for supply can be expanded only by adding labour, fertilisers, etc. Price therefore increases to OP_1. But in the long period more land can be planted with sugar cane.

FIGURE 12.7
Changes in the Price of Cane Sugar Over Time in Response to a Change in Demand

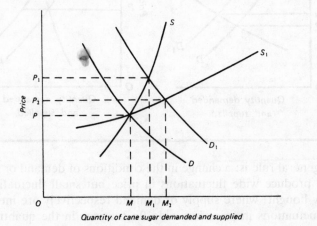

Quantity of cane sugar demanded and supplied

Supply is therefore more elastic, and is represented by the curve S_1. The long-run price falls to OP_2.

(*c*)   *Given free markets, why is the price of butter likely to fluctuate more than the price of margarine?* Generally speaking, the prices of primary products tend to fluctuate between wider limits than the prices of manufactured goods. This is because (i) demand is often more inelastic for primary products, and (ii) supply is usually more inelastic, particularly in the short period. We shall concentrate on supply.

Margarine is processed chiefly from vegetable oils. If the price of margarine falls, these oils can be transferred to other uses, e.g. soap manufacture. The supply of butter, on the other hand, depends chiefly on the number of cows. If the price of butter falls, roughly the same amount of milk still has to be processed into butter, for other outlets are very limited. No real change can take place in the number of cows for some time. This would still apply should the price of butter rise. In short, the supply of butter is more inelastic than the supply of margarine, and the price varies more for a given change in demand (Figure 12.8). The price of margarine rises from OP to OP_1, whereas that of butter moves from OP to OP_2.

FIGURE 12.8
Changes in the Prices of Margarine and Butter in Response to a Change in Demand

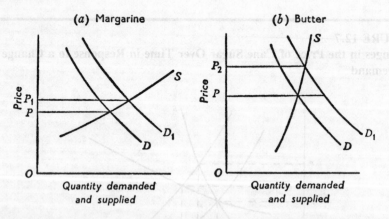

(*a*) Margarine

(*b*) Butter

The general rule is: a change in the conditions of demand or supply will tend to produce wide fluctuations in price but small fluctuations in the quantity bought, where supply or demand respectively are inelastic; and small fluctuations in price but wide fluctuations in the quantity bought, where supply or demand respectively are elastic.

2. *The Elasticity of Supply is Significant with Regard to Taxation*

(*a*) Where the supply of a good is inelastic, the Chancellor of the Exchequer can impose a tax on the producer without it having a great effect on the amount of the good offered for sale. Suppose, for instance, that a person owns a field which is suitable only for sheep-grazing, and that the most any farmer will pay for the use of this field is £10 a year, which the owner accepts. Now suppose that the government puts a tax of £5 a year on this type of land. This means that the owner will have to pay the tax, for the farmer will pay no more, and the land cannot be put to any other use. In fact, the government could tax almost all the rent away before it would make any difference to the number of sheep being grazed on it; but, if all the rent went on tax, the owner might leave the land standing idle (see p.232).

(*b*) The relative elasticities of demand and supply determine the proportion of a selective indirect tax borne by the producer as compared with the consumer (see p.392).

12.5 The Value of the Assumption of Perfect Competition

Since conditions of perfect competition are so rarely met with in real life, it might be asked why economists should choose to assume it for purposes of analysis.

The first reason is that model-building has to start at a simple level. From this first step modifications can be made to the original assumptions to make the model conform more closely to real life. We can illustrate by an example from the physical sciences. The physicist tells us that a body falling freely to earth will accelerate at 32 feet per second. But, by inserting the world 'freely', there is eliminated any resistance by the air or other force. Yet such a condition does not apply to the real world; it can only be produced artificially. On the other hand, it provides the fundamental 'benchmark'. From it the physicist can proceed to work out the rate at which different objects, e.g. a parachute, would fall when allowance is made for air resistance, etc. In exactly the same way the analysis of a private enterprise economy operating under conditions of perfect competition provides a simple jumping-off board from which more complex situations can be analysed as the conditions of perfect competition are relaxed.

The second reason for assuming perfect competition follows from the first. Since certain assumptions have to be made when beginning to build a model, it is desirable to be as realistic as possible, even though they will be modified later. Now, an alternative model could start from monopoly – one seller. Yet, as we shall see later, there can be no absolute monopolist, since all goods are to some extent competitive with one another. In real life, too, a deviation from perfect competition is probably a much nearer approximation than a deviation from monopoly.

Lastly, perfect competition does provide some indication of economic efficiency. Production, for instance, takes place where price (what consumers are prepared to give up at the margin) equals marginal cost (what it costs in factors of production to produce this marginal increment). Moreover, in the long period, production also takes place at minimum average total cost; no super-normal profits are being made. The conditions necessary for perfect competition, e.g. mobility of the factors of production and perfect knowledge, can often be promoted by a government seeking to improve the efficiency of an economic system.

On the other hand, we must not go so far as to say that complete perfect competition would provide maximum economic efficiency. For one thing, it considers only private costs and benefits. But there are likely to be external costs and benefits. Thus it may be efficient for society to produce where marginal costs exceed price if, as (for instance) with an underground railway line which reduces congestion on the roads, there is also a social benefit. Furthermore, to achieve maximum efficiency, perfect competition would have to rule throughout the economy: promoting it in just one part might result in a worse allocation of resources. Above all, our analysis of perfect competition has been conducted for purely static conditions. It may be that some other market form is more adaptable to future change or more conducive to innovation and therefore to growth (see p.176).

13 Monopoly

13.1 Imperfect Competition

What Do We Mean by Imperfect Competition?

In chapter 11 we stated the assumptions of perfect competition and examined their implications. What happens if *any* of these assumptions is broken?

1. Many Small Sellers and Buyers

Suppose that, instead of many sellers, there are only a few, or even one. Each seller now provides a substantial part of the market supply. As a result, the market price will be affected whenever he varies the amount he supplies of the commodity. In other words, he is faced with a downward-sloping demand curve (see p.140).

Similarly, on the buying side, when any buyer takes a significant proportion of the total market supply, he will be faced by a rising supply curve.

In both cases we have some element of 'imperfect competition'. As we shall see, a downward-sloping demand curve has particular significance as regards marginal revenue.

2. Homogeneous Product

Products may not be homogeneous. The seller may split up the market to some extent by (*a*) product differentiation, or (*b*) goodwill. The result will be that even though he raises his price a little, he still retains some of his customers. Again he faces a downward-sloping demand curve. Nevertheless, there may still be freedom of entry to the 'industry' (see Chapter 14).

163

3. Perfect Knowledge, Free Entry and Perfect Mobility of the Factors of Production

A breach of any of these conditions can give rise to demand or supply curves which are not perfectly elastic. Consumers, for instance, may not have complete knowledge of prices ruling elsewhere, e.g. in retail markets. Thus sellers can raise their price without losing all their custom. Similarly, there may not be free movement into the industry. This may arise when again outside firms do not have complete knowledge of the profits being made by existing firms. Or entry may be legally prohibited or made impossible by the inability to obtain essential factors of production. In such cases, existing firms can combine to exert some control over the market supply.

Thus, whenever any of our conditions for perfect competition is broken, some form of 'imperfect competition', indicated by a downward-sloping demand curve or an upward-sloping supply curve facing the individual seller or buyer, results.

Forms of Imperfect Competition

There are many 'shades' of imperfect competition. At one extreme, we have a single producer of a certain product; at the other, the only difference from perfect competition is that firms in the industry are each producing a slightly different brand. The first we call 'monopoly', the second 'monopolistic competition'. In between, we can have just a few sellers of the same or of a slightly different product – 'oligopoly'. The broad market forms are shown in Figure 13.1.

13.2 What Do We Mean by 'Monopoly'?

Comparison with Perfect Competition

Under perfect competition, there are many sellers each producing a very small amount of the total supply of a homogeneous product. The result is that each producer is faced with an infinitely elastic demand curve. It would be nice, therefore, if, at the other extreme, we could define a monopolist, which literally means 'one seller', as a producer who is faced with an absolutely inelastic demand curve.

Unfortunately this is impossible. Because income is limited, goods compete with one another for this income. To a greater or lesser degree, therefore, all goods are substitutes for each other.

FIGURE 13.1
Market Forms

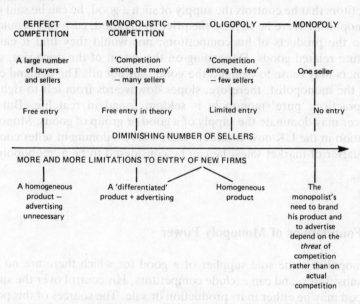

Has the Monopolist's Demand Curve a Constant Elasticity of 1?

It has been suggested, therefore, that the only true monopolist is one who sold all goods and therefore obtained all consumers' spending. The demand curve facing him would then be of unit elasticity at all prices. Any rise in the price of goods would simply mean that, although less were bought, total expenditure was unchanged.

But if we follow this argument through we can see that this definition is untenable for two reasons:

1. Any reduction in output will result in the same receipts, but lower costs. Where, then, does the reduction stop?
2. What the monopolist pays to the factors of production (his costs) is also the income of households (Figure 2.4) which they spend on the goods he produces (see Chapter 26). If he goes on reducing output (in order to lower costs), where do receipts come from?

Monopoly in Practice

Since, therefore, a theoretical definition of monopoly is impossible, we have to consider the situation from a practical point of view. While to some extent all goods are substitutes for one another, there may be essential characteristics in a good or group of goods which give rise to gaps, as it were, in the chain of substitution. If one producer can so exclude competitors that he controls the supply of such a good, he can be said to be a 'monopolist'. Were he to raise the price of his good, customers could not turn to the products of his competitors; nor would they find it easy to substitute related goods. Depending on the extent of the price rise, some customers may cease to demand the good, but not all. The demand curve facing the monopolist, therefore, slopes downwards from left to right.

In practice, 'pure' monopoly is seldom found in real life. But one producer may dominate the supply of a good or group of goods. Monopoly legislation in the UK now considers that, where a dominant seller controls one-quarter of market sales, he can be considered to be a 'monopoly'.

13.3 Foundations of Monopoly Power

A monopolist is the sole supplier of a good for which there are no very close substitutes, and can exclude competitors. His control over the supply of a good may be either in its production or sale. The sources of this power can be classified under four main headings:

1. Immobility of the Factors of Production

Immobility of the factors of production means that new competitors cannot compete with existing suppliers. Such immobility may arise through:

(a) *Legal prohibition of new entrants*. In the seventeenth century James I granted monopolies as a means of raising revenue, but today prohibition of entry of new firms is chiefly confined to the 'public utility' undertakings, e.g. water supply, docks and harbours, and the nationalised industries, e.g. coal-mining, electricity and postal services. For technical reasons, the provision of such goods and services is not suitable to open competition, especially as they are important to the community as a whole.

(b) *Patents, copyrights and trademarks*, with the object of promoting invention and the development of new ideas.

(c) *Government policy of establishing single buying and selling agencies*, e.g. marketing boards.

(d) *Control of the source of supply by one firm*, e.g. minerals, mineral springs, specialist workers (e.g. Emmanuel dress-designers), trade unions and professional associations.

2. Ignorance

A monopoly may persist largely through the ignorance of possible competitors. These may not realise that super-normal profits are being made by the existing firm (whose published profits may not reflect its actual profits). Or they may not be able to acquire the necessary 'know-how' such as is required, for instance, in involved technical processes.

3. Indivisibilities

The original firm may have been able to build up its size gradually, whereas new firms, in order to compete in costs, have to start on the scale already reached by the established firm. Raising the large sums of capital required may prove difficult for new firms.

In some cases, too, the efficient scale of plant may be so large relative to the market that there is room for only one firm. This applies to many of the public utilities, e.g. gas supply, water, electricity generation, telephone communications, etc.

4. Deliberate Policy to Exclude Competitors

Restriction of competition falls into two main groups. On the one hand we have the sources of monopoly power described so far. These have, as it were, resulted indirectly rather than from any deliberate action by producers. In fact, such monopolies can almost be described as 'spontaneous'. We must contrast these 'spontaneous' monopolies with the second kind, the 'deliberate' monopolies, those artificially created with the deliberate object of making super-normal profits by restricting supplies. There is 'contrived scarcity'.

It is essential to distinguish between the two when formulating policy. While the 'spontaneous' monopolies may still abuse their fortunate position in order to make high profits, to a large extent they are inevitable, and usually policy should seek to control rather than destroy them. On the other hand, monopolies solely designed to follow restrictive practices detrimental to the consumer should, where possible, be broken up. In practice, however, it is often difficult to draw a distinct line between the two. While firms may increase production or combine in order to reduce costs through economies of scale, the effect may still be that competitors are forced out.

Deliberate action to exclude competitors takes various forms. Firms producing or selling the same good may combine, or a competitor may be subject to a takeover bid. Monopolies are often formed in the sale of services. Trade unions are primarily combinations of workers formed with the object of obtaining higher wages (see Chapter 16). Certain professions, such as medicine, the law, accountancy and engineering, also have their associations which regulate qualifications, methods of entry, professional conduct and often the scale of fees to be charged. In as much as they can regulate the supply of these services by limiting entrants or by fixing a scale of fees, they must be regarded as a form of monopoly.

Some practices to exclude competitors are highly questionable, taking the form of vicious temporary price-cutting, collusion in submitting tenders, collective boycotts, intimidation of buyers by threats to cut off the supply of another vital product, etc.

13.4 The Equilibrium Output of the Monopolist

The Effect of the Downward-sloping Demand Curve on Marginal Revenue

Consider Figure 13.2. In (a) the producer is selling under conditions of perfect competition. His MR, the addition to total receipts from selling an extra unit, is equal to the full price at which the extra unit sells. For the fourth unit it is the shaded area *A*.

FIGURE 13.2
Marginal Revenue Under Conditions of Perfect and Imperfect Competition

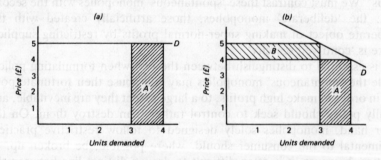

In (*b*), however, the producer is selling under conditions of imperfect competition. If he wishes to sell a fourth unit, for example, he must lower his price from £5 to £4. But this lower price applies not only to the fourth unit but to the first three units as well. Thus, his net addition to receipts is equal to what he gets for the fourth unit, *A*, less what he loses on the three previous units, *B*. Under imperfect competition, therefore, MR is always less than price at any given output.

The Relationship Between Costs, Revenue and Output of a Monopolist

Let us consider another hypothetical manufacturer of lawnmowers, Airborne Mowers. To simplify, we shall assume that it has identical cost curves to Rollermowers. But it differs in that it makes a special type of mower, very popular in a certain district. A patent enables the firm to exclude competitors. In short, in this particular market, it is a monopolist. Since what is supplied is also the market supply, the number put on the market affects the price. Thus if the firm produces only 20 mowers a year, they will fetch £790 each; if it increases total output to 90, the price per mower will drop to £440.

Airborne Mowers has the same problem as Rollermowers – to decide on the output which will give it the maximum profit. But it has an extra complication on the revenue side – as output increases, price falls, not only for the last unit of output, but for the *whole* output. The result can be seen in his marginal receipts (Table 13.1). These figures are plotted in Figure 13.3.

FIGURE 13.3
The Equilibrium Output of a Monopolist

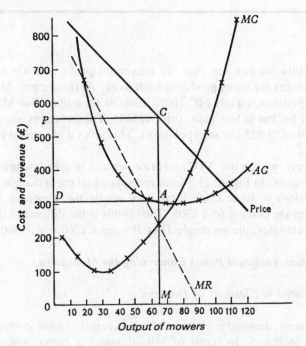

Table 13.1
Costs, Receipts and Profits of Airborne Mowers (in £)

Output per week (units)	Costs			Price per unit	Receipts		Profits
	Total	Average total	Marginal		Total	Marginal	
0	10 000	—	—	—	—	—	−10 000
10	12 000	1200	200	840	8 400	840	−3 600
20	13 400	670	140	790	15 800	740	2 400
30	14 400	480	100	740	22 200	640	7 800
40	15 400	385	100	690	27 600	540	12 200
50	16 750	335	135	640	32 000	440	15 250
60	18 600	310	185	590	35 400	340	16 800
70	21 000	300	240	540	37 800	240	16 800
80	24 000	300	300	490	39 200	140	15 200
90	27 900	310	390	440	39 600	40	11 700
100	33 000	330	510	390	39 000	−60	6 000
110	39 600	360	660	340	37 400	−160	−2 200
120	48 000	400	840	290	34 800	−260	−13 200

By inspection we can see that the maximum profit is made when 65 Airborne mowers are being produced each week. At this output, MR, as in perfect competition, equals MC (both £240 at 65 units). But MR is no longer equal to, but is less than, price (£565). Total receipts are £36 725 and total costs £19 825 (by interpolation). This gives a maximum profit of £16 900.

Alternatively, we can use ATC and price per unit to calculate profit at an output of 65 units. In Figure 13.3 total receipts equal the rectangle *OMCP* — (output x price) = 65 x £565, total cost equals the rectangle *OMAD* (output x average cost) = 65 x £305. Thus profit is the difference between these two rectangles, the rectangle *DACP* = 65 x £260 = £16 900.

Some Important Analytical Points Concerning the Monopolist

1. MR is Related to Elasticity of Demand

As we have seen, demand is elastic when, as a result of a fall in price, total expenditure increases. In terms of MR, demand is elastic when MR is

FIGURE 13.4
Elasticity of Demand and the Monopolist's Output

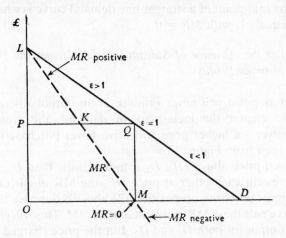

positive. Similarly, demand is inelastic when MR is negative. This is shown in Figure 13.4, where we have assumed a straight-line demand curve for simplicity.

From Figure 13.4 we can draw the following conclusions:

(a) A monopolist will never produce at a price where demand is inelastic. (Here MR is negative; so the monopolist can increase total revenue by reducing output.)

(b) Where a monopolist has no marginal costs (e.g. the owner of a mineral spring gushing from the earth), the MC curve will be horizontal along the *x*-axis. Production will therefore take place where elasticity of demand equals unity.

(c) Where a monopolist firm has marginal costs, it will always produce at a price where demand is elastic. (If MR = MC, MR must be positive, too.)

2. With a Straight-line Demand Curve, the MR Curve bisects the Horizontal Distance between the Price Axis and Quantity Demanded

This can be proved as follows:

Total revenue = Sum of revenue for each unit of output = *LOM* at output *OM*
Total revenue =   Price × Output =   *POMQ* at output *OM*

Therefore *LOM = POMQ*

But area $POMK$ is common. Therefore LPK is equal in area to QMK. But identical angles are equal. Therefore, Δ LPK is congruent with Δ KMQ. Therefore, $PK = KQ$, and thus $OM = $ MD. This also means that $LQ = QD$. Thus the mid-point of a straight-line demand curve is where elasticity of demand equals 1, with $MR = 0$.

3. The Greater the Absence of Substitutes, the Greater the Power of the Monopolist to make Profits

While the monopolist will never produce at an output where demand is inelastic, the greater the inelasticity of demand, the greater will be monopoly power – a higher price will drive fewer purchasers elsewhere. This can be seen from Figure 13.5.

At any given price above OP, D_1 is more elastic than D_2. Since these demand curves cut each other at price OP, the MR of each must be the same at output OM (from proposition (2) above). Suppose the monopolist's MC curve cuts these MR curves at output OM. This will give the same equilibrium output for both D_1 and D_2. But the price charged will be OP_1 for D_1, and OP_2 for D_2. Profits are therefore greater for D_2 (shaded) than for D_1 (nil).

4. The Monopolist can Produce at an Output where MC is Falling even in the Long Period

At an output where MC is falling, AVC must be greater than MC (see Figure 11.1). Under perfect competition, therefore, an output where price = MC (falling) must mean that TVC are greater than TR. There will thus be no production.

With monopoly, however, MR is below price. Thus a profit is still possible provided ATC at the equilibrium output, e.g. OM (Figure 13.5), is less than the price at which the monopolist sells.

5. It is Impossible to Derive a Supply Curve for the Monopolist

Under perfect competition, MC is equated with MR to obtain equilibrium output. Since the producer is faced with a demand curve of infinite elasticity, MR also equals price. There is thus a direct relationship between the amount supplied and price.

A monopolist, too, equates MC and MR, but now MR is less than price. But the MR corresponding to a given price depends upon the elasticity of demand at that price. It is possible, therefore, to have many different outputs at the same price, or many different prices for the same output. Thus we cannot show a *unique* supply at any given price as we can under perfect competition.

FIGURE 13.5
Elasticity of Demand and Monopoly Profits

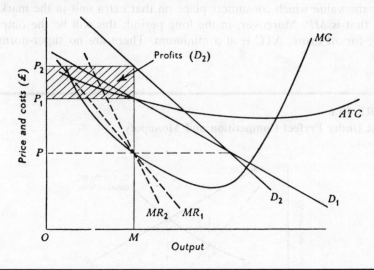

This can be illustrated from Figure 13.5, for at the output *OM* different elasticities of demand give different prices. The reader can construct a similar diagram showing different quantities supplied by the monopolist for the same price according to differences in elasticity of demand.

6. There is no Difference between the Monopolist's Long-period and Short-period Equilibrium Positions

Under perfect competition, the existence of profits in the short period attracts new entrants, and super-normal profits are competed away. Under monopoly, the producer is the industry, and, by definition, no new firms can enter. Thus, even in the long period, the monopolist's profits remain.

13.5 Public Policy and Monopoly

Monopoly and Perfect Competition

Monopoly is an emotive word. It is often assumed that the monopolist, in seeking to maximise profit, will always carry out policies inimical to the consumer. The argument goes somewhat as follows.

Where there is perfect competition, output for all firms in the industry will take place where price = MC, i.e. at *OM* (Figure 13.6). In other words, production is carried to the point where the cost of an extra unit just equals the value which consumers place on that extra unit in the market place, that is *MP*. Moreover, in the long period, this will be the output where, for all firms, ATC is at a minimum. There are no super-normal profits.

FIGURE 13.6
Output Under Perfect Competition and Monopoly

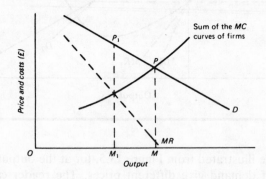

Now suppose a cartel takes over the marketing of the products of all the individual firms. In order to maximise its profits, it will only sell an output where MC = MR, i.e. OM_1, and at a price MP_1. Thus consumers get less of the product and at a higher price than under perfect competition; factors of production are not fully allocated according to the wishes of consumers.

Criticisms of the Above Argument

While there may be much truth in this argument, it is not infallible. For one thing, it makes certain implicit assumptions; for another, it ignores dynamic considerations.

First, it rests on the assumption that the competitive industry's supply curve will be the same as the MC curve of the monopolist. But this is unlikely to be so. A single firm may be able to achieve economies of scale which are not open to the comparatively small firms which comprise the competitive industry. Such economies arise through indivisibility of plant,

increased division of labour, improved co-ordination, and greater investment (since there is now no fear of over-capitalisation of the industry
through rival firms carrying out similar investment).

It is probable, therefore, that the monopolist will, at the relevant market
output, have lower costs than firms producing under conditions of perfect
competition. Indeed, we can envisage a situation where, even though the
monopolist is producing at the maximum profit output, the consumer
nevertheless obtains more of the product and at a lower price than under
perfect competition. Thus, in Figure 13.7, perfect competition between
firms would give an output of OM at price OP. But, since the monopolist
has lower cost curves, OM_1 would be produced at a price OP_1 (and there
would still be super-normal profits!)

Second, our competitive model was purely static in its approach. Profits
were maximised on the basis of given prices of products and factors. No
consideration was given to other influences on the growth of firms over
time.

FIGURE 13.7
**A Monopolist Producing a Larger Output and at a Lower Price than a
Perfectly Competitive Industry**

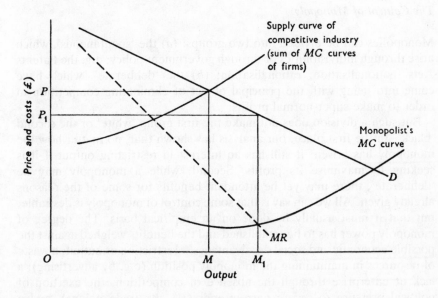

But the *development* of firms depends upon innovation and investment in research. Thus we have to ask the question: 'Are firms more likely to innovate and spend on research if, by being granted monopoly powers, they can be assured of the rewards of their spending?' In other words, are monopolies more conducive to growth than perfect competition? We cannot develop the argument here, but the mere existence of the Patents Acts suggests that there is some truth in it. On the other hand, there have been instances where monopolies have bought up patents in order that they shall *not* be developed in competition with them.

Third, price and output may be more stable under monopoly. Where there are many competing producers, as in agriculture, the reactions of each can bring about sharp swings in the total supply and price of the commodity. In contrast, the monopolist can view the market as a whole in assessing likely future demand, probably finding that only marginal adjustments to supply are necessary. Partly for this reason Marketing Boards have been set up as selling monopolies in certain branches of agriculture.

Finally, in criticising monopoly, we must remember that restriction of output may permit a discriminating monopolist to charge prices which will allow certain markets to be supplied (see pp.182–3).

The Control of Monopoly

Monopolies can be divided into two groups: (*a*) the 'spontaneous', which arise through indivisibilities or through government policy, e.g. the Patents Acts, nationalisation, rationalisation; (*b*) the 'deliberate', which have come into being with the principal object of eliminating competition in order to make super-normal profits.

But such a division does not make the first group 'white' or the second 'black'. In the first place, our analysis has shown that, no matter how the monopoly has arisen, it still has an interest in restricting output if it is seeking to maximise its profits. Second, while a monopoly may be 'deliberate', there may yet be attendant benefits for some of the reasons already given. All we can say is that some control of monopoly is desirable, but that it must usually be done on an empirical basis. The degree of monopoly power has to be established and the benefits weighed against the possible economic and social disadvantages – restriction of output, a waste of resources in maintaining the monopoly position (e.g. by advertising), a lack of enterprise through the absence of competition, the exertion of political pressure to secure narrow ends (e.g. by trade unions), and a redistribution of wealth from consumers to the monopolist.

As a result, monopolies in the UK are regulated rather than prohibited. Yet any policy is fraught with difficulties. An exact assessment of the public benefits and disadvantages resulting from a monopoly is impossible. Very often, too, the decision as to whether a monopoly is useful or anti-social in character depends on circumstances and therefore varies from one period to another (note the fostering of monopolies in the 1930s). Moreover, if legislation is proposed, the term 'unfair competition' has to be closely defined by lawyers, though, for the purposes of control, it really requires an elastic interpretation based on economic issues. Last, government policy in another field may influence the problem of monopoly. Thus tariff protection, by restricting competition from abroad, enhances the possibility of establishing monopolies in the home market.

Broadly speaking, policy can take three main forms:

1. State Ownership

When it is important not to destroy the advantages of monopoly, the problem may best be solved by the state taking it over completely; the public then appears to be effectively protected. Freed from the objective of maximising profit, there should be no tendency for the state-owned industries to use their monopoly position to make high profits. Should, however, such profits be made they would eventually be passed on to the public in lower prices, or in reduced taxation.

In practice, however, lower profits may mask inefficiency in operation or the payment of wages to employees above those in comparable occupations elsewhere. Consequently, provision must be made for the prices charged to be examined by an independent body and for efficiency checks to be carried out.

2. Legislation and Administrative Machinery to Regulate Monopolies

This method is usually employed when it is desired to retain monopolies because of their benefits but to leave them under private ownership.

The Monopolies and Restrictive Practices Act 1948 (since amended) set up a Monopolies Commission to investigate monopoly situations. Upon the Commission's report, a ministerial order can declare certain arrangements or practices illegal. Subjects investigated have included: supply of household detergents, breakfast cereals, bricks, asbestos, wire and fibre ropes, plasterboard, cross-channel sea-ferries, frozen foodstuffs; London rail services for commuters; and proposed mergers, e.g. *The Times* and News International, Lonrho and House of Fraser.

The Act was subject to two main criticisms. First, it specifically excluded investigation of the nationalised industries and trade unions. Second, it did not possess any 'teeth', only civil action following the breach of a ministerial order. Nevertheless, publicity, rather than direct action following an adverse report, usually influenced firms to mend their ways.

3. Breaking Up or Prohibition of the Monopoly

Where the monopoly is on balance detrimental to consumers, policy can take the form of breaking it up or prohibiting it by legislation. Thus the state could reduce the period for which patents are granted or make their renewal more difficult. Similarly, it may pass Company Acts requiring firms to publish profit statements, so that other firms can ascertain quickly if super-normal profits are being made. Alternatively, the state can outlaw attempts to eliminate competition, whether by unfair practices, the formation of cartels or restrictive agreements. Total prohibition was the policy at one time followed by the USA.

In the UK an investigation by the Monopolies Commission led to the Restrictive Trade Practices Act 1956. This: (*a*) allowed manufacturers and traders to enforce *individual* resale price maintenance through the ordinary civil courts; (*b*) banned the *collective* enforcement of resale price maintenance through such practices as private courts, stop lists and boycotts; (*c*) required other restrictive pacts, such as common price and level tendering, to be registered with a new Registrar of Restrictive Trading Agreements appointed by the Crown; (*d*) appointed a new Restrictive Practices Court. The Court sits as three-member tribunals, each consisting of at least one judge and two lay members. For a practice to be allowed, it must be justified as being 'in the public interest'.

But the 1956 Act still permitted individual suppliers to enforce resale price maintenance for their own products. This was amended by the Resale Prices Act 1964, which made minimum resale price maintenance illegal, except for goods approved by the court. So far only minimum prices for books and proprietary medicines have been authorised.

The Monopolies and Mergers Act 1965 strengthened and extended the legislation on monopolies. It permitted the Department of Trade to refer a merger or proposed merger to the Monopolies Commission where it would lead to a monopoly or would increase the power of an existing monopoly. The Act also increased the government's powers to enforce the findings of the Commission (for example, by giving it powers to prohibit mergers or to dissolve an undesirable monopoly).

The Fair Trading Act 1973, as strengthened by the Competition Act 1980, moved the thrust of monopoly policy to *promoting competition*. The Act:

(*a*) Created an Office of Fair Trading under a Director-General. Not only did the Director take over the functions of the Registrar of Restrictive

Trading Agreements, but he now has the responsibility for discovering probable monopoly situations or uncompetitive practices. Thus the Office of Fair Trading provides the minister with information and advice on consumer protection, monopoly, mergers and restrictive practices.

(b) Empowered the renamed Monopolies and Mergers Commission to investigate local as well as national monopolies, and extended its powers of inquiry to the nationalised industries and even to restrictive labour practices (though with limited follow-up powers).

(c) Reduced the criterion for a monopoly situation to a one-quarter (minimum) market share.

13.6 Discriminating Monopoly

A discriminating monopolist is one who can, and does, sell the *same* product at different prices to different consumers.

Examples of discriminating monopoly are: (a) a doctor who varies fees for the same treatment according to estimates of the wealth of the patients; (b) a car manufacturer who sells cars in export markets at a lower price than on the home market (even allowing for differences in taxation); (c) electricity taken during the night for heat-storage and charged at a lower tariff than that consumed during the day; (d) a small builders' merchant who charges the professional builder less for paint and wallpaper than the 'do-it-yourself' amateur.

The Necessary Conditions for Discriminating Monopoly

For discriminating monopoly to be practicable, certain conditions must be fulfilled.

(1) *There must be some imperfection in the market.* Under conditions of perfect competition, discrimination is impossible. But where there are different markets, or where parts of the market are separated by transport costs, consumers' ignorance or national barriers, sellers can exercise some control over the supply in each market, or in each part of the market, separately.

(2) *Elasticities of demand in the markets must be different.* This means that the demand curves must slope differently. As a result, different prices will be charged by the monopolist in order to maximise profits.

(3) *No 'seepage' is possible between markets or different parts of the market.* If an exporter in one country, for instance, sells the good much more cheaply in another country, then either transport costs or physical controls must prevent re-importation to the country of origin.

The Equilibrium Position of the Discriminating Monopolist

Suppose that a discriminating monopolist is faced with two markets, *A* and *B*. The demand curves for each of these markets are shown in Figure 13.8. In order to maximise his profits he will have to decide: (*a*) the total output he will produce; (*b*) how to divide this output between the two separate markets; (*c*) what price to charge in each market. We shall examine each problem in turn.

(*a*)   *What shall be his total output?* Since we assume that the product is homogeneous, the monopolist must consider the MC for the *whole* output irrespective of which market it is sold in. This MC he will equate with the combined MR curve of the two markets (CMR). This curve is found by adding the two MR curves – the output of market *A* for any given MR is added to the output of market *B* for that MR. This is repeated for all values of MR. Thus in Figure 13.8 the monopolist will produce *OQ*. At that output the addition to his cost of producing the last unit just equals the addition to his revenue from selling that unit in either market.

FIGURE 13.8
The Equilibrium Output of a Monopolist Who Sells in Different Markets

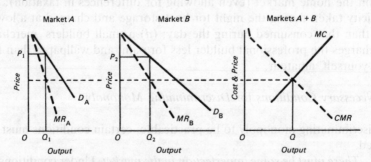

1 For simplicity, straight-line revenue and cost curves have been assumed.
2 Demand is more elastic in market *B* at all prices.

(*b*)   *How shall he divide this output between the two markets?* The monopolist will maximise profits by equating the MC of the *whole* output with the MR in market *A* (MR$_A$) and the MC of the *whole* output with the MR in market *B* (MR$_B$). This means that he will sell *OQ*$_1$ in market *A* and *OQ*$_2$ in market *B*, for the combined output *OQ* (where CMR equals marginal cost) is obtained by summing the output in *A* and in *B*. MR must be the same in both markets, for it has to be equated with MC for the total output. If it were not the same, the monopolist could increase profits by transferring output from where marginal revenue was lower to where it was higher.

(*c*) *What will be the price in each market?* This, too, can be seen from the diagram. An output of OQ_1 in market A will sell at OP_1; an output of OQ_2 in market B will sell at OP_2. Since demand is less elastic in market A than in market B, a smaller quantity is sold and at a higher price in A than in B.

Can Price Discrimination be in the Interest of Consumers?

The term 'discrimination' suggests that consumers are exploited in order to increase the profits of the monopolist. Now price discrimination will enable the monopolist to obtain a higher total revenue (and thus higher profits) than if he merely charged a single price for the whole of the market. But this means he must produce a larger output than with a single price. He is able to do this because, by being able to separate the markets, he does not force down the price in one market by selling extra goods in another market. Indeed, if there were different markets for all units of his product (that is, 'perfect discrimination'), the marginal revenue for each good would be the price at which it sold. The monopolist's output would then be identical with the perfectly competitive output (Figure 13.9).

FIGURE 13.9
Receipts under 'Perfect Discrimination'

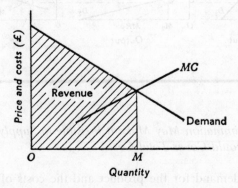

Two points of significance to the consumer follow from this.

1. Price Discrimination May Make it Possible to Supply a Particular Market

Two examples come to mind. British Rail charges all passengers at so much per mile. Main line services are profitable at the standard rate; many local services are not. Local lines are therefore closed down. It is possible, however, that local passengers would be willing to pay higher fares to maintain the service.

Or we can consider a doctor whose services are demanded by both wealthy and poor patients. Their demand curves, D_1 and D_2 respectively, will, with price differentiation, allow the monopolist doctor to supply OM_1 at price OP_1 to the wealthy patients and OM_2 at price OP_2 to the poorer patients. But if he has to charge a single price (and wishes to maximise his profits), he will supply OM at a price OP – and this only to his wealthy patients. This is because his total demand curve is still D_1+2 but, without price discrimination in separate markets, a negative MR_1 outweighs increased revenue from D_2 at the price and output where that becomes effective, K (Figure 13.10).

FIGURE 13.10
How Price Discrimination Allows an Extra Market to be Supplied

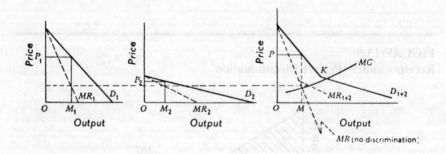

---

2. Price Discrimination May Make it Possible to Supply a Good when no Single Price would Cover Total Costs

Suppose the demand for the product and the costs of producing are as shown in Figure 13.11. Where a single price is charged, no firm could cover its total costs. But it may be possible for a firm (e.g. a public utility) to

FIGURE 13.11
The Possibility of Supply with Price Discrimination

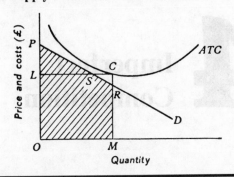

charge discriminating prices and thus cover its costs. If the monopolist could discriminate perfectly between every purchaser, he could produce an output up to the point where $\Delta\ SRC = \Delta\ PLS$, for $LOMC$ are his total costs and $POMR$ would be his total revenue.

The firm might be able to cover its costs by imposing a fixed standing charge on consumers irrespective of the quantity bought. But, if this is impossible, without price discrimination the firm would either have to close down or have its revenue shortfall covered by a subsidy.

14 Imperfect Competition

Perfect competition, we have seen, occurs where identical goods are made by a large number of producers and there is completely free entry to the industry. The opposite market condition, monopoly, is possible where a good which has no close substitutes is made by a single producer who can prevent competitors entering the industry.

Perfect competition and monopoly represent the two extreme market forms. In the real world, however, there is more likely to be a situation of *imperfect competition* somewhere between the two. Here we consider two major possibilities where there are (*a*) many firms, (*b*) few firms competing imperfectly in the market.

14.1 Monopolistic Competition: Imperfect Competition with Many Firms

The Nature of Monopolistic Competition

An industry may consist of many firms each making a product which differs only in detail from that of its rivals. Each firm, since its product is not homogeneous with that of other firms, enjoys some monopoly power. On the other hand, because there is no real gap in the chain of substitution, there is competition from other firms. What we really have is a number of small 'monopolists' competing with one another – 'monopolistic competition'. How does this come about?

Conditions Giving Rise to Monopolistic Competition

On the demand side, we have a situation which is closely akin to monopoly. Few goods are completely homogeneous. Indeed, nearly every firm tries deliberately to give its product some distinction from those with

184

which it competes. This 'product differentiation', as it is called, takes various forms. Special characteristics of the good are extensively advertised, competitions are run periodically, free gifts are offered, distinctive wrappings are used. Or, quite simply, the brand name is splashed across television screens and street hoardings in the hope that constant repetition will lead consumers to prefer the good. Apart from product differentiation, a seller may depend upon 'goodwill' (arising through habit or social contacts), rather than the actual price charged, to retain customers.

Whichever method is used, product differentiation or goodwill, the result is the same. The producer is not faced with a market demand which is beyond control. If the firm raises its price, some customers will buy competitors' brands. But not all customers will do this. Some will consider other brands inferior, and only a large price rise will induce them to change. Similarly, if the firm lowers its price, it will attract only a limited number of customers from rival producers. In short, the producer of a brand good or a seller possessing goodwill is, like a monopolist, faced with a demand curve which slopes downwards from left to right. Nevertheless, demand tends to be elastic. Although there are not perfect substitutes available, there are fairly good ones – the different brands of rival producers.

On the supply side, because entry to the industry is possible, the situation is similar to perfect competition. Where one producer is seen to be making super-normal profits, existing producers tend to copy the product and new competitors start producing a somewhat similar brand.

The Equilibrium of the Industry under Monopolistic Competition

We simplify the analysis by making two important assumptions: (*a*) individual producers can obtain all their supply of any factor at a given price; (*b*) external economies do not affect costs as the number of firms in the group increases. While the latter can be allowed for by subsequent modification, the former is to some degree unrealistic. The industry consists of many but not an infinite number of firms. The demand of one firm for a factor of production may therefore be sufficient to affect its price. Nevertheless, our assumption enables us to analyse a situation where all firms can, in the longer period, achieve identical cost curves, and where cost curves will not rise as new producers enter.

1. The Short Period

In the short period existing firms cannot increase production by employing additional fixed factors, nor can new firms enter. Each firm, therefore, is a little 'monopolist', having a downward-sloping demand curve for its product and producing where MC equals MR. Because there are many firms, each firm can set its price without having to consider the reactions of competitors. This price will be greater than MR, and super-normal profits are made.

2. The Long Period

In monopolistic competition the full long-period equilibrium position is possible only when both firms and the industry are in equilibrium. Whereas for each firm the condition of equilibrium (MR = MC) will apply whatever the output, for the industry we must allow, as with perfect competition, for the entry of new firms and for increased production by existing firms. This is where monopolistic competition differs essentially from monopoly; with the latter, *one* firm is *the* industry.

The increase in supply in the long period will lead to a fall in the price of the good, and the demand curve facing each producer shifts its position downwards to the left, for more producers are now dividing up the total market. At the same time, it is likely that the demand curve will become more elastic, for all products of the group will tend to become more similar to that of the most successful. In other words, each brand becomes a better substitute for other brands.

This will continue until super-normal profits have disappeared. Each firm will be earning only normal profits. (In practice the full equilibrium position is unlikely to be reached. Differences between firms will persist, and most will be earning small super-normal profits.)

A comparison of the equilibrium position of the firm in the short period and the long period under monopolistic competition is shown in Figure 14.1. In the short period output is *OM*, where MR = MC. But the inability to add to fixed factors means that super-normal profits exist, equal to *ABCD*. In the long period the entry of close substitutes, causes the AR curve to fall. Super-normal profits disappear, and the equilibrium output is OM_1, where MC = MR, and AC = AR.

Certain points regarding this long-period equilibrium output should be noted:

(*a*) No super-normal profits are made; as in perfect competition, there is free entry to the industry.

(*b*) The same conditions of full equilibrium hold as in perfect competition – MC = MR (equilibrium of the firm), and AC = AR (equilibrium of the industry). That both conditions hold at the same output is due simply to a mathematic relationship. At an output less than OM_1, AC is falling more rapidly than AR. This means that MC must be pulling down AC more than MR is pulling down AR. In other words, MC must be less than MR. At any output greater than OM_1, AC is rising more rapidly than AR. MC must therefore be greater than MR. The only point where AC and AR

FIGURE 14.1
Monopolistic Competition: Equilibrium of Firms in the Short and Long Periods

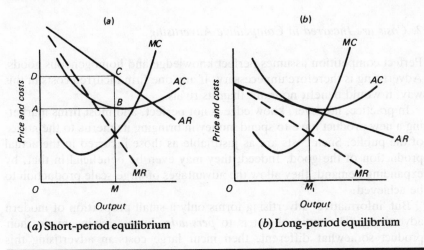

(a) Short-period equilibrium   (b) Long-period equilibrium

are falling at the same rate is at output OM_1 where they are tangential, and here MC is neither less nor greater than MR – it is equal to it.

(c)   Price is greater than MC and MR – a result of the falling AR curve.

(d)   The equilibrium output is less than that under perfect competition. This again is the result of the downward-sloping AR curve, which can be tangential to a U-shaped average-cost curve only at an output less than the minimum average cost.

The Economic and Social Effects of Monopolistic Competition – the 'Wastes of Competition'

1. Even in the Long Period Firms Operate at less than the Optimum Size

Under perfect competition, not only are super-normal profits eliminated, but in the long period each firm is producing where AC is a minimum – the optimum output. At this output factors of production are combined in the correct proportions and the full advantages of large-scale economies are achieved. What happens under monopolistic competition is that firms operate at less than their optimum size and thus there is some waste in the way in which factors of production are used.

But we should not assume from the above argument that monopolistic competition is necessarily a 'bad' thing. Not every consumer will want to buy goods which are identical with those bought by other consumers. Different individuals have slightly different tastes. Thus waste in the use of the scarce resources can be regarded as the part of the price that has to be paid for variety of choice.

2. Costs are Incurred in Competitive Advertising

Perfect competition assumes perfect knowledge and homogeneous goods. Advertising is therefore unnecessary. If any one firm incurred costs in this way, it would benefit no more than its rivals.

In practice, however, knowledge is not perfect, and most firms marketing a new product have to spend money in bringing its merits to the notice of the public. Such costs are as justifiable as those incurred in the actual production of the good. Indeed, they may even be beneficial in that, by expanding demand, they allow the advantages of large-scale production to be achieved.

But 'informative' advertising forms only a small proportion of modern advertising. The main object is to *persuade*. Firms, having made their product somewhat different, then incur large costs in advertising this difference and in persuading the customer that their brand of good is superior to other brands. Put in economic terms, they aim at decreasing the elasticity of demand for their particular product as well as shifting the demand curve to the right. In reality, there may be little basic difference between brands – but labour and other scarce resources are wasted in trying to convince the public that it is otherwise.

In practice it is not always easy to draw the line between informative and persuasive advertising. What is 'one person's meat is another person's poison'; and if you adhere to the principle of allowing people to exercise freedom of choice, then you must accept the concomitant – that they are open to be persuaded. What consumers lack is knowledge of the good, and they are thus easy victims to the pressures of advertising. Today there is only a private body, the Consumers' Association (publishers of *Which?*), to report on goods to subscribers.

14.2 Oligopoly: Imperfect Competition with Few Firms

Pricing where there are Few Firms

In real life many goods and services are produced by just a few firms, e.g. cigarettes, cars, petrol, tyres, screws, detergents, electric cable, synthetic fibres, kitchen tiles and lawnmowers. Here we have 'oligopoly', where pricing and output policy conforms to no given principles. Sometimes one firm is so dominant that its price is more or less followed by the smaller firms. In other cases, firms may be of fairly equal strength but, since their number is small, no one firm can set a price *without considering the likely reaction of its competitors*. If, for instance, it reduces its price, it cannot guarantee that it will win a greater share of the market since other firms may retaliate and cut their prices.

It is impossible, therefore, to predict the exact behaviour of the oligopolist. Whereas with monopoly and monopolistic competition the relationship of marginal revenue and marginal cost determines price and output, the oligopolistic firm has the added dimension of having to make a guess about the reaction of its competitors to a change in price. There are many different assumptions it can make, and each will give a different solution.

Thus there is no single theoretical model to cover the oligopolist's pricing policy. A likely assumption by firms is that price cuts will be matched by competitors, but not price increases. From this has developed the theory of the kinked demand curve.

The Kinked Demand Curve

The oligopolist firm reasons that if it cuts prices, its competitors will follow suit in order to avoid losing customers. On the other hand, if it raises its price, its rivals will do nothing, being content to pick up the extra customers driven away by the price increase. This means that its demand curve is relatively inelastic for price cuts, but relatively elastic for price increases. Thus in Figure 14.2, if the original price is P, the firm would expect to move down along the curve towards D and upwards towards D_1.

For two reasons, the kinked demand curve makes for price stability. First, the oligopolist firm is likely to be conservative in its pricing policy, not changing its price from P. Second, even though its costs change, the firm would not change its price or output. This is the result of the broken marginal revenue curve, MR, which follows from the kinked demand curve. Thus marginal cost can change between MC to MC_1 without exerting any pressure on the firm's policy. Only if costs change more would the firm consider risking the loss of customers by raising its price or risk a price war by lowering its price.

The model, however, does have weaknesses in that: (*a*) it cannot explain how price P was originally determined; and (*b*) there is little empirical evidence to support the assumption that a price cut, but not a price rise, will be matched by competitors – though provided the oligopolist *acts* on this assumption it makes no difference to the outcome.

Oligopoly Policy in Practice

Since in an oligopolistic market situation firms are reluctant to engage in price-cutting, other policies are often pursued in practice.

FIGURE 14.2
The Kinked Demand Curve

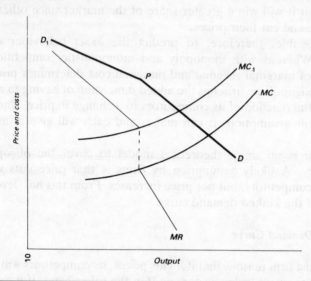

First, the few firms concerned are able and usually willing to come to a tacit agreement on price in order to achieve joint profit maximisation. Often this takes the form of following the price set by the largest firm. Thus Brooke Bond Oxo appears to give the lead in tea prices. The extent to which such an understanding is possible depends on the ability to exclude new firms, for example because production has to be on a large scale from the outset.

Second, non-price competition is prevalent, e.g. through extensive advertising, free gift stamps, competitions, temporary special offers, etc.

14.3 Pricing Policy in the Real World

Difficulties of the MC = MR Principle

Follwing the above brief discussion of oligopoly, we have to admit that in many other cases the strict principle of fixing a price where MC equals MR may not be rigidly adhered to. For one thing the optimum output may be unobtainable because of cash-flow difficulties, the result of the capital market not being perfect. For another, few markets are so perfectly competitive that individual producers have no control over their price and have such an exact knowledge of the shape of their demand curve that MR can be equated with MC at all outputs.

Pricing policy therefore usually follows more pragmatic methods. Sometimes, for example with government contracts, the firm may follow a 'cost-plus' approach, being allowed what is considered to be a fair percentage addition to basic costs to cover overheads and normal profit; or the firm will, by a process of trial and error, seek to charge 'what the traffic will bear', e.g. the 'black-market' ticket seller.

Mark-up Pricing

More usually pricing is on a 'mark-up' basis. Only the cost of manufacturing is calculated accurately, and to this is added a rather arbitrary percentage for overheads in order to arrive at the final selling price. Thus, in selling a book, the publisher calculates the cost of printing and binding, adds a percentage (say 40 per cent) to cover overheads and normal profit, and fixes a final bookshop price which covers these costs plus the author's royalty and the bookseller's margin based on the retail price.

Indeed, this may be the only practicable method when, as is usual, firms are producing more than one product. A publisher, for instance, could not exist on the sales of one book and, in any case, would want the extra security of publishing different types of books. Furthermore, in order to survive, producers have to pay regard to what is known as 'the product life-cycle', which consists of innovation, growth, maturity, saturation and decline (Figure 14.3). In the growth period the product shows increasing

FIGURE 14.3
The Product Life-cycle

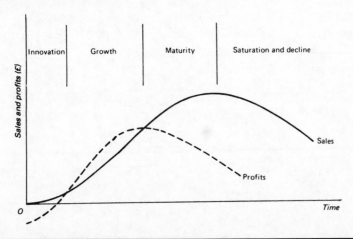

profitability, for the firm enjoys almost a monopoly position. With time, competitors enter: sales increase, but only at the expense of rising advertising costs. Thereafter the market becomes over-supplied or competitors produce improved models, and sales decline. Thus the go-ahead firm will always be planning new products so that one replaces another as each passes through its life-cycle.

With a many-product firm the exact share of overheads attributable to any one product would be difficult, if not impossible, to ascertain. The mark-up method sidetracks this difficulty. Furthermore, it allows control by the cost accountant, especially as regards maintaining cash flow and assuring profitable production. Where pricing is on the MC = MR principle, there is no certainty that total costs are covered.

Part IV

For Whom? How the Factors of Production are Rewarded – the Theory of Distribution

15 The Marginal Productivity Theory of Distribution

15.1 Introduction

Sharing the National 'Cake'

Factors of production co-operate together to produce the national product. Each of these factors is owned by somebody. How much of the cake each individual in the country obtains depends upon (i) how much of the factors is owned, and (ii) the reward each factor receives.

Differences in individual incomes therefore depend upon both inequalities of ownership and inequalities in earnings. It is the latter, concerned with the theory of distribution, which is the subject of this chapter.

Our approach will be as follows. The price of a factor service is determined, like that of a good, by demand and supply. First, therefore, we look at the demand for and supply of factor services in general.

But, as we have seen, factors can be classified according to certain broad and important characteristics. In the chapters that follow, therefore, we shall examine how these special characteristics influence the return to these different factors.

Before proceeding, however, two important points must be made:

(1) Some factors are consumed in one use (e.g. raw materials), while others are durable, rendering services over a period. In what follows we are examining the price of the *service* rendered by a factor, not the factor itself, though of course the two are directly related. This proviso must be borne in mind when, in what follows, we abbreviate by talking about the 'price of a factor of production'.

(2) Here we are concerned only with the reward to factors in a given industry, occupation or district. In other words, we examine how the price of a factor is fixed in a particular market. Analysis by ordinary demand and supply curves is therefore possible. When, as in Chapter 26, it becomes

necessary to examine the economy as a whole, we have to abandon this partial-equilibrium analysis for a more general one, and we then speak of labour, capital, investment, wages and the rate of interest in broad terms.

15.2 The Marginal Productivity Theory: Perfect Competition

The marginal productivity theory is primarily concerned with what determines the *demand* for factors of production. It shows that, under perfect competition, an employer will always pay a reward to a factor equal to the value of its contribution to the product. Its most serious weaknesses are that in the real world perfect competition seldom prevails and that it tends to ignore the supply side. Nevertheless, it does give precision to what determines the demand for a factor, and thus some examination of the theory is a necessary preliminary to a more detailed discussion of the rewards of individual factors in the real world. It is a general theory applying to all factors of production. Illustration, however, is usually in terms of labour and wages, and we shall adopt this practice in the explanation which follows.

Demand of the Individual Firm

The demand for a factor is made up of the individual demands of all the firms using it. Our first task, therefore, is to ask why a firm demands labour and how much it will demand.

Demand for a factor comes from firms. It is a *derived* demand – the factor is not wanted for its own sake, but simply because it can contribute to the production of particular goods. Hence the actual price which a firm is willing to pay for a factor depends upon the addition to its receipts which results from the employment of a particular unit of that factor. By examining this in more detail precision can be given to what constitutes the demand for a factor.

Let us begin by making the following assumptions:

1. There is perfect competition in the market where the product is sold.
2. There is perfect competition in buying the factor – with labour, each firm is so small relative to the size of the market that it cannot, by varying its own demand, alter the wage rate.
3. All workers offering the particular type of labour are homogeneous.
4. In changing output, only the quantity of labour employed is varied; all other factors remain fixed in supply.

The law of diminishing returns (Chapter 10) showed that, as additional quantities of a variable factor (labour) are added to a fixed factor (land), the marginal return (physical product) of that variable factor would

Table 15.1
Schedules of Marginal Physical Productivity and Marginal-revenue Productivity of Labour—Product Sold under Conditions of Perfect Competition

Number of labourers employed (1)	Marginal physical product (50 kg bags potatoes) (2)	Marginal-revenue product (£) (3)
1	2	20
2	14	140
3	38	380
4	26	260
5	15	150
6	13	130
7	12	120
8	10	100
9	8	80
10	4	40
11	0	—

eventually decline. The analysis was conducted in terms of the physical returns to factors (Table 10.1, p.127), and columns (1) and (2) of Table 15.1 are extracted from that earlier table.

But when demanding labour (or any other factor) the firm is not so much interested in the marginal physical product as in the amount of money it will receive from the sale of that product. It pays for a factor because it contributes to ultimate receipts. What it has to ask, therefore, is: 'How much will total revenue increase if an additional worker is employed?' The value of this contribution to total revenue of an additional factor is known as its *marginal-revenue product* (MRP).

The MRP depends not only on the marginal physical product, but also on the price at which the product sells. Under perfect competition, the producer can sell any quantity at a given price. Hence the MRP is equal to the marginal physical product × the price of the product. Thus, in Table 15.1, by assuming that potatoes sell at £10 per 50 kg bag, we can arrive at the MRP in column (3). For example, when 2 labourers are employed, the total physical product is 16 bags, which at £10 a bag yields a total revenue of £160. When 3 are employed, the total physical product is 54 bags, giving a total revenue of £540. The MRP of the third workers is thus £380. Table 15.1 gives the MRP for each additional labourer, and the figures are plotted in Figure 15.1. The MRP curve shows the increase in total revenue as each extra worker is added to the labour force.

FIGURE 15.1
Changes in the Marginal-revenue Product as the Number of Labourers is increased

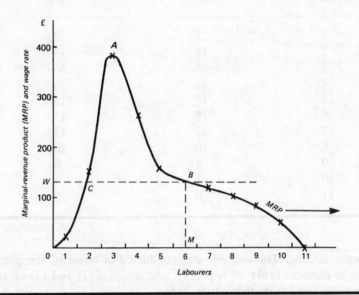

How the farmer decides on the number of labourers to employ can be seen from this example. An extra labourer will be employed so long as the resulting addition to total revenue is greater than the cost of employing the additional worker. In our example, because labour is the only variable factor, the farmer is equating MR and MC.

MR is shown by the MRP curve. But what of MC, the cost of engaging each additional labourer? Here it must be remembered that we have postulated perfect competition in buying factors of production. This means that the farmer's demand for labour is so small relative to the market that he cannot directly influence the price of labour. He has to accept the market wage rate as given, and, at this ruling wage rate, the supply of labour is perfectly elastic. MC and AC are one and the same thing, and are represented by a horizontal straight line equal to the wage rate (Figure 15.1).

The firm therefore equates MRP and the wage rate. Thus, in Figure 15.1, if the wage rate were £130 per week, the farmer would engage 6 workers. If fewer, say 5, were employed, the farmer could add more to receipts than to costs by taking on another worker, for the MRP (£150) would exceed MC (£130). On the other hand, if 7 were employed, the farmer would be paying the seventh worker £10 more than he was contributing to receipts.

Some Difficulties Examined

It might be asked whether the firm can always estimate the marginal-revenue productivity of each factor of production. The following two cases are particularly difficult.

First, with certain factors, such as secretaries, teachers, etc., there is no definite and immediate physical product resulting from their work. How, then, can the marginal physical product, and thus their marginal-revenue productivity, be measured? The answer is simply that they cannot be – but that does not alter the fact that, in practice, a firm proceeds to engage factors as though it can so estimate.

Second, how do we separate the contribution of factors when, for technical reasons, they have to be combined in fixed proportions? In our example this difficulty does not arise. Because labour is the only variable factor, the physical product of an additional worker is measured simply by seeing the difference made to total product. Even when there is more than one variable factor, the marginal product of one factor can be estimated if it is possible to hold the other factors fixed while the one is varied. But where a driver and a lorry, or a carpenter and a plane, have always to be combined together in a fixed ratio, there is the difficulty of distinguishing how much of the additional total product should be attributed to the extra labourer and how much to the extra machine or tool employed.

In practice, this problem arises only in the case of labour, for it is usually possible to vary the proportion of capital employed by such means as giving the driver a larger lorry or providing the carpenter with a mechanical plane. But where an addition to labour necessitates an automatic addition to capital equipment, the marginal productivity theory comes up against a real obstacle. All we can do is measure the MRP to each factor in turn by deducting from the MRP of the whole unit the cost of all the other factors. This will give us what we can call the 'marginal net revenue product' of the particular factor.

15.3 The Determination of the Price of a Factor Service

Like all other prices, the price of a factor service is determined by demand and supply.

Demand

The concept of marginal-revenue productivity gives precision to what determines the demand of an individual firm for a factor.

The *position* of the demand curve of the individual firm will depend upon the following.

1. The Physical Productivity of the Factor

Productivity could be increased through: (a) additional capital being combined with labour, though in the short period some labour might be displaced; (b) technical progress and improved organisation, e.g. increased division of labour, though here again there may be some initial unemployment; (c) higher wages increasing the efficiency of undernourished or discontented workers ('the economy of high wages').

2. The Price of the Product that the Factor is Producing

A rise in the price of the product resulting from an increase in demand would raise the marginal-revenue productivity of labour (see p.216).

3. The Prices of Other Variable-Factor Services Employed by the Firm

In our example above we assumed that there was only one variable factor. But most firms employ, even in the short run, many variable factors – skilled workers, unskilled workers, fuel, raw materials, etc. In order to obtain the maximum return from a given outlay, the firm has to combine its variable factors so that:

$$\frac{\text{MRP}_A}{\text{Price } A} = \frac{\text{MRP}_B}{\text{Price } B} = \ldots = \frac{\text{MRP}_Z}{\text{Price } Z}$$

(See p.130.) It is obvious, therefore, that if the prices of other services, e.g. *B*, rise, the demand curve for *A* (when *A* can be substituted for *B*) will move to the right. Similarly, if the price of *B* falls, the demand curve for *A* will shift to the left.

However, we have so far avoided two complications – the shape of the *demand* curve and imperfect competition in the demand for a factor. Both will be postponed until we consider trade-union activity in the next chapter.

The *industry's demand curve* for a factor service is the sum of the demands of the individual firms. This would be a simple horizontal addition at each given price if we assumed that the price of the product remained unchanged as the quantity of the factor demanded by firms increased. But it is much more realistic to assume that, as firms obtain more of the factor service, the supply of the product will increase and its price fall. The result will be that the industry's demand curve for a factor will fall more steeply than the curve obtained by a straightforward addition of firms' marginal-revenue curves.

Supply

By the supply of a factor we mean the amount which is offered as the reward is varied. Usually we should expect a higher price to extend supply, for factors would be attracted from other industries and occupations. Thus the supply curve normally slopes upwards from left to right (Figure 15.2).

Nevertheless, the actual shape of the supply curve, i.e. the elasticity of supply, will vary according to (*a*) the nature of the factor, (*b*) the institutional background and (*c*) the period of time involved. It is considered in the chapters which follow, where each class of factor is dealt with separately.

Demand, Supply, and the Price of the Factor

The reward of a factor, in this case the wage rate, is determined by the interaction of demand and supply. Thus in Figure 15.2, with demand curve *D* and supply curve *S*, the wage rate is *OW*.

FIGURE 15.2
The Determination of the Price of a Factor

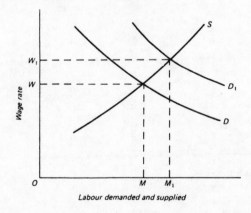

A change in the price of the product will affect the marginal-revenue productivity of the factor. This will be reflected by a change in the position of the demand curve. Suppose, for instance, that the price of the product rises. This will mean that the demand curve for labour will shift to the right, say from D to D_1. As a result, the wage rate is higher, OW_1, and the number employed increases from OM to OM_1.

The Effect of Imperfect Competition on Factor Rewards

The above discussion assumed that there was perfect competition both in the sale of the product and in engaging factors of production. But in the real world such competition may not exist. If, for instance, the firm is selling its product under imperfect competition, the price received will fall as output increases. This means that the marginal-revenue product of an extra labourer will be less than the marginal physical product multiplied by its price, since the lower price applies to all previous units produced.

Similarly, a firm may be the only employer of a factor in a locality, so that, as this firm demands more, the factor price rises not only for the additional factor but for all previous factors. Thus the marginal cost of employing such factors is higher than the market price. In both instances the demand for the factor will be less than it would have been had competition prevailed.

Finally trade unions may exert a monopoly power in the sale of labour, a subject discussed in the next chapter.

16 Labour and Wages

16.1 Why Labour is Treated as a Separate Factor of Production

Labour is the effort, both physical and mental, made by human beings in production. It is the 'human' element which is important.

Because people have feelings and emotions their response to economic forces is different from that of machines. First, whereas a machine which proves profitable can be reproduced fairly easily and quickly, the overall supply of labour does not depend upon its earnings. Other factors are more important in deciding how many children parents have (see p.451). Second, the effort of labour is not determined solely by the reward offered. The method of payment may affect effort, while raising wages may result in less work being offered. Above all, a contented worker will produce more than an unhappy one; thus job satisfaction or loyalty to a firm, rather than a high rate of pay, may be decisive in inducing an employee to work overtime. Third, people have to go where the work is. But labour does not move readily, either occupationally or geographically, in response to job opportunities or the offer of a higher reward. Often such 'immobility' results from strong human contacts. Fourth, workers can combine together in trade unions. Finally, if unemployed for long periods, workers deteriorate physically and mentally.

Both firms and government must have policies which take account of these special characteristics. Training schemes are essential to improve the skill of workers and thus their productivity. Firms must pay particular attention to psychological and social factors in an effort to secure a contented labour force. Furthermore, they must endeavour to co-operate with the workers' trade-union representatives. Above all, firms have to comply with the constraints imposed by government policy.

The government is vitally concerned with labour. It lays down the requirements of the employment contract, supervises working conditions and prescribes the terms under which a worker may be dismissed.

Moreover, it exerts pressure in wage negotiations in order to avoid inflationary wage increases. Most important, it pursues a variety of policies aimed at securing a high and stable level of employment.

This chapter examines these special features though postponing the problem of full employment to chapters 26 and 28.

16.2 Methods of Rewarding Labour

Working for an Employer Usually Eliminates 'Risk-bearing'

Some people are self-employed – window-cleaners, plumbers, solicitors, doctors, etc. As such they are really 'entrepreneurs', taking rewards if demand is high, but accepting the risks of being unemployed or of working for a low return.

The great majority of workers, however, contract out of risk, accepting a wage instead. This wage is received whether or not the product of their labour is sold.

Occasionally, an element of risk-bearing is incorporated in the wage agreement, e.g. by commission payments, bonus schemes, profit-sharing arrangements and the profit-related pay scheme introduced in 1986. Nor must we forget that when a worker is trained for a particular industry, his fortunes are to a large extent bound up with those of that industry. Engine-drivers, for instance, may have to work in other occupations at lower pay with the closing down of many rail lines. Unless a worker is completely mobile, geographically and occupationally, he or she cannot entirely eliminate the economic risks which are inherent in any dynamic economy.

Wages and Salaries

The period of the contract between employer and employee varies. Key research workers or managers may have a contract extending over a number of years. Administrative staff are usually paid a 'salary' on a monthly basis. Shop assistants, typists, lorry-drivers and most manual workers are paid a weekly wage, at least a week's notice terminating employment (more after two years' service) being required. In other occupations the work may be by the day, e.g. casual agricultural labourers, though arrangements guaranteeing a minimum number of hours per week are increasing.

The Wage Rate and Earnings

In what follows reference will be mainly to the *wage rate* – the sum of money which an employer contracts to pay to a worker in return for services rendered. Such a definition includes salaries as well as wages, and makes no distinction between time and piece rates.

Earnings are what the worker actually receives in the pay-packet ('take-home pay') plus deductions which have been made for insurance, income tax, superannuation, etc. In practice, earnings often exceed the rate agreed for a given period of time because this basic rate may be supplemented by overtime working, piece rates or bonus payments.

Time and Piece Rates

Wage rates may be calculated on a time or piece basis, or on a combination of both.

1. Time Rates

Time rates are more satisfactory than piece rates where:

(*a*) a high quality of work is essential, e.g. computer programming;
(*b*) the work cannot be speeded up, e.g. bus-driving, milking cows;
(*c*) there is no standard type of work, e.g. certain car repairs;
(*d*) care has to be taken of delicate machinery, e.g. hospital medical tests;
(*e*) output cannot be easily measured, e.g. teaching, police duties;
(*f*) working long hours may undermine health, e.g. laundry work;
(*g*) the labour is by nature a fixed factor which has to be engaged whatever the output, e.g. secretarial and selling staff;
(*h*) periods of temporary idleness necessarily occur, e.g. repair work.

On the other hand, time rates have certain disadvantages:

(*a*) there is a lack of incentive for better workers;
(*b*) supervision of workers is usually necessary;
(*c*) agreements can be undermined by working to rule and 'go-slow' tactics.

2. Piece Rates

Where output is both measurable and more or less proportionate to the amount of effort expended, piece rates are possible. It is not essential that each individual worker's output should be capable of exact measurement. So long as the output of the group of which he or she forms a part can be assessed, the worker can be attributed with a part of that group product.

The advantages of piece rates are:

(*a*) effort is stimulated;
(*b*) the more efficient workers obtain a higher reward;
(*c*) the need of constant supervision and irksome time-keeping is eliminated;

(*d*) interest is added to dull, routine work;
(*e*) workers can proceed at their own pace;
(*f*) a team spirit is developed where workers operate in a small group;
(*g*) workers are encouraged to suggest methods of improving production;
(*h*) the employer's costing calculations are simplified;
(*i*) output is increased, and the more intensive use of capital equipment spreads overheads.

We see, therefore, that piece rates have advantages for both the employee and employer. Moreover, the lower prices which result benefit the community as a whole. Nevertheless, for the following reasons, they are often disliked by trade unions:

(*a*) workers may over-exert themselves;
(*b*) where piece rates have to be varied according to local conditions or different circumstances, e.g. capital per employee, negotiations for a national wage rate are difficult;
(*c*) variations in piece rates from one place to another undermine union solidarity;
(*d*) the union may lose control over the supply of labour, making it difficult to take strike action or to apportion work in periods of unemployment;
(*e*) piece rates are subject to misunderstanding, e.g. a firm which installs a better machine may be accused of cutting the rate if it does not attribute all the increased output to the effort of labour.
(*f*) workers may resist being shifted from tasks in which they have acquired dexterity (and which therefore produce high piece earnings) even though the current needs of the factory organisation require such a transfer. Thus employers find that piece rates lead to a loss of control over their employees, and many prefer to pay high time rates to obviate this.

3. Combined Wages and Piece Rates

When deciding the basis of the wage rate, both employees and employers want certain guarantees. Workers have a minimum standard of living to maintain, and they desire protection against variations in output which may be outside their control, e.g. weather conditions. On the other hand, the employers providing expensive equipment must ensure that the machines are used for at least a given period of time. The net result is that piece rates are usually incorporated in a wider contract which provides for a minimum basic wage and a stipulated minimum number of hours.

16.3 The Total Supply of Labour

By the supply of labour we mean the number of hours of work offered. There are two separate problems to be considered: the total overall supply of labour available, and the supply of labour to a particular industry, occupation or locality. Here we consider the first.

The total supply of labour will depend upon the following.

1. The Size of the Population

The size of the population sets an obvious limit to the total supply of labour. But while it is influenced by economic factors, e.g. through the birth rate and immigration, it is doubtful, especially in more advanced economies, whether economic factors are of paramount importance.

2. The Proportion of the Population which Works

The working population, the proportion of the population which forms the labour force, is determined chiefly by:

(a) The numbers within the 16–65 age-group.
(b) The activity rates within this group, especially as regards young people and female workers. The tendency over the last twenty years has been for a higher proportion of young people to remain in further education, thus reducing their activity rate. On the other hand, a higher propor- tion of women are now entering the working population. The expan- sion of the service and light manufacturing industries has provided increased job opportunities for women, while the changed attitude to women workers is reflected in the Equal Pay Act 1970 and the Sex Discrimination Act 1975. Above all, the smaller family, the availability of crèches and school dinners, the development of part-time employ- ment opportunities and new labour-saving domestic appliances have allowed married women to work.
(c) The extent to which people over retiring age continue to work, something which is largely influenced by the level of pensions.
(d) The employment opportunities available – the tendency being for the working population to contract in a depression (mainly through withdrawal of married women).

3. The Amount of Work Offered by Each Individual Labourer

Higher rates of pay usually induce a person to work overtime, the increased reward encouraging a substitution of work for leisure. But this is not always so. In addition to the substitution effect, there is also the income effect, and the latter may outweigh the former (see p.58). A higher wage rate enables the worker to maintain the existing material standard of living with less work, and extra leisure may be preferred to more goods. Thus while it is usual to depict the supply curve of labour as in Figure 16.1a, it is possible that, in the short period, it may follow the shape of the curve in Figure 16.1b (see p.209).

FIGURE 16.1
The Relationship Between the Wage Rate and Hours Worked

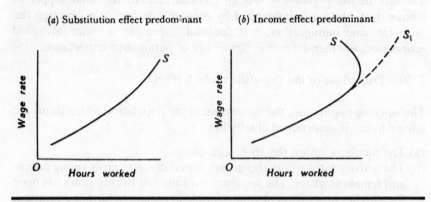

(*a*) Substitution effect predominant   (*b*) Income effect predominant

---

16.4 The Wage Rate in a Particular Industry, Occupation or Locality

In theory the wage rate in a particular industry, occupation or locality will be determined as shown in Chapter 15 by demand and supply. The demand will depend upon the MRP; the supply will depend upon the wage rate being offered.

In practice, this merely provides us with a first approach to the problem, for other considerations have to be taken into account:

1. While marginal productivity explains differences in demand for difference types of labour, more important may be immobilities which split up supply. It is these which have to be considered when we examine the supply of labour to particular industries, occupations or localities.
2. Sociological forces, e.g. workers' attitude to the 'status' of a particular occupation, the preservation of time-honoured wage differentials, blur the long-term economic forces.
3. The strength and militancy of the respective trade unions will influence relative wage rates.
4. Any government incomes policy will modify the extent to which trade unions can secure wage increases.

The Wage Rate and the Immobility of Labour

The supply of labour will depend upon the following.

1. The Response of Existing Labour to a Higher Wage Rate

In the short period an industry may find that the supply curve of labour corresponds to curve S in Figure 16.1b. This has been the case in coal-mining, where, as wages have increased, miners have preferred to enjoy more leisure. In the long period, however, higher wage rates should attract labour from other industries, with the result that the long-period supply curve follows the dashed line, S_L.

2. The Cost of Attracting Labour from Alternative Uses or Localities

Unless there is unemployment, the supply of labour in a particular use can be expanded only by increasing the wage offered. This will attract labour of the same or of a nearly similar kind from other industries, occupations or localities. The extent to which this happens depends upon the elasticity of demand for the products in these alternative uses. If demand is inelastic, higher wages can be offered to hold on to labour, and thus the supply of labour will expand little in response to the wage rise (see p.220).

3. The Mobility of Labour

A rise in the price of a factor should attract it from alternative uses or localities. This may take time, but it is achieved in the 'long period'. With labour, however, there are particular obstacles to moving, and these may mean that the long period is delayed indefinitely. Such obstacles provide frictions to the full and efficient operation of the price system. When they cannot be overcome, the effect is to split up the market into a number of separate occupations and localities with barriers around each.

Thus differences in the wage rates between occupations, or between localities for the same occupation, can frequently be explained by differences in the supply rather than by differences in demand. We are dealing not with one market for labour but with a number of fairly distinct markets.

What are these major barriers? What are the causes of the 'immobility of labour', as it is usually termed?

Workers may be required: (a) to shift from one industry to another; (b) to change occupation; (c) to move home to a different district. Often conditions dictate that all three types of change take place at the same time, but this is not necessarily so. Each presents its own obstacles to workers in their efforts to change jobs.

(*a*) *Obstacles between industries*. Provided that it does not involve a change of occupation or district, a worker can usually move job from one industry to another fairly easily. Secretaries, lorry drivers and porters, for example, are found in most industries. But middle-aged and older workers may experience difficulty. Prejudice or tradition in certain industries may also prove to be obstacles. Women drivers, for instance, would find it difficult to become taxi drivers in London. Moreover, a worker's loyalty to a particular firm may prevent him or her from looking for another job, even though a cut in wages has been suffered (though obviously this does not apply if the worker is made redundant).

(*b*) *Obstacles to a change of occupation*. In changing occupations, obstacles may be encountered in both moving out of the old occupation or in entering a new one. They arise because:

(i)   a high natural ability is required in certain occupations;
(ii)   training is costly and takes time;
(iii)   trade-union or professional-association regulations prohibit entry except under certain stringent conditions;
(iv)   the job in question is repugnant, or alternatively, occupations, e.g. the Church, art and acting, are so pleasant that workers are not drawn into another occupation by the offer of a higher wage rate;
(v)   workers may be too old to learn a new job;
(vi)   workers may prefer to remain unemployed rather than accept a wage below a 'recognised minimum' in an alternative occupation;
(vii)   in spite of prohibiting legislation, there is discrimination on account of sex, colour, social class or religion;
(viii) workers are ignorant of wage rates and opportunities in other occupations.

Of the above, the greatest obstacle to occupational mobility is natural ability. In this respect it should be noted that there can be more mobility between occupations, e.g. storeman and clerk, requiring the same level of innate ability than between doctors and dockers, where there are marked differences in the natural ability and training required. The first is sometimes termed 'horizontal' occupational mobility; the second, where there are non-competing groups of workers, 'vertical' mobility.

(*c*) *Obstacles to a change of district*. When it comes to moving from one part of the country to another, workers have to overcome both real and psychological obstacles. These include:

(i)   the costs of moving, which to many workers represent a considerable capital sum and are incurred even if workers own their own homes;
(ii)   the difficulty of securing accommodation elsewhere on comparable terms, particularly for council and rent-controlled tenants but also for

owner-occupiers having to move into the more expensive housing in southern England;

(iii) social ties of friends, clubs, Church, etc.;

(iv) family ties, such as the children's education;

(v) imperfect knowledge of vacancies or wages paid in other localities;

(vi) prejudice against certain parts of the country, e.g. southerners not wanting to move to the industrial north.'

In Chapter 28 we shall consider some of the ways in which the government tries to reduce occupational and geographical immobility. Here we merely note its effects. Immobility of labour means that wages rates can often be more easily explained by supply conditions rather than by demand. Even if there is competition between employers, differences in supply will lead to differences in the wage rates between occupations (provided there is no counter-balancing difference in demand) and between localities even for the same occupation. Thus solicitors earn more than their clerks because: (i) on the demand side, the services of solicitors are valued more highly; (ii) on the supply side, there are fewer solicitors than clerks, for more natural ability and longer training are required.

The Determination of the Conditions of Employment in the Real World

While demand and supply are the underlying determinants of an occupation's basic wage rate, the actual wage and the conditions of employment are strongly influenced by government intervention, imperfect competition in the labour market and trade-union activity.

The government influences the wage rate through: (i) its minimum-wage regulations in certain industries (see p.213); (ii) the legal protection it affords to workers with regard to conditions of work, e.g. stipulating a written statement of the conditions of employment, prohibiting discrimination on account of sex or race, protecting employees against unfair dismissal, providing for redundancy payments and regulating conditions for health and safety at work; (iii) its efforts to break down illogicalities, etc. sanctioned by customed; (iv) guidelines for wage settlements which it may lay down from time to time in its efforts to combat inflation (see p.363).

Imperfection in the labour market arises where one firm is the major employer in a locality (see above). But mainly it is due to trade unions, which (through the closed shop) can establish what is virtually a monopoly in the supply of a given type of labour. We therefore analyse the economic background to trade-union activity with reference to its strength in negotiating wage increases.

16.5 Trade Unions: the Procedure of Collective Bargaining

Objectives of Trade-Union Activity

Trade unions have many functions. These include:

1. An improvement in working conditions.
2. Educational, social and legal benefits for members.
3. The improvement of standards of work.
4. Obtaining an increase in pay for members by collective bargaining.
5. Co-operation with the government of the day in the furtherance of economic policy.

In this chapter we shall be concerned mainly with the last two functions.

The Process of Collective Bargaining

The process whereby workers settle the conditions of employment with employers jointly through their trade union is known as 'collective bargaining' and, except when the rate of inflation has become critical, the government has followed the principle of allowing the two sides to negotiate on a voluntary basis. For its smooth working, however, certain conditions should be fulfilled. The first is that it must be pursued with good sense on both sides. This is helped considerably where the industry has a tradition of good relations between employers and workers. Furthermore, where there is some accepted criterion to which wage rates can be linked (such as a cost of living index, the wage rates paid in other grades of work and in other trades, or the profits being made by the industry), there can be negotiation from an agreed starting-point as opposed to a heated wrangle where each side tries to grab the best possible terms by threats based upon its strength in the prevailing economic conditions. Second, collective bargaining works better when both sides consist of strong organisations. If all employers in the industry are linked in an association they do not have to fear undercutting of wage rates by outsiders, and if the union can speak for and preserve discipline among all its members, employers know that the agreement will be honoured. Unofficial stoppages damage the reputation of the trade union. To avoid them there must be regular contact between the employer and the union, prompt investigation of grievances at workshop level with members following the procedure for settling disputes.

Thus we come to the third requirement for an efficient system of collective bargaining – an accepted procedure between the parties for dealing with problems as they arise. Such a procedure should, without being so prolonged that it frays patience, exhaust all possibilities of reaching agreement peaceably. A strike or lock-out should come about only after the procedure has been followed to its finality. We can therefore distinguish two stages in the procedure: (1) negotiation; (2) the settlement of disputes.

1. Negotiation

Broadly speaking, the machinery for negotiation falls into three categories.

(*a*) *Voluntary negotiation*. Generally the government has left it to the unions and employers' organisations to work out their own procedures. Today voluntary machinery covers nearly 70 per cent of the insured workers of the UK. Because the organisation of the different unions varies considerably, the recognised procedure differs between industries and trades. However, most industries have some national joint council or committee, completely independent of outside assistance, which thrashes out agreements.

(*b*) *Joint industrial councils*. Usually such voluntary negotiating machinery follows the system of joint industrial councils, composed of representatives of both employers and workers in the industry. These consider regularly such matters as the better use of the practical knowledge and experience of the workpeople, general principles governing the conditions of employment, means of ensuring the workers the greatest possible security of earnings and employment, methods of fixing and adjusting earnings, piece rates, etc., technical education and training, industrial research, improvement of processes and proposed legislation affecting the industry. Although joint industrial councils are sponsored by the government, they are not forced upon any industry, and some important industries, such as iron and steel, engineering, shipbuilding and cotton, which had already developed their own procedure for negotiation, have not formed joint industrial councils. Nevertheless, in 1980 there were some 400 joint industrial councils or bodies of similar character.

(*c*) *Wages councils*. In some industries and trades where organisation of workers, of employers or of both is either non-existent or ineffective, the government has had to intervene. This started in 1909 when trade boards were set up to fix minimum time and piece rates for the 'sweated' trades.

In 1945 they were renamed Wages Councils and today (1986) there are twenty-six covering a variety of industries, such as retailing, catering, hairdressing, clothing and textile manufacturing. The Councils are appointed by the Secretary of State for Employment and are composed of equal numbers of employers' and workers' representatives together with not more than five independent members. Their wages orders are enforceable by law.

Recently Wages Councils have been increasingly criticised as having little relevance to today's employment climate, for instance. The government considers that the ability to pay lower rates to trainees will encourage employers to take on more. Consequently the scope of Wages Councils has now been limited to setting minimum hourly and overtime pay rates for workers over 21 years. Furthermore, Councils now have to consider the impact on jobs of the minimum pay rates set, particularly in areas where pay is below the national average.

In agriculture, wages are fixed by the Agricultural Wages Board, similar to the wages councils' system. Thus about 11 per cent of insured workers are covered by schemes of statutory wage regulation.

2. The Settlement of Disputes

Where negotiating machinery fails to produce an agreement, it is advantageous if agreed procedures exist for ending the deadlock. Three methods can be employed: conciliation, arbitration or special inquiry.

(a) *Conciliation*. In 1974 the Secretary of State for Employment set up an *independent* Advisory, Conciliation and Arbitration Service (ACAS) whose members are experienced in industrial relations. When efforts to obtain settlement of a dispute through normal procedures have failed, ACAS can provide conciliation if this is acceptable to the parties concerned.

(b) *Arbitration*. ACAS can, at the joint request of the parties to a dispute, appoint single arbitrators or boards of arbitration chosen from a register of people experienced in industrial relations to determine differences on the basis of agreed terms of reference.

Alternatively, the Terms and Conditions of Employment Act 1959 allows claims that a particular employer is not observing the terms or conditions of employment established for the industry to be referred compulsorily to an industrial court for a legally binding award.

(c) *Inquiry and investigation*. The Secretary of State for Employment has legal power to inquire into the causes and circumstances of any trade dispute and, if he thinks fit, to appoint a court of inquiry with power to call for evidence. Such action, however, is chiefly a means of informing Parliament and the public of the facts and causes of a major dispute, and is taken only when no agreed settlement seems possible.

The minister's power of inquiry also allows for less formal action in the setting up of committees of investigation when the public interest is not so wide and general.

Neither a court of inquiry nor a committee of investigation is a conciliation or arbitration body but either may make recommendations upon which a reasonable settlement of the dispute can be based.

16.6 Trade Unions and Wages

Trade Union Arguments for Wage Increases

A trade union is likely to base its claim for a wage increase on one or more of the following grounds.

1. A Rise in the Cost of Living

Because inflation reduces their real incomes, workers seek an increase in money wages. But difficulties have arisen. First, wage demands have become an annual event. Second, they are often pitched higher than the rate of inflation, thereby fuelling further inflation (see Chapter 27).

2. A Higher Wage Rate in Comparable Grades and Occupations

The trouble here is that wage differentials are often ingrained in workers' attitudes, whereas they should reflect changes in the demand for and supply of particular types of labour. Furthermore, it is often difficult, indeed impossible, to assess 'comparability', e.g. between a social worker and a computer programmer. On the other hand, if there is a shortage of nurses in national health hospitals owing to the higher pay offered by private hospitals, there is a strong argument for increasing the wage of the state-paid nurse.

3. Profits have Increased

Trade unions feel that they should share in extra profits and here they may be in a strong position (see pp.218, 221).

4. Productivity has Increased

Where output per worker is increasing, there is a rise in the MRP curve, and firms can grant a wage increase (see p.216). But there may be difficulty in apportioning the increased productivity between the workers' efforts and investment in new machines, research, etc. Capital has to receive its share if investment is to continue.

Trade Union Bargaining Limitations

The question must now be answered – how, and to what extent, can trade unions secure increases in the wage rate for their members in conditions of free collective bargaining?

We shall assume that the trade union has a strong member-ship – practically 100 per cent. Workers can thus bargain collectively. As a result, instead of there being a number of sellers of labour in competition with one another, wages are negotiated through one seller, the trade union, which thus becomes a monopolist in selling that particular type of labour.

Broadly speaking, there are three ways in which a trade union can secure a wage increase:

1. It Can Support Measures which will Increase the Demand for Labour

An increase in the demand for labour will come about if the MRP curve is raised. This will result either from a rise in the price of the product or from an improvement in the physical productivity of the workers. Thus the National Union of Mineworkers not only backs the campaign advertising the advantages of solid fuel for central heating, but supports the National Coal Board's exhortations to miners to improve output per man-shift.

The situation is illustrated in Figure 16.2. As marginal-revenue produc-tivity rises from MRP to MRP$_1$, wages of existing workers, ON, rise from OW to OW_1. Alternatively, if there were unemployment, extra men, NN_1, could be employed at the previous wage rate.

FIGURE 16.2
The Effect of a Change in Marginal-revenue productivity on the Wage Rate

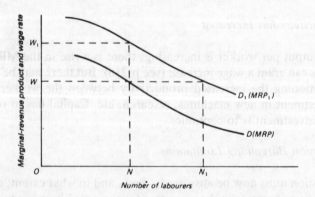

2. *It Can Restrict the Supply of Labour, Allowing Members to Compete Freely in Fixing Remuneration with Employers*

Where a trade union or professional association is sufficiently strong to limit entry, it may also stipulate a minimum wage rate or scale of charges. But it need not do so. The supply of plumbers and electricians, for instance, is restricted by apprenticeship regulations, but many work on their own account and negotiate their own rewards. Similarly, solicitors, doctors, surgeons, accountants and surveyors are given suggested scale fees by their respective associations, but these are not rigidly enforced.

We can therefore analyse this method of securing a wage increase by the simple demand and supply approach (Figure 16.3). Trade-union action reduces the supply of workers in a particular occupation from S to S_1; the wage rate rises from OW to OW_1.

FIGURE 16.3
The Effect on the Wage Rate of Trade-union Restriction of the Supply of Labour

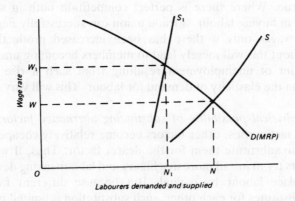

---

3. *It Can Fix a Minimum Wage Rate*

Where wages are raised by the simple process of restricting entry, the individual trade union is usually not greatly concerned about the overall numbers employed. It works simply on the principle that, assuming demand remains unchanged, greater scarcity leads to a higher price.

Most trade unions, however, are faced with a more difficult problem. While they may secure a higher wage rate for their members, their success may turn to ashes in the mouth if, as a result, many members are sacked. Herein is the rub. What we really have to ask, therefore, is *under what conditions can a trade union obtain higher wages for its members without decreasing the numbers employed?*

Once again we have to consider conditions of competition.

(a) *Perfect competition in both selling the product and buying labour.* In the short period, even if there is perfect competition, a firm may be making super-normal profits. Here a strong trade union could, by threatening to withhold all its labour, force the firm to increase wages to the point where the whole of its super-normal profits disappear.

But this could not be permanent. The long-period equilibrium position is one in which there are no super-normal profits and the wage rate is equal to the MRP. A higher wage will represent a rise in costs. Some employers will now be forced out of business (see p.151) and remaining firms will have to reduce their demand for labour until once again the MC of labour (the wage rate) is equal to the MRP. Thus, in Figure 16.3, we assume that OW is the original wage rate fixed by competition and ON the number of men employed – the trade-union membership. Suppose the trade union stipulates a minimum wage of OW_1. In the long period, employment will then be reduced to ON_1. Given a downward-sloping MRP curve, this will always be true. Where there is perfect competition both in selling the product and in buying labour, a trade union can successfully negotiate an increase in wages only if there has been increased productivity: any increase without this will merely lead to members becoming unemployed.

The amount of unemployment resulting from such a rise in wages depends upon the elasticity of demand for labour. This will vary according to:

(i) *The physical possibility of substituting alternative factors.* As the price of one factor rises, other factors become relatively cheaper and the tendency is to substitute them for the dearer factor. Thus, if wages rise, entrepreneurs try to install more machinery and labour-saving devices: that is, they replace labour by capital. But because different factors are imperfect substitutes for each other, such substitution is limited physically. Indeed, if they have to be employed in fairly fixed proportions, little or no substitution is possible. As we saw in Chapter 5, the extent to which substitution can take place largely determines the elasticity of demand.

The degree to which substitution is possible is shown by the slope of the marginal-productivity curve. Where labour is added to another factor, but is a poor substitute for it, marginal productivity falls steeply; where it is a fairly good substitute, marginal productivity falls more gently. Thus in Figure 16.4a labour is not a good substitute for land, and marginal-revenue productivity falls steeply as the number of men employed increases. Demand for labour is therefore inelastic, and a wage rise of WW_1 leads to only NN_1 men being unemployed. Compare this with Figure 16.4b, where

FIGURE 16.4
Substitutability Between Labour and Land

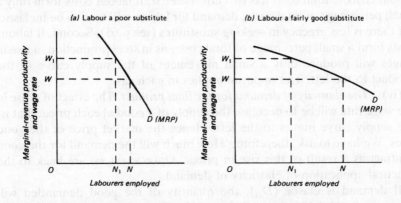

labour and land are better substitutes. Here the same wage leads to much more unemployment.

It should be noted that, since the possibility of substitution increases over time, the longer the period under consideration, the greater will be the change in the labour force.

(ii) *The elasticity of supply of alternative factors*. Under conditions of perfect competition, the cost of a factor to an individual firm will not rise as the firm's demand for that factor increases (see p.141). But when we are analysing a rise in the wage rate of the workers of an *industry*, we must recognise that the whole industry will now be demanding the alternative factors in order to substitute them for labour. This increased demand will affect the price of the alternative factors, and a higher price will have to be paid in order to attract a greater supply. This increase in the price of the alternative factors also limits the extent to which substitution is carried out. Thus if the supply of the alternative factor is perfectly elastic, only the physical considerations referred to above will affect the demand for it; if, on the other hand, supply is inelastic, then it is likely that the quick rise in its price will soon make it uneconomic to substitute it for labour. Once again, the elasticity of supply of the alternative factors will be greater, the longer the period of time under consideration.

Where unemployed labour exists, two conditions prevail that make it difficult for a trade union to obtain a wage increase without reducing the level of employment: (i) a high degree of substitution existing between the union labour and the alternative factor, unemployed labour, particularly if the work performed is unskilled; (ii) an infinite elasticity of supply of the alternative factor, unemployed labour, at least for a time. Hence trade unions are relatively weaker in periods of unemployment.

(iii)   *The proportion of labour costs to total costs.* The proportion of labour costs to total costs has two effects. First, if labour costs form only a small percentage of total costs, demand for labour will tend to be inelastic, for there is less urgency in seeking substitutes (see p.65). Second, if labour costs form a small percentage of total costs, as in steel production, a rise in wages will produce only a small movement of the supply curve of the product to the left. The opposite applies in each case.

(iv)   *The elasticity of demand for the final product.* The effect of a rise in the wage rate will be to decrease the supply of a good at each price: that is, the supply curve moves to the left. Hence the market price of the good rises. We have to ask, therefore, 'How much will the demand for the good contract as a result of this rise in price?' Once again we are back to the practical application of elasticity of demand.

If demand is elastic (D_{el}), the quantity of the good demanded will contract considerably, from OM to OM_1 (Figure 16.5). This will mean a large reduction in the numbers employed. On the other hand, if demand is inelastic (D_{inel}), there will be no great contraction in the quantity demanded – only to OM_2. Here people are willing to pay a higher price for the good (OP_2), and this will cover the increase in wages. In other words, the marginal-revenue productivity of labour has risen.

Elasticity of demand depends mainly on the availability of substitutes. Thus demand in export markets is usually more elastic than in the home

---

FIGURE 16.5
The Extent to which Demand for the Product Contracts as a Result of a Wage Increase

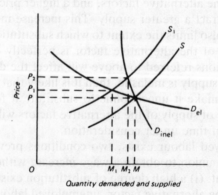

Quantity demanded and supplied

market, for with the former there are often many competing alternative sources of supply from firms in other countries. Consequently, if an industry sells a high percentage of its output abroad, e.g. electronic equipment and aero engines, the trade union is limited in its ability to secure a wage increase.

(*b*) *Imperfect competition*. If there is imperfect competition in selling the product or in hiring labour, the firm is likely to be making super-normal profits. Here it may be possible for the trade union to wring increased wages from the employer without loss of employment. Since it is a monopolist in the supply of labour, the union can insist that the firm shall employ *all* or none of its members at the new wage rate. Thus the firm may be forced to employ workers beyond the point where the MRP = MC. The difference would come from super-normal profits, with the firm working on the principle that 'half a loaf is better than no bread'.

In these circumstances there is a whole range of possible wage rates between the minimum which the workers are prepared to accept and the maximum which employers are prepared to give rather than lose all their labour. The success of the trade union will depend, therefore, upon: (i) the extent to which it can maintain its monopoly position by preventing employers from engaging black-legs, non-union workers, or other sub-stitute labour; (ii) the bargaining ability of its leaders relative to that of the employers. On the one side, the union leaders have to estimate how high they can push the wage rate without employers allowing a strike to take place; on the other, the employers must judge the lowest rate acceptable without a strike. As each is by no means certain as to the other's strength, bluff will play a large part in the negotiations. Such factors as a large order book for the firm's products, costly capital equipment standing idle, or a wealthy strike fund, will obviously strengthen the union's hands. Should a strike actually take place, it is usually because of misjudgement by one side; it is doubtful whether either really gains in the long run by strike action. Thus the strike is a form of 'blood-letting', allowing one or both sides to reassess the position prior to further negotiations.

16.7 Trade Union Co-operation with the Government in the Development of Economic Policy

While the improvement of the conditions of work for its members still remains the primary task of a trade union, the time has passed when it can act independently of government policy, especially as regards full employment and inflation. Accordingly, trade unions are consulted by the government on economic policy and, individually, usually have a voice in saying how industry can be made more efficient. Indeed, through the National Economic Development Council, permanent arrangements exist for consultation at the national level between the government, the CBI and the TUC.

If there is inflation, the government has to give a lead as regards wage increases. When there is full employment labour is in a strong bargaining position, and the tendency is for each union to exploit the situation in order to obtain a wage increase for its members. Unless this increase is accompanied by increased productivity or can be met by a reduction in profits, such a rise in money wages of a particular industry will lead to some increase in the price of its goods.

Initially this rise represents an increase in real wages to the particular workers concerned since it is likely that they will spend only a fraction of their incomes on the goods they produce. But this is not the end of the story. Workers in other industries have not only suffered a relative decrease in money wages, but the rise in the price of the good in the industry where there has been a wage increase represents a decrease in their real wages. The result is that they too ask for increased wages, and these are granted by employers who know they can raise prices (for the extra money wages now being paid by most employers will ensure that the goods are bought at these higher prices). Thus we have a spiral of wages and prices chasing one another. In the UK this process usually resulted in balance-of-payments difficulties, since British exports could not compete in world markets, and imports increase as foreign goods become cheaper relative to home-produced goods. As a result successive governments have had to take action to limit the rate of wage increases (see p.363).

Here it should be noted that when applying an overall policy of wage-increase restrictions, the element of 'fairness' has played a prominent role, in discrimination in favour of lower-paid workers on ethical and social grounds. Thus the government may exercise a considerable influence both over both the general level of money wages and relative wages. This means that the market demand and supply mechanism, while emphasising the basic factors, is an incomplete explanation.

17 Capital and Interest

17.1 Capital

What is 'Capital'?

A schoolteacher earns, say, £250 a week. He also has £900 in the National Savings Bank, yielding him £54 per annum interest (or about £1 a week). We can say, therefore, that his total *income* is £251 *a week*, or £13 054 *per annum*; his *capital* assets are £900.

Thus we see that, whereas *income* is a flow of *wealth* over a *period of time, capital* is a stock of *wealth* existing at any one *moment of time*.

This broad definition of capital, however, has slightly different meanings when used by different people. The ordinary individual, when speaking of his or her 'capital', would include money assets, holdings of securities, the house, and possibly many durable goods, such as the car, the television set, the camera, etc. (sometimes referred to as 'consumers' capital'). The businessman would count not only his real assets (such as his factory, machinery, land, stocks of goods, etc.), but add any money reserves ('liquid capital') held in the bank and titles to wealth (such as share certificates, tax-reserve certificates and government bonds).

But the economist considers capital chiefly as a form of wealth which contributes to production. In other words, he is concerned with capital as a *factor of production*, i.e. as something real and not merely a piece of paper. It is the factory and machines, not the share certificates (the individual's entitlement to a part of them), which are vital to him.

This has two effects. First, in defining capital, the economist concentrates his attention on all producer goods and any stocks of finished consumer goods not yet in the hands of the final consumer. Second, in calculating the 'national capital', the economist has to be careful to avoid double-counting. Titles to capital – shares, bonds, savings certificates, National Savings, Treasury bills and other government securities – must be excluded. Share certificates merely represent the factories, machinery, etc., which have already been counted. Government debt refers to few real assets, for most has been expended on shells, ships, and aircraft in previous wars. The only exception regarding titles to wealth is where a share or bond is held by a foreign national, or conversely where a British national holds a share or bond representing an asset in a foreign country. We then have to subtract the former and add the latter when calculating national capital. Foreign shares or bonds held by British nationals, for example, can always be sold to increase our real resources.

Naturally, 'social capital' (roads, schools, hospitals, municipal buildings, etc.) which belongs to the community at large is just as much capital as factories, offices, etc. And, in order to be consistent, owner-occupied houses have to be included, for they must be treated in the same way as houses owned by a property company (Figure 17.1).

FIGURE 17.1
'Capital' in the Economy

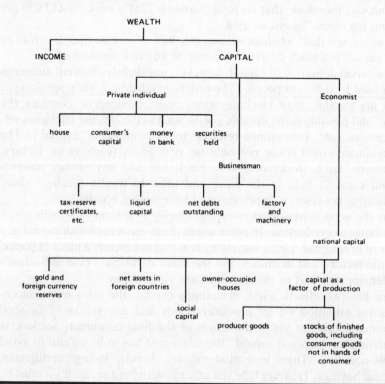

Capital as a Factor of Production

When the economist refers to 'capital', it is usually in the sense of *wealth which has been made by people for the production of further wealth*. This is because capital plays such an important part in increasing production, and therefore in improving living standards. It is in this sense that the term is used from now on.

Increased production occurs because capital – tools, machines, irrigation works, communications, etc. – greatly assists people in their work. Indeed, with modern electronic equipment, machines often take over the actual work. As the use of capital increases, there are three possible gains. First, more current goods can be produced. Between 1980 and 1985 the output of agriculture increased by 11 per cent. But over that period the number of employees *fell* by 11 per cent. There was thus an increased output per employee, due largely to more efficient machines and improved techniques resulting from capital investment in research. Second, instead of simply producing more current goods, people can be released to produce new goods. And, third, people can, as an alternative to more goods, enjoy increased leisure.

The Accumulation of Capital

If capital is so important in adding to our well-being, why do we not have more of it? The answer is simply that we can accumulate capital only by postponing current consumption. In everyday language, more jam tomorrow means less jam today. The accumulation of capital represents an opportunity cost over time – consumption now or greater consumption later? A simple example will make this clear.

Suppose a peasant farmer has been tilling the ground with a primitive spade. By working twelve hours a day he can cultivate two acres. Obviously, if he had a plough which could be drawn by his oxen it would help him considerably. How can he obtain it? Three ways are open to him.

1. He could reduce the land he cultivates to $1\frac{1}{2}$ acres. This would reduce his tilling time by three hours, and he could use this time to make the plough.
2. He could reduce his leisure and sleeping time from twelve to eight hours a day. This would give him an extra four hours for making the plough.
3. He might decide not to consume some of the produce already harvested, exchanging it instead for a plough.

What is important to notice is that, whichever method is chosen, some present sacrifice is necessary. With (1) and (3) he has to reduce his standard of living by having less to eat. With (2) he has to forgo some leisure – in short, he has either to draw in his belt or work harder. But the reward of such sacrifice comes when he has the plough at work. Then, with twelve hours' work a day he can cultivate 4 acres; his standard of living has doubled.

One other point emerges from this illustration. If, owing to the poverty of the soil, sixteen hours were required to dig his two acres, our farmer would have found it much more difficult to find time to make his plough. He would not reduce his food consumption below subsistence level, nor go without essential sleep. In other words, the more fertile his land, the easier it is for him to increase his income. In economics the maxim 'to him that hath shall be given' often holds. Thus a country with a very low standard of living finds it difficult to build up the capital which would improve its living standards and it is for this reason that any aid which can be given to poor countries is so valuable.

Naturally our farmer will have to devote time to repairing the plough. So long as his capital equipment is capable of cultivating four acres, we can say that it is being 'maintained intact'. If it is being increased or replaced in a more efficient form so that more acres are cultivated, capital is 'being accumulated'. Where it is not being maintained (as in wartime), capital is being 'run down' or 'depreciated'.

In practice, it is unusual for the same people to devote so much time to producing consumer goods and so much to the production of capital. Instead, production is organised by applying the principle of the division of labour – some people specialise in consumer goods and others in capital goods.

We can now see why most governments encourage investment, the process of producing capital. Where the proportion of productive capacity devoted to investment falls, there may be serious consequences for living standards in the future. More important, the poverty of many countries is chiefly the result of their lack of capital. Hence the Soviet Union, China, India and Cuba have directly restricted present consumption so that capital development may proceed rapidly under 'five-year-plans'.

17.2 Interest

Investment, i.e. adding to capital goods or stocks, usually first involves obtaining liquid capital. Interest, expressed as a rate, is the price which has to be paid for this liquid capital. What we shall examine here is the rate of interest which has to be paid for liquid capital in a *particular* use or industry. We shall *not* discuss what determines the *general* level of interest in the economy.

The *demand for liquid capital* arises because it is necessary or advantageous to use capital in production. The farmer who sows seed in the autumn and harvests the crop in the summer is using capital in the form of seed. Similarly, a manufacturer needs capital in the form of a factory and machines because, provided demand is large enough, it is cheaper to produce in this way.

Now, as we saw when examining the peasant's decision to make a plough, the accumulation of capital can come about only by postponing present consumption. This can be done directly by the producer himself. The farmer could have obtained seed by putting aside a part of the previous year's harvest; the manufacturer could have secured capital by retaining rather than distributing profits. However, such retentions may be inadequate. In this case funds may be borrowed from other persons who have so saved (that is, forgone current consumption), repaying them later when the product is sold.

The actual demand of the farmer or manufacturer will depend upon the MRP of capital – the addition to profit which, for instance, a farmer thinks will result from adding an additional cow to his herd. Suppose he calculates that profit can be increased by spending £500 on a cow now. To avoid complications, let us also assume that he considers that in eight years' time, when the cow ceases to be worth milking, he will be able to sell it for beef for £500. Assume that the increase in profit (yield from the extra milk less labour and feeding costs) is estimated to be £200 for the year. He would then be willing to borrow the money to buy that cow so long as the interest he had to pay was not more than £200, i.e. not more than 40 per cent. If he bought another cow, the net addition to receipts might be only £190, for the third cow £180, and so on. It is possible, therefore, to draw a curve showing the expected addition to profit which the farmer estimates will be received through adding one more cow. We can call this curve the 'marginal revenue productivity of capital' curve, and the farmer will go on borrowing capital until the rate of interest equals the marginal-revenue product of capital. Hence at different rates of interest, different quantities of capital will be demanded.

Thus in Figure 17.2, when the rate of interest is OR, the farmer will borrow capital to buy 8 cows. If the rate falls to OR_1, he will borrow sufficient capital to buy 11 cows. One point must be emphasised. Because he is producing in advance, the farmer has to base his demand for capital on the *prospective* money yield resulting from its use. His expectations are thus all-important, and we shall have more to say on this subject later.

The sum of the demand curves for liquid capital from all the firms in the industry gives the demand curve for the industry, though some allowance could be made for a fall in the price of the good produced by the capital equipment (see p.201).

The *supply* of liquid funds for *one* use can only be obtained by bidding them away from alternative uses. How much has to be paid for a given quantity relative to other uses will depend upon:

FIGURE 17.2
Demand for Caital and the Marginal-revenue product of Capital and the Rate of Interest

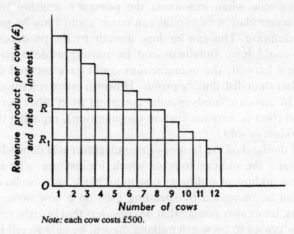

Note: each cow costs £500.

1. whether lenders consider more or less risk is involved;
2. the period of the loan, people preferring to lend for a short period rather than a long one;
3. the elasticity of demand for the product to which capital contributes in alternative uses.

Generally speaking, however, we can expect more liquid capital to be forthcoming the higher the rate of interest offered. We therefore have an upward-sloping supply curve. Thus the rate of interest is fixed by the interaction of the demand and supply curves (as in Figure 15.2).

Once again, however, we must point out that this is only a partial explanation of the determination of a rate of interest. It does not tell us why, for instance, £10 million of liquid capital should be forthcoming at 15 per cent rather than at 8 per cent or at 20 per cent. This will depend upon the general level of interest rates. To discover what determines this benchmark we have to look at the nature of money and government policy (see Chapters 20 and 23).

18 Land and Rent

18.1 'Land' and 'Rent' as General Terms

The Everyday Meaning of 'Land' and 'Rent'

To the economist the terms 'land' and 'rent' have a special meaning. This is just as well, for in everyday speech each can imply different things. Thus if I buy land for farming, it will probably include buildings, fences, a water supply and a drainage system, all of which are really capital. Similarly, I can rent things other than land – a house, television set, gas-meter, building equipment, shooting rights, etc. Rent in this sense simply means a periodic payment for the use of something. It can be termed 'commercial rent'.

Usually, however, rent does refer to payment for the use of a piece of land and, before we consider 'land' and 'rent' in their special economic sense, we must ask what determines how much rent is paid to a landlord.

The Rent of Land in a Particular Use

The problem is similar to the determination of the return on any factor service. The demand for land depends on its marginal-revenue productivity. The curve slopes downwards from left to right for the reasons given in Chapter 15. On the supply side, land, like labour, can usually be put to alternative uses – building factories or houses, growing wheat or barley, raising cattle or sheep, and so on. A given piece of land will be transferred to its most profitable use. If, for instance, the price of cattle rises and that of wheat falls, some land will be transferred from arable to pasture farming. Should the price of cattle rise still further, more land will be transferred, and so on. We can thus draw a supply curve for land in a particular use. It slopes upwards from left to right. The interaction of the demand and supply curves will give the rent actually paid (Figure 18.1).

229

FIGURE 18.1
The Determination of the Rent of a Plot of Land

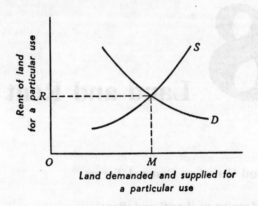

Of course, this assumes: (*a*) that landlords can vary the rent charged any time the demand for and supply of their particular type of land alters; and (*b*) that land can be transferred fairly quickly to a different use. The first assumption is complicated by the fact that rents are usually fixed for a period of years. Only when the lease expires is the landlord free to adjust the rent. The second assumption implies that we are concerned only with the long period in our analysis. But what of the short period when land is a fixed factor? An analysis of this situation is what we are concerned with in the remainder of this chapter.

18.2 Economic Rent – Land and Rent to the Economist

Ricardo's Views on 'Land' and 'Rent'

To explain the special meaning which economists today give to the terms 'land' and 'rent', we have to examine the views of David Ricardo, a classical economist of the early nineteenth century. He was concerned, not with the rent paid to land for a particular purpose, but with the rent paid to land as a whole. Moreover, just as in Chapter 6 we defined land as 'the resources provided by nature' (thereby eliminating improvements by man through the addition of capital), so too it was the 'original and indestructible powers of the soil' that Ricardo emphasised. He pointed out that land in this sense was given freely by nature; its total supply was fixed once and for all.

In this respect, he argued, land was different from the other factors of production, capital and labour. When the price of capital rose, people would be induced to postpone present consumption; the supply of capital would expand. Similarly, a rise in wages would be an inducement to rear and train more children. On the other hand, should the price of capital and labour fall, supply would contract. If no price at all were offered, there would be no supply. Both of these factors have a supply price, more being supplied the higher the price.

But with land as a whole – in the sense of space and natural resources – the same amount is available whatever the price offered. An increase in price cannot bring about an expansion of supply; on the other hand, if the price fell to zero, the same amount would still be available. Land as a whole, therefore, has no supply price. Its return was simply a residual surplus – the difference between receipts and payments of wages for labour and interest for capital. If the price received for the product were high, there would be more left over as rent; if the price were low, there would be less for rent. Rent did not determine the price of the good produced; instead, the opposite was true – rent was determined by price.

'Land' and 'Rent' in Economic Theory Today

On the ambiguities of Ricardo's reasoning we need not dwell. First, it can be argued that the total supply of land is fixed only in the short period; in the long run improved farming techniques and developments in transport are constantly increasing the amount of land which can be put to economic use. Indeed, in this respect there is little difference between land and other factors of production, which likewise can only be increased in the long period. Over a certain period of time – the short period, whatever that may be in months or years – all are fixed in total supply. Second, land, like other factors of production, has alternative uses. It can be used to produce different crops, or as a site for different buildings. The cost of putting it to one use is the yield that could have been obtained had it been employed in another way. Thus, in order to secure it for one purpose, a producer will have to pay a sufficient price to attract it from its best alternative use. It is this allocation of land between its different uses which is the main concern of the economist.

The Nature of the Return to a Fixed Factor

But Ricardo did point out an essential truth – that the return to a factor fixed in supply, i.e. whose supply is absolutely inelastic, will vary directly with variations in the price of the good produced by it. We can illustrate this more clearly by a simple example.

Let us assume: (*a*) a given plot of land on which only potatoes can be grown; (*b*) only land and labour are necessary to grow potatoes; (*c*) the supply of labour for growing potatoes is perfectly elastic because only a small proportion of the total labour force is required.

The return to this plot of land will depend entirely on the price of potatoes. This can be seen from Figure 18.2. When the marginal-revenue product of labour is shown by the curve QN, at a wage of OP, OM workers are employed. The value of the total product is $OMNQ$; the wage bill is $OMNP$ and the return to the plot of land PNQ. If now the price of potatoes increases, the marginal-revenue product of labour rises, in Figure 18.2, to Q_1N_1. OM_1 labourers are now employed at a wage bill of OM_1N_1P. (Each worker still receives the same wage, OP, because the supply of this type of labour is perfectly elastic.) But the return to the given plot of land has increased to PN_1Q_1 The opposite would apply if the price of potatoes fell.

FIGURE 18.2
The Effect of a Change in the Price of a Product of the Rent of Land

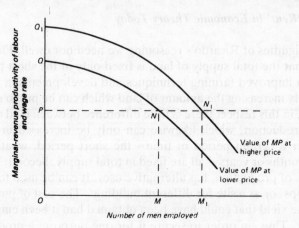

Certain practical conclusions follow from the above analysis:

(i) Because the plot of land will grow only potatoes, it will be cultivated so long as the value of the total product is sufficient to pay the wage-bill. In other words, at the lower price a lump-sum tax on the plot up to QPN could be levied without affecting the output. This is the basis of the much-proposed tax on land.

(ii) The return to land as we have analysed it above – rent in its economic sense – is purely a surplus. It arose because, by definition, our plot of land was confined to one particular use – growing potatoes. The supply of this land offered for sale or hiring will not be affected by a price, simply because nobody has any other use for it. In short, it has no opportunity or transfer cost.

(iii) Once land has been built on, it is largely specific to a given use, and the return to the land and building will be dependent on demand.

(iv) Because land is really space, it is impossible to increase the area of sites in city centres except by building upwards, e.g. as in Oxford Street and the City of London. Such fixity of supply means that rent is largely determined by current demand. Thus in Figure 18.3 it is assumed that the supply of land is fixed at *OM*. This means that the rent is determined by demand: an increase from *D* to D_1 raises rent from *OR* to OR_1. For instance, rents in Oxford Street depend upon the demand for shops there (which in its turn depends upon people's spending) and rents in the City of London depend on the demand for offices there (which in turn depend upon the level of business activity).

FIGURE 18.3
The Determination of Rent when Land is Fixed in Supply

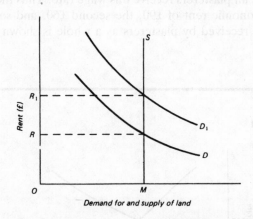

Demand for and supply of land

Economic Rent

The principle of rent being a surplus resulting from the fixed nature of land has a more general application. Economists have adopted Ricardo's concept of land as being symbolic of all factors which, in some way or another, are fixed in supply. The return to such factors is usually discussed under the headings of 'economic rent' and 'quasi-rent'.

'Economic rent' is the term used to describe the earnings of any factor over and above its supply price. Put in another way, it is any surplus over its transfer earnings – what it could obtain in its next most profitable use (its 'opportunity cost', in our earlier terminology). How this idea can be applied generally will now be explained.

The actual rate of return to a factor is the price per period of time at which it is now selling its services. For example, the return to a plasterer is his wage, say £180 per week.

But what is the opportunity cost? Simply what has to be paid to retain it in its present use – that is, sufficient to keep it from going to the best alternative use. Take our plasterer, for instance. His next best occupation may simply be plasterer's labourer, earning £90 per week. He would offer his services as a plasterer, therefore, at anything above £90 per week.

A second plasterer, however, may be a competent bricklayer, and as such earn £120 per week. Therefore, at least £120 per week must be offered for the services of the plasterer. And so we could go on. The supply curve of plasterers to the industry is thus an 'opportunity cost' curve (Figure 18.4).

If in Figure 18.4 we now insert the demand curve, we can obtain the current wage rate to the industry, £180 when *OM* plasterers will be employed. But all plasterers receive this wage rate. Thus the first plasterer receives an economic rent of £90, the second £60, and so on. The total economic rent received by plasterers as a whole is shown by the shaded area.

FIGURE 18.4
Economic Rent

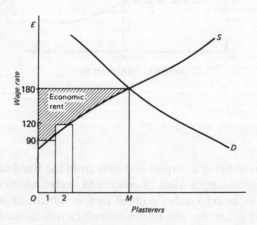

What Determines the Size of Economic Rent?

The size of economic rent earned by a particular type of factor depends upon the elasticity of supply of that factor and how the particular type of factor is defined.

1. The Elasticity of Supply

Elasticity of supply is determined largely by the period of time under consideration and immobilities, some of which cannot be eliminated even in the long period. Both will affect economic rent.

Let us assume that, in the short period, the supply of plasterers is fixed; there is insufficient time for them to move into alternative occupations or for others to move in. In short, there is no alternative occupation – they can either work as plasterers or not at all. Thus all their earnings are economic rent (Figure 18.5).

In the long period, however, other occupations can be trained as plasterers, and existing plasterers can move elsewhere. Sufficient has to be paid – the opportunity cost – to retain plasterers. Thus we have a long-period supply curve of plasterers, and economic rent is smaller (Figure 18.5b).

If the supply of plasterers became perfectly elastic, then economic rent would disappear (Figure 18.5c). Thus economic rent depends upon a less than perfectly elastic supply curve to the industry.

Sometimes the degree of immobility between different uses or occupations persists indefinitely. Building sites for offices in the City of London, for instance, earn rents far in excess of what they could obtain in their best alternative use, say for houses. Simply because such sites are very limited in supply, competition for office accommodation has forced up the rents of

FIGURE 18.5
Economic Rent and Elasticity of Supply

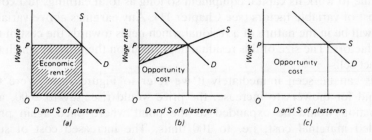

(a) D and S of plasterers
(b) D and S of plasterers
(c) D and S of plasterers

these sites far beyond the possible price which houses could offer. A large part of their earnings is therefore 'economic rent'.

Occasionally, too, we refer to the 'rent of ability'. Many pop singers, film stars, barristers and surgeons have a talent which, to all intents and purposes, is unique, for it cannot be duplicated by training others. Their high earnings, therefore, are almost wholly in the nature of 'economic rent'.

2. The Definition of an 'Occupation', etc.

If we adopt a wide definition of our factor, e.g. land as a whole, the distinction is between employing it or idleness, and thus the whole of its earnings is economic rent. This is what Ricardo had in mind.

If, however, our definition is narrower, e.g. land for a particular use, such as for growing wheat, then the opportunity cost will be larger (e.g. growing barley) and economic rent smaller. Similarly, we could distinguish between cabinet-makers and carpenters, surgeons and doctors, etc. Each would give a smaller 'economic rent' than if the distinction were simply between cabinet-makers and labourers, surgeons and teachers, etc.

Likewise, economic rent will be different whether we are looking at it from the point of view of the industry or the firm. The industry is unlikely to have a perfectly elastic supply curve; thus there will be some element of economic rent in its payment to the factors it hires. The firm, however, will face, in perfect competition, a perfectly elastic supply curve. In this case it will pay the transfer cost to all factors (whose best alternative is another firm); there is thus no economic rent.

Quasi-Rent

For fixed factors, particularly capital equipment, what the firm has to pay to retain them will vary according to the period of time.

In the short period, capital equipment is, by definition, fixed in supply. There is no transfer price. More capital equipment cannot be added; nor can existing equipment be diminished. The firm, as we have seen, will continue to work its capital equipment so long as total earnings just cover the cost of variable factors (see Chapter 11). Any earnings above variable costs will be in the nature of a residual which helps towards the cost of the fixed factors. The size of this residual depends upon the price at which the product sells.

This can be seen immediately if we refer to Figure 11.6. Were the demand for mowers to increase, the price would rise, say to £600, and production would be expanded to the point where once again price equalled marginal cost, i.e. to 100 units. The increased cost of such production would be equal to the increase in total cost, i.e. £5100. But total receipts would have increased by £19 500, and so the fixed factors earn an additional return – the increase in 'super-normal profit', equal to £14 400.

As time passes, however, we move into the 'long period'. If the product has been selling at a high price, the return to the capital equipment will have been high, and this will induce firms to install additional equipment. On the other hand, if the price of the product were low, existing capital equipment will either be transferred to its next most profitable use, or, when it wears out, simply not replaced. In the long period, therefore, earnings of fixed factors are, under perfect competition, equal to their transfer cost; economic rent is eliminated.

To distinguish between economic rent which is more or less permanent and that which disappears over time, the latter is often referred to by economists as 'quasi-rent'. It is not a true rent, for the high return earned by such factors leads to an increase in their supply, and this eliminates the economic rent they earn. True rent refers only to factors which are fixed in supply; even if their earnings are high, identical factors are not forthcoming, and so economic rent persists.

19 Entrepreneurship and Profit

19.1 Entrepreneurship

The Identity of Entrepreneurship and Risk-Bearing

For production to take place, resources must be brought together and set to work. Whoever undertakes this task is often described as 'the entrepreneur'. Usually, however, a somewhat narrower meaning is given to the term.

Organising production can be broken down into two parts. First, there is the task of co-ordination – bringing factors of production together and setting them to work. Second, there is accepting the risk of buying factors to produce goods which will not be sold until sometime in the future – when receipts may not cover costs.

In practice, it is not always easy to separate co-ordination and risk. A farmer, for instance, not only manages and runs the farm, but also accepts the risk involved in deciding what to produce. On the other hand, in a joint-stock company most of the work of coordination is left to a paid board of directors, with a manager playing the major role. Here the risks of the business are borne by the ordinary shareholders. With a public corporation, they are carried by the taxpayers. But neither shareholders nor taxpayers take part in running the business except in a most remote way.

The function of co-ordination, therefore, can be fulfilled by a paid manager. In this respect, management is simply an exceptionally highly skilled form of labour. Thus we narrow our concept of enterprise to cover only bearing those risks of the business associated with ownership.

The Nature of Risks

A firm is always open to the risk of fire, accidents, theft, damage by storm, etc. But these risks are calculable. A mathematician can work out, for instance, the chances of a building catching fire during the course of the year. One cannot say which building will be destroyed in this way, but information is available which states that on average, say, 1 out of every 10 000 will be. Such risks can therefore be insured against. They are thus reduced to a normal cost, and the businessman contracts out of the risk involved.

Certain risks, however, cannot be calculated according to a law of averages. Nobody, for instance, can forecast with certainty how many cold drinks will be sold in Britain next summer. That will depend upon the weather. Similarly, it might be thought that a new 'mini' car would sell profitably. But again there is a chance that this will not be so. The risk of demand being different from that estimated cannot be reduced to a mathematical probability. Such a risk, therefore, cannot be insured against; it must be accepted by those persons whose money is tied up in producing goods for an uncertain demand.

These uninsurable risks are inherent in a dynamic economy. Modern methods of production take time. When an entrepreneur engages factors of production, therefore, it is an act of faith – faith in the estimate of the demand for the product some time ahead. But demand can never be completely certain. People have freedom of choice, and their tastes may change. Many of the factors affecting demand fluctuate even over a relatively short period of time. It is similar on the supply side. Techniques do not stand still; new methods discovered by a rival may mean that, by the time a firm's product comes on the market, it is undersold by a cheaper or better substitute.

Thus there is always some degree of uncertainty, and this involves risk. It is a risk which must be shouldered by those who back with their money the decision as to what shall be produced. The true entrepreneurs, therefore, are those who accept the risks of uncertainty-bearing.

19.2 Profit

How Profit Differs in Nature from other Rewards

The reward of uncertainty-bearing is 'profit'. But profit differs from the earnings of other factors of production. First, profit may be negative. Whereas wages, rent and interest are paid as part of a contract at the time of hiring, profit is received in the future, and then only if expected demand has materialised. Where the entrepreneur has been far too optimistic, a loss is made. Second, profit fluctuates more than other rewards. Thus its size is uncertain, for it feels the immediate impact of booms and slumps. Hence in a boom profits rise faster than wages, while in a slump they fall more severely.

Differences in the Concept of the Term 'Profit'

We must be careful to distinguish four different concepts of the term 'profit':

1. Profit in its Everyday Meaning

To the accountant, profit means simply the difference between total receipts and total costs (see p.132). But because the economist defines costs in terms of alternatives forgone, this idea of profit is amended by deducting, first, the return which the firm would have received on its capital had it been used elsewhere, and second, the value of the entrepreneur's skill in the best alternative line of business.

2. Normal Profit under Perfect Competition

Because uncertainty cannot be eliminated from a dynamic economy, there must be a return to induce people to bear uncertainty. This is true even in the long period. Thus there must be a rate of profit – the price which equates the demand for and supply of entrepreneurship. In the long period under perfect competition, any rent element from profit is eliminated. We then have 'normal profit' – the cost which has to be met if the supply of uncertainty-bearing is to be maintained.

Two modifications should be noted. First, industries differ as regards the uncertainty involved. Where fashions or techniques change frequently, for instance, uncertainty is greater. This would tend to reduce the supply of entrepreneurship in such industries at any given level of normal profit, and thus for them normal profit must be higher. Second, the elimination of the rent element in profit in the long period is only possible if one assumes that entrepreneurs of equal ability are available. In practice, this is not so. Thus there will always be some entrepreneurs earning a rent of ability (super-normal profit) even in the long period.

3. Super-normal Profit

Under perfect competition, the entrepreneur is able to make super-normal profits for a period because new firms cannot enter into competition. Certain factors are fixed in supply. Thus because workers are immobile, it may be difficult to obtain essential skilled operatives. More important, machinery takes time to produce, and for a time those entrepreneurs already possessing it will make super-normal profits. Such profits, therefore, are really the return to factors fixed in supply over the short period, and are thus in the nature of rent – quasi-rent.

4. Monopoly Profit

With monopoly, competitors can be excluded. Certain factors, e.g. diamond-mines, know-how, patents and copyrights, are fixed to the monopolist. Even in the long period, competitors cannot engage such factors, and so super-normal profits persist. The profits of the monopolist are therefore closer to economic rent than to quasi-rent.

The Role of Profit in a Private-enterprise Economy

The world 'profit' is often spoken of in terms of abuse, and persons who make large profits are likely to be regarded as social pariahs. But usually there is little justification for such an attitude, for profits are inseparable from the private-enterprise economy and are vital in making that system work.

We must emphasise, however, that we are discussing only profits under conditions of perfect competition. Given these conditions, super-normal profit is eliminated in the long period (see Chapter 11). Only normal profit – which is really a cost to cover uncertainty-bearing – remains.

Monopoly profit, on the other hand, is not eliminated, even in the long period. Entry into the industry is not free; consequently, profits are not competed away. It may be that such profits stimulate research and allow an industry to expand. But where scarcity has been deliberately brought about, they simply represent an economic rent earned at the expense of consumers by the monopolist owners. Government action is therefore usually aimed at eliminating monopoly profits, and we shall have nothing further to say about them.

Where there is perfect competition, the functions of profits are as follows:

1. Normal Profit is Necessary to Induce Persons to Accept the Risks of Uncertainty

Because uncertainty is implicit in a dynamic economy, some reward is essential to ensure a supply of entrepreneurs to industry. This reward is known as 'normal profit'. Without such profit, no production would take place. It is thus a cost, as essential as the payment of wages to labour.

2. Super-normal Profits Indicate to Entrepreneurs which Industries should Expand and which should Contract

When a firm produces a good which proves to be popular with consumers, it is reflected in the selling price, and therefore in the profits. As a result, it receives super-normal profit over and above normal profit. This is an indication that more factors should be brought into the industry to expand output to meet the wishes of consumers.

On the other hand, should the firm overestimate demand, it may incur a loss. Consumers have shown that they do not want the good, and production should contract.

3. Super-normal Profits Encourage Firms to Increase Production of a Good

Profits not only indicate that consumers want more of a good, they are also the inducement to firms to produce those goods. As we saw in Chapter 11, super-normal profits act as the spur for existing firms to increase capacity and for other firms to enter the industry. On the other hand, when losses are being incurred, firms go out of production and the industry contracts. Thus losses are as important as profits in the operation of the private-enterprise economy.

4. Super-normal Profits Provide the Resources for Expansion

An industry making super-normal profits can secure the factors necessary to expand.

First, profits can be used to provide additional capital ('ploughing back'), and shareholders will respond to a request for further capital (usually made through a 'rights' issue). Similarly, new firms can enter the industry, because investors will purchase the shares or debentures of a company intending to operate in an industry where the level of profits is relatively high.

Second, profits allow expanding firms to offer higher rewards to attract factors. In this way resources are moved according to the wishes of consumers. Eventually, under perfect competition, profits are competed away.

5. Super-normal Profits Encourage Research, Innovation and Exploration

Research, e.g. for new drugs, and exploration e.g. for oil, carry a high risk of failure and therefore of wasted capital expenditure. But the possibility of high returns if successful induces firms to engage in research, especially if new developments are protected for a period from competitors by patents.

6. Profits Ensure that Production is Carried on by the most Efficient Firms

In a perfectly competitive industry, the firm making the largest profit is the one whose costs are lowest. It will have an incentive to expand production and, if necessary, can afford to pay more for factors in order to do so. Less efficient firms must copy its methods, for otherwise they cannot retain factors. Still worse for them, the increased output of the more efficient firm will eventually lower the price of the product. As a result, inefficient firms find that profits become negative – a loss is made.

Thus it can be seen that, under a private-enterprise system, the drive is provided by profits – and the fear of losses. Whether the desire for personal gain is the best of motives may be open to doubt. But, human nature being what it is, it is still the most effective. Uncertainty exists in any dynamic economy, and so there is bound to be scope for profits whether production is organised by private enterprise or by the state. What we have to ask, therefore, is: 'When no personal gain or loss is involved, is there the same incentive to maximise profits or to avoid losses?'

It must be pointed out, too, that under perfect competition, profits are self-destructive. Moreover, in the process of elimination, industry is made more efficient – a form of natural selection.

It is wrong, therefore, to regard profits as being somewhat immoral. The exception is monopoly profits, which do not disappear and do not motivate a full distribution of the factors of production according to the wishes of consumers.

Part V

Money and Financial Institutions

20 Money and the Rate of Interest

20.1 The Functions of Money

What is Money?

It is possible to exchange goods by a direct swap. But barter, as direct exchange is usually termed, is comparatively rare in the modern world. Consider this advertisement in *Exchange and Mart*: 'Ever Ready battery portable in exchange for any pedigree bitch up to two years.' The formidable difficulties in the way of such an exchange are obvious.

In an economy where there is a high degree of specialisation, exchanges must take place quickly and smoothly. Hence we have a 'go-between' – money – a common denominator for all goods. The product of specialised labour is sold, exchanged for money, and this money is then used to buy the many different goods and services required.

Anything which is generally acceptable in purchasing goods or settling debts can be said to be money. It need not consist of coins and notes. Oxen, salt, amber, woodpecker scalps and cotton cloth have at times all been used as money.

In fact, the precise substance, its size and shape, are largely a matter of convenience and custom. But whatever is used, it should be immediately and unquestionably accepted in exchange for goods and services. Thus the use of the particular good should be backed by custom, and people must feel that it will retain its value by remaining relatively scarce.

Legal Tender

Sometimes an attempt is made to confer acceptability by law. In the UK notes have unlimited 'legal tender', in that a creditor must accept them in payment of a debt. But a commodity does not have to be legal tender for it to be money. Nor can legislation ensure that it will be acceptable. In

Germany, after the Second World War, cigarettes were preferred to the Reichsbank mark in payment for goods.

Precious Metal as Money

Most commodities used as money in the past have proved unsatisfactory, especially as exchange economies have developed, for they did not completely overcome the difficulties of barter. Oxen, for instance, were bulky to transport, deteriorated over time, and were costly to store. Moreover, not only were they rarely uniform in size or quality, but they could not easily be divided to purchase goods of small value.

Hence, precious metals eventually replaced other goods as money. Later, in order to simplify transactions, metals were minted into coins of different weights and shapes. The exact amount of money required could now be found by counting instead of by weighing.

Paper Money

In England precious metals and coins were used almost exclusively as money until the middle of the seventeenth century. However, in 1640, Charles I appropriated £130 000 worth of gold held for merchants in the Tower of London. Thereafter gold and silver bullion plate were kept in the strong rooms of the goldsmiths. Eventually, receipts for these deposits were accepted in exchange for goods, and so withdrawal of the actual gold and silver became unnecessary.

This was the origin of the banknote, and paper currency soon began to form an increasing proportion of British money. The paper from which notes are made is comparatively worthless. But people who receive notes are confident that others too will accept them. Notes possess, therefore, the essential characteristic of money – general acceptability. This is true even though, since 1931, it has not been possible in the UK to exchange notes for gold at the Bank of England.

The Functions of Money

Money, it is usually stated, performs four functions:

(1) It is *a medium of exchange*, the oil, as it were, which allows the machinery of modern buying and selling to run smoothly.

(2) It is *a measure of value and a unit of account*, making possible the operation of a price system and automatically providing the basis for keeping accounts, calculating profit and loss, costing, etc.

(3) It is *a standard of deferred payments*, the unit in which, given stability in its value, loans and future contracts are arranged. Without

money there would be no common basis for dealing in debts – the work of such institutions as insurance companies, building societies, banks and discount houses. By providing a standard for repayment, money makes borrowing and lending much easier.

(4) It is *a store of wealth*, the most convenient way of keeping any income which is surplus to immediate requirements. More than that, because money is also the medium of exchange, wealth stored in this form is completely liquid. That is, only money of all possible assets can be converted into other goods immediately and without cost. Or, in the words of the Bible: 'Wine maketh merry; but money answereth all things' (Ecclesiastes 10:19). Indeed, it is this 'liquidity' which is the most distinctive characteristic of money, and it results in money playing an active, rather than a merely neutral, part in the operation of the economy. We must therefore give it further consideration.

20.2 The Demand for Money

What do we Mean by the 'Demand for Money'?

Most people would regard a miser as a crank. To the ordinary person money is wanted not just for counting or to be gloated over, but to be spent on food, clothes, holidays, a car and all the other things which can be enjoyed. In short, it would seem that money is useful only when we are getting rid of it.

But there is somewhat more to it than that. Money was defined as anything generally acceptable in settling debts. But why is it 'generally acceptable'? Simply because everybody has confidence that other people will accept it *immediately* whenever they wish to buy something. Money is, as we have seen, perfectly liquid.

Moreover, no other form of wealth is liquid to the same degree as money. Assets kept in the deposit account of a bank are subject to seven days' notice of withdrawal. Equities and bonds have to be sold before anything else can be bought and this involves payment of the broker's commission and perhaps a capital loss. Or, if a house, car or piano are to be exchanged for something else, it usually means finding a cash purchaser first. Only money can be changed into some other form of wealth without cost or delay.

People want a money balance, therefore, because it is a perfectly liquid asset. It is in this sense that there is a 'demand' for money – *to hold perfectly liquid reserves*. We must now examine why people should want such reserves.

Why People Demand Money

Lord Keynes gave three main reasons for holding money:

1. The Transactions Motive

Both consumers and businessmen hold money to facilitate current transac- tions.

Most consumers receive the bulk of their income weekly or monthly. On the other hand, payments for food, travel and pleasure have to be made each day. Thus a part of money income has to be held throughout the week or month to cover these everyday purchases. How much will this be?

Suppose that I earn £240 a week, all of which is being spent. I receive £240 on the Friday which begins the week, and by the following Friday I have nothing left. Thus my average holding of money is £120. Should it now be decided to pay me monthly, and my spending habits remain the same, my average holding of money, either in cash or in my current account at the bank, would rise to £240. In the same way, if my income doubled but was fully spent, the amount of money I hold would double.

Similarly, a businessman requires money to pay wages, purchase raw materials, and meet other current expenses.

There may be special reasons why the demand for money for the transactions motive may suddenly increase; it does, for instance, at Christmas and holiday periods, or if there is a flurry of activity on the Stock Exchange. Usually the underlying determinants are fairly stable. With consumers, these are the length of time between successive pay-days and the level of income and prices; with businessmen it is the size of turnover. It can be seen, therefore, that the community's demand for money for transactions purposes will be roughly in proportion to the size of the national income.

It should be noted that the value of transactions for which money is required is much greater than the value of money national income. For instance, if the cost of goods to a shopkeeper (including shop expenses) is £100, and these goods are sold for £110, the income from the transaction is £10, whereas £210 in money was required to effect the necessary exchanges. In addition, money is required for what are basically non-income-creating transactions, e.g. switching securities.

2. The Precautionary Motive

Apart from expenditure on regular, everyday purchases, money is required to cover events of a more uncertain nature which may easily occur – illness, accident, unemployment, defects in the car or household appliances, and snap decisions to obtain a cash bargain. Hence both consumers and businessmen usually keep some extra reserve of cash for a 'rainy day' or to make a favourable purchase. The amount held will depend mainly on the outlook of individuals, how optimistic they are, both as regards events and the possibility of borrowing at short notice should the need arise. But, taking the community as a whole, the amount set aside for the precautionary motive is, in normal times, likely to be tied closely to the level of national income.

Keynes termed the money held for the transactions and precautionary motives as 'active' balances. The size of such balances is chiefly dependent on the level of income.

3. The Speculative Motive

Usually the amount of money in existence exceeds what is necessary to satisfy the demand for active balances. But any surplus must be held by somebody, for it must be somewhere! Why, however, should people wish to hold 'idle' balances?

The immediate response of the reader might be 'why not?' As we have seen, money has no carrying costs (e.g. storage, maintenance) and is perfectly liquid. Of all assets, only money confers complete manoeuvrability.

But holding wealth in the form of money has the disadvantage that *it does not provide a yield*. (In periods of inflation, there is the added disadvantage that the value of money is falling, but we can ignore this complication for the time being.) Furniture, jewellery, works of art, etc., afford pleasure; a house can be lived in or rented out. With shares, there is usually a dividend, with bonds, a fixed rate of interest. There is thus an opportunity cost of being liquid – the yield forgone. To simplify, let us refer to this yield as 'the rate of interest'.

Thus, while people might desire liquidity, they have also to think of the cost involved. The higher the rate of interest, the greater the cost of remaining liquid. As the rate rises, so fewer people will be prepared to pay the 'price'; in other words, they will be tempted out of holding money. Thus demand for idle balances is closely related to the rate of interest – the higher the rate, the greater the cost of holding money and so the less will money be demanded.

But the complete answer is less simple than this. Holding money, as opposed to securities, permits speculation. Keynes considered that the main reason why people hold idle balances is to guard against a possible capital loss, as follows.

On any given day it is quite usual for the prices of some securities to rise while those of others fall. But there are periods when the prices of almost all securities move in more or less the same direction. To simplify our explanation, however, we shall concentrate our attention on undated government bonds (fixed-interest-bearing securities); this eliminates time and risk complications.

If people think that the price of bonds is going to rise, they will buy bonds now. Should their forecast prove correct, they will make a capital gain. Similarly, if they think that the price of bonds is going to fall, they will sell bonds. Now the lower the price of bonds, the more will people think that the next likely move will be in an upward direction. As the price rises, so more people will gradually come round to the view that the price is so high that a fall is likely to occur. It follows, therefore, that when the price of bonds is low, people prefer bonds to liquidity; but as the price rises, people move out of bonds in order to hold money.

However, the price of bonds varies proportionately but inversely with the rate of interest. Thus if the current rate of interest is $2\frac{1}{2}$ per cent, £100 $3\frac{1}{2}$ per cent War Loan would be worth £140 on the Stock Exchange, but if the rate were 14 per cent it would be worth only £25.

Thus it is possible to relate the demand for money, not only to the price of bonds, but also to the rate of interest. When people are speculating against the future price of bonds they are speculating against the future rate of interest. Hence we can rewrite our original proposition as follows: when the rate of interest is low (the price of bonds is high), people will prefer to hold money; when the rate of interest is high (the price of bonds is low), people will not wish to hold money. This relationship between the current rate of interest and the demand for idle balances is shown in Figure 20.1.

FIGURE 20.1
The Relationship Between the Rate of Interest and the Demand for Money

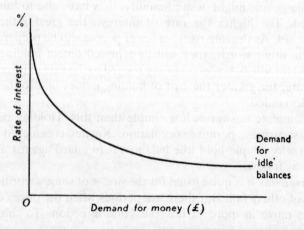

Keynes's emphasis on 'speculative' in this situation is rather unfortunate in that it tends to misrepresent the asset-holder's objective. Some 'speculation' must occur where there is an element of uncertainty, and persons in charge of funds, e.g. pension funds, have, as a minimum, to take precautions to avoid capital loss. In doing so they have to take a view as to the future movement of 'bond' prices generally. The bondholder will compare the interest likely to be earned on the bond over a period with the possibility of any loss in its capital value. If the latter outweighs the former, the bondholder will prefer to hold the money.

Whereas the level of income, the main factor influencing the demand for money for the transactions and precautionary motives, is fairly stable, people's expectations of the future rate of interest, the determinant of liquidity preference for the speculative motive, is far more liable to change. It is this speculation, therefore, which Lord Keynes considered exercises the dominating influence on the level of the rate of interest.

The Demand for Money and Saving

It must be emphasised that the demand for money and saving are quite different things. Saving is simply that part of income which is not spent, and the influences determining it are analysed in Chapter 26. Saving adds to a person's wealth. Liquidity preference is concerned with the form in which that wealth is held. The motives for liquidity preference explain why there is a desire to hold some wealth in the form of cash rather than in goods affording utility or in securities earning income.

20.3 The Supply of Money

The supply of money consists of the following.

1. Coins

These are insignificant in volume being issued for the convenience of effect small, everyday transactions.

2. Notes

From the seventeenth century paper currency began to form an increasing proportion of British money and eventually Parliament had to exercise a strict control over the 'fiduciary issue' – the note issue in excess of the value of gold held by the Bank of England. Today, however, notes, like coins, are regarded as the small change of the monetary system, and so sufficient are always made available for the practical convenience of the public.

3. Bank Deposits

While purchases of everyday goods – bus-rides, newspapers, drinks, etc. – are usually paid for in coins or notes, about 80 per cent (in value) of all transactions are effected by cheque or credit card. When a person writes a cheque, the bank is instructed to transfer deposits standing in his or her account to the person to whom money is owed. Bank deposits therefore act as money.

A large part of these deposits are 'created' by the bank. How banks create deposits and how they can be controlled will be described in the following two chapters.

Other Forms of Money

There is really no hard and fast dividing-line between what is money and what is not. 'True money' confers complete *liquidity* on its holder and, in the last resort, only banknotes and sovereigns do this, for other coins are limited in legal tender. But when considering what serves as money in our economy, the more practical approach is to start from the idea that 'money is what money does'. Is it accepted in payment for goods? If so, it is acting as money. Cheques, as we have seen, are money for this reason, though they represent nothing more than current deposits in a bank. Yet, in advanced economies, cheques form the major part of 'money' in use.

Indeed, although deposits held by bank customers in deposit accounts are subject to seven days' notice of withdrawal, such notice will in practice be waived by the bank with the loss of some interest. Thus sums in deposit accounts can be regarded as 'near' money.

And, in pursuing our argument in the same direction, we find other instruments of credit which, although not 'true money' in the sense that they can be spent anywhere in their present form, nevertheless fulfil the functions of money, if only within a limited sphere. But we must be careful to see clearly how and when they add to the money supply. Deposits can be 'created' by banks only because their clearing system enables them to economise in cash (see Chapter 22). In this the banks hold a unique position; other forms of credit add to the money supply only when they are not covered by cash held idle to an equal amount. Thus, when a person buys a postal order to cover his 'pools' entry, the cash he pays in may be put into circulation again by the Post Office before the order is presented by the pools firm. Thus, to some extent, postal orders can form an addition to the money supply, for they are doing the work of money. This is true, too, of other instruments of credit – credit cards (until the bank account is settled), bills of exchange (especially those 'negotiated', i.e. passed on to a third party to settle a debt), trade credit (particularly when deals between firms are allowed to cancel credit, or if the entitlement to payment is transferred to a third party) and book-entry settlements replacing cash (as occurs, for example, when there is a vertical amalgamation of firms).

'Near' Money

We can carry the above idea further. Any assets possessed can usually be turned into money eventually. Liquidity, therefore, is largely a matter of degree, often depending upon the organisations which exist to make such assets as building society deposits, government securities, shares in public companies and insurance policies liquid. Thus in recent years traders have become more liquid by the development of factor houses to which trade debts can be sold immediately for cash. While assets may have to be sold at some capital loss, they do afford some degree of liquidity to the holder. People possessing first-class shares, for instance, would not need to keep so large a cash balance for the precautionary motive, for they could always sell some in an emergency. In short, the existence of 'near' money means that the demand for 'true' money can be correspondingly less. We shall assume that this has been allowed for in our demand for money curves, which therefore depict the demand for 'true' money.

The Official Definition of the Supply of Money

While there may be no hard and fast dividing-line between money and certain other assets, the acceptance by the government of the view that the money supply is an important influence in the economy has required that it be defined so that it can be measured and monitored as a guide to policy. Two classifications have been adopted.

'Narrow money' refers to money balances which are readily available to finance current spending, that is for transactions purposes. The chosen monetary target is now M0 which consists of notes and coin held by the public and banks, plus banks' holding of cash (till money) and their balances at the Bank of England.

'Broad money' refers to money held for transactions purposes and money held as a liquid asset. It reflects the private sector's holdings of assets which could be converted with relative ease and without capital loss into spending on goods and services. Here the chosen target has been Sterling M3 (£M3) which consists of notes and coins held by the public, plus all private sterling deposits (sight and time) held by UK residents in UK banks. In practice, however, it has proved to be a poor indicator of the effects of government monetary measures and so in 1987 its use as a target was dropped (see p.473).

20.4 The Rate of Interest

We are now in a position to consider the problem postponed in Chapter 17: 'What determines the overall level of interest rates in the economy?' Or, as it is more usually put: 'What determines the *pure* rate of interest, the benchmark around which interest rates fluctuate?'

The Classical Economists' Views

The rate of interest is the price which has to be paid for a loan of liquid capital. The classical economists explained it, therefore, in terms of the demand for and supply of loanable funds. Because investment is profitable, firms *demand* funds for investment. The lower the rate of interest, the greater the number of investment projects which are profitable. Thus total demand for liquid capital consists of the sum of the demands of the individual entrepreneurs at different rates of interest.

The *supply of liquid capital* comes from persons willing to forgo present consumption in order to enjoy it at some future date. To most people, 'a bird in the hand is worth two in the bush'. The classical economists argued, therefore, that in order to persuade people to overcome the inclination to consume immediately a reward in the form of interest had to be offered. The higher the rate of interest, the greater would be the inducement to postpone current consumption, and so the greater would be the supply of loanable funds. Thus we have a supply curve for liquid capital sloping upwards to the right.

The rate of interest, the price of liquid capital, is fixed by the interaction of demand and supply – at the point of intersection of the two curves.

The classical economists' explanation of the rate of interest is too simple:

1. It ascribes to the rate of interest a greater influence on the volume of investment and saving than is justified. Other factors, notably the level of income, are more important (see pp.322–8).
2. It assumes that investment automatically responds to changes in the rate of interest.
3. Since investment and saving as conceived by the classical economists would be fairly stable, their theory cannot explain why fairly short-term variations in the rate of interest occur.
4. It ignores the influence of the government especially on the short-term rate of interest.
5. Most important, it assumes that the whole of income saved is actually lent to entrepreneurs. But besides being reluctant to save, people are reluctant to lend. They prefer to keep their assets liquid in the form of money. It is money as a *liquid* asset that is the starting-point of Keynes's theory of the rate of interest.

The Rate of Interest as a Monetary Phenomenon

Income not spent by an individual is said to be 'saved'. But even after some income has been saved, the choice still has to be made as to what assets will be held. This is because assets differ in the qualities they possess, particularly as regards lender's risk, liquidity and yield.

The greater the lender's risk, the higher the yield required, other things being equal. The exact difference in yield between different types of risk will be decided in the market. We can eliminate this complication by concentrating attention at the extreme end where risk of non-payment of interest and capital is nil – government securities.

Liquidity and yield, too, are usually related inversely. Illiquidity has to be compensated for by a high yield. Complete liquidity, conferred only by money, involves total loss of yield.

But since liquidity is a desirable attribute in an asset, money can be regarded as an acceptable way of holding wealth in comparison with interest-yielding assets. Individuals, therefore, have to arrange their portfolios of assets according to the emphasis they put on liquidity as opposed to interest yield. To eliminate the complication of loans of differing periods, we shall assume that all securities are undated govern- ment stock, which we shall term 'bonds'. Thus there are only two kinds of asset which individuals may hold in storing their wealth – bonds and money. The price of bonds will also give us the rate of interest on riskless, undated securities (see p.252).

On the capital market there will be bonds offered for sale. Some will come out of the existing stock held by people; others will be new bonds arising from current government borrowing. But their price will be determined by demand and supply, just as the price of rubber, tin, wool, cotton and any other commodity is in their respective markets.

People holding money bid on the capital market for the bonds offered. How much money they have will depend upon the total supply of money in the economy and how much they want to hold for the transactions and precautionary motives. At the end of a day's dealing, all bonds may have changed hands. But this need not be so. If the price of bonds is low, some would-be sellers may prefer to hold on to them. On the other hand, if the price of bonds is high, some would-be purchasers may prefer to retain their money.

But, at the end of the day's dealings, a price will have been found at which people have finished dealing – nobody will wish to exchange more bonds against money, and nobody will wish to exchange more money against bonds. There is equilibrium at this price. This price is the inverse of the current 'pure' rate of interest – the benchmark referred to earlier.

The Keynesian Emphasis on Particular Determining Factors

It can be seen from the above that a change in the demand for money relative to bonds, given the stock of money and of bonds, will bring about a change in the rate of interest. Thus if it becomes less attractive to hold money, the rate of interest will fall.

But changes in the relative quantities of money and bonds, i.e. in the sizes of the stocks of each, will also produce variations in the rate of interest. If, for instance, the quantity of money increased and the demand for money and the stock of bonds remained unchanged, it would mean that more money was being offered against bonds, with the result that the price of bonds would rise. Looked at in an alternative way, the owners of wealth could not, at the given rate of interest, be induced to hold the whole stock of money. Thus there would have to be a reduction in the inducement *not* to hold money, i.e. in the rate of interest. Similarly, if the quantity of bonds increased, the demand for bonds and the supply of money remaining unchanged, the price of bonds would fall. Looked at in an alternative way, at the given rate of interest owners of wealth could not be induced to hold the whole stock of bonds. Hence the inducement to hold bonds, i.e. the rate of interest, would have to rise. In practice, stocks, both of money and of bonds, are not subject to great variations except over fairly considerable periods of time.

The supply of money is controlled by the government (see Chapter 23). The supply of bonds coming on to the market comes chiefly from existing stocks of old bonds. In comparison, the flow of new bonds on to the market is small. Current government borrowing, unless it were very large, would therefore have little impact on the rate of interest. Thus, Keynes considered, it is much more realistic to analyse the rate of interest from the point of view of the variable most likely to change over the short period – the demand for money. And here he stressed the role of speculation.

In the market for bonds there will be many people whose main interest will be in their future price. Indeed, as we have seen, Keynes thought that the speculative element dominated all other considerations. If so, then the demand for bonds is largely the result of the present price of bonds. Or the demand for money is primarily a function of the rate of interest.

Instead of approaching the rate of interest through the demand and supply of bonds, therefore, it is possible to approach it through the demand for and supply of money, the alternative asset.

The demand for money depends upon the level of income (transactions and precautionary motives) and the rate of interest (speculative motive), though modern thought would not separate them completely, for people can economise on active balances when the rate of interest is high. But we can combine the demand for each in a single demand curve, adding the demand for active balances (which is largely unaffected by the rate of interest) to the demand for idle balances (which is influenced by the current rate of interest).

This is shown in Figure 20.2. The demand for money for active balances is shown by the distance of the vertical sections of the demand curve from the *y*-axis. Thus if income increases from Y to Y_1, the increase in the demand for active balances is equal to the horizontal difference between the two. To this demand for active balances must be added the demand for idle balances – the sloping portion of the curve.

FIGURE 20.2
The Determination of the Rate of Interest

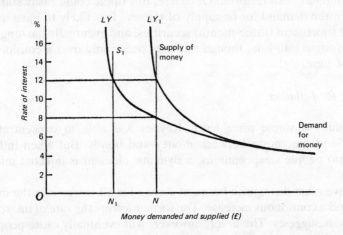

The supply of money is fixed by the government on the banking authorities (see Chapter 23). Suppose it is equal to ON. If the level of income Y, is low, there is less demand for active balances and thus more available for idle balances. The rate of interest is therefore only 8 per cent. With a higher level of income, Y_1, more money is demanded for active balances. This leaves less for idle balances and the rate of interest rises to 12 per cent. And so on.

A smaller supply of money, ON_1 would produce a rate of interest of 12 per cent with Y.

As we shall see, the level of income is influenced by the level of saving and investment. It is through their effect on income that saving and investment have an impact on the rate of interest.

The Structure of Interest Rates

It merely remains to remove our earlier simplification that the only type of security in existence is bonds. In practice, people can put their money into a range of securities each varying in the degree of liquidity and lender's risk involved. These securities can, however, be regarded as fairly close substitutes for one another, and there will be a rate of return on each depending on the demand for that type of security and the supply of it. These rates will be interrelated because, since they are close substitutes, the demand for one type of security will be affected by the rate of return on the security most similar to it. For instance, a rise in the rate of return on short-dated government stock will cause a movement of funds to it from its immediate close substitutes, such as Treasury bills. This sets up a ripple running through the whole structure of interest rates until eventually equilibrium has been restored. Of course, this ripple could easily start by a change in the demand for or supply of money. It is likely to have its first effect on short-term (three-month) securities, and eventually the long-term rate is brought into line, though this may occur only over a considerable period of time.

Allowing for Inflation

By assuming a stable price level, Keynes was able to concentrate on liquidity and the choice between money and bonds. But when inflation enters into people's expectations, a dynamic element is injected into the situation.

First, we must distinguish between a once-for-all increase in the money supply and a continuous increase. The former lowers the rate of interest, as the analysis suggests. The latter, however, will eventually cause people to expect further inflation. It can occur, for example, by the need to finance a recurrent high Public Sector Borrowing Requirement (PSBR).

Second, the expectation of inflation leads people to widen their choice of wealth-holding assets. Apart from bonds, they can hold equities (shares in companies), real property or simply goods. Like bonds, all these incur a loss of liquidity. But whereas bonds valued in terms of money are bound to fall in real terms with inflation, equities, real property and goods have some degree of inflation-hedge. Thus people are likely to switch to holding these alternatives. Equities and real property also afford a yield, but this now tends to be *below* the rate of interest on bonds because investors bid up their prices to obtain the advantage of the inflation-hedge. This difference is referred to as the 'reverse yield gap'.

Smaller holders of wealth are likely to invest in owner-occupied houses, antiques, works of art and, to some extent, goods in general, for these too are expected to carry a 'yield' through inflation. Thus prices of goods rise; in such circumstances, money *does* matter, as the monetarists claim.

In contrast, bonds are not wanted, and their price falls, people requiring a margin to allow for inflation, i.e. a higher yield. In recent years, therefore, although the supply of money has been increased, the rate of interest has risen – in contrast to the Keynesian theory outlined above!

The Weakness of Keynes's 'Idle Balances' Concept

In his theory of interest Keynes implicitly assumed that, given no change in *Y*, any increase in the supply of money would automatically be absorbed into idle balances for liquidity purposes.

But what if extra money encouraged spending on actual goods and services rather than on bonds? In recent years this has proved to be a distinct possibility and we return to it in Chapter 27.

21

The Money Markets and the Capital Market

In Chapter 17 we saw that capital is demanded because of the contribution it makes to production. Hence liquid capital, i.e. loans of money, is required by producers – manufacturers, traders and the government – for varying periods of time. Such funds are provided by persons who not only save a part of their income, but lend all or some of these savings.

Finance is required for different purposes, by different persons and for varying periods of time. This leads to a great variety in the institutions providing loans and in the types of loans arranged. As with goods, markets have sprung up to bring together buyers and sellers.

We shall discuss the subject, however, under the following headings:

1. The money markets, which deal in short-term loans.
2. The capital market, where medium- and long-term capital is raised.
3. The joint-stock banks, which are the major source of working capital, and which exercise a major influence on the system through their ability to create credit.
4. The Bank of England, which exercises overall control on behalf of the government.

It must be emphasised that this separate classification is to a large extent one of convenience to clarify exposition. As we shall see, functions are interrelated, and, especially since 'Big Bang', integrated within the same institution.

In this chapter we are concerned with the first two. For convenience, we also include a description of the work of Stock Markets, though these are mainly markets in existing securities and only indirectly help in providing new loans.

None of the money markets or the capital market is a formal organisation in that buyers and sellers meet regularly in a particular building to conduct business. Instead they are merely a collection of institutions connected, in the case of the money markets, by dealings in bills of exchange and short-term loans and, more loosely in the case of the capital market, in channelling medium- and long-term finance to those requiring it. The complete structure is shown in a very simplified form in Figure 21.1

Not only are there money and capital markets but, within each, there is further specialisation. This will be illustrated later. But, in order to explain

FIGURE 21.1
The Provision of Finance in the UK

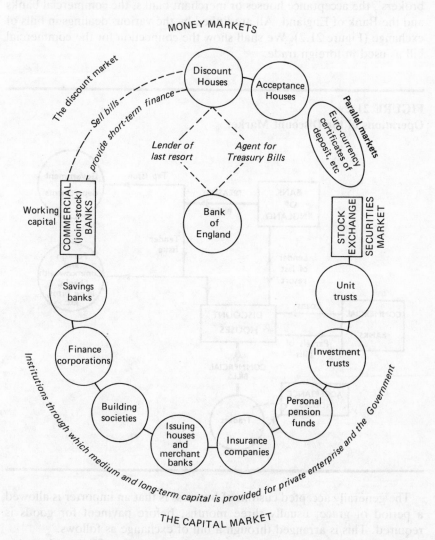

(*a*) the nature of markets in finance, (*b*) how the City of London acquired its expertise, and (*c*) how the Bank of England enters into the market, we commence by looking at the traditional London money market or, as it would be more precisely described today, the *discount market*.

21.1 The Discount Market

The discount market is composed of the discount houses and 'running brokers', the acceptance houses or merchant banks, the commercial banks and the Bank of England. All are linked by the various dealings in bills of exchange (Figure 21.2). We shall show the connection for the commercial bill as used in foreign trade.

FIGURE 21.2
Operations of the Discount Market

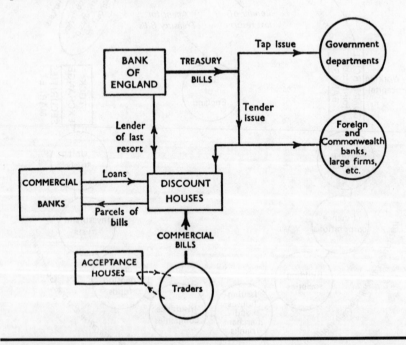

The generally accepted custom of business is that an importer is allowed a period of grace, usually three months, before payment for goods is required. This is arranged through a bill of exchange as follows.

Suppose *A* is exporting cars from London to *B* in New York to the value of £10 000. When *A* is ready to ship the cars, a bill of exchange, as shown in Figure 21.3 is drawn up. This is sent to *B* together with copies of the shipping documents, such as the bill of lading and insurance certificate, to show that the cars have actually been placed aboard the ship. On receipt of the bill, *B* 'accepts' it, by writing 'Accepted' and his signature across the face of the bill, and then returns it to *A*. This acceptance of the bill by *B* is the condition for handing over the original bill of lading, the documentary title to the cars.

FIGURE 21.3
A Commercial Bill of Exchange

£10 000

A's address

29 January 1987

Three months after date, pay to me or to my order Ten Thousand Pounds, value received.

(Signed) 'A'

To 'B',
B's address.

A can now do one of three things: (i) hold the bill until it matures three months after the date of acceptance; (ii) get another merchant to take it in settlement of a debt which *A* owes; or, (iii) sell the bill, usually to a discount house.

Discount Houses

A will probably choose the latter course. So, after endorsing it, he takes it along to one of the London discount houses. Here it will be bought at less than its face-value, the exact amount paid depending on the length of time to maturity, the prevailing short-term rate of interest and the opinion of the discount house as to *B*'s financial standing. Suppose the bill has still three months to run and that the prevailing rate of interest on that class of bill is 12 per cent, the discount house will pay about £9700 for it. This process is known as 'discounting'. It is obvious that through these arrangements the bill of exchange has advantages to all concerned. While exporter A quickly regains liquidity by selling the bill, B obtains three months' credit, during which time the cars will probably be sold.

Discount houses do not usually hold bills for their full currency. Instead bills are assembled in 'parcels' and after about a month sold to the commercial banks who like to have so many falling due each day. There are a few 'running brokers' who act as agents in the process of discounting.

Acceptance Houses

If B is a well-known firm of high financial standing, the accepted bill is, from the risk point of view, almost as good as cash. However, as bills are drawn on firms in all parts of the world, little may be known about B's financial standing. Thus the discount house is either reluctant to discount the bill or will only do so at a fairly high rate of interest. The difficulty can be overcome by getting a firm of international repute to 'accept' responsibility for payment should B default. It is obvious that any firm accepting such a bill must have adequate knowledge of the creditworthiness of the trader upon whom it is drawn. Such knowledge is possessed by the merchant banks, such as Lazard, Baring and Rothschild, who commenced as traders but later specialised on financing trade in particular parts of the world. In their capacity of accepting bills, such merchant banks are known as 'acceptance houses', and for the service they charge a small commission of about $\frac{3}{4}$ per cent, which is willingly paid because the rate of discount on a 'bank bill', i.e. one bearing the name of an acceptance house, is lower than on a 'trade bill' (a bill accepted only by a trader) or on a 'fine trade bill' (where the merchant is of good standing).

In recent years the business of accepting has declined. Originally this was the result of the diminished use of the trade bill in international trade as the commercial banks competed through the cheaper method of the 'reimbursement credit'. With this, B, an importer in New York, asks his own bank to obtain an acceptance credit in London by making itself responsible for payment. Thus the London bank or acceptor there has only to satisfy itself as to the financial standing of the New York bank. This simpler procedure means that reimbursement credits can be granted at very low rates.

Today the business of accepting has declined because of the change in nature of the commercial bill as a means of raising finance.

The Treasury Bill

Discount houses originated to deal in commercial bills of exchange, but their operations were easily extended to Treasury bills when these were introduced by the government. A Treasury bill is really a bill of exchange drawn by the Treasury on itself, usually for a period of three months (91 days), though occasionally two-month bills (63 days) are issued. Since such bills are only a short-term loan, they represent the government's cheapest method of borrowing, the interest being just over 13 per cent. Treasury bills are only issued in high denominations and so are primarily for the institutional investors.

The Impact of Recent Developments

Recent developments have had repercussions on both the discount houses and merchant banks. The restrictions on the lending powers of the banks before 1971 led to the development of other means of short-term borrowing, e.g. internal commercial bills, local authority bills, certificates of deposit, etc. Furthermore, the government has reduced its dependence on short-term borrowing through Treasury bills. Thus the PSBR has been *over* funded by the sale of gilt-edged stock, the proceeds being used to purchase internal commercial bills which are more limited than Treasury bills as a liquid asset base.

Dealings in these short-term instruments are now, therefore, the mainstay of the *discount houses*, though they still tender for the reduced weekly offering of Treasury bills.

The functions of the *merchant banks* have also changed. The work of accepting is not required for Treasury bills or for most of the new short-term instruments since the standing of the borrower is generally known to be first class. Instead, they arrange and underwrite new issues, advise on the terms of 'take overs' and mergers, and pay dividends to stockholders as they fall due. They compete in specialist fields, e.g. property development, in domestic banking business, and also act as trustees and manage investment portfolios. Other functions have resulted from their overseas trading connections. Thus they have important business in the bullion and foreign exchange markets.

The Commercial Banks

The commercial banks fulfil two main functions in the discount market – providing funds to the discount houses and holding bills to maturity.

The discount houses do not themselves have sufficient funds to buy all the bills, commercial and Treasury, offered to them. They overcome this difficulty, however, by borrowing money from the commercial banks at a comparatively low rate of interest. Then, by discounting at a slightly higher rate, they make a small profit. The banks are willing to lend at a low rate because the loans are of short duration, often for only a day, and need not be renewed should there be a particularly heavy demand for cash from their ordinary customers. For the discount houses, the trouble involved in the daily renewal of this 'money at call' and the slight risk of its non-renewal are compensated for by the comparatively low rate of interest charged.

The commercial banks can earn a higher rate of interest if they themselves hold bills for a part of the time they have to run. However, except on rare occasions they do not tender directly for Treasury bills but instead buy them from the discount houses when they still have about two months to run.

The Bank of England

The Bank of England enters the discount market as follows.

First, it is the agency by which the government issues Treasury bills. This issue is achieved by two methods, 'tap' and 'tender'. Government departments, the National Savings Bank, the Exchange Equalisation Account, the National Insurance Funds, and the Bank of England Issue Department, all of whom have funds to invest for a short period, can buy what bills they want at a fixed price, i.e. 'on tap'. This price is not published.

The discount houses and anyone else who wishes to apply (such as Commonwealth and foreign banks) obtain their issue by 'tender'. Every Friday, the Treasury, acting through the Bank of England, invites tenders for a specified amount of bills, usually about £100 million each week. The discount houses compete in their tenders, but always 'cover' the whole of the issue.

Second, the Bank of England is the 'lender of last resort'. When the discount houses are pressed for money because the commercial banks will not renew their 'call money', the Bank of England makes finance available to them. It is convenient, however, if we postpone further discussion of this function to Chapter 23, where the position of the Bank of England as a central bank is considered.

21.2 Parallel Money Markets

With the traditional sources of finance (particularly the clearing banks) becoming increasingly restricted by the monetary authorities in recent years, there was a ready demand even for short-term funds. Here the City of London has showed its adaptability. Specialist money markets developed to meet the specific requirements of particular borrowers and lenders. Indeed, the existence of such markets encourages funds to be lent short-term, for they enable lenders to regain liquidity when desired.

The following are the most important of these comparatively new markets.

1. Inter-bank Deposits

Because money at call and bills of exchange have always been acceptable to the Bank of England as part of the liquidity ratio, clearing banks tended to be connected mainly with the discount market.

Until 1971, however, the other banks – Scottish banks, merchant banks, British overseas banks and foreign banks – were not subject to a liquidity ratio. Brokers therefore established a market so that those banks having funds surplus to their immediate requirements could lend to those who had immediate outlets for such funds, the rate of interest obtained being higher than in the discount market. Eventually the clearing banks participated in the market which has increased in importance. It is described as a 'wholesale' market, as opposed to a 'retail' market where funds are collected directly from the public, e.g. Building Society deposits.

2. Local Authority Deposits

Local authorities borrow on the open market and are willing to make use of very short-term money. Brokers now exist for placing such short-term funds from banks, industrial and commercial companies, charitable funds, etc., with local authorities. Such brokers also deal in longer-term local authority bonds.

Today the market is integrated very closely with the interbank market, as funds from the latter are very often deposited with local authorities.

3. Negotiable Certificates of Deposit

Certificates of deposit enable the banks to borrow for periods from three months to five years. They are like bills of exchange drawn on banks by themselves. For the bank they are for a longer period than an ordinary time deposit, thus facilitating medium-term lending. For the lender they offer a higher rate of interest, while the market in them means that they can be sold whenever cash is required. The market is largely comprised of the discount houses and banks.

4. Euro-currency Balances

Euro-currency deposits are simply funds which are deposited with banks outside the country of origin but which continue to be designated in terms of the original currency.

The most important Euro-currency is the dollar. As a result of the USA's continuing adverse balance of payments, branches of European banks build up dollar balances as customers are paid for exports. These balances are offered to brokers in London, and are placed mainly with companies or banks (e.g. Japanese) operating on an international scale to finance foreign trade or investment.

While the dollar still dominates the market, other European currencies are now dealt in, chiefly the £ sterling, the Deutschmark, the Swiss franc and the Japanese yen.

5. Other Markets

Smaller specialist markets have developed in *finance house deposits* and *inter-company deposits*. Thus finance houses have obtained funds by issuing bills which are accepted by banks and discount houses. Similarly, in periods of tight credit, firms which are short of finance turn towards other companies which temporarily have funds to spare.

21.3 The Capital Market

The unique machinery of the money markets developed in order to supply trade and the government with the short-term finance each requires. Industry, on the other hand, usually obtains its short-term or 'working' capital (to purchase raw materials, pay workers and maintain stocks) from the commercial banks (to be described later), though there are other sources (see p.78).

Long-term capital (to finance investment in buildings, machinery and government projects) is obtained through the capital market. As can be seen from Figure 21.4, this consists of the suppliers of long-term capital on the one hand and those requiring such capital on the other, the two being connected by a number of intermediaries, usually of a specialist nature. Many of these intermediaries were described when the methods by which such capital was raised were discussed in Chapter 6. Here we look briefly at the others.

1. Insurance Companies

Insurance companies receive premiums on the various types of risk insured against. Some of these premiums, such as those for insuring ships and property, are held only for relatively short periods, having, apart from the profit made, to be paid out against claims. But with life insurance, endowments and annuities, premiums are usually held for a long time before the final payment has to be made. Hence insurance companies have large sums of money to invest in long-term securities. These investments are spread over government and other public stocks, the shares and debentures of companies, property, and mortgages. Today 'institutional investors', of which insurance companies are the most important, supply the bulk of savings required for new issues.

FIGURE 21.4
The Capital Market

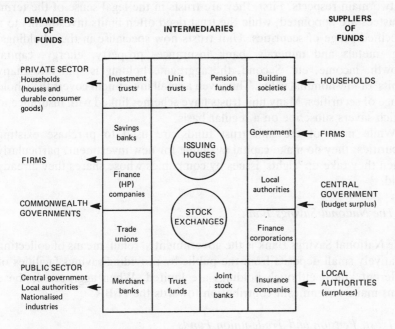

DEMANDERS OF FUNDS — **INTERMEDIARIES** — **SUPPLIERS OF FUNDS**

PRIVATE SECTOR
Households
(houses and durable consumer goods)

FIRMS

COMMONWEALTH GOVERNMENTS

PUBLIC SECTOR
Central government
Local authorities
Nationalised industries

Intermediaries:
Investment trusts | Unit trusts | Pension funds | Building societies
Savings banks | | Government
Finance (HP) companies | | Local authorities
Trade unions | | Finance corporations
Merchant banks | Trust funds | Joint stock banks | Insurance companies

ISSUING HOUSES
STOCK EXCHANGES

HOUSEHOLDS
FIRMS
CENTRAL GOVERNMENT (budget surplus)
LOCAL AUTHORITIES (surpluses)

Notes:

1 Arrows merely indicate direction, not particular intermediaries.

2 Intermediaries collect relatively small amounts of capital, which are channelled to where they are wanted.

3 Some intermediaries are mainly concerned with old issues.

4 Issuing houses assist the movement of funds; Stock Exchanges provide a market in old securities and thus encourage the provision of new funds.

2. Investment Trusts

Investors usually try to avoid 'putting all their eggs in one basket' by having an interest in the securities of many different types of enterprise. However, such spreading of risks requires some special knowledge of investment possibilities and, above all, sufficient resources. The small investor can overcome these two difficulties by buying shares in an investment trust. This invests its capital over a wide range of securities, and after paying expenses of management, the net yield from these investments are distributed as a dividend on its own shares. Thus investment trusts are not 'trusts' in the legal sense, but merely companies formed for the purpose of investment.

3. Unit Trusts

Unit trusts are a development of the investment trust idea, but they differ in two main respects. First, they are trusts in the legal sense of the term. Trustees are appointed, while the trust deed often limits investments to a specified range of securities. Unit trusts now specialise in their holdings, e.g. metals and minerals, bank insurance, property, energy, capital growth, income, etc. Second, the aggregate holding is split into many 'units' of low nominal value. Thus even a small investment covers the whole range of securities. Many unit trusts have schemes linked with insurance to which savers subscribe on a regular basis.

While most of the unit trust funds are used to purchase existing securities, they do make capital available for new investment, particularly when they take up 'rights' issues by companies whose shares they already hold.

4. The National Savings Bank

The National Savings Bank is the government's 'retail' means of collecting relatively small deposits from the public by providing savings facilities of different kinds, although holdings are limited. When aggregated, these sums make a significant contribution towards the PSBR.

5. Trust, Pension and Trade-union Funds

All these accumulate income which is reinvested in government securities, property, shares, etc.

6. Building Societies

These have a specialised function – the supply of long-term loans on the security of owner-occupied dwellings, though sometimes they lend on the security of farms or industrial or commercial premises. Their funds are derived chiefly from money invested in them by the general public, but their shares are not dealt in on the Stock Exchange, being cashable upon notice. Their liquid reserves are usually invested in government stock and local authority bonds.

7. Finance Corporations

The part played by the Industrial and Commercial Finance Corporation in providing funds for industry has already been described (p.86). There are, however, other somewhat similar corporations, whose funds are subscribed by different sources – the banks, the public and the government – which specialise in particular fields, e.g. Finance for Industry (which provides larger funds than the ICFC), the Agricultural Mortgage Corporation and the Export Credits Guarantee Department of the Department of Trade.

8. Finance Houses

These were originally independent companies set up to borrow from the public and banks in order to finance hire purchase of both consumer goods and machinery. Today the industry is dominated by the larger commercial banks. For instance, Mercantile Credit is now part of Barclays Bank, and the United Dominion Trust a part of the Trustee Savings Bank.

21.4 Markets in Securities: the Stock Exchange

History

By the second half of the seventeenth century there was a recognisable market for dealing in securities. This was gradually formalised and in 1773 the Stock Exchange occupied its first settled premises and from 1803 published its *Official List* of prices.

From 1908 its organisation was based on a separation between 'brokers' and 'jobbers'. Brokers acted on behalf of their clients buying from and selling shares to jobbers, the dealers in the shares. This 'single capacity' requirement was designed to protect clients. Whereas brokers worked on a commission basis, jobbers relied on profits from their dealings in UK securities for their income.

Recent Influences

This cosy arrangement was jolted in the early 1980s by two developments.

First, in 1979 government policy put greater emphasis on extending competition throughout the economy, and the Office of Fair Trading frowned upon fixed commissions as a monopolistic practice. Furthermore, the government was keen to maintain and even develop London's invisible earnings capacity (see p.415). The abolition of fixed commissions in New York in 1979 made dealing costs for British institutions lower there than in London, while the ending of exchange control in the same year meant that British investors were unhampered in investing in foreign securities.

The second development was technological – the introduction of electronic information and communication systems. This meant that changes in security prices in a dealing centre in one part of the world could be transmitted and indicated visually on screens in other centres. Thus the three leading centres, Tokyo, London and New York, became one market in which, because of the time difference, dealing took place over almost the twenty-four hours of the day.

Thus the pressure was on the Stock Exchange to revise its fixed commission arrangements and to adopt a less parochial outlook. The actual changes took place on 27 October 1986 and produced such an immediate upheaval that it was referred to as 'Big Bang'.

'Big Bang'

The Stock Exchange agreed with the Secretary of State for Trade and Industry to end fixed commissions. But since this would have forced many brokers out of business it was necessary to end the 'single capacity' rule and allow members to act in a dual capacity both as agents for clients and dealers. The main dealers are termed 'market-makers'.

Market-makers negotiate their own commissions for buying and selling shares, and on the larger orders put through by the institutions can offer attractive terms. While private investors can also negotiate terms, the size of their business is not deemed profitable by the market-makers and commission rates remain much as they were before 'Big Bang'. This leaves room for brokers to earn a respectable living by acting as the retailer for the private investor, providing a personal contact and offering advice and even research.

Further Developments

'Big Bang' proved to be the catalyst for even more far-reaching developments. The government's desire to establish London as an international trading centre necessitated making dealing costs more competitive and so stamp duty on shares was reduced to $\frac{1}{2}$ per cent. But to trade in competition with the larger Japanese and American firms UK dealers had to have access to considerably more capital in order to carry stocks of securities. Thus firms had to merge or, more usually, were taken over by larger financial institutions, such as the merchant banks.

In this, however, 'Big Bang' simply gave impetus to the movement which was already taking place of linking related services in one firm. We can take the major clearing-banks as an example. As was mentioned above, they have already acquired an interest in hire purchase finance and have now followed up their provision of loans for house purchase by acquiring firms of estate agents. The idea has been extended into stock-broking. Market-making, however, has been left to the merchant banks who are less interested in the retail side of finance.

The Stock Exchange Today

We still refer to the 'Stock Exchange' although dealing is no longer on the 'floor of the House'. Instead there is the Stock Exchange Automated Quotation system (SEAQ) which is the electronic market-place of the London stock market. Information from the 64 market-makers on prices and deals made is fed into SEAQ and displayed on screens. This enables the market-maker to quote a selling price and a lower buying price. The difference will be larger when the shares are only dealt in infrequently or where the sale of comparatively few shares can lead to a large fall in price. Unfavourable news, such as a poor monthly balance of payments figure, will cause him to lower prices as a precautionary measure. These new prices would be recorded on the SEAQ screen for the rest of the market.

As noted in Chapter 6, the markets in which securities are dealt in are:

(1) The Stock Exchange, the main market;
(2) the Unlisted Securities Market (USM), a market for smaller companies seeking moderate sums of outside finance.

Both of the above are part of the Stock Exchange. The Over-the-Counter Market (OTC) is independent, but the Stock Exchange is developing a Third Market which will eventually take over present OTC business.

The government has a strong interest in the integrity of the market but opted for allowing the City to regulate itself rather than impose centralised control. The Secretary of State for Trade and Industry appointed a Securities and Investments Board (SIB) which oversees six Self-Regulating Organisations (SRO) and City dealers have to belong to one of these. The Stock Exchange, as a SRO, issues guidelines to members and ensures that these rules are adhered to.

Economic Functions

As the two main UK markets in securities are still subject to the discipline and regulations of the Stock Exchange Council, both are included under the omnibus term of 'the Stock Exchange'.

Critics of the Stock Exchange tend to ignore its real functions and to concentrate on its speculative aspects. It is true that the facilities offered do provide openings for speculation. The fortnightly account allows a speculator to buy securities at the beginning and sell within fourteen days without ever having to put up any money. A speculator who buys securities because he thinks the price will rise is said to be a 'bull'; he hopes to sell them at a profit before the end of the account. On the other hand, a 'bear' sells securities he does not possess because he expects the price to fall before they have to be delivered.

The difficulty concerning speculation is that both optimism and pessimism are contagious and so the market becomes extremely susceptible to both over-confidence and panic. Indeed, expectations are 'self-fulfilling': people who expect the price of securities to rise bid for them, thereby sending up their price, and vice versa. The result is that the prices of stocks and shares may be written up or down not through changes in their earnings prospects but simply through waves of confidence or mistrust.

Even so, we must not forget that some speculation may be advantageous. Expert professional operators tend to steady prices through their function of holding stocks (see below). This also permits securities to be bought and sold at any time, thereby making them more liquid. The great difficulty occurs in distinguishing harmful speculation from genuine investment, for with all investment there is a certain element of risk. In any case the magnitude of the speculative business must not be overestimated. Most purchases represent genuine investment conducted on behalf of investment trusts, insurance companies, pension funds, building societies and private individuals.

The truth is that, for the following reasons, an organised market in securities is an indispensable part of the mechanism of a capitalist economy.

1. It Facilitates Borrowing by the Government and Industry

If people are to be encouraged to lend to industry and the government by the purchase of securities, they must be satisfied that they will subsequently be able to sell easily those investments which they no longer wish to hold. Such an assurance is afforded to any holder of a fairly well-known security by the Stock Exchange, for it provides a permanent market bringing together sellers and buyers.

Thus, indirectly, the Stock Exchange encourages savers to lend to the government or to invest in industry. Indeed, if a new issue receives a Stock Exchange quotation, the chances of its success are considerably enhanced.

2. Through the Market-makers, it Helps to even out Short-run Price Fluctuations in Securities

By holding stocks of shares, a dealer provides in the short run a buffer against speculation by outsiders. This is because he does not merely 'match' a buyer with a seller but acts like a wholesaler, holding stocks of securities. Since he usually specialises in dealing in certain securities, he obtains an intimate knowledge of them. Thus when the public is pessimistic and selling, he may be more optimistic in his outlook and consider that the drop in price is not likely to continue. He therefore takes these securities on to his book. Similarly, when the public is rushing to buy he will, when he considers the price has reached its zenith, sell from his stocks. The effect in both cases is to even out the fluctuations in price, for, in the first case, he increases his demand as supply increases, and, in the second, he increases supply as demand increases.

3. *It Advertises Security Prices*

The publication of current Stock Exchange prices enables the public to follow the fortunes of their investment and to channel their savings into profitable enterprises.

4. *It Protects the Public Against Malpractices and Fraud*

With dealers acting in a dual-capacity, the previous safeguard of a client that his broker acted solely on his behalf was lost. Under the new arrangements there are two safeguards, the open display of prices on the SEAQ screen and the regulations of the Stock Exchange Council as a SRO. The Council insists on a high standard of professional conduct from its members. Should any member default, the investor is indemnified out of the Stock Exchange Compensation Fund.

The *Official List* of securities indicates that the Stock Exchange considers shares are reputable. Permission to deal is withdrawn if any doubts arise about the conduct of a company's affairs.

5. *It Provides a Mechanism for the Raising of Capital by the Issue of Securities*

While the Stock Exchange is essentially a market for dealing in 'old' securities, the success of a new issue to raise capital is enhanced if a promise can be made of a Stock Exchange quotation for it. More directly, brokers and dealers will actively arrange for certain clients to provide capital for firms wishing to expand (see p.86).

6. *It Reflects the Country's Economic Prospects*

The movement of the market acts as a barometer which points to the economic prospects of the country – whether as 'set fair', or otherwise!

22 Commercial Banks

By far the largest part of the business of the commercial banks today is carried on by the 'Big Four'. Thus, unlike the systems of other countries, such as the USA, which are composed of a large number of unitary small banks, Britain has only a few large banks, each having a network of branches throughout the country.

This system of branch banking has two main merits. The first is that the larger unit of operation can enjoy the advantages of large-scale production. The second, and more important, is that there is less risk of failure when financial reserves are concentrated in a large bank than where the banking activities for a particular locality are conducted by a small bank. The fortunes of the small bank are tied up with the fortunes of the locality which, especially if the main activity is farming, may be liable to periodic fluctuations. In short, with a large bank, risks are spread geographically. On the other hand, the large unit has to suffer disadvantages on the managerial side, for usually loans of any size have to be sanctioned by Head Office. This is in sharp contrast to the position of the small unit which can grant even large loans on the spot according to its own judgement, based on its knowledge of local conditions.

22.1 The Creation of Credit

The Cheque System

Banks are companies which exist to make profits for the shareholders. They do this by borrowing money from 'depositors' and relending it at a higher rate of interest to other people. Borrowers are private persons, companies, public corporations, the money market and the government. The more a bank can lend, the greater will be its profits.

People who hold a current account at a bank can settle their debts by cheque. This is a very convenient form of payment. Cheques may be sent safely through the post, can be written for the exact amount, obviate carrying round large sums of money and form a permanent record of payment.

Credit cards possess somewhat similar attributes, and in addition can be used to pay for goods ordered over the phone but usually only up to a stipulated limit.

But the use of cheques and credit cards is, as we shall see, advantageous to banks. Thus, to advertise their business, to induce customers to pay by cheque rather than by cash, and to encourage people to keep sums of money with them, banks perform many services outside their main business of borrowing and lending money – keeping accounts, making standing-order payments, providing night-safe and cash dispenser facilities, paying bills by credit transfers, purchasing securities, transacting foreign work, storing valuables, acting as executors, etc.

The Cheque as a Substitute for Cash

Cheques lead to a reduction in the use of cash. Suppose that I have paid £1000 into my banking account. Imagine, too, that my builder banks at the same branch and that I owe him £500. I simply write him a cheque for that amount, and he pays this into the bank. To complete the transaction, my account is debited by £500, and his account is credited by that amount. What it is important to observe, however, is that in the settlement of the debt no actual *cash* changes hands. A mere book entry in both accounts has completed the transaction.

Perhaps my builder will, towards the end of the week, withdraw some cash to pay workers' wages. But it is likely that most payments, e.g. for building materials, petrol and lorry servicing, will be by cheque. Similarly, while from the £500 still standing to my account I may withdraw some cash to cover everyday housekeeping expenses, the probability is that many of my bills, e.g. club subscription, half-yearly rates, hire-purchase instalments on the car, mortgage repayments, will be settled by cheque or by transfer directly from my account. Furthermore, even where cash is withdrawn, it is often compensated for by cash being paid in.

With the development of the cheque system, the proportion of cash which is required for transactions has decreased. Let us assume a simple model in which the banks operate free of government control but have discovered that in practice only 10 per cent of their total deposits need be retained in cash to cover all demands for cash withdrawals. In short, only £100 of my original deposit of £1000 is needed to form an adequate cash reserve.

The Creation of Credit

It is obvious, therefore, that £900 of my original cash deposit of £1000 could be lent by the bank to a third party without me or anybody else being the wiser. What is not quite so obvious is that the bank can go much further than this – and does!

Let us assume that there is only one bank and that all lending is in the form of advances (see pp.383–4). When a person is granted a loan by a bank manager, all that happens is that the borrower's account is credited with the amount of the loan, or, alternatively, he is authorised to overdraw his account up to the stipulated limit. In other words, a deposit is created by the bank in the name of the borrower.

When the loan is spent, the borrower will probably pay by cheque. If this happens, there is no immediate demand for cash. There is no reason, therefore, why the whole of my cash deposit of £1000 should not act as the safe cash reserve for deposits of a much larger sum created by the bank's lending activities. But the bank must not overdo this credit creation. To be safe, our model has assumed, cash must always form one-tenth of total deposits. This means that the bank can grant a loan of up to £9000. Because it is the only bank, there is no need to fear that cheques drawn on it will be paid into another bank and eventually presented for cash. In general, the deposit to cash multiplier equals:

$$\frac{1}{\text{the reserve asset ratio}}$$

The process of credit creation is illustrated in Figure 22.1. X pays £1000 in cash into the bank. This allows the bank to make a loan of £9000 to B who now settles debts to C and D of £4000 and £5000 respectively by sending them cheques. These cheques are paid into the bank. C withdraws cash rather heavily, £700; but this is compensated for by D, who only withdraws £200 in cash. This leaves £100 cash – enough to cover the average withdrawal which X is likely to make. At the same time as these cash withdrawals are being made, other cash is being paid in, thereby maintaining the 10 per cent ratio.

In practice, there are many banks, but for the purpose of credit creation they are virtually one bank, because they are able to eliminate a large demand for cash from each other by their central clearing arrangements. Moreover, banks keep in line with one another as regards their credit creation. Were one bank to adopt, say, a 6 per cent cash ratio, it would find that because its customers were making such a large volume of payments to persons who banked elsewhere, it would be continually called upon to settle a debt with the other banks in cash at the end of the day's clearing, so that its cash reserve would fall below the safe level.

FIGURE 22.1
How a Bank Creates Credit

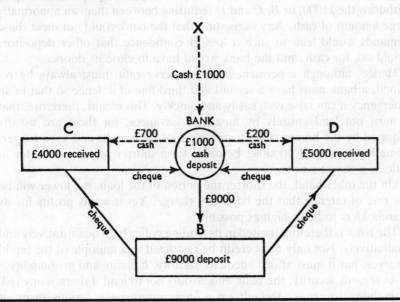

The Effect of Lending on the Bank's Balance-sheet

Suppose that the receipt of the £1000 in cash and the loan to *B* are the sole activities of the bank so far. We ignore shareholders' capital. Its balance-sheet will then be as follows:

Liabilities	£	Assets	£
Deposits:			
deposit account	1 000	Cash in till	1 000
current account	9 000	Advances	9 000
	10 000		10 000

The advance to *B* is an asset; it is an outstanding debt. On the other hand, *B*'s account has been credited with a deposit of £9000 – just as though *B* had paid it in. It can be seen, therefore that *every loan creates a deposit*.

22.2 Considerations Determining a Bank's Lending Policy

In practice, the structure of the bank's assets is more varied than that above. This can be explained as follows.

Creating deposits in order to lend at a profit entails certain risks. In the first place, the loan may not be repaid. Second, and more important, there may be a run on the bank for cash, X (the original depositor) wishing to withdraw the £1000, or B, C and D requiring between them an abnormally large amount of cash. Any suggestion that the bank could not meet these demands would lead to such a loss of confidence that other depositors would ask for cash, and the bank would have to close its doors.

Hence, although a permanent cash reserve ratio must always be retained, a bank must have a second and third line of defence so that in an emergency it can raise cash easily and quickly. This means, therefore, that it must not lend entirely by means of advances, for these are usually required by the borrower for a minimum of six months and even longer. Some loans must, if possible, be made for a shorter period – even for as little as a day at a time.

On the other hand, the shorter the period of the loan, the lower will be the rate of interest that the bank can charge. Yet it wants profits for its shareholders to be as high as possible.

The bank is therefore limited in its lending policy both quantitatively and qualitatively. Not only must credit be restricted to a multiple of the liquid reserves, but it must afford adequate *security, liquidity* and *profitability*.

As regards security, the bank endeavours not to lend if there is any risk of inability to repay. Default on a loan represents a serious error of judgement by the bank manager. While it usually requires collateral, e.g. an insurance policy, the deeds of a house, or share certificates, this is regarded more as a weapon to strengthen its demand for repayment against an evasive borrower than as a safeguard against default. Collateral therefore really assists liquidity; if there were a risk of outright default, the bank would not lend.

Liquidity and profitability pull in opposite directions – the shorter the period of the loan, the greater the bank's liquidity, but the less it will earn by way of interest. The difficulty is resolved by a compromise: (*a*) loans are divided among different types of borrower and for different periods of time; (*b*) the different types of loan are kept fairly close to carefully worked out proportions. In short, the bank, for financial prudence, maintains a 'portfolio' of assets.

22.3 The Distribution of a Bank's Assets

How in practice a bank reconciles the aims of liquidity and profitability can be seen by studying its sterling assets. This is possible because, apart from its cash, buildings and goodwill, loans represent its sole assets. Just as 'sundry debtors' appears on the asset side of a firm's balance-sheet, so debts outstanding to a bank represent assets to it. The position is shown in Figures 22.2 and 22.3.

Bills, which are Treasury bills, local authority and trade bills, are obtained chiefly from the discount houses (though some may be discounted directly for customers) and are held for the remainder of their currency – usually two months.

FIGURE 22.2
The Nature and Distribution of a Bank's Main Assets

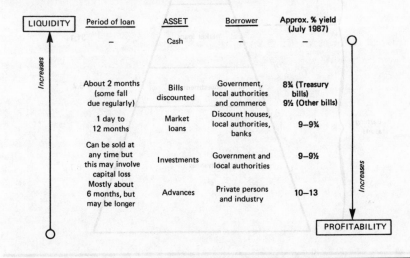

LIQUIDITY	Period of loan	ASSET	Borrower	Approx. % yield (July 1987)
	–	Cash	–	–
	About 2 months (some fall due regularly)	Bills discounted	Government, local authorities and commerce	8¾ (Treasury bills) 9½ (Other bills)
	1 day to 12 months	Market loans	Discount houses, local authorities, banks	9–9¾
	Can be sold at any time but this may involve capital loss	Investments	Government and local authorities	9–9½
	Mostly about 6 months, but may be longer	Advances	Private persons and industry	10–13

Increases (Liquidity) *Increases* (Profitability)

PROFITABILITY

Market loans consist mainly of: (*a*) money at call and short notice which enables the discount houses to discount bills and hold them for a month or so before passing them on to the banks (see p.266); (*b*) loans of less than a year to local authorities; (*c*) certificates of deposit (see p.269); (*d*) short-term loans to other monetary authorities.

Investments are medium- and long-term government securities bought on the open market.

Advances, to nationalised industries, companies and personal borrowers, are the most profitable (1 to 4 per cent above base rate) but also the least liquid of all the bank's assets. The main object of advances is to provide the working capital for industry and commerce. The type of loan preferred is 'self-liquidating' within a period of about six months. A good example is a loan made to a farmer, who borrows to buy seed and fertilisers and to pay wages, and repays the loan when the harvest is sold. Similarly, a

FIGURE 22.3
The Pyramids of Credit

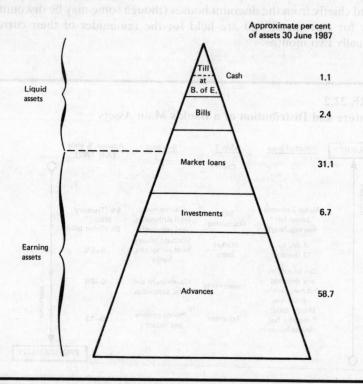

Approximate per cent
of assets 30 June 1987

Till / at B. of E. — Cash	1.1
Bills	2.4
Market loans	31.1
Investments	6.7
Advances	58.7

Liquid assets

Earning assets

manufacturer may borrow to employ additional labour and raw materials just prior to Christmas in order to increase production. When payment is received for those goods the farmer can repay the overdraft. Borrowers are often allowed to 'roll over' their overdrafts.

Banks also make a large number of 'personal loans', usually modest sums to cover exceptional items of personal expenditure. Repayments are spread over the term of the loan, though interest is charged at an agreed rate on the full amount of the loan for the whole of the period.

At one time banks refrained from providing long-term capital for firms, leaving this to the agencies in the capital market. In recent years, however, they have competed successfully in financing such long-term capital projects as the building of additional factory accommodation and the purchase of farms and houses. These fixed assets are the security required, though the bank's main consideration is whether or not the venture is likely to succeed.

It must be emphasised that, apart from cash and bank buildings, these assets are covered only by credit created by the bank. For example, Treasury bills and government securities are paid for by cheques which will increase the accounts of the sellers. If they are new issues, there is an addition to the government account at the Bank of England; if they are old issues, the bank is virtually taking over from somebody else a loan already made to the government. In writing these cheques, the bank increases its liabilities, for book-entry deposits have to be created to cover them. This 'pyramid of credit', created to buy earning assets and to make loans upon a minimum liquid assets basis, is shown in Figure 22.3.

22.4 Modification of the Cash-ratio Approach

The Importance of Liquid Assets as a Whole

Our explanation of how a bank creates credit has followed traditional lines: credit bears a fixed relationship to the cash reserves. This approach is the easiest to understand and underlines the main principles involved.

However, while the basic principles of credit creation still hold true, some modification is necessary to allow for modern banking practice.

Today, banks are more concerned with the general liquidity position when deciding on their lending policy than with one item, cash. This tendency of cash to lose significance originally stemmed from the introduction of the Treasury bill, which, through government support, became almost as good as cash. Improved markets for loans, e.g. the parallel money markets described in Chapter 21, also increase liquidity and, as a result, such loans can be regarded as 'near money'.

External Limitations on the Banks' Lending Policy

Indeed, the monetary authorities (that is, the Bank of England acting as agent for the Treasury) now regard cash simply as the small change of the monetary system, and so they vary it according to the needs of trade.

It follows, therefore, that, if the authorities wish to control the amount of credit which can be created by banks, their attention will have to be directed to the size of the total assets which the banks hold. It is to these external limitations on the banks' lending ability to which we now turn.

23 The Bank of England

The Bank of England, established by Act of Parliament in 1694, remained a joint-stock company until it was nationalised in 1946. But, although started as a private enterprise, the Bank of England has, for the past 200 years, followed policies which have placed the needs of the country as a whole before its own financial interests. Nationalisation merely formalised its position as a 'central bank' – the institution which, on behalf of the government, exercises the ultimate control over the policies of the joint-stock banks and other financial institutions. In the words of the 1959 Radcliffe Report, 'The Bank of England stands as the market operator between the public sector (to which it belongs) and the private sector.' The whole of its capital stock is now owned by the state, and its affairs are regulated by a Court of Directors, consisting of a Governor, a Deputy-Governor and sixteen Directors appointed by the Crown, though not more than four of the Directors can be full-time officers. The members of the Court are distinguished people from finance, industry and commerce, and it is usual for the full-time members to be professional bankers with experience of work in the Bank of England.

23.1 Functions of the Bank of England

We need deal only briefly with most of the Bank's functions.

1. It Issues Notes

The Bank of England is the only ultimate source from which the private sector can obtain cash. It obtains coins from the Royal Mint, but issues notes itself. The *fiduciary issue* (the amount by which the note issue is allowed to exceed the Bank's holding of gold) has ceased to have any relevance. Since 1939 the gold reserves of the Bank have been held in the

Exchange Equalisation Account, and thus today the notes issued are backed almost entirely by Treasury bills, other marketable government securities and commercial bills.

While in England and Wales the Bank of England is the sole note-issuing authority, Scottish and Northern Ireland banks can issue their own notes, though most of these have to be covered by Bank of England notes.

2. It is the Government's Banker

The government has always been the most important customer of the Bank of England. As a result the Bank has acquired the functions of a 'central bank' (see p.286). But it also performs many tasks for the government which spring from the normal banker–customer relationships:

(a) It keeps the central government accounts (the Consolidated Fund and the National Loans Fund) and the accounts of many government departments.

(b) It gives assistance by means of 'Ways and Means' advances if the account goes temporarily 'into the red'.

(c) It manages the government's borrowing through the issue of Treasury bills and government stock. This involves arranging new issues and conversions, paying interest, keeping the registers, and recording transfers.

(d) It advises the government on financial matters.

3. It is the Bankers' Bank

The next most important customers of the Bank of England are the joint-stock banks. The London clearing banks hold cash at the Bank of England and they use the Bank very much as a private customer uses his bank. In particular, they:

(a) draw notes and coin from their balances at the Bank as required;

(b) set off the net payment which has to be made to other banks as a result of the day's clearing by drawing on the balance held at the Bank of England;

(c) take advice on financial matters from the Bank.

4. It Manages the Exchange Equalisation Account (see p.431)

5. It Holds the Gold and Foreign Currency Reserves

The importance of these reserves is that, for a time, they can take the strain when sterling is under pressure. Until 1979 the reserves were protected by various degrees of exchange control administered by the Bank of England.

Today the Bank mainly operates by varying the UK short-term interest rate (see p.474) but, where necessary, it will also arrange loans from other central banks.

6. It has Financial Responsibilities Internationally

(a) The Bank of England maintains close contact with the central banks and monetary authorities of other countries, chiefly with the aim of bringing greater stability to international monetary affairs.
(b) It provides banking services for the central banks of non-sterling countries, e.g. holds and manages their holdings of sterling.
(c) It participates in the work of certain international financial institutions, such as the Bank for International Settlements, the International Monetary Fund, the International Bank for Reconstruction and Development, and the European Monetary Agreement.

7. It Manages the Monetary System of the UK in Accordance with Government Policy

The Bank of England is the central bank of the monetary system of the UK. It is therefore responsible for seeing that the monetary system of the country is working in harmony with the government economic policy. In broad terms, this means varying the cost and availability of credit.

Where people (firms and private persons) can obtain credit on relatively easy terms, the demand for goods (both producer and consumer goods) will normally increase. If there is unemployment, this can be quite a good thing, for the economy will expand and idle resources be put to work (though there is some disagreement as to whether this will be permanent — see pp.359–63). But expansion may be accompanied by rising prices which becomes more serious as we approach full employment.

The Bank of England, therefore, has frequently to adjust the supply of credit to the prevailing economic situation as seen by itself and the Treasury, though the latter will have the last word. We now examine how the Bank seeks to achieve this.

23.2 Principles of Monetary Control

Approaches to Monetary Policy

When the Conservative government took over in 1979, greater emphasis was placed on monetary policy as a means of controlling inflation (See Chapter 27).

Monetary policy can be approached in two main ways: (a) by controlling the supply of credit quantitatively – that is, restraining lending by financial institutions; (*b*) by controlling the *demand* for credit by manipulating its price – that is, varying the rate of interest.

The Old System of Competition and Credit Control (CCC)

The system of CCC initiated in 1971 put the emphasis on controlling the supply of credit *quantitatively*. There were four main weapons:

1. The Minimum Reserve Assets Ratio

The foundation of the policy rested on the ability of the Bank of England to dictate to the banks and other lending institutions their minimum liquidity ratio.

Each bank was originally required to observe a minimum reserve ratio of $12\frac{1}{2}$ per cent of 'eligible reserve assets' (liquid assets as defined by the Bank of England) to 'eligible liabilities' (broadly net bank deposits).

2. Open-market Operations

By buying or selling government securities on the open market, the Bank of England can vary the ability of the banks to create credit. Suppose it sells long-term securities. The increase in the supply offered lowers their price (that is, raises the rate of interest) until the total offering has been bought by the banks or by their customers. But cash will be necessary to pay for them, and so the banks' cash balances at the Bank of England will fall. In other words, the liquid reserve assets held by the banks are reduced and, if previously banks had made loans to the maximum possible extent, they will be forced to squeeze their advances.

Alternatively the Bank of England may put the pressure on the short end of the market by varying the weekly offer of Treasury bills. Inasmuch as these bills are bought initially outside the banks, the cash balances of the bank's customers can be made to fall, and hence the cash of the banks will likewise fall.

3. Special Deposits

The supply of credit can be influenced by calls for special deposits, requiring banks to deposit with the Bank of England a prescribed percentage of their total eligible liabilities. Such special deposits reduce the bank's liquid assets and thus the bank's ability to make loans.

4. Minimum Lending Rate

The minimum lending rate (MLR) was the rate of interest at which the Bank of England would help the discount houses as lender of last resort.

Although the rate was announced each Thursday, it was only changed for compelling reasons and so its effect was to give some stability to interest rates in general.

At various times the above weapons were supplemented by *requests* to the banks to restrict or discriminate in their lending, *funding* operations to reduce overall liquidity by converting government short-term borrowing into long-term debt, and *supplementary deposits* (the 'corset') which required a bank whose interest-bearing deposits had risen faster than a specified rate to place with the Bank of England a given proportion of the excess.

The Weaknesses of CCC

The main purpose of quantitative controls was to reduce the need to raise interest rates, at least in the short term, by causing banks to ration their lending. In practice, quantitative controls only postponed the rise in interest rates needed. At the same time they not only tended to reduce competition but caused funds to move out of the controlled banking sector, while the creation of money substitutes (e.g. the commercial bill of exchange) weakened the role of sterling M3 as a monitor of the money supply. Above all, quantitative controls ceased to be effective in 1979 when exchange controls were abolished for funds could now be obtained from overseas sources.

The Present System (July 1987)

Instead of following a monetary base policy of requiring a $12\frac{1}{2}$ per cent ratio of eligible reserve assets to eligible liabilities, the Bank now adjusts the supply of credit by influencing the short-term rate of interest.

But with the ending of exchange control and the internationalisation of the market in finance, the actual rate is *determined* in the wholesale markets, such as the large inter-bank market. Only when the market is short of cash does the Bank have the whip hand, as a *'lender of last resort'*. This arises as follows.

Because the operations of financial markets depend largely on the creation of credit, any jolt to confidence can have a cumulative destabilising effect. It is recognised, therefore, that the Bank of England will always act to prevent the financial chaos which would otherwise result.

Although its earlier practice of regularly announcing a MLR has now been discontinued, it has the right to indicate in advance the minimum rate at which it will lend for a short period ahead. The kind of situation where this could happen is when a major economic package is announced where interest rates are an important element in the changes envisaged.

Normally, the Bank operates through the discount market. If the discount houses are short of cash to repay money at call, they will have to offer bills, either Treasury bills or eligible bank bills, to the Bank of England and state their price. The Bank of England aims to keep interest rates within an undisclosed band which is moved from time to time in accordance with policy considerations. If, therefore, the Bank does not like the price, it turns them down and the market responds to the Bank's signal, the commercial banks' base rates being adjusted accordingly. Thus while it is the market which proposes short-term interest rates, it is the Bank which has the final word. Twice a day the Bank announces the rates at which it has bought and sold bills.

FIGURE 23.1
The UK Banking Sector

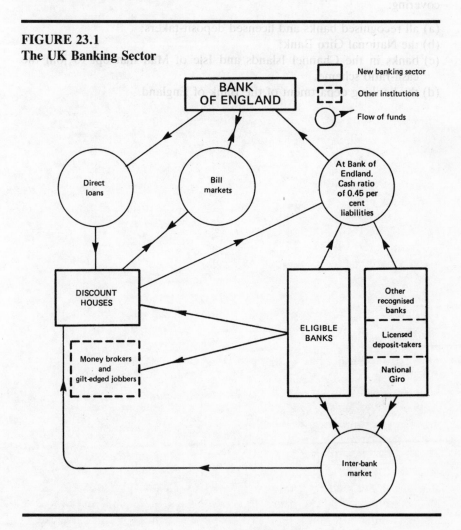

The Bank publishes a list of banks and other institutions whose bills are eligible for discount at the Bank.

Although *special deposits* have been retained and extended to all institutions with eligible reserves of over £10 million, they are only called for in most exceptional circumstances.

How monetary policy is in practice used to regulate the economy is described in Chapter 36.

The Monetary Sector

Monetary policy now embraces a wider monetary sector (Figure 23.1) covering:

(a) all recognised banks and licensed deposit-takers;
(b) the National Giro Bank;
(c) banks in the Channel Islands and Isle of Man that opt to join the cash-ratio scheme;
(d) the banking department of the Bank of England.

Part VI

The Government and the Economy

24 The National Income

In Chapter 2 we summarised the various objectives of government policy. While some of these, e.g. the development of certain industries, the control of monopolies or the protection of workers in 'sweated' industries, can be achieved by intervention in particular parts of the economy, certain broad objectives, e.g. full employment, a stable price level, a healthy balance of payments and adequate growth, require government regulation of the economy as a whole.

But, to be successful, such regulation must be based on adequate information. Hence measurements are made of a variety of items and published yearly in *The United Kingdom National Accounts* (The CSO Blue Book). Later we shall indicate how these figures can be used to plan the economy. For the time being we are concerned with the overall figure – the level of the national income.

24.1 The Principle Upon which Calculation of the National Income is Based

Income, as we have seen, is a flow of wealth (goods and services) over a period of time. If our income rises, we can enjoy more goods and services.

But, to enjoy goods, they must be produced. A nation's income, then, is basically the same as its output over a period. Thus national income is the total money value of all goods and services produced by the country during the year. The question is: 'How can we measure this money value?'

We can approach the problem by studying the different ways in which we can arrive at the value of a table. Figure 24.1 shows that the value of the table can be obtained by taking the value of the final product (£100) or by totalling the value added by each firm in the different stages of production. Thus the output of the tree-grower is what is received for the tree (£30, which, we assume, cost £20 in wages to produce, leaving £10 profit. The

FIGURE 24.1
Value of Total Product Equals Sum of Values Added by Each Firm

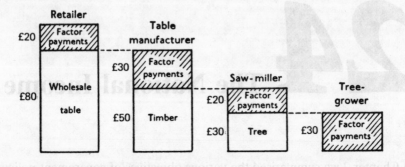

output of the saw-miller is what is received for the timber (£50) less what was paid for the tree. Again, this output (£20) is made up of wages and profit. And so on. The total of these added values equals the value of the final table. Thus we could obtain the value of the table by adding the *output* of the tree-grower (forestry), the outputs of the saw-miller and table manufacturer (manufacturing) and the output of the retailer (distribution).

We could have added up these individual outputs in a different way. Instead of putting them in industry categories, we could have added them according to the type of factor payment – wages, salaries, rent or profit. This gives us the *income* method of measuring output.

Thus, if we assume (*a*) no government taxation or spending, (*b*) no economic connections with the outside world, we can obtain the national income either (1) by totalling the value of final output during the year or, what is the same thing, by totalling the value added to the goods and services by each firm, or (2) by totally the various factor payments during the year – wages, rent, profit.

There is, however, yet another method of calculating the national income. The value of the table in Figure 24.1 is what was spent on it. If the table had sold for only £90, that would have been the value of the final output. The final factor payment – profit to the retailer – would have been only £10 (assuming that the wholesale price had remained unchanged). It follows, therefore, that we can obtain the national income by totalling *expenditure* on final products over the year.

It must be emphasised that the money values of output, income and expenditure are *identical by definition*. They simply *measure* the national income in different ways. This was shown by the fact that factor payments were automatically reduced by £10 when the table sold for £90 instead £100. It can be further illustrated by looking at expenditure in more detail.

Assume the value of the national output (consisting of consumer goods and capital goods) is £1000 million. Factor payments (wages, rent, profit) must therefore equal £1000 million. Suppose, however, that the spending of households on consumer goods (consumption) and the spending of firms on capital goods (investment) does not amount to the income each has received. The result is an addition to stocks – 'unintentional' investment by firms which have, as it were, 'bought in' some of their products.

To summarise, the national income is the national output – the total value of all goods and services produced by the country during the year. We can regard it as:

1. The cost of the national output expressed as the earnings (wages, rent, profit) of all the factors of production combining to produce it.
2. The total amount spent on final goods and services for consumption and investment purposes during the year.
3. The total of the values of the goods and services produced by the various industries, public authorities, etc., during the year.

Before we proceed to examine in more detail the actual process of measuring these three identities, it is convenient if first we consider some of the general difficulties which arise and how they are overcome.

24.2 National Income Calculations in Practice

General Difficulties

Difficulties arise in all calculations of the national income because of the following.

1. The Necessity of Having to make Arbitrary Definitions

(a) *Production*. In calculating the national income, only those goods and services which are paid for are normally included. Because calculations have to be made in money terms, the inclusion of other goods and services would involve imputing a value to them. But where would you draw the line? If you give a value to certain jobs which someone does personally – growing vegetables in the garden, cleaning the car, painting the house – then why not include cleaning one's shoes, driving to work, and so on?

On the other hand, excluding what a person does personally may have the effect of distorting national income figures. As the division of labour develops and the number of exchanges consequently increases, a country's national income can rise even though there may have been no addition to real output! (See also pp.307 and 308.)

An *imputed* money value is included for certain payments in kind which are recognised as a regular part of a person's income earnings, for example goods produced and consumed by a farmer, food, etc., of the armed forces and of domestic servants.

(*b*)   *The value of the services rendered by consumer durable goods.* A table, TV set, dish-washer, car, etc., render services for many years. Should we not, therefore, give a yearly value to such services? Once again we face the difficulties mentioned above of imputing a value and knowing where to stop. A toothbrush, pots and pans, all render services over their life! All such goods, therefore, are included at their full value when they are bought, and subsequent services are ignored.

The one exception is owner-occupied houses. Here the rateable value provides a basis for an imputed value. Including a notional rent keeps owner-occupied houses in line with property owned for letting (income shown as rents or profits of companies) and prevents the national income falling as more people become owner-occupiers!

(*c*)   *Government services.* Education and health services, although provided by the state, are obviously no different from similar services for which some persons pay. Consequently, they are included in national income at cost. But how should we view the work of persons maintaining law and order and defence? The police, for instance when helping children cross the road, are providing a consumer service. But at night their chief task may be guarding banks and factories against theft, and in doing so they are really furthering the productive process. Strictly, therefore, to avoid double-counting, this part should be excluded from output calculations. Nevertheless, because in practice it is impossible to differentiate between the two activities, all police services, and indeed all government services (including defence), are included at cost in the national output (see also p.307).

2. Inadequate Information

The sources from which data are obtained were not specifically designed to provide information for national income calculations. Thus not only do income-tax returns fail to cover the small-income groups, but they err on the side of understatement. Similarly, the *Census of Production* and the *Census of Distribution* are only taken at approximately five-year intervals. Thus many figures must simply be estimates based on samples.

Information, too, may be incomplete. Income-tax returns would not show income from state-owned property or profits of public corporations.

The result is that the national income figure obtained by the three methods of calculation do not coincide. In practice, therefore, the expenditure calculation is taken as the datum, a 'residual error' being provided for the other two to bring them into line (see Table 24.1).

But it is 'depreciation' which presents the major problem, for the figure given by companies, etc., is really only a book figure determined by tax regulations. There is no accurate figure for real depreciation, and thus it is largely the practice now to refer to Gross National Product rather than to National Income (see p.305).

3. *The Danger of Double-counting*

As we shall see, care must be taken to exclude transfer incomes when adding up national income (see p.302), the contribution to production made by other firms when calculating national output (see p.304) and indirect taxes when calculating national expenditure (see p.304).

A fourth way in which a form of double-counting can occur is through 'stock appreciation'. When there is a rise in the general level of prices, the value of stocks of raw materials and goods rises. While this adds to the profits of firms holding such stocks, it represents no increase in real output. Such gains must therefore be deducted from the income and output figures.

4. *Complications Arising from Relationships with other Countries*

Methods of calculating national income must take into account the effects of international trade and international indebtedness.

(a) *Trade*. British people spend some of their income on foreign goods, while foreigners buy British goods. In calculating national *expenditure*, therefore, we have to deduct the value of goods and services imported (since they have not been produced by Britain) and add the value of goods and services exported (where income has been earned by factors in Britain).

(b) *Indebtedness*. If, within a family, a father increases his son's pocket-money, it does not increase the family income. Instead it merely effects a redistribution, the father having less and the son more. But if the boy's income is suddenly augmented by a wealthy aunt who makes him a regular allowance, then the family income is increased. Similarly with the nation; while transfer incomes do not increase national income, payments by foreigners do. These payments arise chiefly as interest and dividends received on loans and investments made abroad. They can be regarded as payments to property abroad owned by British people, e.g. the paper factories of the Bowater Corporation in Canada and the USA. Similarly, interest and dividends have to be paid to foreigners who have invested in Britain.

Table 24.1
Calculations of the National Income of the UK, 1985

A. INCOME

	£m
Income from employment	195 350
Income from self-employment	28 859
Gross trading profits of companies	52 977
Gross trading surplus, public corporations	7 106
Gross trading surplus, general government enterprises	264
Rent	20 541
Imputed charge for consumption of non-trading capital	2 681
Total domestic income	308 778
less stock appreciation	−3 037
GROSS DOMESTIC PRODUCT (income-based)	305 741
Residual error	−3 276
Net property income from abroad	3 400
GROSS NATIONAL PRODUCT	305 865
less capital consumption	−41 846
NATIONAL INCOME	264 019

B. EXPENDITURE

	£m
Consumers' expenditure	213 208
General government final consumption	14 012
Gross domestic fixed capital formation	60 118
Value of physical increase in stocks and works in progress	528
Total domestic expenditure	347 866
Export of goods and services	102 304
Total final expenditure	450 170
less imports of goods and services	−98 603

GROSS DOMESTIC PRODUCT (at *market prices*)   351 567
   less Taxes on expenditure   −56 812
   plus Subsidies   7 710

GROSS DOMESTIC PRODUCT (at *factor cost*)   302 465
   Net property income from abroad   3 400

GROSS NATIONAL PRODUCT   305 865
   less capital consumption   −41 846

NATIONAL INCOME   264 019

C. OUTPUT

	£m
Agriculture, forestry, and fishing	5 485
Energy and water supply	34 335
Manufacturing	76 800
Construction	18 651
Distribution, hotels and catering; repairs	40 384
Transport	12 913
Communication	8 044
Banking, finance, insurance, business services and leasing	42 473
Ownership of dwellings	17 775
Public administration, national defence and compulsory social security	21 599
Education and health services	26 187
Other services	17 978

Total   322 624
Adjustment for financial services   −16 883

GROSS DOMESTIC PRODUCT (income based)   305 741
   Residual error   −3 276
   Net property income from abroad   3 400

GROSS NATIONAL PRODUCT   305 865
   less capital consumption   −41 846

NATIONAL INCOME   264 019

Gross domestic product is simply the output of all resources located within a country irrespective of whether their owners live there or abroad. Hence *net* property income from abroad must be added to gross domestic product to obtain the gross *national* product.

Government Calculation of the National Income

Figures for the national income are obtained at the income, expenditure and output stages (Figure 24.2 and Table 24.1). The results are not identical, because information is not complete, but the proportionate error is small. In practice, the expenditure figure is taken as the datum, and the difference between this and the income and output figures is treated as a residual error.

In deciding whether an item should be included in the calculations one should remember the basic principle: does it represent income earned by expenditure on, or output of goods and services produced by the factors of production of the UK during the year?

1. National Income

National income is the total money value of all incomes received by persons and enterprises in the country during the year. Such incomes may be in the form of wages, salaries, rent, or profit.

In practice, income figures are obtained mostly from income-tax returns but estimates are necessary for small incomes. Two major adjustments have to be made:

(*a*)   *Transfer incomes*. Sometimes an income is received even though there has been no corresponding contribution to the output of goods and services, e.g. through unemployment-insurance benefit, retirement pensions, students' grants, interest on the National Debt, and gifts of money (such as an allowance to a relative) from one person to another. Although most of such incomes would normally be included in income-tax returns, they really represent only a redistribution of income within the nation – chiefly from taxpayers to the recipients. Transfer incomes must therefore be deducted. Otherwise we should have the ridiculous situation where the size of the national income could be increased by raising child benefits, national insurance benefits, etc.

(*b*)   *Income from government activities*. Personal incomes and the profits of companies can be obtained from tax returns. But the government also receives income from its property, while some public corporations make profits. Similarly, local authorities may show a surplus on their trading activities – water supply, housing, transport, harbours and docks, etc. Income earned in these various ways in the public sector must be added in.

FIGURE 24.2
Summary of Gross National Product Calculations

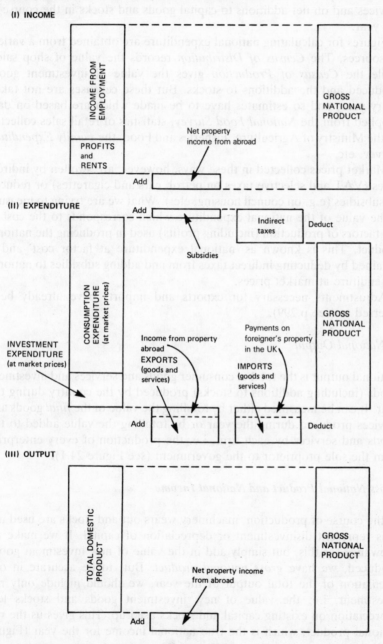

(I) INCOME

INCOME FROM EMPLOYMENT

PROFITS and RENTS

Add

Net property income from abroad

GROSS NATIONAL PRODUCT

(II) EXPENDITURE

Add

Indirect taxes

Deduct

Subsidies

CONSUMPTION EXPENDITURE (at market prices)

INVESTMENT EXPENDITURE (at market prices)

Income from property abroad
EXPORTS (goods and services)

Payments on foreigner's property in the UK
IMPORTS (goods and services)

Add

Deduct

GROSS NATIONAL PRODUCT

(III) OUTPUT

TOTAL DOMESTIC PRODUCT

Net property income from abroad

Add

GROSS NATIONAL PRODUCT

2. National Expenditure

National expenditure is the total amount spent on consumer goods and services and on net additions to capital goods and stocks in the course of the year.

Figures for calculating national expenditure are obtained from a variety of sources. The *Census of Distribution* records the value of shop sales, while the *Census of Production* gives the value of investment goods produced and the additions to stocks. But these censuses are not taken every year, and so estimates have to be made which are based on data supplied from the *National Food Survey*, statistics of retail sales collected by the Ministry of Agriculture, Fisheries and Food, the *Family Expenditure Survey*, etc.

Market prices collected in these ways, however, are swollen by indirect taxes (VAT and selective taxes on petrol, cars and cigarettes) or reduced by subsidies (e.g. on council housing, etc.). What we are trying to measure is the value of the national expenditure which corresponds to the cost of the factors of production (including profits) used in producing the national product. This is known as 'national expenditure at factor cost' and is obtained by deducting indirect taxes from and adding subsidies to national expenditure at market prices.

Adjustments necessary for exports and imports have already been referred to (see p.299).

3. National Output

National output is the total of consumer goods and services and investment goods (including additions to stocks) produced by the country during the year. It can be measured either by totalling the value of the *final* goods and services produced during the year or by totalling the value added to the goods and services by each firm, i.e. the production of every enterprise from the sole proprietor to the government (see Figure 24.1).

Gross National Product and National Income

In the course of production, machinery wears out and stocks are used up. This represent disinvestment or depreciation of capital. If we make no allowance for this, but simply add in the value of new investment goods produced, we have *gross national product*. But, to be accurate in our calculation of the total output of the year, we should include only net investment, i.e. the value of new investment goods and stocks less depreciation on existing capital and stocks used up. This gives us the net national product, which is the true national income for the year (Figure 24.3).

FIGURE 24.3
Gross National Product and National Income

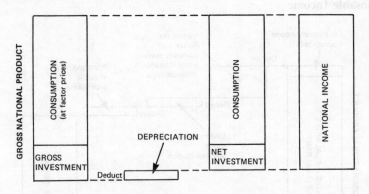

Personal Disposable Income

For some purposes, e.g. an indication of people's current living standards, a measurement of personal disposable income, i.e. what people have to spend after various adjustments have taken place, is more significant. The necessary adjustments to gross national product to obtain personal disposable income are shown in Figure 24.4.

24.3 Uses of National Income Statistics

1. To Indicate the Overall Standard of Living of the People

Welfare is not identical with wealth (see p.10), but wealth bears the closest single relationship to it. Income, the flow of wealth, is therefore the nearest indication of welfare.

Nevertheless, the national income figure cannot be accepted solely on its face-value. Thus although the national income of the UK was £130 000 million in 1978 and £264 000 million in 1985, it does not automatically follow that everyone had doubled their standard of living over that period. The following qualifications have to be made:

(*a*) Some allowance must be made for the rise in the general level of prices from one year to another. Even if we apply the Index of Retail Prices to make the adjustment, it does not completely solve the problem, for there are many difficulties connected with index numbers (see p.366).

FIGURE 24.4
The Relationship between Gross National Product and Personal Disposable Income

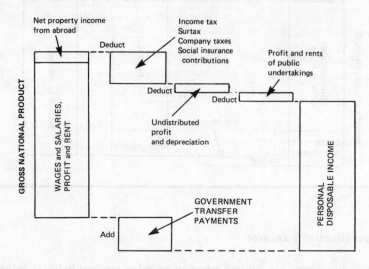

(*b*) Where the population is increasing, we should expect, as there are more producers, that the national income will rise. Average income per head is a better indication of well-being than the overall figure.

(*c*) The standard of living of a person depends upon the quantity of consumer goods and services he enjoys. But the increase in national income may have come about entirely through an increase in the production of producer goods. While these goods may enable a higher standard of living to be enjoyed in the future, they do not increase present welfare. Average personal disposable income might, for this reason, provide a better indication of current living standards, though for the long-run standard of living national income per head is the more satisfactory.

(*d*) The increase in national income may have come about by a surplus of exports over imports. This represents investment overseas, and thus the same remarks as in (*c*) apply.

(*e*) The average income per head figure is merely a statistical average. It does not indicate how the increased national income was distributed; it may have gone entirely to a few rich persons (as in the oil sheikhdoms of the Middle East), leaving the others no better off, or even worse off.

(*f*) An increase in national income may be the result of longer working hours, inferior working conditions, or longer journeys to work (with increased discomfort) as towns expand.

(*g*) Because government spending is included at cost in national income calculations, no distinction is made between expenditure on defence and expenditure on consumer goods and services. As a result, social services, for instance, could be curtailed to pay for a rearmament programme, but national income would be unchanged.

(*h*) The national income figure is swollen when people pay for services which they previously performed themselves. Thus a married woman who returns to teaching but pays someone else to do her housework adds to the national income twice – although the only net addition is her teaching services.

(*i*) Since national income figures are based on private costs and benefits, external costs or benefits do not enter into the calculations. Thus the erection of electricity pylons would be included at cost, no allowances being made for the cost of spoiling the landscape.

(*j*) National income figures do not include the black economy (some estimates would add 10 per cent) where services are exchanged for cash in order to evade taxes.

(*k*) National income includes payments for services necessitated by the stress of modern living, e.g. anti-depressant drugs, clinics for alcoholics.

2. To Compare the Standard of Living of Different Countries

Fairly accurate comparisons of the national incomes of different countries are often necessary for practical purposes. How much help should be given by the rich countries to the very poor? Which are the very poor countries? What contribution should be made by a country when an international body, such as the United Nations, requires funds? What is the war potential of a country?

But when used to compare the standards of living of different countries, national income figures must be subjected to qualifications additional to those mentioned in (1) above:

(*a*) Because figures are expressed in different currencies, they have to be converted into a common denominator. Using the exchange rate for this purpose is not entirely satisfactory, for the rate may not reflect accurately the respective internal purchasing power of currencies (see p.423). More satisfactory is the use of a conversion rate based on the purchasing power parity for a common basket of goods.

(*b*) Different people have different tastes. The cheap loincloth may give as much satisfaction to the Indian as the expensive suit to the Englishman. Similarly, the Canadian has to spend more on heating than the Nigerian. Obviously, neither the Englishman nor the Canadian are better off in these respects – though the national income figures, by valuing goods at cost, would seem to indicate that they were.

(*c*) The proportion of national income spent by different countries on defence varies. Countries which spend less can enjoy consumer goods instead, but average national income does not indicate the difference.

(*d*) Countries vary as regards the length of the average working week, the proportion of women who work, the number of jobs which people do for themselves, the degree to which goods are exchanged against money, and the accuracy of tax returns. Some allowance must be made for each of these factors.

3. To Calculate the Rate at which a Nation's Income is Growing

Is the national income growing? Is it growing as fast as it should? Are the incomes of other countries growing faster? Is there sufficient investment to maintain future living standards? The answers to these and similar questions can be found by comparing national income figures, though for the reasons given above some caution must be observed.

4. To Assist the Government in Planning the Economy

Even capitalist countries now regard some central government planning as essential for achieving full employment, a stable currency and a reasonable rate of growth.

But successful planning requires fairly accurate figures upon which decisions can be based. It is important to know the relative sizes of the various components of the national income and to be able to compare them with past years. Hence *The United Kingdom National Accounts* (The CSO Blue Book) shows, for a number of years: private and public expenditure on consumption and investment; the UK's transactions with the rest of the world; the contribution of each industry to the national product; personal disposable income after tax deductions and transfers; the distribution of personal income before and after tax; the financing of investment; capital formation by sectors of the economy; types of capital formation; expenditure of public authorities. How these figures can be used in planning will be shown in the chapters which follow.

5. To Indicate Changes in the Distribution of Income

While, as a scientist, the economist is not concerned with the 'fairness' of the distribution of income, the government is, for taxation and political considerations. National income figures provide the statistical basis when deciding on such matters.

24.4 Factors Determining a Country's Material Standard of Living

We conclude this chapter with a brief survey of the major factors determining a country's material standard of living. Subject to the qualifications mentioned in the preceding section, this can be defined as the national income per head of the population. For a country having economic relationships with the rest of the world, factors can be classified as internal and external.

Internal

1. Original Natural Resources

Obviously 'natural resources' cover such things as mineral deposits, sources of fuel and power (such as coal and hydro-electric supply), climate, fertility of the soil, and fisheries around the coast, but also included are geographical advantages, such as navigable rivers or lakes which help communications.

While national output increases as new techniques or transport developments allow natural resources to be exploited, the exhaustion of mineral resources works in the opposite direction. Moreover, where a country's economy is predominantly agricultural, variations in weather may cause its output to fluctuate from year to year.

2. The Nature of the People, Particularly of the Labour Force

Other things being equal, the standard of living will be higher the greater the proportion of workers to the total population and the longer their working hours.

But the quality of the labour force is also important. This will depend upon the basic characteristics of the people – their health, energy, adaptability, inventiveness, judgement and ability to organise themselves and to co-operate in production – together with the skills they have acquired through education and training.

3. Capital Equipment

The effectiveness of natural resources and of labour depends almost entirely upon capital equipment. Thus machinery is necessary to extract oil and minerals, a turbine generator to harness a waterfall, and hotels to exploit Spanish sun and beaches. Similarly, the output of workers varies almost in direct proportion to the capital equipment and power at their disposal. Indeed, the most important single cause of material progress is investment, the addition to capital.

4. The Organisation of the Factors of Production

To achieve the maximum output from scarce factors of production they must be organised efficiently. Have we the correct proportion of machinery to each worker? Is the production of the particular good being carried on in the best possible locality? Could the factors be better deployed within the factory? Such questions have to be answered by those organising production.

5. Knowledge of Techniques

Technical knowledge is acquired through capital expenditure on research and invention. Further capital expenditure is necessary to develop discoveries, for example to utilise our present knowledge of nuclear energy. Neverthless, the rapid increase of the standard of living of the UK over the last hundred years has largely been due to the development and application of new inventions such as the steam-engine, the internal-combustion engine, electrical power and electronics.

6. Political Organisation

A stable government promotes confidence and thereby encourages saving and investment in long-term capital projects. Production is therefore greater.

External

1. Foreign Loans and Investments

A net income from property abroad means that a country obtains goods and services from other countries without having to give goods and services in return, and vice versa. Generally speaking, however, welfare from this source is only likely to fluctuate over a long period.

2. The Terms of Trade

Fluctuations in the terms of trade are likely to be far more important in changing material welfare in a short period, especially if the country, as with the UK, has a high level of imports and exports.

By the terms of trade we mean the quantity of another country's products which a nation gets in exchange for a given quantity of its own products. Thus, if the terms of trade move in the nation's favour, it means that it gets a larger quantity of imports for a given quantity of its own exports. This has happened because the prices of goods imported have fallen relatively to those exported. Let us suppose, for instance, that a country exports only cars and imports only wheat. If it exports 10 000 cars at a price of £5 000 per car, the value of its total exports is thus £50 million. If the price of wheat is £50 a bushel, it can import 1 000 000 bushels. Assume now that the price of the cars remains unchanged but that the price of wheat falls to £40 a bushel. The result is that it is now possible to import 1 250 000 bushels of wheat in exchange for the same number of cars. Or the same amount of wheat as previously can be imported but only 8000 cars need to be exported. Thus either an extra 250 000 bushels of wheat or 2000 cars can be enjoyed at home, not, it should be noted, through any increase in productivity, but simply because the terms of trade have moved in favour of the car-manufacturing country.

Thus an increase in the price of oil raises the standard of living of the major exporting countries.

3. Gifts from Abroad

Gifts made to countries for purposes of economic development and defence improve the standard of living of the receiving countries.

25 Full Employment: A Survey of the Problem

25.1 The Nature of Unemployment

The Problem

In the early 1930s people's thoughts were dominated not so much by the threat of war as by the spectre of unemployment. In 1932 there were nearly 3 million workers unemployed in the UK – 22.1 per cent of all insured employees. For certain areas and industries the situation was even more serious. Thus the unemployment rate in Monmouthshire was 36 per cent, and in the ship-building industry generally 62 per cent.

This experience of unemployment of the 1930s dominated Britain's economic policy during the 1950s and 1960s, and full employment was the overriding aim. Keynes's theory that employment was dependent upon the level of aggregate demand for goods and services (Chapter 26) encouraged successive governments to spend to the point where there were more vacancies than unemployed workers to fill them. This produced a state of 'over-full' employment, resulting in inflation, balance-of-payments difficulties, a shortage of skilled workers, high labour turnover, under-investment in new equipment, a failure by industry to adopt new techniques or to switch to the production of high-technology products and an unsatisfactory rate of growth (see Chapter 36). As a result, British industry was in poor shape to withstand international competition during the world recessions of 1974–5 and 1979–82, and by 1987 there were still nearly 3 million unemployed in the UK, 10.4 per cent of the working population.

But although unemployment stated in terms of statistics indicates the extent to which scarce factors are wasted and the numbers who have to be supported from state funds, it does not portray the hopelessness and misery of the unemployed. Many persons without work for years may lose hope of ever finding a job. Skills deteriorate as the period of unemployment increases. It is this aspect of unemployment which makes government action so vital.

The Meaning of a 'Full-employment' Policy

Unemployment is said to occur when persons capable of and willing to work are unable to find suitable paid employment. Important points concerning and arising out of this definition, however, need to be stressed:

1. Unemployment must be involuntary; persons on strike are not reckoned as being unemployed.
2. 'Persons capable of work' must exclude the 'unemployable' – those not capable of work through mental or physical disability. On the other hand, unemployables are usually in the pool of unemployed labour seeking jobs and, where labour is scarce, more use will be made of them – provided that minimum wage regulations do not prevent this.
3. Full employment does not mean that workers will never be required to switch jobs or occupations. Changes in the conditions of demand and supply are bound to occur, and such changes will be more frequent the more dynamic the economy and the more a country is dependent on international trade.

Thus there will always be some workers unemployed. Complete full employment could be achieved only by direction of labour. The question is what percentage of unemployment will conform to 'full employment'?

Sir William Beveridge, who in 1944 formulated a blueprint for full employment, thought that 3 per cent was an acceptable level of unemployment, and in post-war years this has been the minimum rate achieved by both the USA and West Germany. But politicians in Britain considered that such an aim took too little account of the psychological and social effects of condemning more workers than is absolutely necessary to being without a job, even though such unemployment may last for only a short period. Hence until 1974 (except for 1971 and 1972), unemployment was maintained at less than 3 per cent of all employees, and until 1966 was mostly under 2 per cent.

Since 1974, however, unemployment was rising continuously. Inflation and pressure on the balance of payments led to stop–go policies by successive governments. Worse still, world recessions, following rises in the price of oil in 1973 and 1979, added to the problems of British industry in retaining export markets in the face of strong competition from other countries, notably Japan. Above all, the adherence from 1976 to stricter monetary policies with high interest rates had the effect of squeezing firms' profits. Thus while unemployment increased as the fall in demand led to a contraction of production, the situation was aggravated as firms slimmed down their labour force to increase their competitiveness (see Chapter 36).

It has become obvious, therefore, that trying to run the economy at a very low level of unemployment gives rise to problems – inflation, pressure on the balance of payments, a lack of competitiveness and a slow rate of growth – which eventually tend to undermine the objective. Thus the government has to weigh the pros and cons of such a policy. The decision is eventually a political one, but experience since 1970 suggests that any government, whatever its political colour, will have difficulty in achieving only 3 per cent unemployment, though this is likely to be the professed target.

25.2 The Causes of Unemployment

Unemployment may occur for many different reasons, and these must be distinguished if the appropriate remedies are to be applied.

1. Frictional

Unless the economy is completely static, there will always be people changing their jobs. Some merely desire a change of employment or a move to a different part of the country. In certain occupations, e.g. unskilled labour in the construction industry, workers are not employed regularly by any one employer: when a particular contract is completed, labour is made redundant. Occasionally, too, workers are discharged when a factory is being reorganised.

Unemployed workers usually register at the local Jobcentre, forming a pool of labour from which employers can fill vacancies. But. how large should this pool be? If it is too large, workers remain unemployed for longer periods. If it is too small, production is dislocated by bottlenecks in filling vacancies (with employers holding on to labour not currently needed), by job-switching just for the sake of change and, above all, by strikes in support of claims for higher wages.

Frictional unemployment is partly unavoidable, and the grant of unemployment benefit affords the worker some protection against its effects. But positive measures may help. Thus casual unemployment has now been largely eliminated in the docks by required registration of workers and guaranteed minimum weekly payments. It is worth noting, too, that the installation of expensive machinery which must be kept fully employed has quite often had the indirect effect of 'decasualising' labour. In any case, it is easier to minimise frictional unemployment when there is full employment in the economy.

2. Seasonal

Employment in some industries, e.g. building, fruit-picking and holiday catering, is seasonal in character. The difficulty is that the skills required by different seasonal jobs are not 'substitutable'. To what extent, for example, can hotel workers become shop assistants in the January sales? Seasonal employment is not completely avoidable. But it can be reduced if a small, regular labour force will work overtime during the 'season' and admit, say, students during the busy periods. Moreover, the price system may help. By offering off-season rates, hotels at holiday resorts can attract autumn conferences.

3. International

Because the UK is so dependent on international trade, the nation is particularly vulnerable to unemployment brought about by a fall in the demand for her exports. Such a fall may occur because:

(a) *The prices of British goods are too high to be competitive in world markets.* Prices of exports have two components: (i) the home price, (ii) the rate at which the home currency exchanges for foreign currency. Thus if home prices rise, for example because of wage increases, the export market is likely to be hit severely. The demand for exports is usually highly elastic, for substitutes are generally available from competing countries. The effect on employment is shown in Figure 25.1. The wage increase moves the supply curve from S to S_1. Because demand is elastic there is a considerable fall in the demand for the good, from OM to OM_1. The industry and, therefore, employment contract.

Similarly, if at the existing rate of exchange the home currency is too dear in terms of foreign currencies, exports will be expensive to countries importing goods from the country whose currency is overvalued. Here some devaluation of the exchange rate is necessary.

FIGURE 25.1
The Effect on Employment of a Wage Increase in an Export Industry

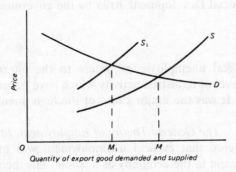

Quantity of export good demanded and supplied

(*b*)   *Incomes of major importing countries may be reduced by a recession or a deterioration in the terms of trade* (see p. 405). If incomes of importing countries fall, their demand for British goods, especially those having a high income elasticity of demand, will be likely to decrease. This is what happened following the increases in the price of oil in 1973 and 1979 (see p. 470).

4. Structural

Structural unemployment, like frictional, results largely from the immobility of labour. Ignorance of opportunities elsewhere or, more likely, obstacles to moving mean that workers do not move to available jobs in other parts of the country. Thus today local authorities in the south of England are, because of the higher cost of housing, finding it difficult to recruit from high unemployment regions.

More serious, however, is occupational immobility resulting from long-term changes in the conditions of demand and supply in certain industries, especially exporting industries.

On the demand side, there may be a change in any of the factors influencing the conditions of demand. The price of substitutes may fall (Dundee jute products have largely been replaced by plastics), or foreign buyers may switch to competitors' goods (British shipyards have been hit by Japanese competition). On the supply side, new techniques or the exhaustion of mineral deposits may make labour redundant. Automation has reduced ICI's demand for workers at Stockton; exhaustion of the better coal seams has led to a closure of pits in south Wales and mid-Scotland.

Where an industry has been highly localised in a particular area, the resulting unemployment may be particularly severe. Thus the depression in the shipbuilding industry is reflected in the unemployment rate for the North region of England in July 1987 being 14.4 per cent, compared with a national average of 10.4 per cent, and this in spite of the region being treated as a Special Development Area by the government.

5. Cyclical

The term 'cyclical unemployment' refers to the alternate booms and slumps in the level of industrial activity which have occurred over the last hundred years. It was the major cause of the high unemployment of the 1930s.

Lord Keynes – *The General Theory of Employment, Interest and Money* (1936) – considered that cyclical unemployment was brought about by inadequate demand in the economy as a whole. His theory has fashioned government policy over the last fifty years.

Recently, however, it has been recognised that a low level of unemployment cannot be achieved simply by demand management. Largely because of the inflation which accompanied a high level of demand, more attention has had to be paid to reducing unemployment by creating conditions which stimulate existing firms to expand and new firms to enter production.

Conclusions

The above discussion suggests that the causes of unemployment can be reduced to: (a) insufficient total demand in the economy; (b) an overall lack of incentive to efficient production; and (c) long-term structural changes in certain industries, often those associated with a particular region.

The first is explained by a 'general-equilibrium' theory which covers the economy as a whole (Chapter 26). The second has led to 'supply-side' economics (pp. 363–5). The third is largely covered by 'regional economics' which applies both a general and partial equilibrium approach in explaining inadequate demand in certain areas (Chapter 28).

26 Cyclical Fluctuations in Income and Employment

26.1 The Link between Spending and Production

When unemployment is *general* throughout the economy, we have to consider the demand for goods as a whole, just as we did when measuring national income. Consumption, saving, investment, wages, profits, etc., must be considered in aggregate terms.

We begin by repeating in simplified form the identity which exists between income and expenditure. Take a simple example. A teacher buys a table from a carpenter. With the money received, the carpenter pays the timber-merchant for the wood, who in turn pays the woodcutter. But where did the teacher obtain the original money to buy the table? Simply from the carpenter, the timber-merchant and the treefeller, who each use part of their receipts to pay fees to the teacher for instructing their children. So with the other goods the teacher buys. Thus there is a circular flow of income – one person's spending becomes another person's income. Spending is therefore necessary for earnings.

The same applies to the economy as a whole; at any one time spending equals income. Suppose, for instance, that in the economy, all production is in the hands of a giant firm which owns all the land and raw materials and employs all the labour. The firm's income consists of the receipts from the sale of its product. Since it owns all the raw materials and land, these receipts must equal what it pays out in wages and what it has left in profits. This was the principle upon which we measured the national income in Chapter 24.

Since spending on goods therefore determines the receipts and thus the profits of firms, it is of vital importance to entrepreneurs. Let us turn back to Figure 2.3, which showed a simplified model of an economic system, but let us concentrate, not on the movements of factors and goods, but on the money payments by firms for factors and on the money payments of households for goods. These money payments are shown in Figure 26.1.

FIGURE 26.1
The Circular Flow of Income

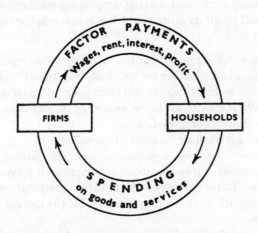

If spending on goods and services is maintained, so can factor payments be maintained; in other words, the profitability to firms of production is unchanged and thus there is no need to vary output. If, however, for some reason or another spending should fall, some of the goods produced by firms will not be sold, and stocks will accumulate. Production is not so profitable, and as a result output is curtailed. On the other hand, if spending on goods and services increases, stocks will be run down. Production has become more profitable and, as a result, output is expanded.

Three important points emerge from our discussion so far:

1. The condition of equilibrium in the economy is a simple one — spending on goods and services equals spending by firms (including profits) on factors of production. Equilibrium exists because then there is no impetus towards a contraction or expansion of production.
2. The level of production, and therefore of employment, is closely related to the level of spending.
3. There is nothing to guarantee that the level of spending will be sufficient to produce an equilibrium level of production where all factors of production are fully employed.

Definitions and Assumptions

Before we show how changes in spending occur, we must tighten up our model by defining terms and making simplifying assumptions.

We define net profit as gross profit less retentions for depreciation.

We assume:

1. *All retentions for depreciation are actually spent on replacement investment.* Thus, when in future we speak of 'investment', it refers solely to net additions to fixed capital and stocks, i.e. net investment.
2. *All net profit is distributed to the owners of the risk capital.* This means that there is no 'saving' by firms.
3. *There is no government taxation or spending.*
4. *There are no economic connections with the outside world; it is a 'closed' economy.* From the above assumptions it follows that: (*a*) the sum of the factor payments is equal to national income (equals national output), as defined in Chapter 24; (*b*) income equals disposable income.
5. *There are no changes in the price level.* Money values of national income are at constant prices; thus any changes in the money value reflect changes in real output.
6. *The level of employment is directly proportionate to the level of output.* In practice, this may not be strictly true; existing machinery, for example, may be able to produce extra output without additional labour. But the simplification does allow the level of employment to be linked directly with the level of national income.

26.2 Reasons for Changes in Aggregate Demand

Aggregate Demand

Our task, therefore, is to discover why changes occur in the national income (hereafter symbolised by Y). Now, as we have just shown, Y depends upon the level of spending, which we shall refer to as aggregate demand (abbreviated to AD). Thus we can find out why Y changes by discovering why AD changes.

Changes in Aggregate Demand

Let us return to our example of the teacher. Most of the teacher's salary will be spent on consumer goods and services – but not all. Some will probably be put aside for a 'rainy day'. That part of income which is not spent we can say is 'saved'. What happens to it? The money could be hidden under the mattress; in this case it is 'hoarded', and is obviously lost to the circular flow of income. But the teacher is much more likely to put it in a bank or building society, for there it is not only safer but earns interest. Is it still lost to the circular flow of income?

So far we have looked only at spending on consumer goods. But spending can also be on capital goods and stocks, usually known as *investment*. Entrepreneurs, as we have seen, go to their banks (and other institutions) to borrow money to purchase capital goods. Thus the sum deposited by the teacher stands a good chance of being returned to the circular flow of income by being 'invested', i.e. spent on additional capital goods or stocks. And if exactly the same amount of money saved by the public is spent by firms on investment, the level of *AD* is maintained (Figure 26.2) and the level of *Y* is unchanged.

FIGURE 26.2
The Level of Income Maintained Through Investment

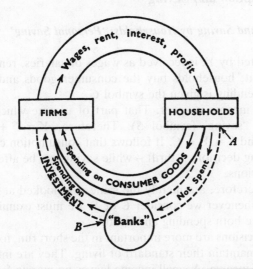

But suppose that the amount of income saved does not coincide with what entrepreneurs wish to invest. This can come about by either a change in the amount invested or by a change in the amount spent by consumers.

Let us first assume that consumers' spending remains constant. If now entrepreneurs reduce the amount they borrow for investment, *AD* is smaller. On the other hand, if entrepreneurs increase their investment, *AD* will be larger. And, as we shall see, the *ultimate* change in the size of *AD* will probably be much greater than the initial change in the level of investment (p.336).

Alternatively, the amount of income spent on consumer goods may alter. Investment, we now assume, remains unchanged. Here, if more is spent out of a given income, AD will increase; if less, AD decreases.

What it is important to recognise is that in an economy where people are free to dispose of their incomes as they please, and where entrepreneurs are largely left to make their own investment decisions, a difference can easily exist between the amount of income 'saved' (that is, which people do not wish to spend) and the amount which entrepreneurs wish to invest. This is because, in their spending, households and firms act for different reasons and mostly independently of one another. Two questions, therefore, have to be asked: (1) What determines spending on consumer goods and therefore 'saving' (at position A)? (2) What determines investment spending (at position B)?

26.3 Consumption and Saving

Consumption and Saving by Households: 'Personal Saving'

Income, denoted by Y, is received as wages or salaries, rent, interest and profits. With it, households buy the consumer goods and services they need. Such spending is given the symbol C.

But not all income is spent. That part of income which is not spent is defined as 'saving' (symbol S). Therefore, $Y = C + S$. Similarly, $C = Y - S$, and $S = Y - C$. It follows that consumption can be affected by active saving decisions – thrift – while saving can be affected by active spending decisions.

C and S, therefore, are merely the same coin looked at from different sides. Thus, whenever we consider C or S, we must examine the factors which influence both spending and thrift.

Spending decisions are more important in the short run, for people's first concern is to maintain their standard of living. They are influenced by:

(1) *Size of income.* A small income leaves no margin for saving. Only when what are considered to be basic needs have been satisfied will some income be saved. Indeed, if current income falls below this level, some spending of past savings or borrowing may take place to maintain the standard of living accustomed to.

But we can go further. As income increases, the proportion spent tends to decrease; or, as it is often put, there is a *diminishing marginal propensity to consume.*

The above conclusions are illustrated in Figure 26.3.

FIGURE 26.3
The Relationship of Consumption and Income

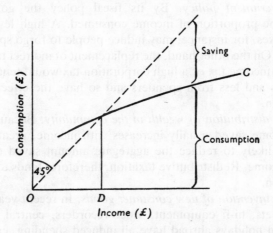

Below an income of *OD*, *C* exceeds *Y*, the difference being covered by spending past savings or by borrowing. At *OD* all income is consumed; it is the 'break-even' income. At higher incomes the proportion spent falls (the proportion saved rises). This diminishing marginal propensity to consume is shown by the decreasing slope of the consumption curve; for any given increase in income, the extra amount spent grows successively smaller.

(2) *The time lag in adjusting spending habits.* In addition to the improved possibility and desire to save as income increases, the marginal propensity to consume may diminish, because it takes time for people to adjust their standard of living as income increases. In the short period, therefore, saving increases.

The above two factors explain the *shape* of the consumption curve – how spending changes as income changes. But we still have to account for the *position* of the curve – what determines the proportion of any given income which is spent. (We had a similar problem when studying the demand curve: the relationship of demand to price determined, through marginal utility, its shape; the conditions of demand determined its position.)

The amount spent out of a given income can vary (that is, the position of the *C* curve may change) as a result of:

(3) *Changes in disposable income.* We have assumed that firms have distributed all net profits and that there is no government taxation or transfers. In practice, both profit distribution and government activity will

affect the size of disposable income, and thus spending. Increased direct taxation, for instance, reduces disposable income and would thus lower the C curve.

(4) *Government policy.* By its fiscal policy the government can influence the proportion of income consumed. A high level of VAT or selective taxes, for instance, may induce people to forgo spending for the time being. On the other hand, the replacement of indirect taxes by a more progressive income tax or a high corporation tax would tend to take more from savers and less from spenders and so have the effect of increasing consumption.

(5) *The distribution of wealth in the community.* Because the proportion of income saved usually increases with income, greater equality of incomes is likely to reduce the aggregate amount saved out of a given national income. Redistributive taxation, therefore, tends to increase total consumption.

(6) *The invention of new consumer goods.* In recent years family cars, television sets, hi-fi equipment, video-recorders, central heating, dishwashers and holidays abroad have all induced spending, especially when backed by intensive advertising.

(7) *Hire-purchase and other credit facilities.* A decrease in the initial deposit or an extension of the period of repayment encourages spending. For this reason, hire-purchase terms have in the past been regulated by the government. Easier bank credit also encourages spending.

(8) *Anticipated changes in the value of money.* It seems reasonable to expect that, if people consider the prices of goods are likely to rise, they are more likely to bring forward their spending rather than save for the future. In fact, during the period of rising inflation 1973–80, the ratio of personal saving to income rose, probably because people sought to re-build the purchasing power of their financial assets.

(9) *The age distribution of the population.* Since most saving is done by people over 35 years of age, an ageing population will tend to reduce the propensity to consume of the community as a whole.

In the long period, people have some concern for their future standard of living, and *thrift* exercises a greater influence on the disposal of income.

The main *factors determining thrift* are:

(1) *Size of income.* As already shown, saving increases as income increases *and* at an increasing rate.

(2) *The rate of interest.* The classical economists considered that, in order to induce people to forgo present for future enjoyment, compensation in the form of interest had to be paid. The higher the rate of interest, the more people would save.

This view, however, is largely rejected by present-day opinion. While a high rate of interest may tempt people to save, actual saving is influenced to a far greater degree by the ability to save (the size of income) and environmental factors (see below). In any case, it must be remembered that much saving is contractual, e.g. by way of pension, insurance and mortgage repayments.

Where people are saving to provide an income for the future and consider that a rise in the rate of interest is likely to be permanent, they may reduce their saving, thereby counterbalancing to some extent any increased saving by persons forgoing present consumption.

(3) *Psychological attitudes.* Some communities are by nature more thrifty than others, providing against sickness, unemployment, old age, and for the education of dependants. Certain people even save beyond these needs, either because it gives them a feeling of power, independence or security, or because they wish to leave something to an heir.

On the other hand, ostentation – the desire to 'keep up with the Joneses' – may provide a motive for a high rate of spending.

(4) *Social environment.* Apart from influencing the general attitude to saving, environment can be a major factor in other ways. Such institutions as the National Savings Bank, building societies, insurance companies, pension funds, unit trusts, etc., are now advertising their schemes extensively. In that they encourage regular thrift, much saving is contractual.

Political conditions, too, influence saving habits. Countries continually threatened by war or revolution do not provide the stable conditions necessary to encourage thrift.

(5) *Government policy.* The government can influence people's attitude to saving in a variety of ways. While some countries may have compulsory saving, the UK tries to stimulate personal saving through the rate of interest, propaganda, income-tax concessions (e.g. on the first £70 interest on National Savings), and special devices (e.g. savings certificates and premium bonds).

On the other hand, it must be remembered that a comprehensive social-insurance and pension scheme or inflation may reduce real personal saving.

Under our simplifying assumptions that all net profits are distributed and that there is no government taxation or spending, all saving is done by households. But in real terms, saving represents the release of resources from present consumption for the construction of factories, machinery, etc. In practice, this release of resources can occur at other points in the income flow where some income is retained and not spent. In order to consider these we temporarily relax assumptions 2 and 3 (p.320). Saving can now be achieved by business and the government.

The distribution of saving in the UK in 1985 is shown in Figure 26.4 (data from the 1987 United Kingdom National Accounts: the CSO Blue Book). It is *personal saving* which fluctuates the most.

FIGURE 26.4
Saving in the UK, 1985 (Before Providing for Depreciation, Stock Appreciations, and Additions to Reserves)

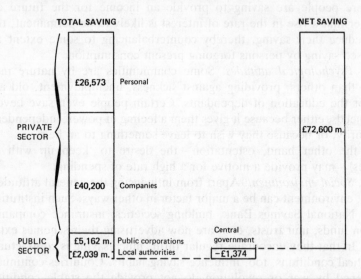

Business Saving

Saving by businesses (which in volume remains fairly stable) is achieved by not distributing to shareholders all the profits made in a year. Some net profits are usually retained, to be 'ploughed back' for the expansion of the business, or to be held as liquid reserves in order to meet tax liabilities, or to maintain dividends in the event of reduced trade, a strike or an increase in taxation. In 1985, business saving amounted to about 62 per cent of total saving.

The chief factors influencing this type of saving are:

(1) *Profits*. When directors are deciding how much profits should be transferred to reserves, they will be guided almost entirely by the size of profits being currently earned. First, a profit is necessary to effect any saving whatsoever, and the larger the profits, the greater the margin for saving. Second, when profits are good, directors are more likely to set aside reserves for expanding the business.

In practice, therefore, company saving is determined principally by the level of aggregate demand, for this represents the receipts upon which profits chiefly depend.

(2) *Subjective factors*. The financial prudence and the energy, en-

terprise and ideas of the directors regarding expansion will influence the extent to which retained profits are invested. Thus some directors may retain liquid reserves, not because they have ideas for expanding the business, but as a source from which dividends can be maintained in lean years, thus avoiding criticism from shareholders.

(3) *Estimated future prices.* Not only do rising prices increase profits and thus optimisim, but they are an incentive to save out of current income in order that investment goods can be purchased now rather than later on.

(4) *Government policy.* An increased tax on *distributed* profits or a 'dividend freeze' would be likely to increase company saving.

Government Saving

Central government saving is achieved chiefly through a 'budget surplus', revenue exceeding current government expenditure. The surplus may be necessary:

(*a*) To provide for the government's own investment and loans to local authorities.
(*b*) To cover the needs of the nationalised industries, whose capital is now largely provided by the Treasury.
(*c*) To ensure that, with personal and business saving, total saving will so cover total investment that aggregate demand will be sufficient to produce full employment without inflation (see pp.348–9).

Between 1974 and 1987 central government expenditure exceeded its income; there was a budget deficit, i.e. net dis-saving.

Public corporations are similar in many ways to ordinary businesses. But as their operations are more directly under government control, and because most of their capital requirements is provided by the Treasury, their saving and investment are included under the public sector.

Local authorities, too, may have a budget surplus. In practice, however, they account for only about $3 \frac{1}{2}$ per cent of total saving, their capital needs being mainly met from the Public Works Loan Board and from private saving through loans floated on the open market.

Thus, in the public sector, spending is determined chiefly by government policy, economic and political.

Conclusion

In the private sector, spending (and therefore saving) depends upon (*a*) the level of income, i.e. the size of *AD*, (*b*) other factors influencing the amount spent out of income. In comparison with changes in *AD*, these other factors are fairly stable. Hence the main factor affecting short-term changes in consumption spending is the size of *AD*!

We have therefore to look elsewhere for the reason why *AD* changes. It is to be found in the comparative instability of the other form of spending – investment.

26.4 Investment Spending

What do we Mean by 'Investment'?

Investment is spending over a given period on the production of capital goods (houses, factories, machinery, etc.) or on net additions to stocks (raw materials, consumer goods in shops, etc.).

It is important to distinguish between this definition and what is usually referred to as 'investment' by laypeople. In national income analysis, investment takes place only when there is an actual net addition to capital goods or stocks. It cannot be applied to putting money in the bank or to the purchase of securities. This is true even when new securities are bought, though here there is a strong presumption that the money is required to finance real investment in factories, machinery, etc.

It should be noted that the definition above would cover 'gross investment', since it makes no allowance for the depreciation of existing capital assets. But, as already explained, we are analysing in terms of national income (net national product) *not* gross national product. Investment in our model, therefore, must be limited to *net* investment, i.e. gross investment less depreciation.

Investment in the Private Sector of the Economy

While in the private sector some investment in housing is undertaken by owner-occupiers who add garages, rooms, etc., to their property, the amount is insignificant relative to investment by businesses (see Figure 26.5).

The level of investment by firms is governed by the expected yield relative to cost, changes in techniques, changes in the rate of consumption and government policy.

1. Expected Yield Relative to Cost

Entrepreneurs spend on new capital equipment when they think that the cost will be justified by the addition to revenue which will directly result. In short, marginal-revenue productivity must at least equal marginal cost.

Whereas marginal-revenue productivity in the case of labour can be estimated fairly accurately, it is not so with capital. Capital equipment lasts a long time, and the return to it is spread over many years. This involves

FIGURE 26.5
Investment in the UK, 1985 (Domestic Fixed Capital Formation)

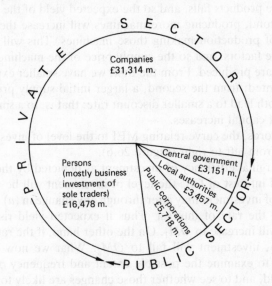

uncertainty. Is demand for the product likely to change? Are competitors likely to enter the market? Will the present methods of production become obsolete? The return to the capital equipment over its life, therefore, can be no more definite than a series of yearly yields which the entrepreneur reasonably *expects*. It is usual to discount these yields to their present value and to express the return over the initial cost as a rate. This rate will be referred to as the *marginal efficiency of investment* (symbol 'MEI').

We can give more precision to this term by a simple example. Suppose a machine costs £1000. It has a working life of four years, during which the entrepreneur expects that it will add £400 each year to receipts. We could find a single rate of discount which would make the £400 received during the first year plus the £400 received during the second year plus the £400 received during the third year plus the £400 received during the fourth year just equal to the initial cost of £1000. This rate of discount is the MEI. (In our example, it is about 22 per cent.) If the MEI is greater than the rate of interest – the cost of borrowing the original £1000 – the entrepreneur will buy the machine; if it is less, he will not.

In the above example, we have shown how the marginal efficiency of a *particular* machine is determined. But what of the marginal efficiency of new capital *in general*? How will this vary as the capital equipment of the community increases or decreases?

For two reasons it can be expected that the MEI will fall as the stock of the community's capital increases. First, as more machines are produced, so will the products made by those machines increase in supply. Thus the price of those products falls, and so the expected yield of the machine will also fall. Second, producing more machines will increase the demand for the factors of production making those machines. This will increase the price of those factors, and so the supply price of the machines is likely to rise as more are produced. From the first, we have smaller expected yields to be discounted; from the second, a larger initial supply price as capital increases. Both lead to a smaller discount rate: that is, to a smaller MEI as the supply of capital increases.

In other words, the curve relating MEI to the level of investment slopes downwards from left to right (Figure 26.6).

With a marginal efficiency of investment as depicted by the curve *MEI* and a rate of interest of *OR*, the level of investment will be *OM*.

The level of investment may alter through any change in (*a*) the expected yield, or (*b*) the rate of interest. Thus if expected yield rises to MEI_1, investment will increase to OM_1. On the other hand, if the rate of interest rises to OR_2, investment will fall to OM_2. What we now have to do, therefore, is to examine the possible extent and frequency of changes in expected yield, and to see whether those changes are likely to overshadow changes in the rate of interest.

FIGURE 26.6
The Determination of the Level of Investment

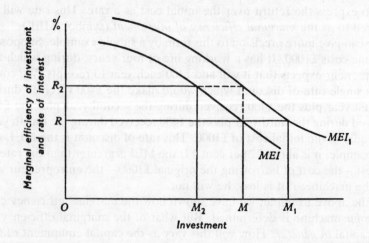

Let us look first at the *expected yield*. We have already shown that this is clouded in uncertainty because the entrepreneur will have to look far into the future to estimate changes in the demand for his product and to allow for possible changes in methods of production. Upon what can he base his estimates?

The simple answer is that he has little definite to go on. His estimate of the earning power of an investment over, say, the next five years can be only tentative, and allowance will have to be made according to the confidence he has in its accuracy. The main factors influencing his decisions are: the level of current income; the course of Stock Exchange prices; the future price level; and government policy. Let us consider each in turn.

In making his estimate, the entrepreneur will most likely commence from the position about which he does have some definite knowledge – the present. If current demand for his goods is buoyant, and has been so for some time, future prospects will probably look rosy. On the other hand, if present demand is low, he will think twice before adding to his productive capacity. But the current demand for goods as a whole depends chiefly upon the current level of AD. Investment is likely to be higher, therefore, the higher is AD.

Prices of shares on the Stock Exchange influence investment decisions in two ways. First, uncertainty in estimating the expected yield means that investment decisions are influenced considerably by prevailing moods of optimism or pessimism. An entrepreneur will be unwilling to extend his factory if current Stock Exchange prices value businesses, particularly those similar to his own, unfavourably. Second, when its share price is high, a company will find it easier and cheaper to raise capital through a 'rights' issue.

As regards the price level, if the entrepreneur thinks that prices in future are likely to be higher, then more investment is likely now. Not only will the value of the factory or machine appreciate, but expected yield will be higher through the rise in the price of the product.

Political instability and changes in government policy add to uncertainty. The former discourages investment, particularly by foreign companies operating in the country. The possibility of the latter has to be allowed for in an entrepreneur's expectations. Is corporation tax likely to be increased? Will the government carry out a disinflationary policy to curb future price rises?

This brings us to the *rate of interest*, the cost of investment. If it rises, marginal projects cease to be viable, and so the level of investment falls. This applies even if funds come from internal reserves, for the opportunity cost – the return on the best alternative, e.g. government securities – has to be considered. To Keynes, therefore, the long-term rate of interest was a major factor in determining the level of investment.

However, we must not assume a *precise* relationship. While the prevailing rate of interest could be decisive for projects where the yields extend far into the future, e.g. houses and office blocks, and for investment by small firms, practical considerations may loom large with other investment.

For one thing investment decisions, especially for large firms, are mainly the result of long-term planning. Any alteration of plans because of a change in the rate of interest might throw the whole programme out of phase. For another, firms allow a considerable safety margin when deciding on investment, probably expecting to recover costs within five years. This margin is thus sufficient to absorb a relatively small rise in the rate of interest. Even the holding of stocks may not be affected by the rate of interest. Convenience is more likely to decide the minimum held. In any case the rate of interest may be only a small part of the cost of holding stocks, warehousing, etc., being relatively far more important. Finally, a part of any increase in interest charges would be covered by reduced tax liability.

Nevertheless, when in 1979 interest rates rose sharply, many investment projects became marginal, and stagnation was prolonged because these could not bear the higher cost.

Even so, it is probably pessimistic expectations which are the prime cause of investment stagnation. Thus in the world depression of 1980–2, it is doubtful whether a lower rate of interest would have been significant in achieving any great increase in investment except for its psychological boost to expectations.

This implies that, compared with entrepreneurs' expectations, the rate of interest plays a secondary role in determining the level of investment. Moreover, uncertainty means that expected yield is subject to frequent reappraisal. In other words, changes in expectations may cause the MEI curve to change so frequently and by so much that it outweighs the effect which a movement in the rate of interest may have on the level of investment. We can illustrate from Figure 26.6. A rate of interest OR and a marginal efficiency of investment curve MEI would give a rate of investment OM. A rise in the rate of interest to OR_2 should reduce investment to OM_2. But this assumes that there is no change in the position of the MEI curve. If, for example, as the rate of interest rises to OR_2, revised expectations cause the MEI curve to move to MEI_1, investment will remain at OM. Expectations may be such that, in a slump, a low rate of interest does little to stimulate investment, while in a boom a high rate does not discourage it. It is the fickleness of business expectations which gives investment a central role in the determination of the level of employment.

2. Changes in Techniques

New technical developments, such as the internal-combustion engine, nuclear energy, the microchip and North Sea gas and oil, give an added impetus to investment. On the other hand, it has to be recognised that the possibility of new techniques rendering existing capital equipment obsolete must be allowed for by the entrepreneur when estimating the MEI.

3. Changes in the Rate of Consumption: the 'Accelerator'

Our conclusion in (1) above, that the rate of investment was tied fairly closely to the size of aggregate demand, is capable of further refinement. Changes in the rate of investment are closely linked, not to the absolute level of consumption, but to changes in the *rate* of consumption. A simple example will explain.

Suppose that 1000 machines are fully employed in producing bicycle tyres and that the life of each machine is ten years. This means that 100 machines have to be replaced each year and the industry making this type of capital good must have a yearly capacity of 100.

Now suppose demand for bicycles increases so that the demand for tyres increases by 10 per cent. If there is no excess capacity for producing tyres, it can be seen that 100 new machines, in addition to the replacement requirement, are needed immediately. In this year, therefore, 200 tyre-making machines must be produced. Thus although the increased demand for consumer goods was only 10 per cent, it led to a doubling of the capacity of the industry making the machines.

If consumption of tyres now remains constant at the new level, production of the machines will have to contract sharply, for until the extra machines wear out in ten years' time, only the annual replacement of 100 machines will be required.

Taking this example as it stands, three conclusions can be drawn.

(*a*) Variations in the rate of consumption will produce changes in investment on a magnified scale. Usually changes in consumption are the result of variations in the level of *AD* (known today as recession and recoveries). But they may also be brought about by such factors as changes in hire-purchase facilities, the boom in hire-purchase commitments being followed by stagnation for two or three years while repayments are made.

(*b*) Swings in the level of production are much greater in the producer-goods industries than in the consumer-goods industries. The longer a machine lasts before it has to be replaced, the greater will be the swing. Thus in our example, if the machine for making tyres lasts for twenty years, the 10 per cent increase in demand for tyres would necessitate a trebling of the capacity of the tyre-machine industry.

(*c*)   A single change in the level of consumption can produce a built-in mechanism whereby changes in the level of investment will be repeated subsequently at fairly regular intervals.

Nevertheless, when we look at the assumptions which are implicit in our example, it loses some of its precision. In the first place, although we stated that there was no excess capacity in the tyre-producing industry, the opposite was assumed in the tyre-machine-making industry – the 100 per cent increase in demand will be met by the production of 100 extra machines. If extra tyres can be produced by using idle machines or by double-shift working, then there will be no need to increase the number of machines. On the other hand, if there is no surplus capacity in the tyre-machine-making industry, the increased demand for bicycles may simply find its outlet in higher prices, and investment will not increase. Second, the model fails to allow for the expectations of entrepreneurs. An increase in the demand for bicycles may have been anticipated by building up stocks or by holding excess capacity in reserve. On the other hand, it may be thought that the increase in demand is unlikely to be permanent, in which case the extra machines would not be bought.

In practice, induced investment may result, not only from an increase in consumption, but from an autonomous increase in investment. Thus it is more accurate to say that the accelerator depends upon changes in *AD* rather than simply on changes in the level of consumption.

4. Government Policy

To be complete we must again relax our assumption of no government taxation or spending. Government policy may directly influence private investment. Banks have been instructed from time to time to restrict credit for certain types of investment. Should it desire to stimulate private investment, the government may give subsidies (e.g. for restoring old houses, or improving farm buildings), raise investment or depreciation allowances in tax assessments, and revive the optimism of entrepreneurs by lowering the rate of interest and, more important, by increasing its own spending.

Investment in the Public Sector

This includes not only the capital expenditure of the central government, but also that of the nationalised industries and local authorities.

Much of central government investment is fairly stable, depending chiefly on policy commitments – road construction, school and hospital building, etc. To some extent, too, the nationalised industries, in deciding whether to invest, may be expected to include external benefits, e.g. getting the unemployed back to work.

Local authority investment, however, may react to changes in the rate of interest, especially where finance is raised on the open market. Spending on new houses in particular may vary with the rate of interest. If, after applying government grants, the cost of borrowing is not covered by the rents charged, the difference has to be found from the rates. But because the rates are not a buoyant form of taxation, a rise in interest charges must usually be met from higher rents. Indeed, a high rate of interest can reduce local authority house-building to mere slum-clearance requirements.

For the purpose of adjusting aggregate demand, public investment is subject to direct government control. Indeed, it is usually included within the global figure of 'government spending'.

Conclusion

By influencing expectations, the current level of income will play a part in determining the rate of private investment. Moreover, investment will bear some relationship to the rate of change of income.

But, in order to simplify our analysis, we shall ignore these connections between investment and the level of income and assume that all investment is autonomous. In other words, investment decisions of firms are based on a number of considerations, and changes in investment are not automatically induced by income changes.

26.5 Equilibrium Through Changes in the Level of Income

The Restoration of Equilibrium

We must now follow through what happens when, for some reason, intended saving and investment become unequal. A simple arithmetical example will help. We shall assume:

1. $Y = 10\ 000$.
2. At this level of income there are unemployed resources.
3. Consumption spending by households is $\frac{6}{10} Y$ (disposable income) at all levels of Y. (In practice, consumption is more likely to be about 90 per cent of disposable income, but our assumption will make the diagrams clearer.)
4. Any increase in Y does not affect the proportion of Y spent by any change in the distribution of Y.
5. Investment spending by firms is autonomous: that is, it is independent of the level of income. Initially the rate of investment (I) = 4000.
6. All figures are in £ million.

Initially, in period 0, the economy is in equilibrium:

$$AD = C + I = 6000 + 4000 = 10\ 000$$
$$Y = C + S = 6000 + 4000 = 10\ 000$$

Now suppose that, in period 1, the rate of I increases by 2000 to 6000. AD is now 12 000. The receipts of entrepreneurs rise to 12 000, and stocks of goods decrease. As a result entrepreneurs expand production – factor payments equal 12 000 = Y (Period 1). This expansion of Y has come about solely because I is greater than planned S. Similarly, a contraction of Y will occur if I is less than planned S.

The 'Multiplier'

But this is not the end of the expansion. An increase in Y to 12 000 will mean that more workers are employed, and they, too, will have income to spend. Thus $C = \frac{6}{10}$ (12 000) = 7200. Together with $I = 6000$, this gives a new AD of 13 200. Thus, in period 2, Y increases to 13 200. And so it continues. We can illustrate how the process works in real life from Nevil Shute's *Ruined City*. After years of idleness, the shipyard obtained an order for three tankers:

> The small, returning ripple of prosperity had not passed unnoticed in the district; a shop, long closed, reopened to sell meat pies, cooked meats, black puddings and small delicacies. It did a good trade over Christmas. Small articles began to be sold at the door for the first time for many years; a man who gleaned a sack of holly in the country lanes disposed of it within an hour, a penny for a spray. A hot roast chestnut barrow came upon the streets, and did good trade.

In our example the process will only come to an end when Y has expanded to 15 000. At this level of income, $S = 6000$ – sufficient to match $I = 6000$. Because $S = I$, this is the new equilibrium level of Y.

The sequence outlined above is shown in Table 26.1 and in Figure 26.7.

It will be noted that the increase in Y is much larger than the original increase in I. The ratio

$$\frac{\text{Increase in } AD}{\text{Initial increase in } I}$$

is known as the 'multiplier'.

To see what the size of the multiplier depends upon, we can concentrate on changes in C, S and Y. As we are referring to changes, we shall prefix our symbols with the sign Δ. These changes are shown in Figure 26.8.

Table 26.1
The Effect of an Increase in the Rate of I on the Level of Y

Period	C	I	S	Y
0	6 000	4 000	4 000	10 000
1	6 000	6 000	4 000	12 000
2	7 200	6 000	4 800	13 200
3	7 920	6 000	5 280	13 920
4	8 352	6 000	5 568	14 352
.	.	.	.	.
.	.	.	.	.
.	.	.	.	.
n	9 000	6 000	6 000	15 000

FIGURE 26.7
The Effect of an Increase in the Rate of Investment on the Level of Income

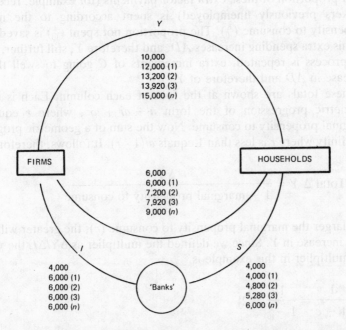

FIGURE 26.8
Increases in Consumption, Saving and Income Resulting from an Increase in the Rate of Investment

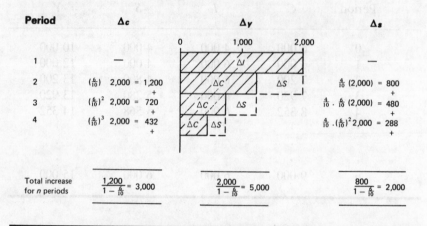

Period	Δc	Δy			Δs
1	—				—
2	$(\frac{6}{10})$ 2,000 = 1,200 +				$\frac{4}{10}$ (2,000) = 800 +
3	$(\frac{6}{10})^2$ 2,000 = 720 +				$\frac{4}{10} \cdot \frac{6}{10}$ (2,000) = 480 +
4	$(\frac{6}{10})^3$ 2,000 = 432 +				$\frac{4}{10} \cdot (\frac{6}{10})^2$ 2,000 = 288 +
Total increase for *n* periods	$\frac{1,200}{1-\frac{6}{10}} = 3,000$	$\frac{2,000}{1-\frac{6}{10}} = 5,000$			$\frac{800}{1-\frac{6}{10}} = 2,000$

Figure 26.8 is explained as follows. The initial ΔI leads to an increase in Y. A proportion of these extra factor payments (for example, received by workers previously unemployed) is spent according to the marginal propensity to consume $(\frac{6}{10})$. The proportion not spent $(\frac{4}{10})$ is saved.

This extra spending increases AD, and therefore Y, still further. And so the process is repeated, extra increments of C going to swell the total increase in AD and therefore of Y.

These totals are shown at the foot of each column. Each is really a geometric progression of the form $a + ar + ar^2$, where r equals the marginal propensity to consume. Now the sum of a geometric progression to infinity where r is less than 1 equals $a/(1 - r)$. It follows, therefore, that:

$$\text{Total } \Delta Y = \frac{\Delta I}{1 - \text{marginal propensity to consume}}$$

The larger the marginal propensity to consume (c), the greater will be the total increase in Y. Since we defined the multiplier as $\Delta Y/\Delta I$, the value of the multiplier in this example is

$$\frac{1}{1-c} = \frac{1}{1-\frac{6}{10}} = 2\frac{1}{2}$$

This can be verified visually in Figure 26.8, where the shaded area equals the total increase in Y. If the proportion of income spent fell to $\frac{1}{2}$, the shaded area would be smaller. Our analysis points to the reason for this. When the fraction of income consumed falls, a higher proportion is saved. Thus income does not have to expand so much in order to bring intended saving into line with investment.

This brings us to the basic difference between saving and investment in the process of income creation. Whereas an increase in investment will, other things being equal, automatically produce an increase in saving, an addition to saving need not lead to an increase in investment. Instead, when the desire to save increases with no similar increase in investment, income merely contracts until what is saved from it equals investment.

Diagrammatic Exposition of Changes in the Equilibrium Level of Income

Employment, we have assumed, varies directly with the level of income (AD), which itself depends upon spending on consumption and investment. If this total spending is equal to income, firms do not make losses and can continue employing the same amount of labour. If total spending is less than income, then firms make a loss because they are getting back less than their expenses of production, and so production is reduced. If total spending increases, then firms more than realise their expectations and production is expanded. This is explained in Figure 26.9.

The income-expenditure line, at an angle of 45°, traces all points where expenditure is equal to income (the same scale being chosen for both the x- and y-axes). Therefore, any point on this line will represent an equilibrium level of income.

The line C shows consumption expenditure at different levels of income. In our example $C = \frac{6}{10}Y$. To this we have to add investment expenditure of 4 000 at all levels of income. Thus the line $C + I$ is vertically distant 4 000 above the C line at all levels of income.

In equilibrium, $Y = AD = C + I$. The only point where this can occur is where the $C + I$ line cuts the 45° line. Here

$$AD = Y = 10\ 000$$

When I increases to 6000, the $C + I$ line moves vertically by 2000 to $C + I'$. AD immediately increases to 12 000, and so does Y. Of this income, $C = 7200$, which, with $I = 6000$, means that AD and Y increase to 13 200. This expansionary process continues until AD and Y are equal to 15 000.

FIGURE 26.9
The Effect on Income of a Change in Investment

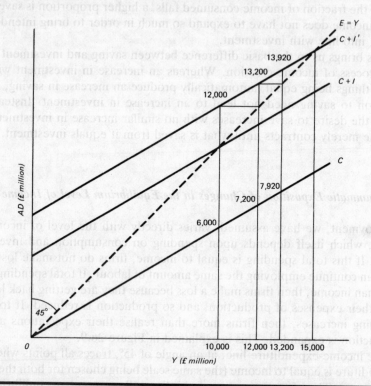

The Effect of a Diminishing Marginal Propensity to Consume

So far we have assumed that the marginal propensity to consume is
constant at all levels of income. But, even if the propensity to consume
diminishes as income increases, the principle of the multiplier is the same.
The only difference is that the calculations are more complicated because,
for each period increment, we have to apply a smaller multiplier, since the
marginal propensity to consume diminishes as income increases.

26.6 The Effect of Changes in Consumption

An Autonomous Change in Consumption

So far we have analysed what happens to AD when there is an increase in autonomous investment. But the result is exactly the same if there is an autonomous increase in consumption, investment remaining unchanged.

Suppose, for instance, that C increases by 2000 at all levels of Y. That is, $C = 2000 + \frac{6}{10}Y$. This simply means that the original $C + I$ curve (Figure 26.9) would move vertically upwards by 2000 to the $C + I'$ position (as with an autonomous increase in I equal to 2000). The increase in C is subject to the same multiplier effect, and thus Y increases as before to 15 000.

The Paradox of Thrift

But what is the situation when there is a decrease in the propensity to consume, i.e. an increase in saving? Here we have what is often called the 'paradox of thrift'.

As we have seen, saving occurs because all income is not spent on consumption; people are limiting their demand for consumer goods. In real terms, they are saying that they will free factors from the production of goods for present consumption so that they can produce capital goods – houses, roads, factories, power stations, machinery, etc. As we saw in Chapter 16, the acquisition of capital involves forgoing present consumption. In this respect, therefore, thrift is a virtue.

But when our peasant farmer reduced present consumption in order to make his plough (see p.225), he automatically carried out investment with the time at his disposal. However, as we have seen, in a modern economy decisions to save and decisions to invest are carried out for different reasons by two different sets of persons – households and firms respectively. When intended saving is greater than investment, not all factors released from producing goods for present consumption are used to produce capital goods. Some are unemployed. From the community's point of view saving can only be in capital goods or additions to stocks. When factors are unemployed there is no real saving – what they could have produced is lost to the community for ever.

What happens, as we have seen, is that income falls until it has reached that level where intended saving out of income just equals investment. Thus, if additional saving is not matched by additional investment, thrift is a curse, not a virtue, for it leads to a reduced standard of living as factors become unemployed and fewer consumer goods are produced.

Indeed, the fall in consumption is likely to have an adverse effect on firms' expectations. Therefore investment itself falls, causing an even greater fall in income. Thus the real paradox of thrift is that, in these circumstances, we can end up with less saving than we originally started with.

Summary

Employment depends upon the level of AD – the total amount of money spent on the goods produced. AD fluctuates according to the relationship between intended saving and investment, so that eventually actual saving equals investment:

1. AD expands if
   (a) investment increases but saving remains unchanged;
   (b) saving decreases but investment remains unchanged.
2. AD contracts if
   (a) the rate of investment decreases but the rate of saving remains unchanged;
   (b) the rate of saving increases but the rate of investment remains unchanged.

In practice, investment is more liable to frequent change than saving. Whereas entrepreneurs' expectations are highly sensitive to new conditions, people's spending habits are fairly stable.

26.7 Government Spending and Taxation

We can now relax our assumption that there is no government activity. The government raises taxes (symbol T). T is a leak out of the circular flow of income, similar to saving.

But government spending (symbol G) is an injection into the flow of AD. Therefore, $AD = C + I + G$. This is shown in Figure 26.10.

G performs the same role as other forms of spending. Any increase in G will be subject to the multiplier. This can be illustrated from Figure 26.9. If, instead of the increase in I, the increase in AD took the form of $G = 2000$, the $C + I'$ line would be simply $C + I + G$, and the new level of Y would still be 15 000.

The effect of taxation is a little more difficult to analyse. However, we shall simplify by assuming: (a) taxes are not related to income (that is, they are imposed autonomously by the government as lump sums); (b) households spread the burden of any change in the level of taxation between consumption and saving.

Suppose $AD = C + I + G = 9000 + 4000 + 2000 = 15\ 000 = Y$; assume also that there is no T. Thus disposable income still equals Y, $C = 9000$ and $S = 6000$. The government now decides to raise 2000 by taxation. Does this mean that Y falls back to 10 000? The answer is 'no'. Disposable income now equals $Y - T$: that is, there is an initial fall to 13 000. As a result there is an initial fall in C ($\frac{6}{10}$ x 13 000) to 7800. But this fall in C is subject to the multiplier; thus the total fall in Y equals

FIGURE 26.10
The Circular Flow of Income and Government Spending and Taxation

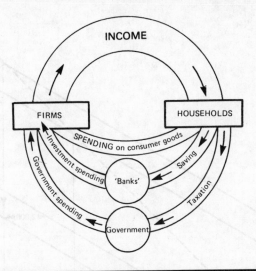

$1200 \times \frac{10}{4} = 3000$, giving $Y = 12\,000$ with $C = 6000$, $I = 4000$ and $G = 2000$. The reason why Y does not fall to $10\,000$ is that part of the burden of T falls on S, which is already a leak from the circular flow of income.

Figure 26.11 illustrates the above diagrammatically. A tax of 2000 reduces disposable income. Consumption is therefore now only what it would be if disposable income were 2000 smaller at all levels of income. Thus the C curve moves downward vertically from C_0 to C_1 by 1200.

It should be noted that in moving from a budget deficit of 2000 to a balanced budget, the government has reduced Y by 3000. Similarly a budget deficit of 2000 from $Y = 12\,000$ would increase Y by 3000. As we shall see, budgetary policy can be an important weapon in securing full employment or in combating inflation.

26.8 The Effect of Foreign Trade

We can now relax our assumption of a closed economy.

Let us assume that the production of consumer and investment goods is at a given level, and that there is unemployment. Now imagine that British firms obtain orders to supply £2000 worth of capital equipment to the USA. As a result, in the British economy AD and Y expand initially by

FIGURE 26.11
The Effect of an Increase in Taxation on Disposable Income and Consumption

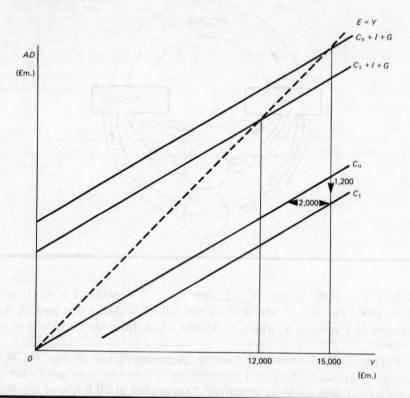

2000 – paid out in wages, salaries and profits, the cost being covered by entrepreneurs borrowing the money.

But this is not all. Of the initial 2000 increase, 1200 will be spent and 800 saved. The 1200 spent now becomes income of other persons, who in their turn spend 720 and save 480. So we could go on. The position is exactly the same as with investment – additional spending by persons abroad on British exports has a multiplier effect depending upon the marginal propensity to consume. In this case, as a result of the initial additional spending of 2000 on exports, *AD* increases by 5000.

Increased spending on imports, given the conditions of unemployment stipulated above, works in exactly the opposite way. There is now more spending on foreign goods, and less on British. As a result, foreign rather than British workers supply goods for the home market. Less expenditure on home-produced goods means that income is taken out of the circular flow, and AD contracts. As before, the initial loss of income is multiplied according to the marginal propensity to consume.

We can summarise the position as follows. Expenditure on exports is equivalent to an addition to investment – income is generated in producing goods which do not become available on the home market. Expenditure on imports, on the other hand, is a leak from the circular flow of income similar to a reduction of consumption. Hence we can combine the effect on AD of changes in investment, exports and imports as follows:

$$\text{Increase in } AD = \frac{\text{Increase in } I + \text{Exports} - \text{Imports}}{1 - c}$$

The above explanation, however, does assume that both exports and imports are autonomous, i.e. they bear no precise relationship to the level of income. We shall continue this assumption with exports, though it could be that these decline as income expands, since it is now easier to sell on the home market.

But imports are likely to form a proportion of consumer spending, and therefore of income. Thus if we assume that imports form $\frac{1}{6} C$, we can say that the 'propensity to import' is $\frac{1}{10} Y$. We can now treat this import leakage in the same way as saving. Whatever the cause of the initial expansion in Y, leakages occur because some of this increased Y will be saved and some will be spent on imports. Thus, when m represents the *marginal* propensity to import, we have:

$$\text{Change in } AD = \frac{\text{Change in } I + \text{Change in exports}}{1 - c + m}$$

Suppose, for instance, that income is in equilibrium at 10 000. There is no foreign trade, and $C = 6000$ and $S = 4000$. At any income above this the marginal propensity to import is $\frac{1}{6} C = \frac{1}{10} Y$. If there are now exports of 2000, the increase in Y will be 2000 $1/(\frac{4}{10} + \frac{1}{10}) = 4000$.

The analysis of this section indicates why, during the 1930s, many countries tried to solve their unemployment problems by pushing exports (which increase income and therefore employment) and by discouraging imports (which decrease income). A little reflection will show, however, that such a restrictionist policy merely 'exports' unemployment to other countries. Nowadays we realise that countries must co-operate with one another in fighting unemployment (see pp.410–11, 431–2).

26.9 An Explanation of Cyclical Fluctuations

So far in this chapter we have been concerned with building up a theoretical model showing how fluctuations in AD (national income) can occur. We must now use this model to explain such fluctuations and the unemployment connected with it. In particular, the following questions must be answered: Why do the upswings and downswings occur? Why are they cumulative? Why do they eventually come to an end and reverse their direction? Why may this happen before full employment is reached? Why are the capital-goods industries and export industries more severely hit? Why do prices eventually rise in the upswing? We concentrate our attention on the private sector.

The Upswing

Let us start from the bottom of the depression. Until now there has been a cumulative downswing. What causes the upturn? Why does AD begin to increase?

As we have seen, AD can increase because (*a*) investment, but not saving, increases, (*b*) saving, but not investment, decreases, (*c*) exports increase in value more than imports. For the following reasons, all three changes become more likely as the level of income continues to fall.

Investment may revive for a variety of reasons. Stocks may have run low. Fixed equipment wears out and replacement cannot be postponed indefinitely. Additional fields of profitable investment arise as, with time, new techniques or even new industries are developed.

Saving decreases because the marginal propensity to consume increases as income falls. People may even spend past savings in order to maintain their standard of living.

Imports tend to fall in value and exports to increase. This occurs because (*a*) lower income means a fall in the demand for imports, (*b*) lower relative wages and costs, produced eventually by unemployment, lead to lower prices and therefore to increased overseas demand for exports (see p.428). This process is strengthened if other countries' incomes are expanding. Indeed, with international trade assuming a greater significance, cyclical fluctuations now tend to be worldwide.

But this is not all. When investment increases, the initial effect on AD is magnified by the multiplier. Moreover, a revival in one part of the economy is likely to make firms more optimistic elsewhere. They, too, begin to reinvest. The upswing is cumulative.

Added impetus is provided by the accelerator. Until now, firms have been reluctant to replace their machinery. Thus the increase in demand for consumer goods finds them short of productive capacity. The acceleration principle shows the marked effect that this has on the capital-goods industries. The climb back to greater prosperity gathers momentum as the revival spreads.

The Break in the Boom

Why should the upswing fizzle out? The reason is that the increase in *AD* begins to level off. This happens because both the proportion of income consumed and investment eventually fall.

As income increases, the marginal propensity to consume falls. Not only do people spend a smaller proportion of their income as income rises, but it is likely that more of that income is going to profit-recipients who are likely to spend a smaller proportion of their income than wage-earners. The result is that, unless investment increases to match increased savings as income expands, the expansion in income will come to an end.

But even if there is increasing investment, it is doubtful whether it will be sufficient to maintain the *rate of increase* of *AD*. If it is not, the accelerator comes into operation. Then the level of investment falls back to where it is just sufficient for replacement purposes only, no additional capacity being required. In addition, new fields of investment, e.g. through the invention of new techniques or the development of new industries, can be expected to become exhausted. There is thus a built-in mechanism which is likely to cause investment to tail off.

But even without this, all types of investment may fall simply because firms become less optimistic. Normally this is brought about by the slackening off in demand for the reasons just given. Nevertheless, there are other factors at work. When investment is running at a high rate, the confidence of entrepreneurs is vulnerable to even minor setbacks. Capital may prove to be less profitable than expected because it has been invested by different entrepreneurs in competing products so that, relative to total demand, there is over-investment. Or the government, fearing that inflation will develop, raises the rate of interest. While this may have little direct effect on large firms – they can bear the extra cost or expand out of their liquid reserves – they are bound to wonder how it will affect the purchasers of their products. Although proposed investment may not be cancelled, it could be postponed.

Finally, at some stage in the boom, factors may arise which cause exports to fall or imports to increase:

1. As incomes expand, not only are more imports demanded, but goods which might have been exported are diverted to the home market.
2. The nearer a country approaches full employment, the greater is the tendency for costs and prices to rise (see p.356). Her exports, therefore, becomes less competitive.
3. Important buyers of exports may suffer a depression before the home country. As a result, their demand falls. This is particularly serious for

a country so dependent on international trade as the UK. When this happens, *AD* falls – a slump has been 'imported' (see p.316).

Thus we see that both the recession and the boom contain the seeds of their own destruction.

The Downswing

The break in the boom is followed by a downswing which can gather momentum. Falling expenditure in one part of the economy leads to reduced expenditure elsewhere. The multiplier is working in reverse! Pessimistic expectations of entrepreneurs are therefore justified, and the drop to the bottom of the depression is a sharp one. Nor will interest policy prove effective. While a rise in the rate of interest may check a boom, a decrease is unlikely to halt a depression. As expectations of entrepreneurs grow more pessimistic, so the MEI curve falls to the left, and this outweighs any reduction of the rate of interest aimed at restoring investment (see p.332).

Eventually, however, for the reasons already given, the bottom is reached, and the upswing begins. The cycle varies both in the time taken and its severity.

26.10 The Control of Cyclical Unemployment

To combat cyclical unemployment, *AD* must be maintained at an adequate level. The responsibility for this must rest with the government. First, only the government can exercise the powers, particularly as regards collecting the statistics and information necessary for adequate planning. Second, the government's own spending forms such a large proportion of *AD* that, to a great extent, it can be used to balance variations in the private sector. Third, the knowledge that the government is committed to a full-employment policy will eliminate much of the uncertainty from which cyclical fluctuations begin.

A Brief Analysis of the Task

In order to make our explanation simpler, we shall assume a closed economy.

Employment depends upon the level of national income (*Y*). If the level of *AD* is too low, the economy will be in equilibrium where *Y* is below the full-employment level. Thus the government's task is to estimate the level of *AD* that will produce full employment, and then arrange that *AD* is increased to this level.

In terms of Figure 26.10, this means that the government must increase the size of injections – *C*, *I* and *G* – relative to the size of the leaks – *S* and *T*. The multiplier will enlarge any change made to produce a new equilibrium where *AD = Y*. This must be the full-employment *Y*.

The same requirement can also be shown on a 45° diagram (Figure 26.12). Full employment requires *Y* to equal *OE*. An *AD* as shown by *C + I + G′*, however, will produce equilibrium where *Y = OF = OZ*. If we look at the situation from the full-employment level of *Y*, there is a deficiency of *AD* equal to *LM* – the 'deflationary' gap. The government has to raise the *AD* curve to *C + I + G*.

FIGURE 26.12
Equilibrium Levels of Income

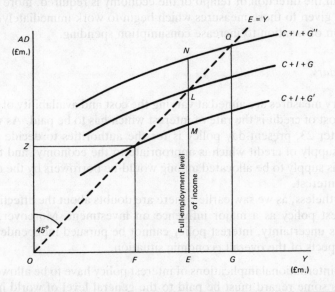

The Nature of Government Action

The role of the government in controlling the economy can be likened to that of the driver of a car going to work in a city. At no time can the car run on its own without some direction, and the driver has to make the necessary adjustments continuously. From time to time, too, he or she is concerned with more definite alterations, varying pressure on the accelerator and changing gear. The driver may even modify the route, making detours to avoid traffic congestions.

But in all these manoeuvres, different drivers act differently. Some use the gear lever rather than the accelerator in changing speed. Others estimate that the traffic congestion will not be so bad as to warrant a detour. Nor does the same person do exactly the same things each day. The driver knows many different routes to work and, being flexible, makes use of them as he or she thinks fit.

So it is with the government. Like the driver guessing the traffic congestion along the route, the government has to work from incomplete information in estimating what change in *AD* is necessary to produce the desired result and the extent to which the measures it adopts will produce that change. It has two main types of control – monetary and fiscal – but it usually has to combine them in different ways. Not only does one reinforce the other, but a different emphasis has to be placed on each at different times in order to meet the needs of the prevailing situation. Where a quick change in the direction or tempo of the economy is required, more weight must be given to those measures which begin to work immediately, e.g. a reduction of taxation to increase consumption spending.

1. Monetary

Monetary measures are aimed at varying the cost and availability of credit.

The cost of credit is the rate of interest which has to be paid. As we saw in Chapter 23, present-day policy is for the authorities to decide on the overall supply of credit which is appropriate to the economy, and then to allow this supply to be allocated among would-be borrowers by the market rate of interest.

Nevertheless, as we saw earlier, there are doubts about the effectiveness of interest policy as a major influence on investment. Moreover, apart from this uncertainty, interest policy cannot be pursued independently of other aspects of the overall economic situation.

(*a*) The international implications of interest policy have to be allowed for. Thus some regard must be paid to the general level of world interest rates. If, for instance, Britain retained interest rates which were low in relation to those of the rest of the world, there would be an outflow of sterling balances, with a consequent lowering of the sterling exchange rate.

(*b*) The PSBR may be so large, that a high interest rate is necessary to attract loans (see p. 353). It must be remembered, however, that this adds to the burden of servicing the National Debt, necessitating higher taxation.

(*c*) The rate of interest does not discriminate in its operation, e.g. as between firms which export a high proportion of their output and those which do not, and projects of high social value (e.g. slum clearance) and those of less certain merit (e.g. gaming casinos).

Even so, interest policy can still play a part in regulating the economy. It can be applied quickly and to a fine degree and, if implemented early, can provide advance warning of the authorities' intentions. Indeed, the psychological effects of changes are probably much more important than their direct effect on the cost of long-term investment. Finally, because the rate of interest affects the flow of funds internationally, any changes have an impact on foreign exchange rates and thus on the competitiveness of exports.

The *availability of credit* is concerned with the overall level of liquidity and selective controls. The former is now linked to the declared ceilings on increases in the money supply and reflects the more recent emphasis on allowing the rate of interest to rise in order to curb the demand for bank credit (see pp.291, 474).

In contrast, selective controls are really only effective when the interest rate is being held below the 'market' rate. Because demand for credit exceeds the supply, some allocation by controls is then necessary. Such credit controls have been exercised mainly by restrictions on bank advances and hire purchase.

2. Fiscal

Indirectly, fiscal policy can influence private consumption and investment by changing the type of taxes levied. Thus a switch from indirect to direct taxation would tend to increase consumption, for it would mean greater spending power for poorer people (those having a high propensity to consume). Similarly, a movement away from taxes on firms would tend to increase investment through improved profitability.

More directly, spending may be influenced by budget policy. Today the budget is regarded, not as the means by which revenue is raised to meet estimated expenditure for the year, but as the weapon to adjust AD to the output which can be produced by the resources available. Reducing taxation will increase disposable income. Provided this increase is not all saved, spending will increase (expanding income according to the multiplier). In terms of Figure 26.11, the C curve will rise. Thus, if government spending remains unchanged, the curve $C + I + G$ will rise (Figure 26.12).

Attention must be paid to the phrase 'if government spending remains unchanged'. Budgetary policy is essentially one of adjusting the relationship between government taxation and expenditure. As we have seen, taxation represents an appropriation by the government of a part of private incomes. The amount so appropriated is retained in the circular flow of income only in so far as it is spent by the government. Hence AD will be increased if taxation is less than government spending and vice versa. If previously the budget were balanced, there will now be a budget deficit, and vice versa.

Such a policy is not without its difficulties. First, the convention of annual budgets tends to dictate the timing of major adjustments. However, 'mini' budgets are possible, while the 'regulator' does allow the Chancellor to vary VAT by 25 per cent and other indirect taxes by 10 per cent at any time. Second, reducing taxes may, because of administrative difficulties, take time to be effective. With PAYE, for instance, new tax tables have to be distributed. Thus reliefs will often have to concentrate on putting extra purchasing power quickly into the hands of consumers, e.g. by reducing National Insurance contributions and indirect taxes. Taxation, too, has objectives other than that of adjusting AD – redistributing income, for instance. But a rise in taxation may have to be achieved by increasing indirect taxes because of possible disincentive effects of high income tax. Thus policies can conflict. Third, overall budgetary policy makes it difficult to direct demand into those districts and industries where unemployment is highest. Again we see the necessity of having a variety of measures which can be applied to the needs of a particular situation. Finally, the deficit may be so large and persistent that it can only be financed by raising the rate of interest to attract loans, or by creating money, which may have inflationary consequences (see p.353).

Nevertheless, budgetary policy does allow the national product to be divided between private and communal uses according to their relative priorities. There are certain tasks which can be undertaken better by the state than by private enterprise, and the government must decide on the proportion of the national product which shall be devoted to these – defence, justice, social welfare, roads, health, etc. Thus taxation policy can be regarded as a means by which private demand is adjusted to release resources for the needs of the public sector. If there is full employment, excessive private demand will leave insufficient resources to meet the needs of the public sector. Thus taxation must be increased – or public expenditure be reduced. If, on the other hand, private demand is insufficient to employ fully resources which are not required by the public sector, taxation must be reduced. Such a policy for full employment avoids *direction* of resources. Once the essential claims of the public sector on the economy have been met, the rest of the national product can be produced through the price system. Thus the main advantages of that system – the efficiency which springs from the profit motive, individual choice, the accurate assessment of consumers' wants, and the provision for those wants – are retained.

Weaknesses of Keynes's Theory

Keynes wrote his *General Theory* against a background of the high cyclical unemployment of the 1930s. As we have seen, his basic remedy was to expand AD, mainly by budgetary deficit policy.

But Keynes's preoccupation with maintaining a high level of employment led him, and in particular his followers, to under-emphasise its pressure on the price level and the balance of payments. Nevertheless until the early 1970s governments were able to restrict the rate of unemployment to 3 per cent by 'fine-tuning' the economy, imposing temporary 'stop' policies whenever expansion led to balance-of-payments' difficulties.

However, as the rate of inflation and then the level of unemployment increased together, Keynes's views came under increasing scrutiny. For one thing he had under-played the side-effects of a large PSBR which high government spending had given rise to. If it was covered by borrowing from the banks, it increased their liquidity and thus the supply of money. If it was covered by borrowing outside the banks, the rate of interest would rise. This could cause private investment to fall, 'crowded out' by the increased public spending!

But a more important criticism of Keynes was that his theory of the price level under-estimated the impact on AD of increases in the money supply and gave insufficient weight to the role of trade unions' inflation-expectations in the wage-bargaining process. Furthermore, since expanding AD to achieve a high level of employment is inhibited by the threat of inflation, more attention has to be paid to increasing employment by incentives to increase production. This 'supply side' approach is in line with the evidence that Britain is suffering from a high degree of structural unemployment. It is these problems which we analyse in Chapters 27 and 36.

The Meaning of 'Full Employment' Today

While in our presentation in this chapter of the Keynesian theory of unemployment we have, for the sake of clarity, shown the full-employment level of income as a single point, it is, in the real world, a too simplistic and static approach. The incompatibility of government objectives – price stability, a strong balance of payments, full employment and growth – means that policy has to consider the full implications of seeking to maintain a high level of employment. Before full employment is reached, inflationary and balance-of-payments difficulties are likely to occur. Thus in practice there is now no precise target full-employment level of income which can be achieved by 'fine-tuning' the economy. Instead, the 'full-employment' position has to be determined politically according to the emphasis placed by the government on the other objectives.

27
Inflation

The prices of goods can, as we have seen, rise or fall relatively to each other owing to changes in demand or supply. At times, however, it is observed that the prices of *all* goods generally are rising or falling, apart from variations in their relative prices. We say then that there is a rise or fall in the general level of prices, or, what is the same thing, a fall or rise respectively in the value of money.

The situation over the last forty years, however, has been one of constantly rising prices. It is therefore the problem of inflation that we concentrate on in this chapter.

27.1 The Effects of Inflation

Today the control of inflation is given priority in government policy. To appreciate why, we have to look at the effects of rising prices or – what is the same thing – a fall in the value of money. It is then necessary to consider the causes of inflation and the possible remedies that can be applied.

Possible Benefits

At one time a gently rising price level was not viewed with too much concern. It improved the climate for investment and so helped to maintain aggregate demand. Moreover, it tended to reduce the real burden of servicing the National Debt: while interest payments are fixed in money terms, receipts from taxation increase as money national income rises.

The snag, however, is that, once started, the rise in prices is difficult to contain. At first it becomes uncomfortable, producing undesirable results, both internal and external. Eventually the rate of inflation increases. The

354

situation is then serious, for it is much more difficult to reverse the trend. Indeed it can develop into runaway inflation.

Internal Disadvantages

1. Income is redistributed arbitrarily. Not only does inflation reduce the standard of living of persons dependent on fixed incomes, e.g. pensioners, but it benefits debtors and penalises lenders (unless the loan is 'inflation-proofed'). Thus the stability upon which all lending and borrowing depends is undermined.
2. Interest rates rise, both because people require a higher reward for lending money which is falling in value and also because the government is forced to take disinflationary measures.
3. Investment is discouraged by government anti-inflation policy. In practice, controls imposed on prices are more effective than those on costs, particularly wages. The result is an erosion of profits and a disincentive to invest.
4. Saving is discouraged because postponing consumption simply means that goods cost more if bought later.
5. Inefficiency is encouraged because a buoyant sellers' market blunts competition as higher prices obtained for their products allow even inefficient firms to survive.
6. Inflation generates industrial and social unrest since there is competition for higher incomes. Thus, because of rising prices, trade unions ask for annual wage rises. Often, demands exceed the rate of inflation, anticipating future rises or seeking a larger share of the national cake to improve their members' real standard of living. Those with the most 'muscle' gain at the expense of weaker groups.
7. The rate of inflation tends to increase, largely because high wage settlements in anticipation of higher future prices help to bring about the very rise which people fear.

External Effects

Inflation can create serious difficulties for a country dependent on international trade, as Britain has discovered over the past thirty years.

1. Exports tend to decline because they are relatively dearer in foreign markets.
2. Imports tend to increase because foreign goods are relatively cheaper on the British market.
3. Higher money incomes in the UK increase the demand for imports and tend to decrease exports because the 'soft' home market makes it less vital for manufacturers to seek outlets abroad for their goods.

4.   An outward movement of capital may take place if price rises continue since foreign traders and financiers lose confidence in the pound sterling maintaining its current rate of exchange.

While the above effects are uncomfortable, it is possible to live with a moderate rise in prices. The snag is that where rising prices are thought likely to continue, people bring forward their spending, thereby producing the very price rise feared – an example of 'self-justified expectations'. So the process gathers momentum, stimulated still further by demands for higher wage increases.

27.2 Causes of Inflation: a Simplified Statement

Prices rise when there is excess purchasing power for goods available at current prices. But what brings about the excess of purchasing power? Experience of inflation over the last thirty years suggests that there is no single cause. We can begin, however, by distinguishing initiating impulses on both the demand and supply sides.

1. Demand-pull

The Keynesian analysis of the determination of the level of activity suggests that, if there is cyclical unemployment, the situation can be improved by increasing aggregate demand (AD). We can use Figure 27.1 to explain how this will affect the price level.

At low levels of output there is surplus capital and labour, and so supply can be expanded at constant cost: the aggregate supply curve, AS, is horizontal. But as the full employment output Y_f is approached, firms' costs begin to rise as less efficient labour is employed and bottlenecks occur in the supply of components. At full employment, output cannot be increased and the AS curve is vertical.

AD can be expected to *expand* as the price level falls: given no change in the money supply, cash balances increase in real terms and so consumer spending increases. There is also less transactions demand for money, so that the rate of interest falls and investment increases. The AD curve therefore slopes downwards to the right.

Thus, if AD is *increased* when output is at a low level, e.g. by an increase in government spending, output expands at constant prices. Eventually, e.g. when the AD curve has moved from AD to AD_1, the price level begins to rise. Any increase in AD when there is full employment produces a truly inflationary situation.

This last situation is covered in Figure 26.12. The $C + I + G''$ curve gives an AD which is more than sufficient to produce full employment.

FIGURE 27.1
The Relationship Between the Price Level and Total Output (Aggregate Supply)

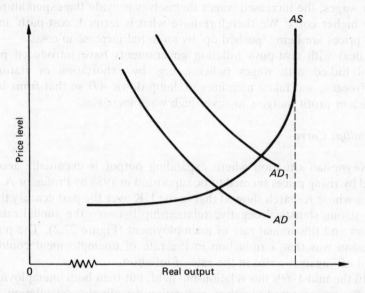

Since output cannot rise above *OE*, there is an inflationary gap of *NL* and prices rise. To cure this *demand-pull* inflation it would seem that the government has simply to lower the curve to *C + I + G*, thereby reducing *AD* from *EN* to *EL*, giving a full-employment level of income, *OE*.

2. Cost-push

The rise in prices can start on the supply side, e.g. through an increase in the price of imports. Thus the four fold rise in oil prices in 1973–4 triggered off world-wide inflation.

More usually, however, cost-push inflation has followed on from demand-pull. Once prices start to rise as the government pursues a full-employment policy, trade unions seek compensating wage increases. Indeed, the scale of their demands tends to increase in order to allow for future price rises. Furthermore, the current practice is for such demands to be presented yearly, even in excess of the rate of inflation and without any justifying increase in productivity.

Where the level of activity is high employers tend not to resist such demands, feeling that product prices can be raised to cover them. In practice, their expectations are justified, for unless the government imposes financial restraints to make it more difficult for firms to cover higher wages, the increased wages themselves provide the expenditure to justify higher costs. We therefore have what is termed 'cost-push' inflation – prices are being 'pushed up' by an initial increase in costs.

To deal with cost-push inflation governments have introduced price control linked with wages policies, e.g. by exhortation or statutory wage-freezes, and taken measures to damp down *AD* so that firms have insufficient profit margins to cover high wage increases.

The Phillips Curve

The Keynesian situation where expanding output is eventually accompanied by rising prices seemed to be supported in 1958 by Professor A. W. Phillips whose research showed that in the UK over the past century there was a strong statistical negative relationship between the annual rate of inflation and the annual rate of unemployment (Figure 27.2). The policy conclusion was that a reduction in the rate of unemployment could be 'traded off' against a rise in the rate of inflation.

Until the mid-1960s this relationship held, but then both unemployment and inflation increased together, a situation described as 'stagflation'.

Inadequacy of the Keynesian Explanation

The weakness of the Keynesian approach is that it is too static, allowing nothing for expectations. Instead of inflation being merely a condition of excess demand at the full-employment level, it is a *process*. An initial price rise generates demands for wage increases from trade unions in key industries even though there had been little increase in productivity and irrespective of the fact that some of their members were already unemployed. Moreover, wage rises awarded in the growth industries are in practice conceded in declining industries, e.g. shipbuilding, steel, cars, etc., through the annual process of wage bargaining. Indeed, it is asserted that any norm urged by the government merely reinforces an across-the-board increase since it is interpreted as a minimum for all workers.

But increased wages push up prices still further, thus leading to new demands for wage rises, often geared to an *expected* higher rate of inflation. In short, there is an inflationary spiral. Thus the remedy is not a simple piece of surgery to remove excess fat, but rather a fight against a cancerous growth.

Thus an alternative theory of inflation embodying expectations was required. This has been built up by the 'monetarists', led by Professor Milton Friedman.

FIGURE 27.2
The Phillips Curve

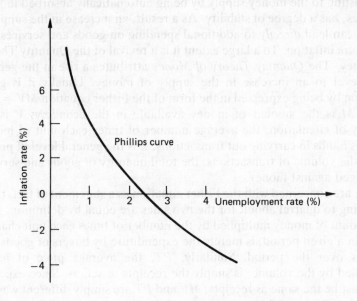

27.3 Monetarism

The current monetarist explanation of inflation has three main elements: the direct connection between the money supply and *AD*; inflation expectations as a cause of the inflation process; and a 'natural rate of unemployment' hypothesis. We will explain each in turn.

The Money Supply and AD

It was observed that there was a positive correlation between increases in the money supply and the rate of inflation. But is there a causal connection? Does an increase in the money supply *directly* increase *AD*?

As we have seen (pp. 257–61) Keynes considered that the supply of money did not enter directly into spending decisions. In the short run these were dependent upon the level of income; over time they would be affected by long-term factors, such as social example, thrift habits, contractual commitments to regular saving, etc. Any increase in the supply of money simply found its way into 'idle' balances, making it easier to be liquid for speculative purposes. Its impact, therefore, is on the rate of interest. Aggregate demand (AD) will expand only indirectly, through a lower rate of interest leading to more investment spending.

In contrast, Milton Friedman holds that the demand for money, instead of adjusting to the money supply by being automatically absorbed in 'idle' balances, has a degree of stability. As a result, an increase in the supply of money can lead *directly* to additional spending on goods and services and thus *cause* inflation. To a large extent it is a revival of the Quantity Theory of Money. The *Quantity Theory of Money* attributes a rise in the general price level to an increase in the supply of money. Usually it is given precision by being expressed in the form of the Fisher equation $MV = PT$, where M is the amount of money available in the economy, V is the velocity of circulation, the average number of times each unit of money changes hands in carrying out transactions, P is the general level of prices, and T the volume of transactions, the total quantity of goods and services exchanged against money.

If we are concerned with the Fisher equation as a statement of fact, there is nothing to quarrel about, for the two sides are equal by definition. MV, the amount of money multiplied by the number of times each unit changes hands in a given period, is merely the expenditure by buyers of goods and services over the period. Similarly, PT, the average price of goods multiplied by the volume, is simply the receipts of sellers. Since expenditure must be the same as receipts, MV and PT are simply different ways of expressing the same thing.

But as an explanation of what *causes* changes in the price level, the Quantity Theory is only valid if T and V can be assumed to be constant. It is regarding V – which can be looked upon as the demand for money in reverse – that Keynes and Friedman clash.

The monetarists consider that people maintain a fraction of their nominal income in cash balances. An increase in the money supply results in their having larger cash balances than they require, and so run them down by spending. Such spending increases AD and money incomes until cash balances are equal to their former fraction. Nor does this surplus cash have to be spent on bonds (as Keynes holds). Wealth can be held in many forms: cash which yields liquidity, 'bonds' which yield interest and possible capital appreciation, and consumer goods which yield utility. People distribute their spending according to their marginal preferences for those different forms of yield (which in turn can be influenced by their expected rate of inflation).

Thus any increase in the money supply is likely after a little while to lead to some increase in the demand for consumer goods, resulting in a rise in their prices.

FIGURE 27.3
The Effect of Inflation-expectations on the Rate of Unemployment

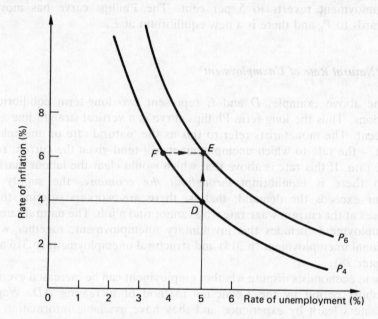

Inflation Expectations

Once inflation expectations enter into wage negotiations, the monetarists hold that increasing *AD* will not achieve a *long-term* decrease in the rate of unemployment but simply result in higher inflation. In short there is no trade-off between inflation and unemployment as in the Keynesian model (Figure 27.3). We refer again to the Phillips curve.

In Figure 27.3 we assume that the rate of inflation is 4 per cent and the rate of unemployment is 5 per cent. This position at *D* is stable because wage-bargainers have expected 4 per cent to be the inflation rate.

The government now decides that it wants to reduce the unemployment rate to 4 per cent and accordingly increases *AD*. Prices rise to 6 per cent inflation at *F*, but money wage rates do not rise. Thus firms, enjoying increased profitability, increase output so that initially unemployment falls to 4 per cent on curve P_4.

But this is only a short-term position depending on the fact that workers tend to concentrate on nominal money-wages rather than real wages – the 'money illusion'. Eventually, however, they realise that real wages have fallen and in their next wage negotiations they obtain a 6 per cent rise in money wages to cover what they expect to be the rate of inflation. The recovery in real wage-rates increases costs, so that firms reduce output and unemployment reverts to 5 per cent. The Phillips curve has moved outwards to P_6 and there is a new equilibrium at E.

The 'Natural Rate of Unemployment'

In the above example, D and E represent two long-term equilibrium positions. Thus the long-term Phillips curve is a vertical straight line at 5 per cent. The monetarists refer to this as the 'natural rate of unemployment' – the rate to which unemployment will tend given the current real wage rate. If this rate is above that which would clear the labour market when there is equilibrium *throughout the economy*, the supply of labour exceeds the demand; that is, there are workers offering their services at the current wage rate who cannot find a job. The natural rate of unemployment includes this involuntary unemployment, together with frictional unemployment (p.314) and structural unemployment (p.316 and Chapter 28).

Some economists dispute whether employment can be increased even in the short period by the Keynesian method of increasing AD. Wage-bargainers learn by experience and they have available information by which they can *predict* the future rate of inflation. Thus the correct expected rate of inflation is embodied in their wage settlements. This assertion of 'rational expectations' rather than a mere adaptation to a new inflation rate means that the long-period Phillips curve also depicts the short-period situation.

27.4 Policy Implications of Monetarist Theory

Monetarist theory originated as an explanation of how increases in the supply of money led directly to increases in AD and thus to rising prices. Even with cost-push inflation, extra money is necessary to accommodate wage increases. Thus the first condition for keeping inflation in check is strict control over the money supply.

A major difficulty here is that 'money' is difficult to define (see p.255) and policy has to be based on an imperfect money index (see p.473).

But, as we have seen, the theory goes further to show that expanding AD to reduce unemployment will only be successful for as long as there is a fall in real wage rates. This may occur in the short period owing to the 'money illusion', but eventually labour incorporates a revised higher expected rate of inflation in its wage negotiations. Indeed, if the 'rational expectations' view applies, there is not even a short-term improvement in unemployment through an increase in AD.

Government policy must be directed to convincing the trade unions that the trend of the future rate of inflation is downwards. This is not easy for until wage negotiators can actually see a falling rate of inflation, they interpret a wage increase which falls short of their expected rate of inflation as a cut in real wages. Yet wage-restraint is the 'least-cost' policy for controlling inflation. The difficulty is that voluntary restraint soon breaks down, and statutory wage and price freezes have to be imposed in an attempt to break the inflation spiral. But the rigidity in the economy which results means that even these cannot last long.

An alternative approach is to reduce inflation expectations by announcing strict monetary and fiscal targets for the medium-term future. The extent to which such a policy reduces rational expectations largely depends on how far unions are convinced of the government's resolve to hold to its targets. In this respect it should be noted that if the government sets a limit to the PSBR it virtually has to have a wages policy for the public sector, and its determination to restrict wage increases here will have its impact on the private sector.

Unfortunately the change in the economic climate takes time to be realised especially when in the past trade union negotiators have been consistently successful in obtaining inflationary wage increases. In the meantime there may be a sequence of unsuccessful strikes and a prolonged period of unemployment. This is the 'high cost' alternative.

27.5 Supply-Side Measures

The introduction of the hypothesis of a 'natural rate of unemployment' suggests that, since expanding AD is ineffective in reducing unemployment, less emphasis should be placed on demand and more attention given to supply. Reducing the costs of production would mean that a greater output could be supplied at any given price level, i.e. the AS curve shifts to the right. Put in an alternative way, the objective is an eventual reduction in the natural rate of unemployment.

Policy to achieve this embraces a variety of incentives usually included under the umbrella term 'supply-side economics'. It integrates longer-term micro measures within the overall macro policy.

Costs can be lowered by:

(a) reducing national insurance contributions – an *ad valorem* tax on employing labour;
(b) improving the supply of labour through training, encouraging flexible working hours to allow part-time workers to enter the labour force, and restricting by law the power of trade unions to call strikes;

(c) giving grants for relocating to a Development Area (see p.373)
(d) improving the mobility of labour (see pp.371, 373)

Incentives to increase enterprise and effort include:

(a) reducing the marginal rate of income tax (though here a negative income effect may reduce the supply of labour);
(b) reducing corporation tax, thereby encouraging investment and the undertaking of entrepreneurial risks;
(c) making it easier for new and smaller firms to obtain capital, e.g. by 'start-up' allowances, income tax concessions to investors through the Business Expansion Scheme.

Indeed many supply-side measures encourage long-term growth of the economy. Thus a lowering of the rate of interest and investment allowances stimulate capital development, while one of the aims of privatisation is to improve economic performance through competition in the market economy.

27.6 Concluding Observations

This chapter has discussed the difficulty of achieving a low rate of unemployment without making the rate of inflation uncomfortable.

The Keynesian solution puts the emphasis on reducing unemployment by expanding AD. Its success depends largely on achieving an effective policy to restrain rises in real wages which are not matched by increases in productivity.

In contrast, monetarist policies centre on strict control of the money supply and *supply-side* economics. The monetarist approach rests on two hypotheses – a stable demand for money and a natural rate of unemployment – both of which still require empirical verification. However, the experience of Britain and other Western economies in recent years does seem to indicate a link between an increase in the supply of money and, after a time-lag, an increase in the rate of inflation. What is certain is that without increases in the supply of money, inflation cannot continue.

Few economists, however, would go so far as to say that the increase in the supply of money was the *cause* of an inflation. As we have seen, there is no *single* cause. Excess AD may be generated in a number of ways apart from spending newly-created money. It may come from increased government spending, or arise on the cost side through wage demands or higher import prices. The tendency, therefore, is to favour a pragmatic approach combining control of the money supply with other policies.

This is consistent with the fact that inflation cannot be considered in isolation from employment and economic growth. Control of inflation may be the prior condition for a healthy economy, especially for the UK which is so dependent on maintaining exports. But in the final analysis the extent to which priority is given to inflation is a political decision.

How actual policies have varied and been implemented in the UK over the last thirty years are described in Chapter 36.

27.7 A Note on Measuring Changes in the General Level of Prices

The difficulty in measuring changes in the general level of prices (that is, in the value of money) is that different kinds of prices – wholesale prices, retail prices, security prices, import prices, etc. – change differently. If we tried to measure changes in all prices, therefore, our task would be stupendous. But more than that, it would lack practical significance. Suppose, for instance, that security prices rose considerably, other prices remaining unchanged. A measurement of the general level of prices would show a rise, but this would be of little interest to the manual worker who owns no securities.

When measuring changes in the value of money, therefore, it is usual to concentrate on changes in the prices of those goods which are of most general significance – the goods bought by the majority of people, for it is upon the prices of these that the cost of living really depends.

Method of Measuring Changes in the Value of Money

Since we are mainly interested in the extent to which the value of money has altered between one date and another, it can be measured as a relative change by means of an *index number*. The steps are as follows:

1. A base year is selected. This is now referred to as the 'reference date'.
2. In order to ensure that the same goods are valued over the period under consideration, a 'basket' of goods, based on the current spending habits and income of the 'typical' family is chosen.
3. The basket is valued at prices, and expressed as 100.
4. The same basket is revalued at current prices.
5. The cost of the current basket is then expressed as a percentage of the base year. Thus if the cost of living had risen by 5 per cent, the index for the current year would be 105.

In practice, the prices of the selected goods are compared, their percentage changes being 'weighted' according to the relative expenditure on the particular commodity in the base year. Suppose, for instance, that there are only two commodities, bread and meat, upon which income is spent. The index between two years is calculated as follows on page 366. The price in year II is expressed as a percentage of the price in year I. This is multiplied by the appropriate weight to give a 'weighted price relative'. These weighted price relatives are then totalled and divided by the total of the weights to give the new index number.

| | YEAR I | | | | YEAR II | | |
	Price	Units bought	Expend-iture	Weight	Price	Year II as % of year I	Weighted price relative
Bread	30p	5	150p	10	45p	150	1,500
Meat	150p	11	1,650p	110	180p	120	13,200
				120		120)	14,700
							122.5

Index

Year I (base)　　100

Year II　　　　　122.5

Difficulties in Calculating Index Numbers

The method outlined above of calculating changes in the value of money has obvious snags:

(1) The basket and the weighting are merely an arbitrary average. Different income groups have widely different baskets, and even within the same group the amount spent on each good varies. Thus a change in the Index of Retail Prices does not affect all people equally.

(2) The basket becomes more unreal the further we move from the reference date (at present January 13, 1987 = 100). For instance, an increase in income gives a different pattern of expenditure, new goods are produced and the quality of goods changes, and spending is varied according to relative price changes. The Index of Retail Prices tries to overcome this defect by revising the weights each January on the basis of the *Family Expenditure Survey* for the previous year.

(3) Technical difficulties may arise both in choosing the reference date and in collecting information. For instance, the reference date may coincide with abnormally high prices, while the development of discount stores may upset standardised methods of collecting prices.

Thus an Index of Retail Prices is merely an indication of changes in the cost of living. But if we bear its limitations in mind, it is the most useful measurement we have of changes in the value of money.

28 Regional and Occupational Unemployment

28.1 The Effects of the Immobility of Labour

The Nature of the Problem

Even where there is considerable unemployment, there will still be some job vacancies. Thus, while in June 1987 the number of persons unemployed (seasonally adjusted) was 2 925 300, there were in existence 233 300 vacancies.

The reason is that conditions of demand and supply change. Tastes change, incomes rise, foreign competitors produce at a lower prices, etc. As a result, demand is buoyant for some goods and slack for others. On the supply side, technological change leads to redundancies. Thus in the UK since the Second World War, we have had a buoyant demand for consumer durable goods, services, electronic equipment, high technology products, etc., and a considerably reduced demand for coal, cotton goods, iron and steel, ships, etc. The demand for factors of production is a 'derived' demand; if the demand for a good decreases, the demand for the workers producing that good will also decrease.

Moreover, because of the localisation of industry, these differences in demand relative to resources are carried over into regions, some regions enjoying a high level of economic activity whereas others are depressed. This can be seen from Table 28.1, where some regions had unemployment rates well above the national average.

Causes of the Regional Problem

The regional problem can take many forms, but in the UK we can distinguish two major causes:

(1) *The particular region may be endowed with poor natural resources.* The Highlands of Scotland is an example. But more general are agricul-

367

Table 28.1
Seasonally Adjusted Percentage Rate of Unemployment by Region, July 1987

United Kingdom	10.4
Region:	
South-East	7.4
East Anglia	7.7
South-West	8.5
West Midlands	11.5
East Midlands	9.4
Yorks and Humber	11.7
North-West	13.0
North	14.4
Wales	12.7
Scotland	13.4
N. Ireland	18.3

tural regions which do not attract those expanding industries normally associated with a rising national income, e.g. Cornwall and Devon. Here income per head lags behind the level prevailing in the rest of the country.

(2)   *A region's basic industry is either stagnant or in decline.* Such a region suffers relatively from a high rate of unemployment, a low level of income, slow growth of income, a low activity rate (particularly of female workers), a high rate of outward migration, and an inadequate infrastructure. In contrast, other regions may be expanding so rapidly that they become congested and their further development entails the construction of new social capital. Often inflationary pressures arise. Although decaying and expanding regions are opposite situations, their problems are linked and policies for each cannot be considered in isolation. While the type of region in (1) is characterised by simply having a level of income below the national level, that in (2) has a *falling* level of income and a rising unemployment rate. It is the latter type of regional imbalance, therefore, which creates the greater problem and is the subject of the rest of this chapter.

Correction of Regional Imbalance Through the Price System

The classical model considers that industries, like trees in the forest, grow, decline, and eventually rot away. But there will always be new industries growing to which the resources of the decaying industries can transfer.

Thus workers who become unemployed will be moved by the price system to other jobs. The fall in the price of a good through a decrease in demand, and the consequent fall in the demand for the workers producing it, will lead to a relative deterioration in their wages. On the other hand, wages should rise where demand is buoyant (assuming that AD is adequate throughout the economy as a whole). This change in relative wages should have two effects: (*a*) a movement of workers from low-wage to high-wage industries; (*b*) a movement of industries from high-wage to low-wage areas.

Weaknesses of the Classical Theory

The attraction of the classical theory is that economic efficiency and the correction of an imbalance can be brought about by the free play of market forces. Yet in suggesting that a government regional policy is largely superfluous, the theory has serious weaknesses:

(1)   Factor markets adjust much less perfectly than the theory implies. Labour is immobile (see pp.209–11), while factor prices, especially wage rates, tend to be resistant to any downward movement. Moreover, national wage-bargaining weakens the response to the price signals of regional imbalance. Finally, the information available to factor markets is often imperfect. Thus capital markets tend to be centralised in the more prosperous regions of a country. If such markets operate with a bias against, or with imperfect knowledge of, investment opportunities in the peripheral regions, there may well be no injection of investment to cover savings in these regions.

(2)   The assumption of constant returns to scale which is implicit in the theory may not hold. Manufacturing in particular is characterised by increasing returns to scale over the relevant output range so that high-wage regions may also generate high returns to capital. Thus firms, like labour, may migrate to the prosperous high-wage regions. Indeed, as communications improve, these regions may gain with the progressive opening of trade at the expense of the decaying region. Thus the south-east region of England has benefited from its close connections with the EEC.

(3)   External costs are ignored. Not only is there a loss of social capital and a disintegration of communities in the depressed regions, but congestion and inflationary pressures may be generated in the expanding areas. Moreover, those workers who do move from the depressed regions are mostly the young or more enterprising. As such they are often the leaders of the community. The result is that the region becomes still further depressed *and* thus unattractive to new industries.

(4)   The theory ignores the fact that migration from the depressed regions leads to a loss of income there. The multiplier effect of reduced consumer spending and investment serves to depress the area still further.

28.2 Broad Outline of Government Policy

First-aid Measures

Where an area is depressed, the government can give first aid by placing its contracts there, e.g. for defence equipment, and awarding it priority for public-works programmes – schools, new roads, hospitals, the physical regeneration of urban areas, etc. Subsidies may also be granted to secure contracts, for example, to build ships.

Long-term Policy

In the long term, however, the government must take measures that will, on the one hand, encourage the outward movement of workers, and on the other induce firms to move in to employ those workers who find it difficult to move and also to halt further degeneration of the region. The first is usually referred to as 'workers to the work', the second as 'work to the workers'.

28.3 Workers to the Work

General Considerations

Taking workers to the work is basically a micro approach to overcome market frictions, chiefly the immobility and imperfect knowledge of labour. In pursuing this policy, however, the government must bear in mind the following:

(a) Unemployment arising through immobility is far more difficult to cure when cyclical unemployment also exists, for an unemployed person has little incentive to move if there is unemployment even in the relatively prosperous areas.

(b) Other government interference in the economy may add to the problem of immobility. Thus high rates of income tax whittle away monetary inducements to move and unemployment benefit may reduce the incentive to seek a job elsewhere. Similarly, rent control and residential qualifications for local authority housing priorities lead to difficulties in finding accommodation.

(c) Even owner-occupiers in depressed regions may be restricted in mobility by the much higher cost of housing in the prosperous areas.

(d) Many changes of both occupation and area take place in a series of ripples. Thus an agricultural labourer may move to road construction to take the place of the labourer who transfers to the building industry.

The government's first task must be to improve occupational mobility. Entry into certain occupations should be made less difficult, e.g. by giving information on opportunities in other industries and occupations and by persuading trade unions to relax their apprenticeship rules. More important, people must be trained in the new skills required by expanding industries – currently the responsibility of the Manpower Services Commission.

Improving the geographical mobility of workers to the more prosperous regions operates chiefly under the government's Employment Transfer Scheme. This consists of granting financial aid towards moving costs, providing information on prospects in other parts of the country and giving free fares to a place of work away from the home town.

28.4 Work to the Workers

While a 'workers-to-the-work' policy has a role to play in correcting regional imbalance, it suffers from: (i) an exclusive concern with unemployment to the neglect of other consequences of regional imbalance; (ii) a failure to recognise the macro effects of the outward movement of workers.

Thus taking work to the workers is now regarded as the policy most likely to effect a long-term solution to the problem for it reduces regional differences in income and the rate of growth as well as in unemployment. By helping the more immobile workers, such as older people and married women, it stimulates the activity rate. It also avoids forcing workers to leave areas to which they are attached, relieves the growing congestion in south-east England, and prevents the loss of social capital resulting from the depopulation of depressed areas. Above all, it works in harmony with Keynesian macro theory. The 'multiplier' operates for regional economies in much the same way as it does for the national economy. Moving unemployed workers and their families reduces spending in the area (e.g. because unemployment benefits are no longer being drawn) and this gives rise to a negative multiplier. In contrast, moving firms into the area generates spending power and produces a positive multiplier, variously calculated at between 1.25 and 1.5.

On the other hand, a policy of locating firms in depressed areas may involve them in higher costs. Their desire to establish plant in the south-east is to secure location advantages, such as a supply of skilled workers, easier and less costly communications, contact with complementary firms and nearness to EEC markets. The government, therefore, has to offer financial inducements to offset these extra costs.

To induce firms to establish or expand in an Assisted Area (Figure 28.1),

FIGURE 28.1
Great Britain Assisted Areas

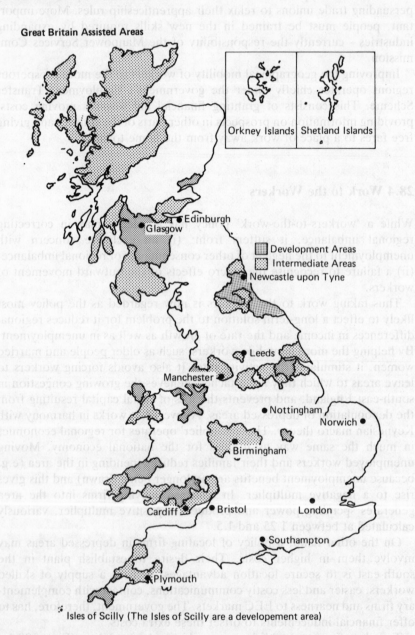

Great Britain Assisted Areas

Orkney Islands   Shetland Islands

Edinburgh
Glasgow

Newcastle upon Tyne

Development Areas
Intermediate Areas

Leeds

Manchester

Nottingham

Norwich

Birmingham

Cardiff   Bristol   London

Southampton

Plymouth

Isles of Scilly (The Isles of Scilly are a developement area) the government may use either the carrot or the big stick. Today it concentrates on the former, though there has been some oblique compulsion through planning regulations (see below). In 1984 new measures were introduced which put more emphasis on actual job-creation rather than on straight investment. There are now two main types of grant.

Regional Development Grants are given *automatically* for projects in development areas which provide a service. The level of grant is calculated in two ways according to whichever method is most favourable to the applicant:

(a) 15 per cent of eligible capital expenditure subject to a grant per job limit of £10 000 for each *new* job created; or
(b) £3000 for each new full-time job created.

Where firms employ fewer than 200 workers, a 15 per cent grant of eligible expenditure up to £500 000 is given whether or not new jobs are created.

Regional Selected Assistance is available on a *discretionary* basis in both development area and intermediate areas. Grants, which are negotiable, take two main forms:

(a) project grants, based on the capital cost of a project or on the number of jobs to be created within three years; and
(b) training grants of up to 40 per cent of the costs of training directly associated with the viability of a project.

In addition to these grants, other incentives include:

(i)   help for transferring key workers;
(ii) factories for renting on favourable terms, such as an initial rent-free period;
(iii) loans at favourable rates of interest; and
(iv) grants towards the cost of reclaiming derelict land in certain designated areas.

All these incentives are in addition to the investment incentives (through tax concessions) available to manufacturing and service industries throughout the whole country.

Assistance (£2000 million to date) is also obtained from the EEC's Regional Development Fund, set up in 1975, and loans are available on favourable terms from the European Investment Bank and the European Coal and Steel Community. Depressed areas also benefit from aid given to the unemployed by the European Social Fund.

The Department of Industry controls the Industrial Estates Corporation which supervises government-sponsored industrial estates in England. Similar schemes operate in Scotland and Northern Ireland.

More recently the government has established some twenty-five 'enterprise zones' in areas of physical and economic decay, including the

London docklands, Swansea, Manchester, Clydebank, Belfast and Hartle-pool. Each zone covers up to 500 acres and firms there enjoy special benefits, e.g. exemption from general rates and simplified planning procedures.

Through its *planning powers* the government can indirectly use some compulsion. Consent of the local planning authority is necessary for any new building or addition to an existing building. More important, until 1981 an Industrial Development Certificate or an Office Development Permit could be required before floor space over a certain size was created outside assisted areas. While such controls might force firms to consider alternative locations, they are purely negative and may result in firms deciding not to expand but to carry on in their present obsolete premises, or, with multinational firms, setting up branches in less restrictive environments abroad, for instance, in the EEC.

In the dispersal of industry the government has set an example. Thus the Department of Health and Social Security is centred in Newcastle, the National Giro in Bootle, and the Driving and Vehicle Licensing Centre in Swansea.

Regional Planning

While development area policy deals with special areas needing extra help, there is now a trend towards planning for larger regions each with an infrastructure which is attractive to industry and management in that it features: good executive housing; educational, cultural and recreational facilities; first-class shops and hotels; and a modern road network, rail services and airport. The aim is to secure a broad-based industrial structure, with special consideration being given to service industries.

The whole country is divided into ten regions (eight for England and one each for Scotland and Wales). Each region has an Economic Planning Board, consisting of civil servants from the main government departments concerned with regional planning, whose task is to formulate plans and co-ordinate the work of the various departments.

Primary responsibility for regional development lies with the Department of Industry which has an Industrial Development Unit to help with the appraisal, negotiation and monitoring of projects referred to it.

Regional Policy in the Context of the EEC

A healthy integrated Community – at both economic and political levels – is possible only if progress is made towards reducing disparities in economic opportunity between regions within the Community. Indeed, while the foregoing reasons for regional policy are all relevant at the Community level, additional considerations apply:

(a) Physical controls are more difficult to apply in the EEC context. Not only are they at variance with the objective of greater mobility within the EEC, but firms have the option of relocating in a prosperous region of another member state.

(b) The depressed peripheral regions of Scotland, Northern Ireland, Southern Italy, etc, are more distant from the expanding centre of the Community – South-east England through to north-east France and eastern West Germany – than they are from the centres of their own countries. This Community 'centre' forms a concentrated market to which industries are likely to be increasingly attracted, thereby adding to its dominance.

(c) The EEC embraces regions exhibiting wider economic disparities than in any one member-state. Moreover, regional problems are more heterogeneous, for example, whereas the UK depressed regions are mainly industrial, Italy has many depressed agricultural areas.

These additional considerations mean that the formulation of an effective EEC regional policy is a difficult task. Not only must it respond quickly as new regional problems arise, but it has to be linked with, and be complementary to, the individual nation's regional policy. Indeed EEC policy should also co-ordinate the regional policies of member-states, for example, a physical control in one country must not be undermined by a firm being able to locate in another country.

It follows, therefore, that regional policy must be handled to a substantial degree at the Community level and be wide-ranging in the measures employed so that one reinforces the others. Above all, to achieve greater equity, it must envisage substantial transfers of income through incentive funds which are in addition to those provided by the member-states.

28.5 An Appraisal of Regional Policy

Although the UK has had a regional policy for fifty years, disparities still persist in the rates of unemployment between different areas. Indeed, such disparities have widened in recent years. With the onset of the world recession, there has been less incentive for firms to ease their labour problems by locating in the Development Areas, while workers have had less inducement to move to the relatively prosperous regions since these had fewer unfilled vacancies.

But the nature of regional policy itself has contributed to this situation. The emphasis has been on aid to manufacturing industry. Thus since 1972, one-quarter of all aid has gone to the chemical industry where investment has created hardly any new jobs. On the other hand, natural growth is in the service industries, enabling them to weather a recession more successfully. Yet not until 1973 did policy move towards encouraging service firms to transfer the bulk of their office work to regions outside the south-east.

Furthermore, the average cost of a job created is too expensive at £35 000. Financial incentives have been weighted on the side of investment, encouraging firms to substitute capital for labour. While this view ignores the multiplier effects on income through induced consumption spending, an additional subsidy related directly to job-creation would be more effective in relieving unemployment and to a limited extent this has been implemented in the new Regional Assistance Grant. There is a danger, too, that investment grants encourage investment in inherently unsuitable firms which are already in Development Areas. Replacing them with special lower rates of corporation tax would do more to link aid with financial viability.

It should be noted also that concentrating on inter-regional differences has diverted attention away from problems within regions. Thus London now has more unemployed than the whole of the north-east region, with a rate of unemployment of up to 15 per cent in certain districts, such as Poplar.

The most favourable assessment which can be made of policy, therefore, is that without it disparities between regions would be greater.

28.6 Recent Changes in Development Area Assistance

The government has now recognised that there was only a minimal contribution to labour employment of many projects receiving *automatic* Regional Development Grants. Hence in 1988 it was announced that no further applications would be accepted, though schemes in the pipeline would ensure that such regional assistance would continue at a high level until 1991.

In future there would be increased Regional Selective Assistance on a *discretionary* basis, particularly for medium or small firms who show that they genuinely need money in order to proceed and that their projects are viable.

29 Government Finance

29.1 Government Expenditure

Limits to Government Spending

Today taxation takes about 40 per cent of the gross national product – a remarkable increase over the last seventy years. Even Lloyd George's famous budget of 1910 sought to produce only £200 million, about 10 per cent of the national income. The pressure on the government is always to spend more, not less. Today people demand a full range of government activities.

But this does not mean that the government can curry favour with the electorate by a continuous increase in its spending. Goods and services in the economy as a whole are limited. In practice, therefore, the government is in the same position as everybody else. It can only secure more of the goods and services by allowing the private sector less.

Many items of government expenditure, e.g. retirement pensions, interest on the National Debt, grants to local authorities, are impossible to avoid; by nature they are basically contractual. It may seem, therefore, that the government has merely to estimate its expenditure and then impose taxes to cover it. But this is not the case. Contractual items of government expenditure may be likened to the outgoings of the ordinary individual on necessities – rent, food, fuels, etc. 'Cutting one's coat according to one's cloth' takes place at the margin on such items as a new television set, a longer holiday, or a larger car. So it is with the government. How much can we afford for the Arts Council? How much can we give to sport? Can university education be maintained this year? Can we reduce National Insurance contributions? The economic problem confronts everybody, private persons and the government alike. In the last resort, how the national product is to be divided between the public and private sectors is a political decision.

The Distribution of National Expenditure

Government spending can be classified under the following headings:

(1)   *Defence*. Defence, which must be given priority, is today largely determined by treaty commitments, e.g. NATO, SEATO. Spending on it accounts for one-ninth of all government spending.

(2)   *Internal security*. This covers spending on the police, law enforcement and the fire brigades.

(3)   *Social responsibilities*. Provision must be made for the adequate education of citizens, and some protection must be afforded against the hazards of sickness, unemployment and old age by means of the health services, unemployment benefits and pensions.

(4)   *Economic policy*. The government is now responsible for maintaining the level of employment and securing a steady growth of the national product. It grants subsidies to agriculture and industry, gives help to areas of high unemployment, trains workers, and sets up Jobcentres. Most of the capital requirements of the nationalised industries are now provided by the Treasury.

(5)   *Miscellaneous*. The largest single item under this heading is interest on the National Debt, but there is also expenditure on colonies and the consular services, grants to local authorities and aid to less-developed countries.

How Government Expenditure is Financed

In the same way that firms have to pay for both variable and fixed factors, so the government has to spend not only on recurrent, one-use goods and services, but on goods whose services are rendered over a long period. Regular yearly expenditure, charged on the Consolidated Fund, should be met out of regular yearly income. But capital spending (charged on the National Loans Fund), on such items as loans to nationalised industries and less developed countries, is more fairly financed by borrowing. These projects render services over a period of years, and so they are financed by borrowing, interest and capital being repaid in the future, thereby allowing the burden to be shared by all persons receiving benefits from them in both the present and the future.

Current expenditure is met from two main sources:

1.   Miscellaneous receipts, chiefly interest on loans, rents on Crown Lands, and charges on goods and services (such as the charge on prescriptions and for dental treatment).
2.   Taxation, described in more detail later.

Capital expenditure is mostly met by government borrowing, though until 1970 'budget surpluses' provided an increasing proportion.

Government borrowing takes the form of:

(1) *Short-term loans*. These loans are mostly obtained by the sale of Treasury bills. Originally Treasury bills were used to bridge the time gap between expenditure and receipts from taxation, but later they became a major means of government borrowing, because it is cheaper to borrow short than long. Nevertheless, inflationary effects resulted, and in recent years the government has, as far as possible, followed a 'funding' policy, converting short-term into long-term debt (see p.290).

(2) *Medium- and long-term loans*. These are represented by stock having a minimum currency of five years. They include undated stocks, such as $3\frac{1}{2}$ per cent War Loan, which since 1951 have fallen in value as the rate of interest has risen.

(3) *'Non-market' borrowing* through national savings certificates, premium savings bonds, etc., and the deposits of the National Savings Bank.

29.2 The Modern Approach to Taxation

Taxation and Government Policy

Until the end of the nineteenth century the functions of the state were concerned mainly with defence and law and order. Taxation was levied primarily for revenue purposes, those taxes regulating trade having been abolished in the previous century.

To meet the vast increase in government spending over the last fifty years, higher rates of taxation have been imposed and new taxes introduced. These additions have, as we shall see, provided new means for promoting economic and social policies. Briefly, by its fiscal measures, the government can:

1. *Exercise an overall control over the economy*, mainly with the object of achieving full employment. To secure this, the government:
   (a) adjusts individual taxes in order to influence consumption, saving and investment;
   (b) varies the relationship between its own expenditure and revenue through a budget surplus or deficit (see Figure 29.1).
   Both were discussed in Chapter 26.
2. *Promote economic growth*, by such measures as giving generous taxation allowances for investment expenditure.
3. *Modify the influence of the price system*, in order to:
   (a) protect an 'infant' industry;
   (b) develop a vital industry;
   (c) cushion the impact on an industry of fundamental changes in the conditions of demand and supply;

FIGURE 29.1
Public Income and Expenditure, 1987–8

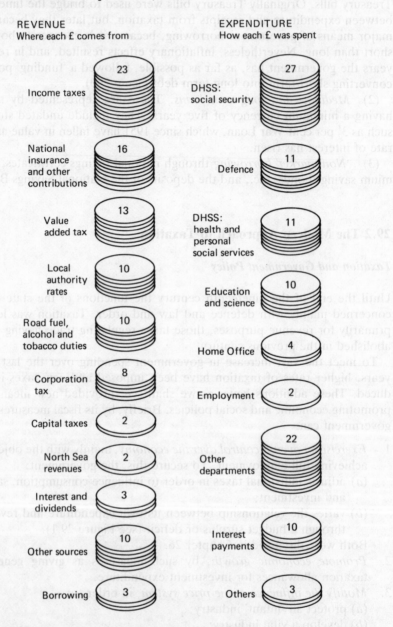

REVENUE
Where each £ comes from

EXPENDITURE
How each £ was spent

Income taxes — 23

DHSS: social security — 27

National insurance and other contributions — 16

Defence — 11

Value added tax — 13

DHSS: health and personal social services — 11

Local authority rates — 10

Education and science — 10

Road fuel, alcohol and tobacco duties — 10

Home Office — 4

Corporation tax — 8

Employment — 22

Capital taxes — 2

North Sea revenues — 2

Other departments — 22

Interest and dividends — 3

Other sources — 10

Interest payments — 10

Borrowing — 3

Others — 3

Cash totals of revenue and expenditure £173 billion

(*d*) increase trade with the EEC;

(*e*) improve the terms of trade by levying an import duty on goods whose supply is less elastic than the demand for them;

(*f*) improve the balance of payments by imposing duties to restrict imports (these points are discussed in Chapter 30); and

(*g*) compensate for external costs and benefits, e.g. protecting health by taxing cigarettes.

4. *Achieve greater equality in the distribution of wealth and income.*

5. *Secure minor objectives*, such as increasing individual responsibility for government (by ensuring that everybody pays some tax).

The Attributes of a Good Tax System

In his *Wealth of Nations* Adam Smith was able to confine his principles of taxation to four simple canons. Stated briefly, these were: persons should pay according to their ability; the tax should be certain and clear to everybody concerned; the convenience of the contributor should be studied as regards payment; the cost of collection should be small relative to yield.

While today the main purpose of any tax is usually to raise money, the additional uses of taxation have rendered Adam Smith's maxims inadequate. Indeed, objects other than revenue may take priority. Thus when the purchase tax was introduced in 1940 it was primarily to discourage spending and only secondarily to raise revenue. Ideally, therefore, a modern tax should have all the following attributes:

1. Productive of Revenue

All taxes cost money to collect and are unpopular. The yield of any tax, therefore, should at least cover the cost of collection, with something to spare to offset the vexation caused. In practice, too, a single tax with a high yield is better than a number of taxes each having a small yield, for the latter make the tax structure complicated and not easily understood.

Normally, too, the Chancellor should be able to estimate the yield of a tax with a fair degree of accuracy. This is particularly important if the budget is to be used for the purpose of adjusting overall demand. In this connection it is useful to the Chancellor if some taxes can be adjusted to produce an immediate yield, or, if lowered, afford an immediate relief.

2. Certain to the Taxpayer

Not only should a taxpayer know exactly when and where tax has to be paid, but he or she should find it difficult to evade payment. Indirect taxes score heavily here.

3. Convenient to the Contributor

Bad debts and evasion are reduced if the time and manner of tax payment are related to how people receive and spend their incomes. Thus it is convenient to pay income tax through the PAYE system, and indirect taxes when goods are bought.

4. Impartial between One Person and Another

All persons similarly placed should pay the same tax. Thus while non-smokers do not pay the selective tax on tobacco, all smokers do.

Yet, although there is impartiality in this sense, the old concentration of indirect taxes on a few goods – chiefly tobacco, alcoholic drink and motoring – did penalise severely certain forms of spending. Thus people who obtain most of their pleasure from cycling and dining out still receive many benefits from state expenditure, benefits which are largely paid for by their smoking, drinking and car-driving neighbours! One of the objects of introducing VAT was to broaden the tax base.

5. Adjustable

A tax should be capable of variation, both up and down, according to changes in policy.

6. Automatic in Stabilising the Economy

Varying the relationship between government expenditure and revenue is one of the major weapons for keeping the economy on an even keel – with full employment but a stable price level. Thus the overall level of taxation is used to vary the amount of purchasing power in the hands of the public. Usually the Chancellor of the Exchequer has to make a deliberate adjustment in the budget, but it would be helpful if taxes could operate automatically in the required direction.

To some extent they do. Thus when money income increases, so does the yield from both income tax and VAT. This has a disinflationary effect. The opposite occurs when money income decreases.

7. Unharmful to Effort and Initiative

This attribute has become of increasing importance with the growth of direct taxation. High rates of income tax, for instance, may induce taxpayers to take their income in the form of leisure or reduce their willingness to undergo training or to seek promotion.

However, in practice there is little statistical evidence to support this view. Where people have fixed money commitments, e.g. hire-purchase instalments, mortgage repayments, school fees and insurance premiums, they may be compelled to work *harder* in order to meet them when income is reduced. Furthermore, if we assume that high income tax is a disincentive to effort, we infer that persons always look upon work as distasteful and leisure as a pleasurable alternative. This may be true for the majority, but there are many who work because they derive enjoyment from it. Last, we have to remember that most people are not free to vary their hours of work except as regards overtime. The normal working week is often an agreement on a national basis between trade unions and employers' associations.

The disincentive effect is more likely to occur when there is a sudden jump in the rate of tax between one income level and another. People reduce their effort at the higher-taxed income level. This is a psychological reaction, for they are not forced to consider whether their standard of living will fall – as happens when there is a general rise in the rate of tax. In other words, the disincentive occurs when the marginal rate of tax exceeds the average rate.

Even with indirect taxes, care must be taken that certain 'incentive goods' – cars, video recorders, deep-freezers, dish-washers, etc. – are not taxed so heavily that they are priced beyond the reach of persons who would otherwise work overtime in order to secure them.

High direct taxes can also affect enterprise and efficiency. A higher money reward is usually necessary to induce a person to devote time to training and study or to incur the cost of moving a home to secure promotion. It follows, therefore, that where the wage differential between skilled and unskilled labour is eroded by income tax, incentives are proportionately reduced. Similarly, entrepreneurs are only prepared to accept risks if the rewards are commensurate. Direct taxes, therefore, act as a brake on the initiative of workers and on the willingness of entrepreneurs to accept risks.

On the other hand, high taxation of profits and income means that the penalty of inefficiency is not borne entirely by shareholders, for a large part falls on the government through loss of revenue.

8. Consistent with Government Policy

While the tax structures should not be subject to frequent change, individual taxes must be constantly reviewed to see how they could be used to promote government policy or to prevent their working out of harmony with it. In reaching its decision, the government has to consider the balance of advantage, setting off any loss of revenue against expected gains. It must have in mind such problems as: What tax reliefs should be given to exporters? Should rates be reduced (instead of increased as at present) for people who relieve road congestion by building their own garages? Should the income from work be taxed at a lower rate than investment income to encourage effort? Will an indirect tax, by raising the cost of living, increase wage-push inflation?

Indirect taxes can be made adaptable to specific objectives of policy, e.g. cigarettes bear a selective tax and exports are zero-rated under VAT.

9. Minimal in its Effect on the Optimum Allocation of Resources

The imposition of an indirect tax on a *particular* good results in resources not being perfectly allocated according to the real preferences of consumers. In the long period, under perfect competition, no super-normal profits are made – the cost of producing the good is just equal to people's valuation of it. Moreover, consumers have allocated their outlay according to their preferences, so that marginal utility relative to the price of the good is equal in all cases. A tax on one good destroys the equilibrium, for the price of the good rises (unless supply is absolutely inelastic). This results in a redistribution of consumers' expenditure and thus of the factors of production. In addition, there will be some dislocation of the industry concerned, the extent depending upon the elasticity of demand for the product (see p.390).

Finally, selective indirect taxes result in greater loss to the consumer than an income tax that raises an equivalent amount. Unlike an income tax, selective indirect taxes change the relative prices of goods. This means that consumers have to rearrange their pattern of expenditure. This substitution involves a loss of satisfaction in addition to that suffered through the reduction in income.

Direct taxes, too, may affect the supply of factors, particularly capital, to industry. It may be that high taxation discourages saving; it certainly reduces the power to save. This is not serious for large companies, but the major source of capital for the small private company or sole proprietor is the owner's personal savings out of income. Normally firms which are making the largest profits will be the more likely to want to expand. Thus income tax and corporation tax deprive small, risky, but often progressive companies of much-needed capital.

Not only that, but high direct taxes may repel foreign capital. Although the deduction of income tax on dividends may be refunded, the company still has to bear corporation tax on profits (at 35 per cent). The amount available to shareholders is therefore less, and the declared dividend correspondingly smaller. Consequently, people may prefer to invest in companies operating in countries where there is a higher return to capital – a higher return which is the result, not of superior efficiency, but simply of the lower taxes payable.

10. Equitable in its Distribution of the Tax Burden

Taxes can be classified according to the proportion of a person's income which is deducted:

(a) *A regressive* tax takes a higher proportion of the poorer person's income than of the richer. Indirect taxes, for instance, which are a fixed sum irrespective of income (e.g. television licences), are regressive.

(b) *A proportional* tax takes a given proportion of one's income. Income tax is now proportional for the first £19 300 of taxable income, 25 per cent of every pound being taken in tax.

(c) *A progressive* tax takes a higher proportion of income as income increases (Figure 29.2). Thus income tax, which is 40 per cent of taxable income above £19,300 is progressive.

FIGURE 29.2
The Difference Between Regressive, Proportional and Progressive Taxes

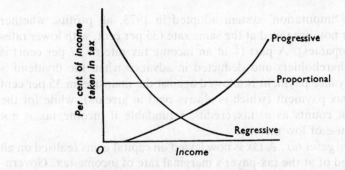

Justification for taxing the rich higher than the poor rests on the assumption that the law of diminishing utility applies to additional income, and that an extra £50 affords less pleasure to the rich person than to the poor person. Thus taking from the rich does not involve such a hardship as taking from the poor. Generally this can be accepted as true, but we can never be sure, simply because there is no absolute measure of personal satisfaction.

29.3 The Structure of Taxation

Because certain objectives of taxation conflict with one another, no single tax is completely perfect. Consequently there must be a structure of taxation, combining a number of taxes which the government can vary from time to time according to changes in the emphasis on different objectives.

The following classification of taxes is based on the method of payment:

1. Direct Taxes

With these taxes the person makes payment direct to the revenue authorities – the Inland Revenue or the local authority. Usually each individual's tax liability is assessed separately.

(*a*)   *Income tax*. Income tax was first levied in 1799, but it was repealed soon after Waterloo. Reintroduced in 1842, it has since been continuous.

In 1988 the standard rate is 25 per cent of taxable income. 'Taxable income' is arrived at after allowing deductions depending on marital status and other personal circumstances. Above taxable income of £19 300 however, the rate is 40 per cent.

(*b*)   *Corporation tax*. In 1965 the profits tax was replaced by a corporation tax.

Under the 'imputation' system adopted in 1973, all profits, whether distributed or not, are taxed at the same rate (35 per cent, with lower rates for small companies). A part ($\frac{27}{73}$ at an income tax rate of 27 per cent) is imputed to shareholders and deducted in advance when the dividend is paid. This advance payment is allowed against the mainstream 35 per cent corporation tax payment (which is always paid in arrears), while for the shareholder it counts as a 'tax credit', refundable if income tax is not payable because of low income.

(*c*)   *Capital gains tax*. A tax is now levied on capital gains realised on all assets disposed of at the tax-payer's marginal rate of income tax. Government securities, owner-occupied houses, cars, National Savings Certificates and goods and chattels worth less than £3000 are excluded.

Where the net gains from the disposal of assets do not exceed £5000 (1988) in any year, no tax is payable.

(*d*)   *Inheritance tax*. Inheritance tax has now replaced estate duty. It applies to lifetime gifts as well as to legacies, though the former generally bear only half the latter's rate of tax. The rate of duty is now 40 per cent (1988). Gifts made seven years before death are exempt from tax.

(*e*)   *Other taxes*. These consist of stamp duties (payable on financial contracts), motor-vehicle duties, a petroleum revenue tax and a mineral-rights duty, but only the first three are important. All except motor-vehicle duties are collected by the Inland Revenue.

Local rates, levied by district councils, are also a direct tax.

Direct taxes yield nearly two-thirds of total revenue. Their great merit is that, in so far as they are progressive and assessed according to the individual's particular circumstances, they ensure that the heaviest burdens are placed on the broadest backs. Their progressive character also gives additional weight to their role as a 'built-in stabiliser'.

Their main disadvantage is that, when the rate of tax is high, there may be certain disincentive effects. As a result, indirect taxes also have to be levied.

2. Indirect Taxes

Indirect taxes, on goods and services, are so called because the revenue authority (Customs and Excise) collects them from the sellers, who, as far as possible, passes the burden on to the consumer by including the duty in the final selling price of the good (see p.392). They may be *specific* (that is, a fixed sum irrespective of the value of the good) or *ad valorem* (that is, a given percentage of the value of the good).

Indirect taxes may be divided into:

(a)   Customs duties on imported goods, which are levied at EEC rates on goods from countries outside the EEC.

(b)   Excise duties on home-produced goods and services, e.g. beer, whisky, petrol, cigarettes and gambling.

(c)   Value-added tax (VAT): an *ad valorem* tax introduced in 1973 to replace purchase tax and selective employment tax. It is levied on most goods and services at each stage of production at a basic rate (now 15 per cent). Thus, using Figure 24.1 (p. 296) as an example, the VAT at 15 per cent paid by the consumer on the table in the shop would be £15, making a total purchase price of £115. The VAT, however, would have been paid at each stage of production as follows: tree-grower £4.50; saw-miller £3; table manufacturer £4.50; retailer £3. In practice, each producer pays to the Customs and Excise the full 15 per cent tax of the goods as invoiced by him *less* the VAT paid by his suppliers of materials, etc., as shown on their invoices. Thus, for instance, the retailer actually sends to the Customs and Excise £15 *minus* the £12 VAT charged on his cost of £80, ie. £3.

Some goods, e.g. food (except meals out), coal, gas, electricity, the construction of buildings, books, newspapers, public transport fares, medicines on prescriptions, are zero-rated. This means that the final seller charges no VAT and can reclaim any VAT invoiced by intermediary producers. Other goods, e.g. rents and medical services, are 'exempt'. Here no VAT is charged by the final seller, but any VAT paid by an intermediary, for example for building repairs, cannot be reclaimed.

Apart from harmonising with the EEC indirect tax system, the main merit of VAT is that it is broader based than the old purchase tax. Because the latter was applied to a comparatively narrow range of goods, for example cars and consumer durables, the yield did not increase proportionately with consumer spending. Moreover, since VAT covers most forms of spending, it does not distort consumer choice to the extent of the old purchase tax (see later).

On the other hand, it can be argued that a general tax on spending is regressive, for it hits those on lower incomes hardest. This is tempered somewhat, however, by zero-rating goods which can be regarded as necessities.

Through indirect taxes all citizens have to pay something towards government spending, and this tends to promote responsibility. Such taxes give a certain and often an immediate yield and can be adjusted to specific objectives of government policy. On the other hand, by being regressive, in that they fall more heavily on the poorer sections of the community, they undo some of the redistributive effects of direct taxes.

29.4 The Incidence of Taxation

What do we Mean by the 'Incidence' of a Tax?

So far we have considered only the *formal* incidence of a tax – how the tax is distributed between the various taxpayers. Thus direct taxes, we saw, are progressive, falling heaviest on the higher income groups. Indirect taxes, on the other hand, are regressive as regards consumers, though the direct incidence falls on producers or distributors who actually pay the tax to the Customs and Excise.

But the economist is chiefly concerned with the *effective* incidence – how the real burden of a tax is distributed after its full effects have worked through the economy.

In the case of *direct taxes* we have seen that, with some qualifications, both income tax and corporation tax adversely affect effort, enterprise and risk-bearing, economy in expenditure, and saving (see pp.382–3).

An increase in income tax can be passed on only by those workers who can secure some addition to their wages by way of compensation. For this to happen, they must be in a strong bargaining position. Certain conditions must be fulfilled (see p.220), the chief one being that the demand for the good they produce is fairly inelastic. The increase in the price of the good that results from the higher wages will be borne mainly by consumers – which really means workers in other groups who are not in such a strong bargaining position.

Similarly, in the short period, when supply is fairly inelastic, an increase in a tax on profits will be borne chiefly by producers (see p.232). But in the long period, when some entrepreneurs transfer from the riskier enterprises (which the tax hits hardest), there will be changes in the relative supply of goods, and consumers of those goods whose production involves the most risk will, according to their elasticity of demand, have to bear a part of the tax.

A tax which falls on monopoly profits, however, cannot be passed on. There has been no change in the demand or supply curves, and the monopolist is already producing where profits are a maximum. Hence if the monopolist has to pay, say, a 20 per cent tax, the equilibrium position will be unchanged; four-fifths of maximum profits are still better than four-fifths of anything less.

With *indirect taxes* the effective incidence can be analysed more precisely. An indirect tax may be *general* or *selective*. A sales tax levied across the board on all goods and services at a standard rate would be a *general* indirect tax. In the British system VAT comes closest to such a tax in that it is levied at a basic rate on most goods and services. The important point is that relative prices remain unchanged and the consumer cannot switch to a substitute which is relatively cheaper because it bears no tax. If the government wishes to reallocate resources, therefore, it must do so by using the proceeds of the tax to subsidise certain industries, or by imposing additional excise duties on goods whose consumption it would like to curtail, e.g. tobacco. A few goods, e.g. alcohol, petrol, cars, and also tobacco, because they are such excellent revenue-raisers, are subject to special taxes. Any tax which is levied at a higher rate on certain goods is termed *selective*.

When a tax is selective, the following questions become important: What is the effect of imposing a selective tax on the size of the particular industry? How will the burden of such a tax be ultimately distributed between the producer and consumer?

We begin by explaining how the imposition of a tax can be shown diagrammatically.

The Diagrammatic Representation of a Tax

Theoretically, the effect of a tax can be analysed on either the demand or the supply side. No matter which is chosen, the same new equilibrium position for price and output will result. Later we shall prefer one method to the other according to the particular problem being analysed.

Suppose a specific tax is imposed on *buyers*. At price *OP*, without tax, *OH* was demanded. A tax equal to *t* is now imposed. If the same amount *OH* is to be demanded, price must fall by the amount of the tax to *Ot*. We can carry out a similar procedure at each different price. The effect of the tax, therefore, is to lower the demand curve to D_1, which is vertically equidistant from the demand curve *D* by the amount of the tax (Figure 29.3a).

FIGURE 29.3
The Representation of a Tax

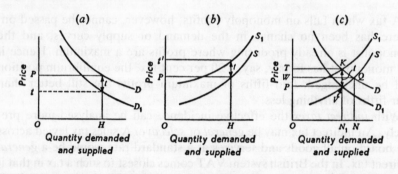

Similarly, if the tax is levied on *producers*, the same amount *OH* (Figure 29.3b) will be supplied only if price rises by the amount of tax to *Ot*. Thus, as with demand, we have a new supply curve, S_1, vertically equidistant from the curve *S*, but to the left of it, by the amount of the tax.

When we combine (*a*) and (*b*) it can be seen that it makes no difference whether the effect of the tax is shown on the demand or supply sides (Figure 29.3c). The new equilibrium output ON_1 is the same, both demand and supply having contracted from *ON* as a result of tax *t*. Total expenditure changes from *ONQW* to ON_1KT, but the latter includes tax receipts of *PVKT*.

The Effect of an Indirect Tax on the Size of an Industry

The greater the elasticities of demand and supply, the greater will be the effect of a tax in reducing production. We can show diagrammatically that this is true.

1. Elasticity of Demand

Before the tax is imposed, total output is *OM* (Figure 29.4). The effect of the tax is to raise the supply curve from *S* to S_1. Two demand curves are shown, D_a being less elastic than D_b at price *OP*. The effect of the tax is to reduce output to OM_1 where demand is D_a, and to OM_2 where it is D_b. In the latter case consumers will probably switch to buying substitutes.

FIGURE 29.4
The Relationship Between Elasticity of Demand and Production when a Tax is Imposed on a Good

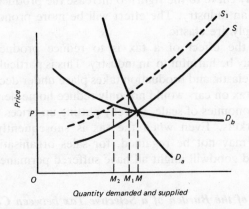

Quantity demanded and supplied

2. Elasticity of supply

Before the tax is imposed, total output is *OM* (Figure 29.5). The effect of the tax is to lower the demand curve from *D* to D_1. Two supply curves are shown, S_a being less elastic than S_b at price *OP*. The effect of the tax is to

FIGURE 29.5
The Relationship Between Elasticity of Supply and Production when a Tax is imposed on a Good

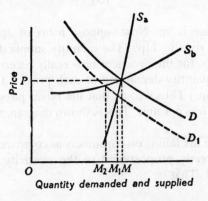

Quantity demanded and supplied

reduce output to OM_1 where supply is S_a, and to OM_2 where it is S_b. In the latter case producers will probably turn to producing alternative goods.

This proposition has important practical applications.

(*a*) The government may use a subsidy (which can be illustrated by moving the supply curve to the right) to increase the production, and thus employment, of an industry. The effect will be more pronounced where demand and supply are elastic.

(*b*) Because the effect of a tax is to reduce production, even a temporary tax may be harmful to an industry. This is particularly so where home demand is elastic and production takes place under decreasing costs. Thus a selective tax on cars would not only reduce home demand, but, by doing so, lose economies of scale, thereby putting up prices to both home and foreign markets. Even when the tax is subsequently withdrawn, foreign markets may not be regained, for sales organisation, servicing arrangements and goodwill might all have suffered permanent harm.

The Distribution of the Burden of a Selective Tax between Consumers and Producers

When a good is subject to a selective tax, it does not mean that its price will rise by the full amount of the tax. Consider the following demand and supply schedules for commodity X:

Price of X (pence)	Demand (000lb)	Supply (000lb)
12	60	150
11	70	130
10	80	110
9	90	90
8	100	70

The equilibrium price is 9p. Now suppose a tax of 3p per unit of X is imposed. The price rises to 11p. (The quantity supplied to the market at 11p is only 70 000 lb, for the producer now really receives only 8p a unit. Alternatively, the quantity demanded at each price is that for which the price is greater by 3p.) Thus we see that the buyer pays 2p more and the supplier receives 1p less per unit. This is shown diagrammatically in Figure 29.6.

The amount of the tax falling on consumers as compared with that falling on producers is directly proportional to the elasticity of supply to the elasticity of demand. That is:

$$\frac{\text{Consumers' share of tax}}{\text{Producers' share of tax}} = \frac{\text{Elasticity of supply}}{\text{Elasticity of demand}}$$

FIGURE 29.6
The Distribution of a Tax Between the Buyer and the Seller

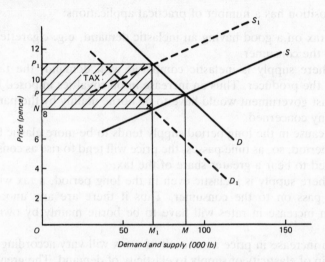

That this proposition is likely to be true can be seen from the following argument. When a tax is imposed, the reaction of the producer is to try to push the burden of the tax on to the consumer, while similarly the consumer tries to push it on to the producer. Who wins? Simply the one whose bargaining position is stronger. This will depend upon the ability to switch to producing substitutes if the price falls as compared with the ability to switch to buying substitutes if the price rises. Now the possibility of substitution largely determines elasticities of supply and demand. Thus the relative burden of the tax paid by producers and consumers depends upon relative elasticities of supply and demand.

The proposition can be proved geometrically as follows. As a result of the tax, price rises from OP to OP_1, and the quantity demanded and supplied falls from OM to OM_1.

$$\text{Elasticity of supply at } OP = \frac{M_1M/OM}{NP/OP}$$

$$\text{Elasticity of demand at } OP = \frac{M_1M/OM}{PP_1/OP}$$

$$\frac{\text{Elasticity of supply}}{\text{Elasticity of demand}} = \frac{M_1M}{OM} \times \frac{OP}{NP} \times \frac{OM}{M_1M} \times \frac{PP_1}{OP} = \frac{PP_1}{NP}$$

$$= \frac{\text{Increase in price (burden of the tax) to the consumer}}{\text{Decrease in price (burden of the tax) to the producer}}$$

This proposition has a number of practical applications:

(*a*) A tax on a good having an inelastic demand, e.g. cigarettes, falls mainly on the consumer.

(*b*) Where supply is inelastic compared with demand, the tax falls mainly on the producer. Thus an increase in oil royalties imposed by one Middle East government would have to be borne mainly by the particular oil company concerned.

(*c*) Because in the long period supply tends to be more elastic than in the short period, so, as time passes, the price will tend to rise as consumers are required to bear a greater share of the tax.

(*d*) Where supply is inelastic even in the long period, a tax will take longer to pass on to the consumer. Thus if there are any unoccupied houses, an increase in rates will have to be borne mainly by owners of property.

(*e*) An increase in price as a result of a tax will vary according to the relationship of elasticity of supply to elasticity of demand. The greater the elasticity of supply relative to the elasticity of demand, the greater will be the price rise.

The Distribution of the Benefit of a Subsidy

The grant of a subsidy ('negative tax') can be analysed similarly by moving the demand or supply curve to the right. More of the good will now be traded, and the benefit of the subsidy to consumers as compared with that of producers is directly proportional to the elasticity of supply to the elasticity of demand. That is:

$$\frac{\text{Consumers' share of subsidy (fall in price paid)}}{\text{Producers' share of subsidy (increase in the price received)}}$$

$$= \frac{\text{Elasticity of supply}}{\text{Elasticity of demand}}$$

Part VII

International Trade

30 The Nature of International Trade

30.1 Introduction

How International Trade Arises

International trade arises simply because countries differ in their demand for goods and in their ability to produce them.

On the demand side, a country may be able to produce a particular good, but not in the quantities it requires. The USA, for instance, is a net importer of oil. On the other hand, Zambia and Kuwait do not require all the copper and oil, respectively, which they can produce. Without international trade most of their deposits would lie untapped.

On the supply side, as we have already shown, both workers and localities are better at producing some goods than others. Nor can the advantages that they possess be easily transferred. What happens, therefore, is that they specialise in producing those goods in which they have the greatest relative advantage and exchange the goods they make for all the other things they want.

The same applies to countries. Factors of production are not evenly distributed throughout the world. One country may have an abundance of land; another may have a skilled labour force. Capital, oil, mineral deposits, cheap, unskilled labour and a tropical climate are other factors possessed by different countries to different degrees.

Nor can these factors be transferred easily from one country to another. Climate, land and mineral deposits are obviously specific. Labour is far more immobile internationally than within its own national boundaries, for additional obstacles are encountered – difference in language, immigration quotas and regulations, ignorance of opportunities, trade-union prejudice against foreign workers, unfamiliar customs and living conditions. Capital, too, moves less easily; political instability in some countries or simply ignorance of possibilities may prevent investors from moving funds abroad. In addition, governments may restrict the movement of capital because it imposes a strain on the balance of payments.

Because factors are difficult to shift, the alternative – moving the goods made by those factors – is adopted. What happens, therefore, is that countries, if the terms of trade are appropriate, specialise in producing those goods in which they have the greatest comparative advantage, exchanging them for the goods of other countries. Thus international trade arises.

Why Make a Separate Study of International Trade?

So far we have said nothing that is different in principle from trade between persons or between localities within a country. A carpenter who makes a chair exchanges it through the price mechanism for the food and other goods needed. Similarly, cars made in Oxford are exchanged for washing-machines made in South Wales. Why then, apart from the fact that longer distances are involved, do we treat separately the exchange of cars made in Britain for the wool produced in Australia?

The answer is that although the same theoretical principles apply, international trade gives rise to different problems. Exporters lack knowledge of foreign markets, find demand more difficult to predict, and have to cope with differences of language, weights and measures, government regulations, and changes of currency. Such factors tend to reduce the volume of international trade. Above all, since goods have to cross frontiers and be paid for in the currency of the country selling them, international trade may be regulated by governments for both economic and political reasons (see p.407). What we have to do, therefore, is to show the theoretical gains which result from international trade and then indicate why our theoretical argument has to be modified in practice.

30.2 The Advantages of International Trade

1. It Enables Countries to Obtain the Benefits of Specialisation

Specialisation by countries improves the standard of living for all, enabling a greater variety and a larger number of goods to be consumed.

(*a*) It is obvious that, without international trade, many countries would have to go without certain products. Iceland, for instance, has no coal, Britain no gold or aluminium, and Sweden no oil.

(*b*) More important, many goods can be enjoyed which, if produced at home, would be within the reach of only the very wealthy. In Britain this would apply to bananas, spices, oranges, peaches and indeed to most of the goods imported. How international trade can benefit people in this way is explained by economists in what is usually known as the 'law of comparative costs'. This shows that countries can gain by specialisation and trade in certain commodities providing that there is some difference in the relative costs of producing those commodities. The following imaginary examples will explain.

Suppose that there are two countries, *A* and *B*, producing just two commodities, wheat and cars. Each has the same amount of capital and the same number of labourers, but *A* has a good climate and fertile soil compared with *B*. *B*'s workers, on the other hand, are far more skilful. As a result, *A* has an *absolute* advantage in producing wheat, and *B* in producing cars. All factors are fully employed.

When both countries divide their factors equally between the production of wheat and cars, they can produce as follows:

Country	Wheat(units)	Cars(units)
A	500	100
B	100	500
Total production	600	600

But if *A* specialises in producing wheat and *B* in cars, total production would be 1000 wheat and 1000 cars. There is thus a net gain of 400 wheat and 400 cars to be shared between them (see p.402).

Here the gains are obvious, because *A* is better at producing wheat whereas *B* is better at producing cars. But suppose *A* has skilled labour and capital also, and is better at producing both wheat and cars, as follows:

Country	Wheat (units)	Car (units)
A	500	300
B	400	100
Total production (no specialisation)	900	400

Are there still gains to be achieved by specialisation?

Provided the rate at which cars can be exchanged for wheat lies within certain limits (see p.402), the answer is 'yes'. The reason for this is that *A*'s superiority in producing cars is far more marked than her superiority in producing wheat. In the production of the former she is three times as efficient, but with the latter only one-and-a-quarter times. Here *comparative*, rather than absolute, advantage is what is really important. The result is that if *A* specialises in producing cars, leaving *B* to produce wheat, total production will be 800 wheat and 600 cars.

Suppose now that world conditions of demand and supply are such that 2 wheat exchange for 1 car: that is, the price of cars is exactly twice that of wheat. *A* now exchanges 200 cars for 400 wheat, giving her a total of 400 wheat and 400 cars, and *B* 400 wheat and 200 cars.

It can be seen, therefore, that through specialisation *B* is 100 cars better off. But has specialisation improved *A*'s position? She now has 400 cars but only 400 wheat, a gain of 100 cars but a loss of 100 wheat. To produce the cars she has gained would have taken $\frac{1}{6}$ of her factors of production, but the loss of wheat represents only $\frac{1}{10}$ of her factors. In effect, therefore, specialisation has increased *B*'s productive capacity. Alternatively, we can say that if *B* gave up 100 wheat, by her own efforts she would obtain only 60 cars, whereas through exchange she gets 100.

The above argument can be put in terms of opportunity costs. If there is no specialisation, *A* has to give up 3 cars in order to produce 5 units of wheat. On the international market, however, the terms of exchange are such that 3 cars can obtain 6 units of wheat. It will obviously pay *A*, therefore, to specialise in producing cars and to obtain wheat by exchange. Similarly with *B*. For 4 units of wheat she can, by her own efforts, obtain only 1 car. On the world market she gets 2 cars. It will thus pay her to specialise in producing wheat and to obtain her cars by exchange.

It must be emphasised that the law of comparative costs merely shows possibilities on the supply side – how two countries can specialise to advantage when their opportunity costs differ. But until we know the terms upon which goods can be exchanged, we cannot say definitely whether specialisation will take place or, if it does, to what extent (see p.439).

It is the difference in relative prices which moves goods between countries. Hence, although a country may be favourably placed to produce certain goods, a large home demand and thus a relatively high price may mean that it is a net importer of that good (as the USA is of oil). It must also be remembered that few advantages in production are permanent. Climate and, to a large extent, mineral deposits persist, but new techniques can make factors more productive. Thus India now exports cotton goods to Britain! In any case, the above explanation must be amplified to allow for:

(i) *Transport costs*, which reduce the gains postulated by the law of comparative costs and therefore make for less specialisation. Indeed, it is conceivable that transport costs could more than offset *A*'s superiority in producing cars so that *B* found it better to produce her own requirements.

(ii) *The more realistic conditions where many countries and many products enter international trade.*

(iii) *Interference by nations with the free movement of goods* by customs duties, quotas, exchange control, physical control, etc. (see pp.406–7).

(iv) *The possibility of diminishing returns setting in as the production of a good increases.* The theory as stated assumes that, at all stages of production, wheat can always be produced instead of cars by both *A* and *B* at a constant ratio. Thus at any output, *A* can have 5 wheat instead of 3 cars and *B* 4 wheat instead of 1 car. But it is likely that as *B* increases her output of wheat, diminishing returns set in, for inferior land and labour have to be used. Thus instead of getting 4 additional wheat for 1 car, she receives only 3, and later only 2, and so on. The same applies, too, as the production of cars is increased by *A*. Eventually, therefore, it pays to specialise no longer. *A* can obtain her wheat cheaper by producing herself than by buying it on the world market, and the same applies to *B* as regards cars. Diminishing returns, and thus increasing costs, usually mean in practice that there is only partial specialisation – up to the point where opportunity costs are less than those offered by the terms of trade. Thereafter it is better for a country to produce the good itself. Most countries, in fact, both produce and import the same goods (e.g. the UK and agricultural produce).

2. By Expanding the Market, International Trade Enables the Benefits of Large-scale Production to be Obtained

In contrast to those goods where diminishing returns soon set in as output increases (see above), there are many products (e.g. aircraft, cars) which are produced under conditions of decreasing cost. Here the home market is too small to exploit fully the advantages of large-scale production. This applies particularly to small countries such as Switzerland. In such cases, international trade lowers costs per unit of output.

3. International Trade Increases Competition and thereby Promotes Efficiency in Production, Particularly where otherwise a Monopolist might gain Control of the Home Market

As we have seen, any limitation in the size of a market makes it easier for one seller to gain control. In contrast, international trade increases competition. A government must always consider the risk of a monopoly developing when it gives protection to the home industry by tariffs, etc.

4. International Trade Promotes Beneficial Political Links with Countries

Examples of this occur in Western Europe with the EEC, and within the Commonwealth where trade is still an important link.

30.3 The Terms of Trade

The Limits of the Exchange Rate

In our example, *A* specialises in producing cars and *B* in producing wheat. By her own efforts, *A* could have 5 wheat for 3 cars. Obviously, therefore, she will not specialise in cars if, by exchange, she receives less wheat than this. Similarly, *B* will not specialise in producing wheat if she has to give up more than 4 wheat for 1 car.

Thus for specialisation to be beneficial to both *A* and *B*, the rate at which wheat exchanges for cars must lie somewhere between the upper limit of $\frac{5}{3}$ and the lower limit of 4.

Determination of the Exchange Rate

But how is the actual rate of exchange (which we assumed to be 2 wheat for 1 car) determined?

The answer is quite simple. When we say that 2 wheat exchange for 1 car, we are really comparing relative values. Hence the price of cars will be twice that of wheat. Their relative prices will be fixed in the market, like all other prices, by demand and supply. We can explain by developing our simplified example still further.

Suppose *A* and *B* are the only two countries engaged in trade and that only two commodities, wheat and cars, are produced. Through specialisation, but before exchange, *A* has 600 cars and *B* has 800 wheat. As the relative prices of wheat and cars change, so we have the following imaginary demand and supply schedules:

Price (exchange ratio) wheat : cars	A		B	
	Wheat de-manded	Cars offered	Cars de-manded	Wheat offered
3:1	1,500	500	100	300
$2\frac{1}{4}$:1	900	400	240	540
2:1	650	325	325	650
$1\frac{3}{4}$:1	350	200	400	700

It can be seen that, given the conditions of demand and supply as shown in the above schedules, only at a price of 2 wheat to 1 car is there market equilibrium. The example could be extended to cover more than two countries and more than two commodities.

For both *A* and *B*, the rate at which wheat exchanges for cars represents the *terms of trade*. If there are changes in demand or supply, so that more wheat has to be given for a car, then the terms of trade have improved so far as A is concerned, but have worsened for B. On the other hand, if less wheat has to be given for a car, the terms of trade have improved for *B* but worsened for *A*.

Changes in the Terms of Trade

The terms of trade, therefore, are the rate at which a country exchanges its exports for imports. Where goods are traded internationally, this rate is fixed by (*a*) world conditions of demand and supply, and (*b*) the currency exchange rate, i.e. monetary influences. Long-term changes in the terms of trade are brought about by changes in the conditions of either demand or supply. Thus, in our example, if there is a large increase in *A*'s demand for wheat, the price of wheat will move nearer to the higher limit of $\frac{5}{3}$:1. Likewise, if there is a decrease in *A*'s demand for wheat, the price will move nearer to the lower limit of 4:1. Or, if the conditions of supply change so that *A* can produce 1000 cars instead of 600, she would probably be willing to supply more cars in exchange for a given quantity of wheat, and so the price of wheat rises, the terms of trade moving in favour of *B*. On the other hand, if *A*'s skilled labour emigrates and tends to be replaced by unskilled labour, she may be able to produce only 500 cars instead of 600, and the price of cars rises. The terms of trade move in favour of *A*.

Examples of how changes in the terms of trade can originate in the real world are:

1. Changes in the Conditions of Demand

(*a*) Demand may increase through industrial development. Thus the increased demand for oil has improved the terms of trade for oil exporting countries.
(*b*) A large increase in world demand for oil, without any corresponding increase in production, would improve the UK's terms of trade.
(*c*) A decrease in demand for basic raw materials resulting from world recession can, when their supply is inelastic, bring about a large fall in the price. This was a factor helping to improve the UK's terms of trade in 1980.

2. Changes in the Conditions of Supply

(*a*) Technical improvements may increase supply, e.g. in agriculture during the 1970s and 1980s. Where demand is inelastic, the price of a good may, as a result, fall considerably, improving the terms of trade for net importers of foodstuffs.
(*b*) Political or labour unrest or war in a country which is the main producer of a good, e.g. Chile (copper), may raise world prices and so

improve the terms of trade for other major producing countries, e.g. Zambia.

(c) Producers of a particular good may form a selling monopoly, e.g. the Organisation of Petroleum Exporting Countries (OPEC), thereby forcing up the price of their product.

How *currency* exchange rates are determined is explained in Chapter 32. Basically they reflect the relative demand for exports and imports. Thus the improvement in the sterling exchange rate in 1980 was a reflection of Britain becoming self-sufficient in oil, enabling her to reduce imports and even to become a net exporter.

But the currency exchange rate is also influenced by capital movements. Some of the 1987 improvement in the sterling exchange rate resulted from the movement of short-term capital to London because foreigners had increasing confidence in the £ sterling as the price of oil was stabilised at around $18 a barrel.

Thus a country's terms of trade can change even when there have been no real changes in the conditions of demand and supply simply because the value of its currency has altered on the foreign exchange market.

Measurement of the Terms of Trade

The terms of trade express the relationship between the price of imports and the price of exports. In practice, however, our interest is centred on this relationship not so much at any one time but rather as it changes over a period of time. We therefore measure relative changes in the terms of trade from one period to another.

Because countries import and export many goods, and the prices of different goods move in different ways and by varying amounts, we have to measure changes in the price of imports and exports as a whole by index numbers. And, it must be remembered, these are subject to certain defects (see p.366).

In practice, therefore, the terms of trade are measured as follows:

$$\frac{\text{Index showing average price of exports}}{\text{Index showing average price of imports}} \times \frac{100}{1}$$

Actual figures for recent years are given in Table 30.1.

When a country's exports become cheaper relative to her imports, she will have to give more goods in exchange for a given quantity of imports. It is then said that the terms of trade have 'deteriorated' or 'become less favourable'. If the opposite occurs, the terms of trade are said to have 'improved' or 'become more favourable'. Table 30.1 shows that the terms of trade for the UK have held fairly steady since 1979.

Table 30.1
The Terms of Trade of the UK, 1979–86 (Base Year 1980)

Year	Export unit-value index (1)	Import unit-value index (2)	Terms of trade (1) ÷ (2)
1979	87.6	90.9	96.4
1980	100.0	100.0	100.0
1981	108.8	108.2	100.5
1982	116.2	116.7	99.6
1983	125.7	127.5	98.6
1984	136.0	139.7	97.4
1985	143.5	145.2	98.9
1986	136.6	134.0	101.9

Results of Changes in the Terms of Trade

The direct effects of an improvement in a country's terms of trade are beneficial. First, she obtains more imports for a given quantity of exports (see pp.310–11). Second, her balance of payments may be improved. Suppose, for instance, that Britain's imports and exports are equal in value, now suppose that the price of imports in sterling falls, but the price of Britain's exports in sterling remains unchanged. If Britain's demand for imports is inelastic, the direct effect will be to improve the balance of payments, for less will be spent in sterling on imports. Similarly, if the demand for her exports were inelastic and their price in sterling rose, Britain's balance of payments would improve.

But the indirect results may make an improvement in the terms of trade, especially for a developed country, seem less desirable.

First, countries whose terms of trade have worsened may not be able to afford to buy the exports of the countries whose terms of trade have improved. For example, suppose that the price of wheat falls from £110 to £100 a tonne, but that an exporting country finds that demand increases only from 900 000 to 950 000 tonnes. Total expenditure on wheat drops, therefore, from £99m. to £95m. But this expenditure equals approximately the income of farmers who are exporting the bulk of their crop. As a result of the fall in income, their demand for imports from a country such as the UK would drop.

Second, the fall in income will also mean that less is spent on their home-produced goods, thereby reducing profits. To the extent that their firms are owned by British shareholders, lower dividend payments reduce the UK's invisible earnings.

Third, a fall in the incomes of less developed countries may mean that the loss be made good by increased aid.

Fourth, the economies of countries which are dependent on foreign trade may be subjected to frequent adjustments if there are swings in the terms of trade. If, for instance, the demand for raw wool is inelastic and its price fluctuates, incomes will be greater in Australia when the price of wool is high, and smaller when the price of wool is low. This has far-reaching effects on a policy aimed at a stable level of income and employment.

30.4 Free Trade and Protection

The Advantages of Free Trade

The theory of comparative costs shows how every country can enjoy a higher standard of living when each applies the principle of the division of labour to the production of goods. Theoretically, it seems to follow that trade should be as free as possible, for only then can the maximum specialisation according to the law of comparative advantage take place. In practice, however, we find that all countries follow policies which, to varying degrees, prevent goods moving freely according to differences in relative prices.

Methods of Controlling International Trade

1. Customs Duties

Customs duties, for example the common external tariffs of the EEC, are both revenue-raising and protective. They become protective when the imported good bears a higher rate of tax than the similar home-produced good.

2. Subsidies

While countries which subscribe to the General Agreement on Tariffs and Trade (GATT) cannot follow a policy of 'dumping' by giving direct subsidies to exports, the volume and pattern of international trade may be influenced indirectly by other means, e.g. government assistance to the shipbuilding industry. Less obviously, high welfare benefits, such as child benefits, by keeping down labour costs, may distort comparative costs by giving one country a price advantage over another which would not be justified by the real cost of producing.

3. Quotas

If demand is inelastic, the increase in price resulting from a customs duty will have little effect on the quantity imported. Hence when the government wishes to restrict the importation of a good to a definite quantity, quotas can be imposed. Compared with duties, quotas have two main disadvantages:

(a) As a result of the artificial shortage of supply, the price may be increased by the foreign supplier or by the importer. Hence unless the government also introduces price control, it is they who gain the advantage and not the public.

(b) Quotas make for rigidity in the economy, for they are calculated on a formula, usually based on volume of imports over a given period, which grows increasingly out of date with time. This penalises the efficient firm wishing to expand.

To avoid having formal quotas imposed on its good, 'voluntary' export restrictions may be agreed (e.g. on the import of Japanese cars to the UK).

4. Exchange Control

A tighter check on the amount spent on imported goods can be achieved if quotas are fixed in terms of foreign currency. This necessitates some form of exchange control (see p.427). All earnings of foreign currency or claims to foreign currency have to be handed over to the government and goods can be imported only under licence. Thus the government, not the free market, decides the priorities for imports.

5. Physical Controls

A complete ban – an embargo – may be placed on the import or export of certain goods. Thus narcotics cannot be imported, while the export of strategic goods to Iron Curtain countries is forbidden. Similarly, imposing strict technical standards for certain goods (e.g. milk) and regulating the importation of live animals (e.g. dogs and parrots) make trade more difficult.

Reasons for Government Control of International Trade

In general, trade is controlled because governments think and act nationally rather than internationally. Although people as a whole lose when trade is restricted, those of a particular country may gain.

Many reasons are put forward to justify control. Occasionally they have some logical justification; more usually they stem from a narrow interest seeking to gain an advantage. We can examine the arguments, therefore, under three main headings: (1) those based on strategic, political, social and moral grounds; (2) those having some economic basis; (3) those dependent on shallow economic thinking.

1. Non-economic Arguments

(*a*)   *To encourage the production of a good of strategic importance*. Where a nation is dependent on another for a good of strategic importance, there is a danger of its supply being cut off in the event of war. Thus one argument for subsidising aircraft production in the UK is to ensure the survival of plant and skilled labour.

(*b*)   *To foster closer political ties*. As a member of the EEC, Britain must impose a common external tariff as part of a movement towards political as well as economic unity.

(*c*)   *To prosecute political objectives*. Trade can be a weapon of foreign policy, e.g. in 1982 the USA stopped the export of high technology products to the USSR following the imposition of military rule in Poland.

(*d*)   *To promote social policies*. Although in the past, Britain has subsidised agriculture mainly for strategic reasons, today the purposes are basically social – to avoid depression in rural districts and a further movement to already congested towns.

2. Economic Arguments Having some Justification

(*a*)   *To improve the terms of trade*. The incidence of a selective tax is shared between producer and consumer according to the relative elasticities of supply and demand (see p.292). A government can therefore levy a tax on an imported good to improve the terms of trade if demand for the good is more elastic than the supply, for the increase in price is borne mainly by the producer, while the government has the proceeds of the tax. In practice this requires that: (i) the producing country has no alternative markets to which supplies can be easily diverted; (ii) her factors of production have few alternative uses; (iii) the demand for the exports of the country imposing the tariff must be unaffected by the loss of income suffered by countries who now find their sales abroad reduced.

(*b*)   *To protect an 'infant industry'*. It may be possible to establish an industry in a country if, during its infancy, it is given protection from well-established competitors which are already producing on a large scale. It is argued that the guaranteed home market will enable it to get over its teething troubles and in time it will be so strong that it can compete on equal terms with the rest of the world. Britain's car industry, for instance, benefited from such protection. The difficulty is that most industries come to rely on such protection, so that tariffs are never withdrawn, e.g. American duties on manufactured goods imposed in the eighteenth century are still in existence today. Moreover, often industries are encouraged which, without protection, would have no chance of survival. This leads to a maldistribution of the resources of a country.

(*c*) *To enable an industry to decline gradually.* Fundamental changes in demand for a good may severely hit an industry. Such, for instance, was the fate of the British cotton industry in 1975. Restrictions on imports can cushion the shock, but in practice many industries do not make use of the breathing-space to restructure.

(*d*) *To correct a temporary balance-of-payments disequilibrium.* A temporary drain on gold and foreign currency reserves may be halted by controlling imports. But if the depletion of the reserves is due to fundamental and lasting causes, other measures should be used (see Chapter 33).

(*e*) *To prevent 'dumping'.* Goods may be sold abroad at a lower price than on the home market. This may be possible because: (i) producers are given export subsidies; (ii) discriminating monopoly is possible (see p.179); or (iii) it enables the producer to obtain the advantages of decreasing costs. People in the importing country benefit directly from the lower prices. If, however, the exporter is trying to obtain a monopoly position which can be exploited once home producers have been eliminated, then there is a case for giving the home market some protection.

3. Economic Arguments having little Validity

(*a*) *To retaliate against tariffs of another country.* A retaliatory tariff may be used to influence another country to change its restrictive policy. The difficulty is that countries often retaliate by imposing still higher duties, with everybody losing.

(*b*) *To maintain home employment in a period of depression.* When there is a general depression in world trade, countries have tended to place restrictions on imports in order to ensure that income is spent on home-produced goods, thus providing employment at home. The difficulty is that other countries retaliate, thereby leading to an all-round contraction in world trade. GATT endeavours to prevent this from happening (see p. 410).

(*c*) *To protect home industries from 'unfair' foreign competition.* The demand that British workers must be protected from competition by cheap, 'sweated' foreign labour is frequently heard, usually from narrow interests – the industry and its workers facing competition. When economic analysis is applied, however, the argument can be seen to have little justification, and any protection given to an industry must be on other grounds, e.g. home workers cannot move to other occupations or industries:

(i)　It is the antithesis of the whole principle of comparative costs, which says that a country should specialise where it has the greatest relative advantage. That advantage may be an abundance of land, capital, tropical climate, minerals – or of cheap labour.

(ii)　Carried to its logical conclusion, the USA should refuse to import British cars because wages in Britain are much lower than in the USA.

(iii)　Low wages do not necessarily denote low labour costs. Wages may be low because labour is inefficient, i.e. because productivity is low. What we have to look at is the wage cost per unit of output. Thus the USA can export manufactured goods to the UK even though her labour is the most highly paid in the world. The threatened industry can compete by improving productivity and thereby lowering wage-cost per unit.

(iv)　A tax against a poor country with cheap labour merely makes the country poorer and its labour cheaper. The way to raise wages (and the price of the good produced) is to increase demand in foreign markets.

(v)　If imports from poor countries are restricted, other help has to be given. They prefer 'trade to aid'.

(vi)　Protection, by reducing the income of the poorer countries, means that they have less to spend on Britain's exports.

(vii)　The policy breeds retaliation.

In conclusion, we must emphasise that any restriction of trade has a social cost – a lower standard of living. But there may be other benefits – economic, political and social. Usually the economic gains are doubtful. Others cannot be measured, and it has to be left to the politicans to decide where the balance of advantage lies. But it must always be remembered that protection creates vested interests, which oppose any subsequent removal.

The General Agreement on Tariffs and Trade (GATT)

At Geneva in 1947 twenty-three nations drew up the General Agreement on Tariffs and Trade (GATT). The objectives were: (*a*) to reduce existing trade barriers; (*b*) to eliminate discrimination in international trade; (*c*) to prevent the establishment of further trade barriers by getting nations to agree to consult together rather than take unilateral action. It operates as follows.

Member nations meet together periodically to try to agree on a round of tariff reductions. Here the 'most-favoured-nation' principle applies. This means that if one country grants a tariff concession to another it must apply automatically to all the other participating countries. Thus if the EEC agrees to reduce her tariff on American automatic vending machines by 5 per cent in exchange for a 5 per cent reduction in the American tariff on EEC man-made fibres, then both concessions must be extended to every other member of GATT. This principle of non-discrimination also means that bilateral agreements and retaliatory tariffs against another country are out of harmony with the GATT.

Today (1987) there are 92 member nations, accounting between them for four-fifths of the world's trade. Through the organisation a progressive reduction in existing tariffs has been achieved, and the principle has been established that problems of international trade should be settled by co-operative discussion rather than by independent unilateral action. But difficulties have arisen.

(1) The principle of reciprocity means that low-tariff countries have to begin from an inferior bargaining position, and the concessions they can make are thus limited. Such countries may therefore prefer a low-tariff regional arrangement, such as the EEC.

(2) In certain circumstances the 'most-favoured-nation' principle may deter a country from making a tariff reduction to another country for the simple reason that it has to be applied to all.

(3) The Articles of the Agreement have had to be waived to allow for special circumstances – balance-of-payments difficulties, protection of agriculture, the establishment of 'infant' industries in the less developed countries, and the discriminatory character of the EEC.

(4) While the GATT has been successful in dealing with tariffs and many physical barriers, it has been by-passed by the new forms of protection – voluntary restraint agreements, orderly marketing arrangements, subsidies for special groups of exports, and trading requirements as conditions for overseas investment.

(5) The GATT rules will eventually have to be extended to cover services, which now account for a quarter of world trade.

31

The Balance
of Payments

31.1 Paying for Imports

Differences in Currencies

Occasionally, international trade may take the form of a barter arrangement, one country agreeing to take so much of another country's produce in exchange for so much of its own. Normally, however, exchanges are arranged by private traders who, according to relative prices, decide whether it is profitable to export and import goods.

But each country has its own currency – Spain (pesetas), France (francs), the USA (dollars), the UK (£ sterling), and so on. Even though currencies may have the same name, they are still different. Thus the pounds of Egypt, Syria and the UK are quite different from one another. This difference is important in international trade for two reasons: (*a*) sufficient foreign currency has to be obtained to pay for imports; (*b*) a rate has to be established at which one currency will exchange for another. The first will be considered forthwith, the second in the chapter which follows; but neither is independent of the other.

How are Imports Paid For?

We can best answer this question by first considering the purchases made by an individual, say Mrs Jones. Each week she buys a variety of goods. What is important for our purposes, however, is that there are at least seven sources from which she can obtain the money to pay for them.

The first and most usual source is the week's earnings, hers and her husband's, and Mrs Jones pays the shopkeeper on the spot with this money. It must be noted, however, that what in fact Mrs Jones is really doing is exchanging the goods which she and Mr Jones have specialised in producing for all the other goods needed. Thus, if Mr Jones is a tailor, the suits he makes are sold, and it is from the money thus obtained that Mrs Jones buys the goods the family needs. Furthermore, money is often earned, not by making goods, but by performing a service. Thus Mrs Jones herself may work a day each week for a shopkeeper, sending out accounts and answering correspondence. Last, interest on savings may provide some current income. Provided that all the weekly expenses are met out of this combined weekly income, we should say that the Jones family was 'paying its way'.

It might happen, however, that Mrs Jones's expenditure was not covered by the current weekly income. This might occur, for instance, because she bought a costly good, such as a washing-machine, which was not a regular item of weekly expenditure. In such circumstances Mrs Jones would have to raise the money from other sources. First, she could draw money from her National Savings account or from any other 'nest-egg' which she had by her. Second, she could sell some goods from her household stock, such as the piano or the television set, for which she had a less urgent need. Third, she might be able to borrow the money from a friend or, what amounts to the same thing, ask the shopkeeper to forgo payment for the time being. Finally, if she were extremely fortunate, she might be able to obtain a gift of money, say from a doting father. Such methods of payment would be fairly satisfactory for a good which is in use over a long period, provided that her savings were gradually replenished, or the assets sold were replaced by assets of equal value, or that the loan was repaid during the lifetime of the good. Where, however, this does not happen, either because insufficient savings are put by out of weekly income or because the over-expenditure is a frequent occurrence, we would say that Mrs Jones is 'not paying her way'. In time her savings would run out, her home would be sold up, and she would be unable to obtain any more loans or credit from the shopkeeper.

Broadly speaking, a nation trading with other nations is in exactly the same position as Mrs Jones. The same alternatives are open to it in paying for goods it imports. The main source is money received from the sale of current exports. Figure 31.1 shows how an export earns foreign currency. In normal times importing and exporting are done by firms, and payments are arranged through banks, who exchange the currency of one country for the currency of another *provided that they have the necessary reserves of that currency*. Such reserves are earned by customers who export to foreign countries.

Let us assume that £1 sterling exchanges for $1.60 and that there are no currency restrictions. Suppose a British merchant *X* wishes to import cotton from *A* in the USA to the value of £10 000. The American exporter requires payment in dollars, for all payments, e.g. workers' wages, have to be made in dollars. Hence the importer goes to a bank, pays in £10 000 and arranges a 'documentary credit'. The bank cables its branch in New York,

FIGURE 31.1
How Exports Pay for Imports

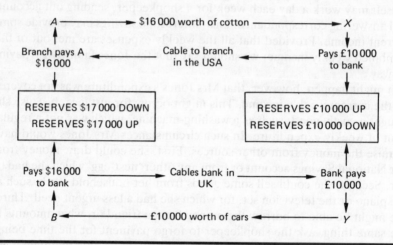

authorising it to make the equivalent dollar payment to *A* on production of the necessary documents, e.g. the bill of lading. (Most banks have branches in foreign capitals; if not, they engage local banks to act for them.) But how is it that the branch has dollars available to honour the draft?

We can see this if we imagine that another British firm *Y* has sold £10 000 worth of cars to an importer *B* in the USA. This firm wants payment in £ sterling. Hence the American importer of the cars pays $16 000 into a bank in the USA, and the same procedure follows. It is obvious that the two transactions – buying cotton from the USA and selling cars from Britain – balance one another. The British bank's branch has had to pay out dollars, the American sterling. The British bank has received sterling, the American bank dollars. If the two get together, their requirements match. (In practice, it is more likely that they would meet their needs through the foreign-exchange market.) Thus the dollars needed for paying for the cotton are obtained by selling the cars and vice versa. In short, exports pay for imports.

'Exports' in the Wider Sense

In this connection the term 'exports' needs qualification. In the same way that Mrs Jones received payment for the service of sending out the shopkeeper's accounts, so a nation may receive payment, not only for the goods it exports, but also for services rendered to other countries. Goods exported are termed 'visible exports', because they can be seen and recorded as they cross the political boundaries between countries. Services performed for people of other countries, however, are called 'invisible exports', because they cannot be seen and recorded as they cross frontiers. Nevertheless, since both goods and services involve payment by persons of the importing or receiving countries to persons in the exporting country, they are both 'exports' in this wider sense.

The main sources of invisible earnings and payments are:

1. *Government expenditure abroad*, e.g. overseas garrisons, diplomatic services.
2. *Shipping services*, e.g. an American travelling in the *Queen Elizabeth II* or shipping exports in a British merchantman.
3. *Civil aviation.*
4. *Travel*, e.g. sterling required by an American tourist for spending on a visit to London.
5. *Other services*, e.g. royalties earned on books and records, income from the transactions of overseas oil companies which ship direct from wells and refineries abroad to other countries.
6. *Interest, profits and dividends from overseas investments.*
7. *Private transfers*, e.g. remittances to relatives abroad.

Payments for any of the above transactions involve changing into another country's currency. Thus they represent 'imports' to the paying country and 'exports' to the receiving country.

31.2 The Balance of Payments

Most countries give an account each year of their monetary transactions with the rest of the world. The accounts presented are known as 'the balance of payments'. The balance of payments for the UK for the year ended 31 December 1985 is given in Table 31.1.

The Current Account

The current account shows, on the one hand, the foreign currency which has been *spent* on *imported goods* and *invisibles* in the course of the year, and, on the other, the foreign currency which has been *earned* by *exporting goods* and *invisibles*.

That part of the current account which shows the payments for just the goods exported and imported is known as the *visible balance* (formerly the *balance of trade*). Where the value of goods exported exceeds the value of goods imported, we say that there is a favourable visible balance. Too much, however, must not be read into the terms 'favourable' and

Table 31.1
The Balance of Payments of the UK, 1985 (£m)

CURRENT ACCOUNT

Visible trade

Exports (f.o.b.)	+78 051
Imports (f.o.b.)	−80 162
Visible balance	−2 111

Invisibles (net)

Government	−1 285
Sea transport	−1 157
Civil aviation	+ 353
Travel	+ 574
Financial and other services	+7 327
Interest, profits and dividends	+3 400
Private and government transfers	−3 499
Invisible balance	5 713
CURRENT BALANCE	3 602

FINANCIAL ACCOUNT

Transactions in external assets and liabilities:

Investment abroad (net)	−15 092
Borrowing abroad (net)	9 554
Official reserves, addition to	− 1 758
TOTAL	− 7 296
Balancing item	+ 3,694
	− 3 602

'unfavourable'. They are derived from the mercantilists of the sixteenth century who thought that a country's wealth depended upon it having a favourable balance of trade. In the first place, we have to know the reasons for the unfavourable balance. It may be brought about, for instance, by an increased demand for raw materials – which will later be exported in the form of manufactured goods. Second, a favourable or unfavourable visible balance can be reversed when the invisibles are taken into account.

When we add net income (+ or −) on the invisible items to the visible balance, we have what is known as the *current balance*. These items are shown in Table 31.1.

There is no special reason why earnings from goods and invisibles exported between 1 January and 31 December in any one year should equal expenditure on the goods and invisibles imported during that period. In fact, it would be an extraordinary coincidence if they did so. How often does what you earn during the week tally *exactly* with what you spend?

The current account is therefore likely to show a difference between earnings and expenditure. When the *value* of goods and invisibles exported exceeds the *value* of goods and invisibles imported, we say that there is a surplus current balance; when the reverse occurs, we say that there is a deficit current balance. The importance of the current balance is that it shows how far a country is paying its way.

However, the current account is only part of the statement covering a nation's overseas financial transactions. Capital flows must also be scrutinised. As we shall see, a current deficit need cause no alarm if it is covered by borrowing which will be put to a productive use. On the other hand, a current surplus may be insufficient to offset a heavy drain on the reserves through the outward movement of short- and long-term capital. The balance-of-payments statement must be examined as a whole.

Investment and other Capital Flows

If the current-account transactions were a country's only dealings with the world, the balance-of-payments accounts would be quite simple. A surplus of £100 million, for example, would add that amount to the reserves or allow the country to invest that amount overseas or to pay off short-term borrowings from the International Monetary Fund (IMF) or other foreign creditors. A deficit of £100 million would reduce the reserves by that amount or have to be financed by disinvestment or short-term borrowing abroad.

However, there are other flows of money into or out of a country which affect its ability to build up reserves or to pay off government debts. These are flows of capital – leaving Britain for investment or loans abroad, and coming into Britain for similar purposes. Whereas the current account covers income earning and spending in the course of the year, 'investment and other capital flows' deals with the movement of *capital* in and out of the country.

Short-term capital movements are those which arise from the transfer of liquid funds to and from Britain. Because London is a world financial market centre, foreigners hold bank balances or short-term bills there. These short-term funds can move quickly from country to country to take advantage of higher interest rates or to guard against an exchange rate depreciation. They are thus often referred to as 'hot money'.

Long-term capital investment by British residents in factories or plant overseas (whether directly or by the purchase of shares), or a loan by the British government (e.g. to a less-developed country or an international institution) leads to an outflow of capital. Similarly, investment in the UK by persons overseas or borrowing from abroad by the British government, local authorities, nationalised industries or companies leads to an inflow of foreign capital.

Any movement of capital out of Britain gives rise to a demand for sterling; a movement into Britain from abroad leads to the receipt of foreign currency.

No distinction is made between short- and long-term investment in presenting the overall balance of payments. In fact much of Britain's overseas investment is financed by short-term capital borrowed from foreigners, e.g. from the pool of Euro-currency deposited in London. To the extent that this occurs, there is no net outflow of foreign currency. Britain's overseas investment which is undertaken in order to make a profit is, in fact, like private business ventures. And, just as the shopkeeper borrows from the bank to cover the holding of stocks before Christmas, so the UK borrows to finance investment overseas in factories, plantations, oil-wells, nickel-mines, etc.

Thus the UK's balance-of-payments accounts concentrate on what is really significant to Britain – the extent to which currency flows as a whole influence the £ sterling exchange rate and her reserves of gold and foreign currencies.

The Financial Account

The Financial Account sets out the currency flow generated by capital movements.

Net investment abroad (£15 092 m.) consisted of direct investment (£3937 net) and portfolio investment (£11 155 net). In addition, official reserves were increased by £1758 m. Thus the total net demand for foreign currency was £16 850 m.

This demand was covered by borrowing abroad (mostly private, but some government) of £9554 m. net, the current balance of £3602 and a balancing item of £3694 m. (Figure 31.2).

The *balancing item* arises as follows. When the total effect of recorded capital transactions is added to the current balance, the total never adds up exactly to the amount of foreign currency the country has in fact gained or lost, which is known precisely to the Bank of England. Government spending overseas, for instance, is easier to record exactly than the foreign

FIGURE 31.2
The Balance of Payments, 1985

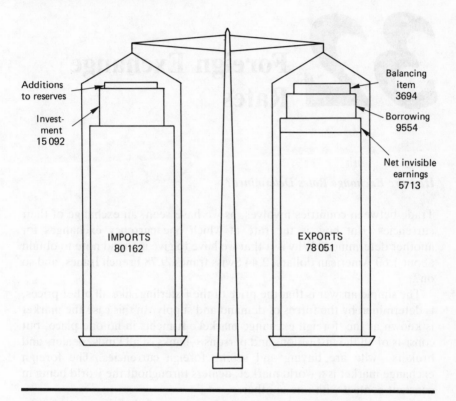

spending of people taking holidays abroad. Exports, too, may go abroad in December, but payments for them come in the following February.

A 'balancing item' is therefore added to make up the difference between the total value of the transactions recorded and the precise accounts kept by the Bank of England. If the balancing item is '+', it means that more foreign currency has actually come in than the estimates of transactions have indicated. When there is a '−' balancing item, the opposite is the case.

32 Foreign Exchange Rates

How are Exchange Rates Determined?

Trade between countries involves, as we have seen, an exchange of their currencies. But how is the rate at which one currency exchanges for another determined? Why is it that we have to give a pound note to obtain about 1.60 American dollars, 2.44 Swiss francs, 9.78 French francs, and so on?

The simple answer is that the price of the £ sterling, like all other prices, is determined by the forces of demand and supply. In this case the market is known as the 'foreign exchange market'. It meets in no one place, but consists of all the institutions and persons – banks of all kinds, dealers and brokers – who are buying and selling foreign currencies. The foreign exchange market is a world market, dealers throughout the world being in constant contact with one another.

Let us assume that we have 'freely fluctuating exchange rates': that is, rates are not fixed by governments, but are free to move from day to day according to changes in the conditions of demand and supply. To discover how a change in the exchange rate can come about, we can glance once again at the mechanism of foreign payments.

When the British merchant wished to import cotton from the USA (see p.413), the bank provided the necessary dollars for payment. These dollars, we saw, were obtained from its branch in the USA, and this branch in its turn had received them from an American importer of cars who had deposited them in exchange for the £ sterling needed to pay the British motor firm. Let us assume that the existing exchange rate is $1.60 to the £ sterling and that trade is such that the same quantity of dollars is both demanded and supplied.

The situation, we imagine, now changes. Imports of cotton from the USA increase in value, but exports of cars remain the same. The bank now finds that because more dollars are being demanded than are being deposited, its reserves of dollars are depleted. In short, the demand for dollars exceeds the supply. It is possible that the bank will be able to find on the foreign exchange market another bank or dealer who is receiving more dollars than pounds sterling. But if its experience is typical of the rest of the market, i.e. there has been a general increase in the demand for dollars relative to pounds, it will be able to replenish its reserves of dollars only by offering more pounds sterling in exchange. The dollar thus appreciates in value, say, to $1.58 to the pound. (As we shall see later, this will, to a large extent, bring a self-correcting mechanism into operation as regards the lack of balance between the value of imports and the value of exports.)

Arbitrage

We have concentrated our attention on the rate of exchange between the dollar and the pound. But there is also an exchange rate between the pound and the Deutsche mark, the French franc, and so on; and all these rates are linked with one another. If, for instance, £1 = $2 and $1 = 2 marks, then £1 must equal 4 marks. Otherwise, what are known as *arbitrage operations* by foreign exchange dealers would bring the rates into line. Thus suppose in London 5 marks can be obtained for the pound. A dealer would buy marks for pounds in London, sell them for dollars in New York, and exchange the dollars for pounds, making 25p profit on the deal. This would not last for long, because the world market in foreign exchange is so perfect that the increased demand for marks in London would soon bring the price there into line with the world price.

What are the Factors upon which the Demand for or Supply of Foreign Currency Depend?

It can be seen that an increased demand for dollars by people in Britain is one and the same thing as an increase in the supply of sterling being offered for dollars. An increased demand for dollars may be counteracted by an increased demand for sterling (that is, an increased supply of dollars) by Americans. For the sake of simplicity, we concentrate our attention on the factors leading to a demand for sterling by Americans. These factors are:

(1) To pay for the import of goods from Britain.
(2) To pay for 'invisibles', e.g. a tour of Britain, government spending on troops in Britain, etc.
(3) To meet capital movements into Britain (see p.418).

What are the Underlying Economic Forces Influencing how much Foreign Currency is Demanded and Supplied?

So far we have merely indicated the items for which foreign currency will be demanded or supplied. Now we examine the economic forces which determine how large each of these items will be. They are:

1. Relative Prices

The chief factor affecting trade, both visible and invisible, is the price of home-produced goods as compared with the price of similar goods abroad. If, for example, American prices are high, Americans will wish to import cheaper British goods, whereas the British will prefer home-produced goods to American. The increased demand for sterling will, in a free exchange market, so raise the value of the £ sterling that eventually the prices of British goods are in line with those of the 'high-cost' American producer.

Some economists, notably Professor Gustav Cassel in 1922, carried this argument a stage further. They said quite categorically, in what became known as the *purchasing power parity theory*, that the value of a foreign currency in terms of another depends mainly on the relative purchasing power of the two currencies in the respective countries. In other words, the exchange rate settles at the level which makes the purchasing power of a given unit of currency the same in whatever country it is spent.

For example, suppose that there is only one commodity, a type of machine, and this machine sells for £200 in Britain and for $330 in the USA; then the rate of exchange would be 1.65 dollars to the pound. If now the price in Britain rises to £220, the rate of exchange will be 1.50 dollars to the pound. Thus a fall in the internal purchasing power of a currency through a rise in the general level of prices leads to a corresponding fall in its foreign exchange value. Or, mathematically, the purchasing power parity theory says that:

Foreign exchange price of £ (e.g. in dollars)

$$= \frac{\text{USA price level}}{\text{British price level}}$$

When we are considering the long period, there is considerable truth in this theory. If, for instance, there is an inflation of prices in Britain relative to the USA, there will be less demand for British exports, but an increased demand for American imports. As a result, the price of the £ sterling falls in terms of the dollar. But, particularly in the short run, to say that overall purchasing power is the sole factor governing exchange rates is a gross over-simplification. The theory fails to allow for the following:

(*a*) Not all goods enter into international trade. Quite a number, for instance the Indian's loincloth, satisfy local and particular wants. Others, like houses, railway travel, gas and electricity, haircuts and personal and professional services, cannot be transported easily from one country to another. The prices of such goods may rise considerably, whereas those of exports remain the same. Eventually, export industries will be forced by competition to pay higher wages, etc., but owing to immobility and imperfections of the market, this may take a very long time to come about. In the meantime exchange rates will not be affected – in spite of the statistical rise in the general level of prices.

(*b*) Such factors as indirect taxes, subsidies and transport costs may change the prices of goods within a country but not affect exchange rates in the way the theory predicts. Suppose a 100 per cent tariff is placed on an important import, the demand for which is not absolutely inelastic. The price in the home market would rise, but since less foreign currency would be spent on it, the exchange rate would tend to improve!

(*c*) A change in the exchange rate may originate in factors quite independent of the internal price level. When national income rises, for instance, imports are likely to increase in value relative to exports. As a result, the external value of the currency will depreciate. Similarly, a change in the terms of trade may affect the exchange rate. The 1986 fall in the price of oil, for instance, led to the £ sterling depreciating on the foreign exchange market.

(*d*) The theory ignores the effect of movements of capital upon the exchange rate, an influence which is particularly important in the short period (see p.424).

The purchasing power parity theory is not therefore a complete explanation of what determines exchange rates. But this does not mean that the theory has no value. Since imports and exports are the major items in a country's balance of payments, it draws attention to what, in the long run, is the dominant influence on exchange rates – how the internal price level moves relative to that of other countries. Indeed, there is a close link between this and the movement of capital for speculative purposes, for the latter is likely to reinforce changes in the exchange rates originating in the current account of the balance of payments.

The fundamental link between internal price levels and the external value of currencies is only too vividly illustrated by Britain's experience since 1945. During this period the basic cause of the fall in the foreign exchange value of the £ sterling has been her inability to maintain the £'s internal value.

2. Relative Money Incomes

When a country's money income expands, its demand for imports increases. Potential exports also tend to be diverted to the home market.

3. Long-term Investment Prospects

People can invest capital in foreign countries either by buying the bonds of foreign governments or the equities of companies there, or directly by building factories abroad as offshoots of parent companies in the UK. The chief factor influencing such investment decisions is how the prospective yield compares with that which could be obtained elsewhere.

Political risks, e.g. of default on loans, or changes in government policy, e.g. a swingeing increase in corporation tax, have also to be assessed by those investing overseas.

4. The Rate of Interest

Short-term capital moves from one country to another as changes take place in the rate of interest being offered by each. The government can therefore vary interest rates to attract or repel foreign capital as it sees fit.

5. Expected Future Movements of the Exchange Rate

Inflation in a country will be interpreted by foreign holders of its currency as being likely to lead also to a fall in the external value of the currency. Selling of the currency follows, thereby helping to bring about the fulfilment of those expectations!

6. Government Expenditure

Military expenditure and economic aid abroad now provide large sources of supply of certain currencies, e.g. the American dollar and the £ sterling, to foreigners.

It can be seen, therefore, that exchange rates are not dependent on any single factor. The only safe generalisation which can be made is that the value of a currency depends upon all the forces which give rise to the purchase or sale of that currency in the foreign exchange market.

33

The Correction of a Balance-of-Payments Disequilibrium

33.1 Alternative Approaches

When do Corrective Measures become Necessary?

Taken as a whole the balance of payments must always balance. Foreign currency necessary for making payments abroad must have come from somewhere. If earnings from exports and invisibles are insufficient, the balance must be achieved by drawing on the gold and foreign currency reserves or by borrowing.

In the short period a withdrawal from the reserves may not be serious. It could easily happen that, just prior to 31 December, the date usually chosen for drawing up the accounts, imports of raw materials were running at a high rate. Later, when the goods manufactured from these raw materials are sold abroad, the reserves will be replenished. Reserves of gold and foreign currencies are held for this very purpose – to provide a 'cushion' when current earnings are temporarily insufficient to cover payments abroad. Even individuals usually carry spare cash to bridge the gap between income and spending.

Alternatively, a less-developed country may run an adverse balance of payments for a number of years. The deficit is covered, not by drawing on reserves, but by borrowing. Loans are used to buy capital equipment. Eventually, this equipment will allow the country to export goods which will cover the interest due on the loan and then the repayment of the loan itself. Once again, the balance-of-payments deficit need not be frowned upon: it is just good business – like a firm obtaining a loan from the bank.

But the situation is different when year after year a country is running a balance-of-payments deficit and there is little likelihood of it being able to reverse the trend. This disequilibrium between credits and debits is then said to be of a 'fundamental nature'. If not corrected, reserves will run out. Other countries will refuse to lend to the country in difficulties – they

doubt whether the spendthrift will ever be in a position to repay. Action
has to be taken, therefore, to remedy the situation.

A Broad Analysis of the Problem

A first-aid measure is for the authorities to force up the short-term rate of
interest in order to reverse the outward flow of short-term capital.
Furthermore, reserves could be strengthened by borrowing from the IMF
and other central banks. This would help to restore confidence in the
currency.

Eventually, however, exports must be increased in value and/or imports
decreased in value.

There are two basic policies which can be follows: (1) reducing expenditure on imports; (2) switching expenditure, so that foreigners spend more
on British exports and Britons spend less on imports in favour of
home-produced goods. Both policies can be implemented simultaneously
(though with a different emphasis on each), but it is easier to clarify the
issues by considering them separately.

33.2 Reducing Expenditure on Imports: Deflation

The Difficulty of Increasing Exports

A government may adopt policies to promote exports. Thus the British
government guarantees payment through the Export Credits Guarantee
Department and provides information on developing markets abroad.
Moreover, banks may be asked to discriminate in favour of exporters when
granting loans. Although under the terms of GATT it is impossible to grant
direct tax reliefs, incentives can be incorporated in indirect taxes, for
example zero-rating VAT on exports.

Increasing the value of exports by such means, however, takes time and
is largely only marginal to the problem. The main immediate thrust would
need to be made on reducing expenditure on imports. This may be
achieved by both physical controls and the deflation of home income.

Physical Controls

Physical controls may be exercised through import duties and quotas or by
exchange control.

1. Import Duties and Quotas

Tariffs may be levied to increase the price of imports. But if demand is
inelastic imports will not be greatly discouraged or the expenditure on

them in terms of foreign currency greatly decreased. Sometimes, therefore, an import quota in terms of volume is imposed.

However, physical controls reduce the advantages of free trade, while the efficiency of home industry may be impaired by its protection from foreign competition. Moreover, they displease other countries and are likely to attract retaliation.

2. Exchange Control

Exchange control may be introduced for the following purposes:

(*a*) to limit the amount of foreign currency spent on imports;
(*b*) to discriminate against those countries whose currencies are 'hard' (that is, cannot easily be earned by exporting to them), and to favour those countries whose currencies are 'soft' (because they buy exports from the country concerned);
(*c*) to distinguish between essential and non-essential imports;
(*d*) to control the export of capital.

Exchange control is essential when a country's currency is over-valued – that is, its declared exchange rate is higher than it would be if it were determined on the foreign exchange market. What this really means is that foreign currencies are valued below the market price – and so they have to be rationed.

Pegging the rate at a high level, however, may be advantageous to the country concerned, particularly if her demand for imports and supply of exports is inelastic. In such circumstances the balance of payments would not be improved by reducing the external value of the currency (see pp.432–5).

Nevertheless, exchange control suffers from many of the disadvantages associated with rationing. Inefficient home firms are protected from foreign competition. Regulations are evaded and 'black markets' in the currencies occur. Many administrators are needed who could be more productively employed elsewhere. Moreover, it can lead to uncertainty in international trade. Countries may find their regular markets closed, and firms cannot plan ahead because of uncertainty as to whether they will be allowed to purchase their raw materials from a hard-currency area. Furthermore, the confidence of foreigners is impaired if any attempt is made to prohibit the movement of their funds out of a country. Finally, when people are prevented from buying in hard-currency countries, it often means that they are forced to purchase dearer or inferior goods elsewhere.

Deflation of Home Income

Since imports increase as income expands, one way in which the value of imports can be brought into line with that of exports is by reducing income.

Such a deflationary policy would also tend to put a brake on any rise in home prices. More important, it allows adjustment to take place without altering currency exchange rates. This has the advantage that it facilitates international trade by removing the uncertainty associated with fluctuating exchange rates when negotiating long-term contracts or making loans.

But there are serious disadvantages:

1. Unless home prices are flexible downwards, a deflationary policy can only succeed at the expense of creating unemployment. In practice costs, particularly wage rates, prove to be rigid, so that home prices are sticky.
2. There is a low income-elasticity of demand for many imports, e.g. basic foodstuffs, raw materials and manufactured components.
3. Any reduction of imports to Britain represents a loss of exports by other countries. Deflationary effects on their economies may result in a reduction in their demand for imports, thereby reducing British exports. In short, deflation is a 'beggar-my-neighbour' policy where the benefit is uncertain even to the deflating country.

The Gold Standard

The old gold standard was basically such a deflationary mechanism for correcting a balance-of-payments deficit. All major currencies had a declared value in terms of gold. If, for instance, Britain had a balance-of-payments deficit, foreign currency would be demanded. But the sterling exchange rate could not fall a great deal because it soon became cheaper to pay for imports with gold.

Purchases of gold were paid for by cheques drawn on the commercial banks, who drew gold from the Bank of England. This lowered their cash reserve and so, unless the Bank of England restored the position by buying securities on the open market, the commercial banks had to reduce their lending activities.

Furthermore, the Bank of England's power to issue notes was limited by its gold reserves and the fiduciary issue. Hence, in order to protect its reserves, the Bank raised the bank rate. Other interest rates moved in sympathy.

Higher rates of interest attracted foreign capital, thereby halting the export of gold. But, by discouraging investment, they also set in motion a deflationary process. It was assumed that the contraction of income would result in a fall in costs, and thus lower home prices. In practice, as noted above, this proved difficult. As a result, restoration of balance-of-payments equilibrium was achieved, not so much by expanding exports, but, as incomes fell, by a reduction in imports. Eventually the resulting unemployment did produce a fall in costs and, as exports became cheaper relative to foreign goods, the flow of trade was reversed.

In the meantime, however, the deflationary process caused severe suffering. Rather than continue with this, the UK and most other countries abandoned the gold standard in the 1930s.

33.3 Expenditure-switching: Depreciation of the Exchange Rate

Expenditure-switching by Exchange-rate Adjustment

The great merit of the gold standard was that, in maintaining stable exchange rates, it facilitated trade. Its big disadvantage was that a country could not follow an independent internal monetary policy in order to promote full employment.

But balance-of-payments policy can take the form of expenditure-switching, with foreigners spending more on British exports and Britain spending less on imports. While some switching can be enforced by government control of import expenditure (see pp.407, 427), the most effective method is to alter the relative prices of imports and home-produced goods.

Prices of internationally traded goods are composed of: (a) the home producer's price, and (b) the exchange rate. Thus British exports can be made more competitive in world markets by lowering the rate at which the £ sterling exchanges for foreign currencies. Because fewer units of foreign currency have now to be given up to obtain £1, foreigners can buy British exports more cheaply. Similarly, imports to Britain now cost more in terms of sterling, encouraging Britons to switch to the relatively cheaper home-produced goods. Provided that, taken together, the demand for both exports and imports is sufficiently elastic, there will be a correction of Britain's balance-of-payments deficit (see pp.433–4).

Such corrective exchange-rate adjustments occur automatically through the forces of demand and supply in a freely operating foreign exchange market. Thus if the USA's exports to Britain are greater in value than the USA's imports, the demand for dollars will increase, for British importers will be wanting them to pay for those imports. Consequently the exchange rate will move against sterling. This will raise the price in sterling of Britain's imports from the USA, and lower the price in dollars of British exports to the USA. Demand responses to these price changes tend to bring about equality in value of British imports and exports.

Advantages and Disadvantages of Exchange Depreciation as a means of Correcting a Balance-of-Payments Disequilibrium

Exchange depreciation has the advantage that this correction is effected without the tribulations of deflation. Instead a country can follow its own internal monetary policy – even inflating if it thinks that this is desirable in the interests of reducing unemployment.

Moreover, with freely fluctuating exchange rates (when the value of the currency 'floats'), the correction is secured without the many controls which are often necessary when the exchange rate is 'pegged' (see p.427) because reserves do not have to be protected. Indeed, there is less need for a country to carry gold and foreign currency reserves.

Unfortunately, fluctuating exchange rates are themselves not without disadvantages.

First, the demand for exports and imports may be so inelastic that the balance-of-payments disequilibrium is made worse by depreciation rather than better (see p.433). Supply, too, may be so inelastic that a country cannot take advantage of the expanded demand for its exports which follows a fall in the exchange value of its currency (see p.434). It should be emphasised, however, that such conditions are possible rather than likely in the real world.

Second, fluctuating exchange rates may deflect a government from pursuing policies to maintain the internal purchasing power of its currency. Instead export prices are made competitive by foreign exchange depreciation. Unfortunately such depreciation tends to be continuous, for, as the prices of imports also rise, home costs and prices are increased, giving a push to further inflation through wage demands, etc.

Third, freely fluctuating exchange rates encourage speculation, thereby making movements more frequent and pronounced. Speculative capital moves according to the holder's estimate of the future value of currencies. Similar speculation occurs with trade. Foreign importers of British goods who expect the price of sterling to depreciate delay paying for the goods as long as possible, a situation described as 'lags'. British importers of foreign goods make their payments in foreign currency as soon as possible, described as 'leads'. The importance of speculation is that it can bring about the very rise or fall in the exchange rate that was expected. On the other hand, dealers who quote fixed 'future' prices for foreign currencies on the 'forward' market serve, to some extent, to even out exchange rate fluctuations.

Finally, fluctuating exchange rates add to the normal uncertainties associated with foreign trade for this usually involves granting credit and even entering into long-term contracts. By the time an exporter receives payment for his goods, the exchange rate may have moved so adversely that the expected profit has been turned into a loss. In such circumstances the exporter may prefer not to take the risk of trading with somebody in another country. Although arrangements can usually be made with a dealer to supply 'forward exchange' (that is, the foreign currency can be obtained at a given future date at an agreed price) trade may still not be worth while through the additional cost involved.

Similarly, fluctuating exchange rates can discourage long-term investment overseas.

33.4 Managed Flexibility

The Exchange Equalisation Account

When Britain left the gold standard in 1931, she followed a policy of flexible exchange rates. Nevertheless, to cancel out fluctuations in the exchange rate brought about by movements of short-term capital, the government set up the Exchange Equalisation Account.

The Account operates by the simple application of the laws of price. It has a stock of gold and foreign currencies (mostly borrowed against Treasury bills), and this stock is either replenished or offered on the market according to whether short-term capital is moving into or out of London. For instance, a movement of capital into London from the USA would increase the demand for the £ sterling and drive up its price; the Account can prevent this rise by offering pounds in exchange for dollars. The value of the pound would not change but the Account would add to its stock of dollars. On the other hand, if there were a movement of capital out of London, the Account would offer dollars in exchange for pounds, thereby reducing its stock of dollars and increasing its holding of pounds.

The knowledge that such an Account exists to even out exchange fluctuations has done much to prevent speculation in the value of the pound. Provided it has adequate reserves of foreign currency, the Account can allow that value to appreciate or depreciate within its discretion, and this it now does according to the policy of the monetary authorities (see p.432).

The International Monetary Fund (IMF)

The major defect of a system of freely fluctuating exchange rates is that it tends to discourage international trade. Countries therefore attempted to stabilise the exchange value of their currencies, and an international code of behaviour to achieve this was drawn up at the Bretton Woods conference in 1944. This established the International Monetary Fund (IMF) and the International Bank for Reconstruction and Development (IBRD, the 'World Bank').

A system of 'managed flexibility' was operated through the IMF. Each member country (140 in 1987) agreed that eventually it would maintain free convertibility of its currency at an agreed rate and contribute its quota of currency to a pool held by the IMF. From these reserves, the IMF could make foreign currency available to a country running a short-term balance-of-payments deficit. Should this balance-of-payments disequilibrium prove to be 'fundamental', devaluation of the country's currency was possible under agreed rules.

The Bretton Woods agreement worked tolerably well for twenty-five years. But it suffered from two main weaknesses:

1. The pressure of exchange adjustment fell almost entirely on debtor nations (which were forced to devalue) rather than on creditor nations (which could have eased part of the burden by revaluing).
2. In spite of Keynes's arguments at Bretton Woods, little provision was made for the expansion of international liquidity necessary to service increasing world trade.

We consider each of these.

Exchange Adjustment

While the UK and, later, the USA were frequent 'persistent debtor' nations, West Germany and Japan were 'persistent creditor' countries. Both the latter countries, however, proved reluctant to revalue their currencies, fearing that the rise in the price of their exports which this would entail would make them uncompetitive in world markets.

The result was that, in order to maintain the existing exchange rate the UK in particular had to deflate the economy whenever balance-of-payments difficulties arose. To some extent this could be regarded as the penalty which she had to pay for her inability to prevent prices rising as the economy expanded. Furthermore, the 'stop' policy had to be carried further since an initial weakness of the £ gathered momentum because sterling was held as a reserve currency (see later).

The decisive step was taken in June 1972, when once again sterling came under pressure as the British economy expanded. The Heath government would not allow the maintenance of a fixed exchange rate to stand in the way of economic expansion. Thus the 'pegged' pound was abandoned, and instead the pound was allowed to 'float', its value being arrived at according to the day-to-day demand for and supply of sterling on the foreign exchange market. Eventually all other major trading countries adopted floating exchange rates, though these are not completely market-determined. Instead they are influenced by the operations of each country's equivalent of the UK's Exchange Equalisation Account.

Conditions Necessary for Successful Exchange Depreciation/Devaluation

Where countries maintain an agreed rate of exchange between their currencies (e.g. as in the European Monetary System; see p.444), depreciation takes the form of a once-for-all reduction in the value of a country's currency by definite government decision, and is known as *devaluation*. But both depreciation (through the mechanism of the foreign exchange market) and devaluation involve a reduction in the rate at which a country's currency exchanges for other currencies, so that, in examining the effects, the same broad principles apply.

Let us suppose that the UK trades only with the USA and that she has a persistent balance-of-payments deficit. The value of the pound falls from $1.65 to $1.50. Whether such depreciation is successful or not will depend upon the answers to the following questions.

1. What is the Elasticity of Demand for Exports and Imports?

The effect of the devaluation will be to make British exports cheaper in terms of dollars to the American buyer and imports from America dearer in terms of pounds to the British buyer.

A British good formerly selling in the USA for $1.65 need now cost only $1.50. This fall in price should lead to more British goods being demanded, and, if elasticity of demand is greater than unity, more dollars will be earned.

Similarly, an American good worth $1.65 formerly cost the British buyer £1. After the depreciation, the price will rise to £1.10. But will this mean that we have to spend more *dollars* on our imports? The answer is 'no'. (Suppose that you are on a camping holiday in the USA and that the pound is devalued. Would your bread, camp site, etc., change in price?) The worst possible situation is when demand for imports is absolutely inelastic; then the same quantity of imports will be demanded and the same amount of dollars spent on them. Otherwise there will be some contraction of demand (because the price in terms of pounds has risen) and then expenditure in dollars will fall.

The two elasticities of demand for exports and imports must be considered together. Even if the demand for imports is absolutely inelastic (so that the same amount of foreign currency is spent on them), the balance of payments will not deteriorate provided that there is a gain of foreign currency from an increased demand for exports.

What is the probable situation in the real world for the UK as regards the elasticities of demand for imports and exports? Demand for imports is likely to be fairly inelastic. Most of Britain's imports are necessities – foodstuffs, raw materials and essential components. Indeed, if exports expand, demand for raw materials will increase. Offsetting this is a likely fall in British demand for luxuries and foreign travel on account of the greater cost, home-produced goods and holidays now being more competitive.

On the other hand, the demand for British exports as a whole is probably elastic. Not only could the UK undersell exporting competitors, e.g. in cars, electrical equipment, etc., but the lower export price resulting from depreciation would convert what were formerly 'potential exports' into real exports. Moreover, such items as tourism are likely to have a highly elastic demand. But it must be remembered that the price of exported goods will not fall by the entire amount of the depreciation. Their home price will rise when they are made from imported raw materials or components.

2. What is the Elasticity of Supply of Exports?

It is on the supply side that the greatest obstacles to a successful depreciation are likely to be encountered. The fall in the price of exports will probably lead to an expansion of demand, but this will provide no lasting cost advantage if the supply of exports cannot be increased without the home price rising. Here the reaction of labour to the effects of depreciation is crucial. The increase in the cost of imports raises the cost of living. There is thus a strong temptation to demand wage increases. Moreover, labour is in a strong position, because demand for exports should increase following the depreciation. If the trade unions exploit their position, the resultant rise in wages could soon wipe out the cost advantage which Britain had gained and further depreciation would occur.

It should be noted, however, that where demand for British exports is inelastic, then inelasticity of supply may not be detrimental. The exporter need not reduce the price in terms of foreign currency to foreign importers, and British earnings of foreign currency may not fall.

3. What is the Elasticity of Supply of Imports?

If foreigners are dependent on the British market, and supply is inelastic, then they may be willing to reduce their prices. This may reduce Britain's expenditure of foreign currency, though in volume imports are almost as great.

4. What is the Nature of British and American Investments with Each Other?

Suppose British investments in the USA are mostly in the form of shares in companies there. Profits will be earned in dollars and so there will be no loss of foreign currency after depreciation.

On the other hand, if American investments in the UK are in stock with interest fixed in sterling, the USA will lose by depreciation of the pound, for she gets fewer dollars than formerly in invisible earnings.

5. Will Countries Fear Further Depreciation?

Depreciation reduces the value of sterling securities held by foreigners, including the sterling balances held in London. In the first place, this may destroy confidence in sterling, undermining London's position as a banking centre. Business is transferred elsewhere, and invisible earnings are lost. Second, unless positive measures are taken to correct the underlying inflation, foreigners will fear further depreciation and so hasten to remove their capital from London, bringing about what they fear.

The above arguments suggest that, for a country like Britain, depreciation provides no escape from dealing with inflation. It may entail a serious deterioration in the terms of trade, a large amount of additional exports having to be given to achieve a small gain in the balance of payments. Indeed, where demand for both imports and exports is highly inelastic, depreciation may cause the balance of payments to deteriorate still further. In this case, a country has to resort to physical controls to reduce imports.

33.5 International Financial Arrangements

International Liquidity

Just as money in our pockets or at the bank is necessary to finance our everyday purchases, so people dealing in international markets require reserves of an acceptable form to finance international trade.

The one form this is always acceptable in is gold. Unfortunately, the supply of gold is not increasing fast enough to keep pace with the expansion of world trade and the corresponding need for larger reserves. In the past, the difficulty has been overcome by holding reserves in other currencies – dollars and sterling. These were convertible into gold, and were known as 'reserve currencies'. Holding reserve currencies instead of gold had the additional advantage that a rate of interest was earned, whereas there is no return on holding gold.

The willingness to hold a reserve currency, however, only lasts as long as there is little possibility of the reserve currency being devalued. Persistent balance-of-payments deficits undermine confidence in the currency concerned, and there will then be a tendency to move out of the reserve currency. This is what happened in 1972 and 1973, first to the £ sterling, and then to the dollar.

To some extent the shortage of international liquidity has been made good by economising on the reserves through pooling arrangements, e.g. in the IMF and by the central banks of the Group of Ten. But such pooling arrangements proved inadequate in the speculation against the pound in June 1972. A new form of reserve to provide *additional* assets became essential.

Special Drawing Rights (SDRs) – in contrast to the ordinary drawing rights of the IMF – are such an addition. Beginning in 1970 they have been issued by the IMF as a line of credit to members in proportion to their quotas. The value of SDRs is expressed in terms of a basket of sixteen major currencies weighted according to their international importance and calculated according to their daily value on the foreign exchange market.

Both the IMF and its members have agreed to honour SDRs. Thus a member country can use them to purchase foreign currency in order to support its exchange rate, and countries with a strong balance of payments can be required to accept SDRs up to twice their own quota allocation.

At present (1987), with the recession in world trade and the reduced requirement for reserves with the general adoption of floating exchange rates, there is no pressure on international liquidity. But the creation of SDRs has established an important principle – that internationally created credit could be used to finance world trade – and the creation of SDRs is likely to be the major source of extra international reserves in the future. Indeed it has been suggested that SDRs could be created as a means of giving aid to the less developed countries.

The International Bank for Reconstruction and Development (the World Bank)

Whereas the IMF makes short-term funds available to meet a temporary balance-of-payments deficit, the World Bank provides long-term finance for reconstruction and development – the building of roads, irrigation schemes, power stations, etc. – especially in the less developed countries.

Funds are obtained by: (1) a 'quota' subscribed by member nations roughly in proportion to their national incomes; (2) borrowing on the international market by the issue of bonds backed by the quotas of members.

Countries which can satisfy the Bank that they have economically sound projects may borrow from the Bank for a period of five to twenty-five years at a rate of interest which is as low as possible having regard to the Bank's ability to borrow.

The poorer less-developed countries can borrow from the *International Development Association* (IDA), an affiliate of the World Bank. Funds are provided almost entirely by its wealthier members and so loans are interest-free, only a service charge being levied.

34 The European Economic Community

34.1 Background to the EEC

Supra-national Organisations

The two world wars convinced statesmen in Western European countries that some form of political unity was desirable, and in 1949 the Council of Europe was created – the basis, it was hoped, of a European parliament. But organisations with definite functions – the Organisation for European Economic Co-operation (founded in 1948), the North Atlantic Treaty Organisation (1949) and the Western European Union (1954) proved more fruitful than did the Council of Europe with its broad aims.

Although these organisations involved co-operation, they were merely voluntary associations, not federal bodies exercising supra-national powers in the interests of members as a whole. Although federation was the ultimate aim of European statesmen, they realised that it could only proceed piecemeal and on a functional basis. The first supra-national organisation, the European Coal and Steel Community (ECSC), was formed in 1951 to control the whole of the iron, steel and coal resources of the six member countries – France, West Germany, Italy, Holland, Belgium and Luxembourg. The old divisions created by inward-looking national interests were thus broken down.

The success of the ECSC led to the setting up in 1957 of the Atomic Energy Community (EURATOM), a similar organisation, for the peaceful use of atomic energy, and the European Economic Community (EEC), an organisation to develop a 'common market' between the six member countries. All three communities have now been brought within the EEC.

437

Britain's Attitude to the EEC

When first offered membership of these organisations, Britain refused to join. Not only would joining the EEC have weakened Commonwealth ties, but she was also unwilling to forgo the right to follow independent policies in economics and defence. Instead, with six other nations, she joined the looser European Free Trade Area (EFTA).

Contrary to Britain's expectations, the EEC grew in strength, for difficulties were resolved as they arose. Moreover, Britain's trade with EEC countries increased at a faster rate than that with EFTA, since her goods were more complementary to their economies. Accordingly, after protracted negotiations, the UK joined the EEC in 1973. The other members are now: France, West Germany, Italy, Belgium, the Netherlands, Luxembourg, Denmark, the Irish Republic, Greece, Spain and Portugal.

34.2 Institutions of the EEC

The essential point to grasp is that the 1957 Treaty of Rome set up a 'Community' with its own form of government and institutions.

There are four main institutions:

1. The Commission

This is the most important organ of the EEC. Its seventeen members (two from the UK) serve for four years. Once chosen, however, the members of the Commission act as an independent body in the interests of the Community as a whole, and not as representatives of the governments that have nominated them.

The Commission is responsible for formulating policy proposals, promoting the Community interest, trying to reconcile national viewpoints and implementing Community decisions.

2. The Council of Ministers

Each member country sends a cabinet minister (usually the foreign secretary) to the Council of Ministers. This is the supreme decision-making body. Its task is to harmonise the Commission's draft Community policies with the wishes of member governments. Proposals and compromise plans are exchanged between the Council and the Commission. If the Council becomes deadlocked, the Commission reconsiders the proposal in order to accommodate the views of the opposing countries. Originally it was intended that the Council decisions should be on a weighted majority basis, but proposals affecting vital national interests now have usually to be unanimous.

3. The Court of Justice

This consists of ten judges appointed by agreement of member governments for six-year terms. Its task is to interpret the Treaty of Rome and adjudicate on complaints, whether from member states, private enterprises or the institutions themselves. Its rulings are binding on member countries, Community institutions and individuals.

4. The Assembly, or European Parliament

This is a body of 518 elected members (81 from the UK). Members sit according to party affiliation, not nationality. The assembly debates Community policies and also examines the Community's budget. It can dismiss the Commission by a two-thirds majority.

Special Institutions

Apart from the four main institutions above, there are also special institutions to deal with particular policies, e.g. the Economic and Social Committee, the European Investment Bank etc.

A newly created *European Council* is a meeting of the heads of member states three times a year. The major problems confronting them are reviewed in an informal and pragmatic way. The object is to suggest loosely defined strategies in which each member takes into account the impact of its own policies on the others.

34.3 Economic Objectives of the EEC

The overriding aim of the EEC is to integrate the policies of its member countries. Its economic policy is based on two main principles: (1) a customs union, and (2) a common market.

1. A Customs Union

We have to distinguish between a free-trade area and a customs union. The former simply removes tariff barriers between member countries but allows individual members to impose their own rates of duty against outsiders. A customs union goes further. While it too has internal free trade, it also imposes common external tariffs.

The EEC has a customs union, since this is essential for an integrated common market. Otherwise goods would enter the market through low-duty countries and be re-sold in those imposing higher rates.

2. A Common Market

In essence the common market of the EEC envisages goods and factors of production moving freely within the Community through the operation of the price system; only in this way can the full benefits of the larger market be realised.

However, it is recognised that this takes time to accomplish. Member countries had already developed their own individual taxes, welfare benefits, monopoly policies, methods of removing balance-of-payments imbalances, full-employment policies, and so on. Such differences could distort the working of the free market system because they would give some members advantages over others. For example, suppose Britain taxed refrigerators but not binoculars. This would weight the possibilities of trade against Italy (which has a comparative advantage in producing refrigerators) and in favour of West Germany (which has a comparative advantage in producing high-grade binoculars).

Alternatively the comparative advantage of some countries may lie in the expertise of the professional services they can provide. Usually this means that such services have to be taken to where the customer is (e.g. 'know-how' regarding property development). There must therefore be mobility of labour within the market, e.g. for property developers.

Policy has therefore been directed towards the gradual introduction of 'harmonisation' measures, examples of which are:

(a) *A Common External Tariff* (CET) by which members impose tariffs on imports from non-member countries at the same rates.

(b) *A common agricultural policy* (CAP) – see below.

(c) *Removing barriers to trade and the movement of persons and capital between countries.*

(d) *Uniform rules on competition.* To prevent the distortion of competition in trade, uniform regulations have been introduced to cover price-fixing, sharing of markets and patent rights.

(e) *A common transport policy.* By regulating such items as freight rates, licences, taxation and working conditions, the EEC can seek to ensure that transport undertakings compete on an equal footing. Any hidden advantages enjoyed by one country would distort the free movement of goods within the Community.

(f) *Harmonisation of tax systems.* As has already been shown, some standardisation of taxation is necessary in order to remove any 'hidden' barriers to trade. This applies particularly to indirect taxes.

In the EEC value-added tax (VAT) is the basic form of indirect tax, and it is proposed that eventually all member countries will levy it at the same rates.

No proposals exist for harmonising income taxes, but most countries have adopted the 'imputation' system of corporation tax (see p.386).

(g) *Complete monetary integration.* As we have seen, countries can adjust the prices of imports and exports by varying the exchange rate. If this were allowed within the EEC, it could enable a member to obtain a competitive advantage over others by depreciating its currency. Thus through the European Monetary System (EMS) – the 'snake' – all currencies have fixed exchange rates within narrow limits. To date (1987) the UK has not seen her way clear to join (see below).

(h) *A common regional policy.* Just as one nation cannot allow depressed areas to persist, so the EEC is expected to help regions of high unemployment. Northern Ireland and southern Italy are two such regions. Apart from the establishment of a regional development fund, however, little has so far been done to integrate policies designed to encourage industries to go to problem areas.

34.4 Advantages of Belonging to the EEC

Several advantages can accrue to countries by forming a common market:

1. Increased Possibilities of Specialisation

The EEC provides a market of 320 million people, larger than that of the USA. This allows economies of scale to be achieved, especially as regards sophisticated products requiring high initial research expenditure, e.g. computers, nuclear reactors, supersonic aircraft and modern weapons. Member countries now combine to cover research costs, e.g. for *Concorde* and the *European Airbus*. These economies of scale should enable EEC firms to compete more effectively in world markets.

2. Increased Efficiency

Keener competition in the larger market can result in greater efficiency. Within the EEC there are no trade barriers which in effect protect inefficient firms. Free trade means that goods and services can compete freely in all parts of the market and that factors of production can move to their most efficient uses, not merely within but also between countries.

On the other hand, it must be recognised that protective duties may reduce competition from outside the market.

3. A Faster Rate of Growth

In the EEC's first fifteen years the GNPs of the six original members grew twice as fast as that of the UK, giving them (Italy apart) a higher GNP per head than Britain's. To a large extent this faster rate of growth was the result of increased economies of scale and competition enjoyed by the EEC countries. But it is also possible that the EEC generates growth by the mood it engenders.

4. Political Benefits

As already explained, the ultimate objective of the original advocates of European co-operation was some form of political union. A Western Europe which could speak with one voice would carry weight when dealing with other major powers, particularly the USA and the Soviet Union. Moreover, the integration of defence forces and strategy would give its members far greater security.

34.5 Problems Facing the UK as a Member of the EEC

While Britain's membership of the EEC can secure important benefits and allow her to influence its future development, there do exist special problems.

1. The CET could lead to the Diversion of Trade toward less efficient EEC Suppliers

The duties imposed by the customs union may allow firms within the common market to compete in price with more efficient firms outside.

Suppose, for instance, that the same machine can be produced by both the USA and West Germany, but because the American firm is more efficient, its machine is 5 per cent cheaper. In these circumstances Britain would, other things being equal, import from the USA. As a member of the EEC, however, Britain would have to discriminate against the American machine by the appropriate CET, say 10 per cent. This would make the German machine cheaper, and so trade would be diverted to the less efficient producer.

2. The CAP is an Increasing Drain on the Community Funds

Before joining the EEC Britain imported food at the lowest world price that could be found. In so far as the UK producer could not make an adequate living by selling at free market prices, British policy consisted of granting *deficiency payments* (financed out of taxation) sufficient to raise the price received by the producer to a level set out in an Annual Review. The consumer paid a low price for food and the world had free access to the UK market. The taxpayer paid for the farmers' support.

But because the Community could not function satisfactorily if the cost of food to consumers differed appreciably in various parts of it, there has to be some equalisation of prices. However, if this occurred through competition between producing countries it could destroy many small farmers, particularly in France and West Germany. In addition, because demand for agricultural products tends to be inelastic, changes in the conditions of supply can have far-reaching effects on the incomes of farmers.

The CAP seeks to support farmers' incomes by maintaining prices on the home market through a variety of protective devices at the Community's external frontier. Three prices are fixed for each product:

(a) a *target price*, which, it is estimated, will give farmers an adequate return in a normal year;
(b) a *threshold price*, which is used as the basis for assessing levies on imports; and
(c) the *intervention price*, at which surplus supplies are bought up by various agencies to be disposed of outside the EEC, e.g. butter sold to the Soviet Union.

In practice, however, giving farmers a guaranteed price above the market clearing price for all they can produce simply encourages over-production (Figure 34.1).

In Figure 34.1, the market-clearing price would be OP. However, if the guaranteed intervention price is OP_1, the demand curve becomes horizontal, D_i, at this price. At price P_1, consumers take OQ_1, but farmers supply OQ_2. There is thus an excess supply of Q_1Q_2 which is bought for storage by the authorities at a cost of $P_1 \times Q_1Q_2$. The increase in farmers' incomes is shown by the shaded area.

If these stores were used as buffer stocks to make good deficiencies in supply when harvest were poor, at least some of the cost could be recouped. In practice, however, the artificially high price has encouraged additional supplies as techniques have improved. The result is that we have embarrassing butter mountains, beef and corn stocks and wine lakes which have to be sold off on the world market at a low price, e.g. wheat and butter to Russia.

FIGURE 34.1
The Effect on Supply of a Guaranteed 'Intervention' Price

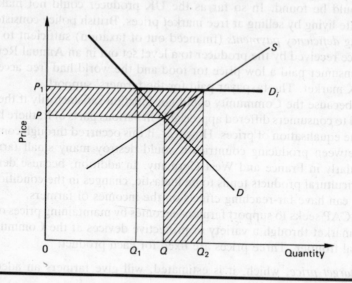

In addition, the distortion of the normal pattern of international trade in foodstuffs widens the gap between the rich and poor countries because the latter are often food producers.

Obviously the CAP confers greater benefits on countries in which agriculture is important (e.g. France) compared with countries which are relatively more dependent on manufacturing (e.g. the UK, West Germany).

3. The Adoption of the European Monetary System may not be in Britain's best Interests

As we have seen, countries can adjust the prices of imports and exports by varying the exchange rate. If this were allowed within the EEC, it could enable a member to obtain a competitive advantage over others by depreciating its currency. It is agreed, therefore, that eventually all currencies will have fixed exchange rates within narrow limits. This is achieved through the European Monetary System (EMS), except for the UK, which has not yet joined.

The importance of stability of exchange rates can be seen in the operation of the CAP. Intervention prices are stated in terms of an accounting unit, the Agricultural Unit of Account (AUA), and are then translated into national currencies by using a reference rate (in the case of sterling, the 'green pound').

If exchange rates are fixed, this raises no difficulties. But if the exchange rate varies – as sterling does since Britain is outside the EMS – an appreciation, say, of sterling would leave the green pound undervalued. The intervention price when converted into sterling would now be high in Britain. Therefore, to discourage other EEC farmers exporting to Britain to obtain the high intervention price, border taxes, known as monetary compensatory amounts (MCAs), are levied. Similarly, to restore their competitive position, British farmers are given MCAs for their exports to other EEC countries.

In the above case, if the green pound were revalued in line with its value on the foreign exchange market, MCAs would be eliminated. It would also lower food prices in Britain, but reduce the incomes of British farmers.

The difficulty for Britain in joining the EMS is that, since she is a major oil exporter, the sterling exchange rate tends to fluctuate with the price of oil on the world market, and this price may vary considerably, especially when OPEC countries fail to agree. To maintain a fixed parity within the EMS, therefore, Britain might have to revert to 'stop-go' policies (see also p.471).

4. There is Insufficient Control over the Community Budget

A Community budget is necessary to meet the costs of administration and policies requiring expenditure, e.g. CAP and regional assistance. There are three main sources – agricultural levies, import duties on non-Community goods and a VAT of just over 1 per cent.

Today over 70 per cent of the budget is spent on agricultural support, and this is increasing. As a result, annual Community expenditure exceeds receipts, necessitating a rise in the VAT yield.

Some revision of the CAP system is essential but this is politically difficult for countries where the farming lobby is important. Yet Britain can see that, unless firm action is taken to deal with the CAP problem, there will be a continuous increase in the VAT rate and spending on other Community policies, e.g. the regional and social funds, will suffer.

Part VIII

Some Current Economic Problems of the UK

35

The Population of the UK

In many ways it would have been more satisfactory to have examined in an early chapter the population of the UK – the people who comprise 'households', the consumers of finished products and the suppliers of the factors of production. But in order to proceed beyond a mere description it is essential to apply certain principles of economics, and so it was first necessary to examine these.

We shall look at the problems of composition, size and industrial and geographical distribution of the population. But first we must describe briefly how it has grown over the last 200 years.

35.1 The Growth of Population

Changes in the Rate of Growth

Table 35.1 shows how the UK's population has grown since 1801. It can be seen that in the nineteenth century it roughly doubled every fifty years; but over the first half of the twentieth century it increased by less than one-third. In fact the rate of growth averaged just over 13 per cent per decade during the nineteenth century, and only 5 per cent during the twentieth century.

There are thus three main questions which have to be answered: (*a*) Why was there such a rapid growth of population during the nineteenth century? (*b*) Why did the rate of growth fall off so markedly during the first half of the twentieth century? (*c*) What is likely to happen to the population during the remainder of the twentieth century?

Causes of Changes in the Rate of Growth

The factors influencing population changes are shown in Figure 35.1. On the one hand, we have the natural increase – the excess of births over

449

Table 35.1
Population (in 000s), 1801–1981

Date	Great Britain (England, Wales and Scotland)	Northern Ireland
1801	10 501	—
1851	20 816	1 443
1901	37 000	1 237
1951	48 854	1 371
1971	53 832	1 528
1981	54 128	1 547
1985 (est.)	55 060	1 558

FIGURE 35.1
Factors Influencing Population

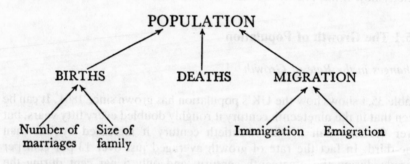

deaths; on the other, migration – the balance between immigration (inwards) and emigration (outwards). In fact, apart from the years 1931–41 and 1951–7, Britain has lost by migration on average about half a million people each decade. The changes in the rate of growth, therefore, are chiefly the result of changes in the natural increase.

The reason for the rapid rate of increase during the nineteenth century was that, while the birth rate remained high, there was a considerable fall in the death rate. The latter was the result of improved medical knowledge, sanitation and water supply, and chiefly of general advances in the standard of living following the agricultural and industrial revolutions.

But the situation changed in the twentieth century. The death rate did not fall so rapidly. More important the birth rate fell considerably. The reason for this was a fall in the average size of family – from between five and six children to just over two. A variety of factors contributed to this:

1. Improved methods and social acceptance of birth control.
2. The increased economic burden of parenthood due, for instance, to the gradual raising of the school-leaving age.
3. The higher standards which parents generally set themselves for their children's welfare.
4. The growth of competing alternatives to children, such as holidays, foreign travel, the cinema and the motor-car.
5. The emancipation of women, politically, economically and socially, with the consequent desire to be free from home ties.
6. The momentum which social example, smaller houses and advertisement provided when once the movement towards smaller families had started.

Britain's Future Population

In 1949 the Royal Commission on Population estimated that unless there were a change in people's attitude to the size of family, or immigration on a considerable scale took place, Britain's population would be declining absolutely in numbers by the end of the century!

It seems, however, that such a decline is unlikely to occur. Until recently, people were building slightly larger families, the result of younger marriages, greater economic prosperity, increased government help to families and more facilities for young mothers to resume work.

But the 1981 census revealed that the rate of increase of the population over the previous ten years had dropped to a mere 0.3 per cent. While external emigration had been a contributory factor, the fall in the rate of increase 1971–81 was mainly due to a fall in the birth rate. Indeed after the 'baby boom' of the early 1960s, the actual number of births each year fell until 1977. Not only has the marriage rate fallen and people are now getting married older, but they are leaving it longer after marriage before starting their families. After the first child, the second comes more quickly, but the 3+ children family has halved proportionately since 1971. This change in the pattern of family building has been brought about largely by the desire of married women to shorten the period when they are not available for work.

As a result, the average size of family has fallen to around the 2.19 level, at which the population would just be replacing itself.

While any projections of population are dependent upon the reliability of assumptions, especially as regards births and migration, it now seems

likely that the population of the UK will be in the region of 59 million at
the end of the century.

35.2 The Age Distribution of the Population

The decline in the rate of increase in the population during the twentieth
century has brought about a change in the age composition of Britain's
population compared with a hundred years ago. This is shown in Figure
35.2.

FIGURE 35.2
**Changes in the Age Distribution of the Population of Great Britain,
1851–1985**

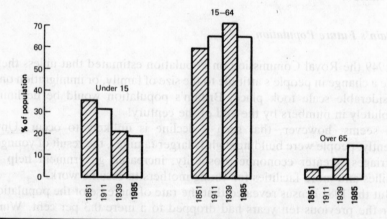

The two factors which have brought about this ageing population are:

1. The lengthening of life due to the various factors which have led to a
    fall in the death rate.
2. The fall in the birth rate at the end of the nineteenth century and the
    consequent fall in the number of births each year between 1911 and
    1941.

The trend has continued. In 1985 the 15–64 age-group formed
about 66 per cent of the population, and those under 15 years and those
over 65 years, 19 per cent and 15 per cent, respectively. By the end of the
century, the working age-group could form only 60 per cent of the total
population; but, through the fall in the number of births after 1964, those

under 15 years will account for only 18 per cent, and those over 65, for 22 per cent.

The Economic Effects of an Ageing Population

It should be noted that a part of this trend is due to the fall in mortality and is a normal development. To some extent, therefore, we are forced to adjust ourselves to these changing circumstances, and, if we try to prevent them by a rapid increase in the birth rate, we shall increase the size of the population – which may give rise to further problems (see pp.458–9). We must therefore provide for:

1. An Increased Dependence of Retired Persons on the Working Population

Current wants can only be provided for by current production. An ageing population means that the proportion of workers to consumers is falling. Whereas in 1851 there were over 12 workers to every person over 65 years of age, in 1981 there were only just over 3. One particular result will be the increased burden of retirement pensions, more pensioners have to be supported by proportionately fewer contributors. This highlights the importance of economic growth.

2. A Changing Pattern of Consumption

An ageing population means, to take extreme examples, that bath-chairs will be wanted in place of prams, walking-sticks in place of hockey-sticks, tea in place of milk. For many of these new 'wants', consideration has to be given well in advance. Today almost one-quarter of British households consist solely of pensioners and, when planning a housing programme, we have to provide the smaller units and sheltered housing they require. Similarly, the fall in births since 1964 has resulted in fewer school places and teachers being required.

3. Increased Demand on the Social Services

Where old people are more numerous and live longer, their children find greater difficulty in caring for them. Thus there is an increasing need for the state to provide home-care services (such as 'meals on wheels' and home helps) and old people's homes. There is also a greater demand for advice from Citizens' Advice Bureaux, since older people need more help in sorting out difficulties relating to housing, gas and electricity bills, social security benefits and so on.

Similarly, older people make greater demands on the health service, those over 75 years, for instance, costing four times as much per head as the average person. Thus government expenditure has to be increased and diverted towards the special types of medical care and hospitals required by old people, e.g. hip operations, geriatric wards.

4. Less Mobility of Labour

An older labour force is less mobile. In the past, expanding industries have obtained labour from young people just starting their working lives, while the decaying industries have declined fairly quietly by natural wastage – not replacing workers as they leave or retire. However, where the working population is static in size, expanding industries have to draw older workers from the declining industries. 'Teaching old dogs new tricks' and moving them to new areas is not always easy (see pp.371, 373). A high level of unemployment increases the difficulties, for it is the older workers in the declining industries who are likely to remain out of a job the longest. Thus both the government and firms must provide training schemes and relocation incentives.

5. The Possibility that the Community will become less Progressive

An older population tends to be less progressive. While older people are more patient and experienced than younger people, the latter excel in energy, enterprise, enthusiasm and the ability to adapt themselves and to learn new skills.

In addition to the direct economic results, decisions having political implications have to be taken as a result of the ageing population. To what extent should younger generations be augmented by a liberal immigration policy, bearing in mind the social stresses which could arise? Can adequate defence be provided by the use of more sophisticated weapons, or will the falling proportion of young people necessitate conscription? Should television and radio programmes give greater weight to the type of entertainment preferred by old people? And, since older people own the larger share of the nation's capital but are adverse to taking risks, should the state assume responsibility for providing funds for the riskier types of enterprise, such as North Sea oil-prospecting and development, the building of nuclear power stations and the exploration of outer space?

35.3 The Size of the Population

From 1981 to the end of the century, the UK's population is expected to increase by just over 5 per cent to 59.6 million. Is this a good or a bad thing? To lay bare the issues, it is helpful if we glance briefly at certain important theories of population.

The Malthusian Theory of Overpopulation

Until the middle of the eighteenth century the population of Britain grew slowly. But, from then on, growth became more rapid, and in 1798 Thomas Malthus's first essay on *The Principle of Population as it Affects the Future Improvement of Society* made it a major subject of discussion.

Malthus began from two postulates: (i) that the passion between the sexes is necessary and will remain nearly in 'its present state'; and (ii) that food is necessary to human existence. Given these two postulates, his arguments forced him to conclude that: (i) the population will, if unchecked, double itself every twenty-five years; and (ii) the means of subsistence can, at a maximum, increase by only the same amount every twenty-five years. In other words, while population multiplies in a geometric progression, food supplies increase in an arithmetic progression.

The first conclusion was based on information collected by Malthus on the populations of various countries. But the second was supported by no evidence whatsoever. In order to substantiate it, Malthus appealed to the 'known properties of land'. Here he was virtually relying on the *law of diminishing returns*, though that was not precisely stated until some fifty years later.

From these two conclusions the important result followed that the power of population to increase was 'infinitely greater than the power of the earth to produce subsistence for man'. In short, the population would always tend to outgrow its food supply.

Since people cannot live without food, what, Malthus asked, kept population within its means of subsistence? The answer he found in certain 'checks'. First, there were 'positive checks', involving misery – famine, war, disease. Second, there were 'preventive checks' – which, with one exception, all involved 'vice', including contraception. The exception was 'moral restraint', by which was meant deliberately refraining from marrying at an early age. Since this was a remote possibility, the outlook for civilisation was gloomy: in the long run mankind could only expect a subsistence level of existence. Moreover, social policies to alleviate poverty would be self-defeating.

Malthus's 'Blind Spots'

Although at the beginning of the nineteenth century Malthus's views were widely accepted, the final tragedy of starvation, the logical outcome of his two conclusions, has not occurred. Where, therefore, did Malthus go wrong?

First, we must note that to some extent his argument was illogical, for he did not deal with the fact, well known at the time, that, in spite of the rapid increase in the population over the previous fifty years, people on the average were no worse off. This showed that the means of subsistence must at least have increased in proportion. Had Malthus possessed a precisely formulated law of diminishing returns, he could have based his argument on a fixed total supply of land which would sooner or later make itself felt as the population increased.

Second, Malthus was preoccupied with people as consumers. He failed to see that, by and large, a consumer is also a producer, for 'with every mouth God sends a pair of hands'. Here again a fixed supply of land with consequent diminishing returns could have overcome this objection.

Third, Malthus did not foresee change. On the one hand the geometric increase in Britain's population did not come about, because of emigration and above all because of the reduction in the size of the family. On the other hand, improved agricultural techniques and the vast increase in imports meant that Britain's food supplies were not limited to increasing in an arithmetic progression.

Thus Malthus's arguments have validity only when there are fixed resources, such as land or energy reserves. It is, for instance, the limited supply of land which brings about a Malthusian situation in the Far East today.

The Concept of an 'Optimum Population'

To Malthus, increasing numbers were a bad thing, as they pressed on the means of subsistence and lowered the standard of living. But his views lost ground towards the middle of the nineteenth century, for, as the capital investment of the industrial revolution began to yield benefits, the standard of living was seen to be keeping pace with the increase in population.

Indeed, at the turn of the century, Professor Edwin Cannan showed that population could be too small to take full advantage of available technical knowledge. For example, a larger population might justify large-scale production, with more use being made of division of labour, specialised machines and technical discoveries. In short, a doubling of the population could lead to more than doubling production.

Since, therefore, population can either be too large or too small, there must be an intermediate point where it is just right: the optimum population at which, given existing technical knowledge, capital equipment and possibilities of exchange with other countries, average output per head is at a maximum. Thus, with reference to Table 10.1 (p.127), the optimum population for the example given would be four labourers. It follows that any country is over- or underpopulated if its population is respectively more or less than the optimum.

But the concept of an optimum population is not without difficulties. In the first place it is unjustifiable to specify 'given existing technical knowledge, capital equipment and possibilities of exchange' and then to speculate as to what production would be if the population were larger or smaller. Had the population increased differently, these variables themselves would have been different. The same mistake is apparent in J. S. Mill's argument in the middle of the nineteenth century that the world would have been better off if, with the improvements that had taken place, population growth had been less. The truth is that such improvements would not have taken place, for a large and rapidly growing population accumulates knowledge and equipment differently from a smaller or slowly growing one. Even more important is that, from the practical point of view, the concept is of little help. Any optimum population at which a country was aiming would only remain the optimum so long as technical knowledge, etc., did not change. Thus, before an optimum was achieved some new figure would have taken its place. All that can be done, therefore, is to consider the present composition of the population, forecast the population which will result from it, and then relate this population to likely changes in capital accumulation and technical discoveries.

We now apply this procedure to a study of Britain's population.

The Advantage to Britain of an Increasing Population

An increasing population has certain advantages which stimulate growth:

1. It Increases the Size of the Home Market

The additional output needed for a larger population should benefit industries working under conditions of decreasing costs, e.g. those producing aircraft, computers, nuclear reactors. It should be noted, however, that this applies only if the extra output is provided by existing firms and not by additional firms entering the industry. Moreover it is possible to obtain large-scale economies by specialising on a narrow range of goods and exporting, as in Switzerland.

2. It Facilitates Labour Mobility

With an increasing population, unemployment resulting from the immobility of labour presents fewer problems. This is because the decline of older industries is slower and can be covered by natural wastage with fewer redundancies, while expanding industries can obtain most of their additional workers from new entrants to the labour force.

3. It Encourages Investment

An increasing population makes it easier to maintain the level of replacement investment. More than that, the extra consumer demand necessitates additional investment in machinery, factories, schools, houses, transport, etc. Consequently it stimulates improved techniques, thereby accelerating the replacement of existing equipment.

4. It Promotes Vitality

By weighting the age distribution in favour of youth, an increasing population ensures more workers per retired persons and makes for energy, mobility, inventiveness and willingness to accept new ideas.

It should be noted that the disadvantages of a decreasing population could be stated as the opposite of these.

The Disadvantages of an Increasing Population

Against the advantages given above it is necessary to set certain disadvantages which may make it difficult for an increasing population to raise present living standards. Resources have to be used in adding to capital equipment instead of in producing consumer goods or improving existing buildings.

Moreover, the observation that 'with every mouth God sends a pair of hands' ignores two important facts. The first is that not every person is a producer – for a time the additional mouths have to be provided with food, education, etc., by the working group. The second is more important: an increase in the number of people on a fixed amount of land may bring the law of diminishing returns into operation, with a consequent fall in living standards.

It is the law of diminishing returns which pinpoints the problem of increasing numbers. In the Far Eastern countries there is simply a lower output per head, as extra people have to obtain their subsistence from a fixed amount of land. But for Britain the law of diminishing returns does not apply in this basic way. The law assumes no technical improvements, but improved techniques in agriculture have enabled Britain in recent years to raise her self-sufficiency in her principal foodstuffs from 50 per cent to 90 per cent.

As far as Britain is concerned the law of diminishing returns is significant in three ways. First, Britain is still very dependent on imports for the raw materials, special types of machinery, base metals, consumer goods (e.g. cars, cameras) and certain sorts of food and drink (e.g. fruit, wine) that she requires. What Britain has to ask, therefore, is: can exports be increased sufficiently to pay for the extra imports required by the larger population without a severe deterioration in her terms of trade especially when North Sea oil runs out?

Throughout the nineteenth century Britain proved that this was possible. Indeed, a balance-of-payments surplus allowed her to invest heavily abroad. But since then the problem of finding and holding foreign markets has become more difficult.

Second, the growth of population accompanied by increasing real income puts pressure on space for amenity and recreational purposes, as, for example, more houses with spacious gardens are demanded and access to the countryside is sought.

Third, with population growth, environmental problems intensify. As city congestion increases and more open space is required for housing, roads and industry, arguments for conservation and control of pollution gain momentum.

Conclusion

At present Britain is managing to support increasing numbers while improving living standards. But the rate at which the future population is growing must be watched by the government and, if necessary, influenced by immigration policy, the level of child benefits and family income supplements. Furthermore, social as well as economic considerations have to be taken into account.

In the Far East a Malthusian situation exists. While the death rate is falling through better medical services, the birth rate remains high. By the end of the century an almost doubled population could be seeking to live with little increase in land. Possible solutions are birth control, improved agricultural techniques, the development of export industries, and economic aid from developed countries.

35.4 The Industrial Distribution of the Working Population

The Working Population

The UK's population in 1985 was 55 060 000 persons. Of these, 16 442 000 males and 11 150 000 females are described by the Department of Employment as 'the working population' (Table 35.2).

The working population consists of persons over school-leaving age who work for pay or gain or are claiming unemployment benefit. It therefore includes both employees and self-employed persons, even if they are over retirement age or are working only part-time, and members of the armed

Table 35.2
Total Working Population, UK 1975–85 (000s)

	1975	1979	1985
Total employees in employment	22 710	23 157	21 466
HM Forces	336	314	325
Self-employed persons	1 993	1 903	2 623
Unemployed	838	1 234	3 179
Total working population	25 877	26 609	27 593
of whom: Males	16 162	16 215	16 442
Females	9 715	10 394	11 150

forces. Excluded are: (*a*) children under 16 years of age and students above 16 years of age who are receiving full-time education; (*b*) persons, such as housewives, who do not work for pay or gain; (*c*) persons who, having private means, e.g. from investments or gifts, do not need to work; (*d*) retired persons; (*e*) work-seekers who do not claim benefit, e.g. housewives who are ineligible.

The main changes in the working population since 1975 are:

(1) An overall increase of nearly $1\frac{3}{4}$ million (7 per cent). Thus today the working population covers one-half of the total population.

(2) Of this increase, $1\frac{1}{2}$ million have been in female workers. Here the main cause has been the expansion in the service industries. Forty per cent of female workers are part-time (compared with only 5 per cent males). In the UK, the activity rate of women of 16–60 years of age is 66 per cent, higher than all other countries except for Japan and the Scandinavian countries.

(3) Self-employment has increased by 630 000 (32 per cent), largely through the active support of the government. It occurs mostly in agriculture, construction, distribution, catering and other services.

Changes in the Industrial Distribution of the Population

Table 35.3 shows significant changes in the industrial distribution of employees between 1971 and 1985:

(1) a 23 per cent decrease in the primary (extractive) industries – agriculture, mining and fishing;
(2) a 26 per cent increase in services;
(3) a 32 per cent decrease in manufacturing industries.

Table 35.3
Employees in Employment by Industry: UK 1971–1985

	1971		1985	
	Total (000s)	Per cent	Total (000s)	Per cent
Agricultural, forestry and fishing	432	2.0	338	1.6
Energy and water supply	797	3.6	613	2.8
Manufacturing industries	8 085	36.5	5 533	25.8
Construction	1 207	5.5	970	4.5
Distribution, hotels, catering and repairs	3 678	16.6	4 471	20.8
Transport and communication	1 550	7.0	1 304	6.1
Banking, insurance and other financial services	1 336	6.0	1 972	9.2
Other services	5 036	22.8	6 266	29.2
All industries and services	22 121	100.0	21 467	100.0

SOURCE *Social Trends*, 1987.

The basic explanation of the first two changes is an increase in real income over the period, and in this respect it is merely a reflection of a continuous trend. As a result, spending moves to those goods having a high income elasticity of demand. In 1901, for example, the average worker spent 60 per cent of his income on food; by 1985 it had fallen to 24 per cent, of which one-fifth went on meals bought outside the home. Today the provision of services now covers three-fifths of all employees.

The decrease in manufacturing has largely been the result of the uncompetitiveness of British products in world markets brought about by (a) the greater technical efficiency of Japan, (b) the inability to contain wage costs relative to competitors, (c) the appreciation in the value of the £ sterling after 1979 as the result of the export of North Sea oil.

Technical advances and increased mechanisation also help to explain the relative falls in agriculture, energy supply, construction, transport and communications (e.g. increased car ownership), and manufacturing. In contrast, services are more labour-intensive and less highly-capitalised.

35.5 The Geographical Distribution of the Population

Geographically, the population of the UK is dominated by two features: it is *concentrated*, and it is *urban*.

The Concentrated Nature of the Population

As a result of the industrial revolution, industry migrated to the coalfields in the Midlands and north of England. And today, even though electricity frees industry from being located on the coalfields and the basic industries of these areas have declined, they still remain important centres of industry and population (see Figure 35.3). There are two main reasons for this. First, many industries remain on account of acquired advantages, particularly the availability of labour. Second, new industries have been attracted by the government's Development Area policy.

During the twentieth century, the main areas of natural expansion have been the Midlands and south-east England, particularly in the counties around London. The Midlands expanded with the demand for light engineering and electrical products and for motor-vehicles, but the area has recently suffered some stagnation with the decline in the motor and other manufacturing industries. On the other hand, London, always a relatively wealthy area, has expanded outwards as production of goods having a high income-elasticity of demand has moved nearer to their main markets. In addition, the development of government and financial services has attracted population, and this tends to have a multiplier effect as other industries move in to provide for their needs. The proximity of south-east England to the Continent has also attracted industry and population, especially since 1973 when Britain joined the EEC.

Certain rural counties, although not of high density, have also shown a high rate of growth, particularly Norfolk, Suffolk and Cornwall.

The Urban Nature of the Population

This concentration of population is in towns (unlike the Nile and Ganges deltas which consist mainly of concentrated rural communities). Over three out of every four persons in Britain live in an urban area. More than this, 30 per cent of the population lives in the seven conurbations (continuous built-up areas) of Greater London, south-east Lancashire (Manchester), west Midlands (Birmingham), central Clydeside (Glasgow), west Yorkshire (Leeds and Bradford), Merseyside (Liverpool) and Tyneside (Newcastle).

Nevertheless, over the last thirty years, the proportion of the total population in rural areas has increased, reversing the trend towards town life of the previous 150 years. As cities grow, retailing and commerce

FIGURE 35.3
Distribution of the Population of the UK

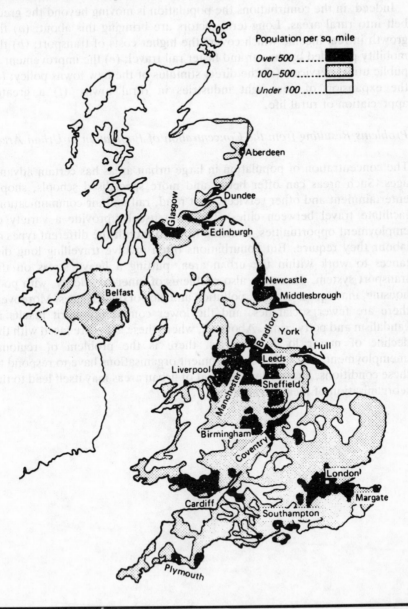

Population per sq. mile

Over 500 ....

100–500 ....

Under 100 ....

Aberdeen

Dundee

Glasgow

Edinburgh

Belfast

Newcastle

Middlesbrough

Bradford

York

Hull

Leeds

Liverpool

Sheffield

Manchester

Birmingham

Coventry

London

Cardiff

Margate

Southampton

Plymouth

compete for central sites. The consequent rise in land values pushes the residential population outwards. Moreover, as real income increases, people can afford houses with more space in the suburbs. Thus *inner*-city areas have been losing population.

Indeed, in the conurbations the population is moving beyond the green belt into rural areas. Long-term factors are bringing this about: (*a*) the growth in real income which covers the higher costs of transport; (*b*) the mobility provided by the car and faster rail travel; (*c*) the improvement in public utility services; (*d*) the direct stimulus of the new towns policy; (*e*) the expansion of new light industries in rural towns; (*f*) a greater appreciation of rural life.

Problems Resulting from the Concentration of Population in Urban Areas

The concentration of population in large urban areas has certain advantages. Such areas can offer better and more specialised schools, shops, entertainment and other services. Fast road, rail and air communications facilitate travel between cities. They can usually provide a variety of employment opportunities, enabling firms to recruit the different types of labour they require. But conurbations often involve travelling long distances to work within the urban area, putting a heavy stress on the transport system. There are also problems of inner-city decay, with poor housing, inadequate schools, pollution and lack of open spaces. Moreover, there are fewer social ties, and the lower community spirit results in vandalism and petty crime. Above all, where these areas are faced with the decline of major local industries, there is the problem of regional unemployment. Not only do government organisations have to respond to these conditions, but the development of urban areas may itself lead to the reorganisation of local government.

36

Growth, the Balance of Payments, Inflation and Unemployment

Since the Second World War the main economic aims of government policy have been: (1) full employment; (2) a healthy balance of payments; (3) a satisfactory rate of growth; (4) a steady price level. What successive governments have discovered is that it has been impossible to achieve all four aims simultaneously.

The theoretical analysis set out in this book indicates that to some extent these aims are mutually incompatible, for success in one of them creates difficulties in achieving others. Full employment, for instance, is dependent on an adequate level of aggregate demand. As aggregate demand is increased, so spending on imports rises and home-produced goods are diverted from exports to the home market. Thus the balance-of-payments position becomes less favourable. Full employment also means that eventually less efficient labour have to be employed, bottlenecks occur in the supply of certain factors of production, and trade unions are in a stronger position to bargain for wage increases. Thus, on the cost side alone, there are forces which make for a rise in the price level as full employment is approached.

In essence, therefore, the government is somewhat like a juggler who is endeavouring to keep four balls in the air simultaneously. At any given moment, one is going up, a second has reached its peak, a third is on the way down and the fourth is being passed from one hand to the other to be given a new upward thrust.

Nevertheless, other developed economies are in the same position, and it has to be admitted that most of them, particularly West Germany and Japan, have been more successful than Britain in achieving these objectives.

36.1 Economic Growth

The Meaning of 'Growth'

Economic growth can be measured roughly by increases in the real gross national product (GNP) per head of the population. However, when people talk about 'growth' they are thinking chiefly of the difference it makes to the standard of living rather than to output itself. Allowances have to be made, therefore, for the defects of GNP as an indication of the standard of living (see Chapter 24).

While year by year measurements of GNP reflect the effects of short-term recessions and recoveries, 'growth' usually refers to the rate at which output is increasing in the long term – even when full employment is being sustained. Thus growth can be defined as the rate at which *potential* output is *increasing* over time. Even with full employment of resources, advanced economies can achieve an annual growth rate of 3 per cent.

How is Growth Achieved?

There are three basic causes of growth:

1. A Rise in the Productivity of Existing Factors

In the short run productivity may be raised by improvements in organisation which secure, for example, more division of labour and economies of large-scale production, or a more intensive use of capital equipment (e.g. the adoption of shift-working). Physical improvements for the labour force, e.g. better food and working conditions, may also increase productivity.

In the longer run more significant increases can come with education and the acquisition of capital skills. These really represent, however, an increase in the capital invested in labour.

2. An Increase in the Available Stock of Factors of Production

(a) *A rise in the labour input.* The size of the labour input can increase relative to the total population through either an increase in the number of hours worked per worker, or an increase in the ratio of the working population to the total population. The first is hardly likely to be a cause of growth in normal conditions, for as living standards improve the tendency is to demand more leisure. The second, however, may come about by an increase in the percentage of the population of working age and by changing attitudes to work (see Chapter 16).

(*b*) *Development of natural resources.* North Sea natural gas and oil, for instance, have allowed Britain to obtain fuel supplies from fewer factors of production, enabling resources to be transferred to other output and thus promoting growth.

(*c*) *Additional capital equipment.* Here we must distinguish between 'widening' and 'deepening' capital. Widening capital – adding similar capital equipment – is necessary if the labour force increases, in order to maintain the existing capital – labour ratio and thus output per head. Suppose 10 men, digging a long ditch, have 5 spades between them. If the labour force is increased to 20 men the capital–labour ratio falls from 1:2 to 1:4 unless 'widening' takes places – that is, unless another 5 spades are provided to maintain the existing ratio. 'Widening' does not increase productivity; it simply prevents diminishing returns to labour setting in.

'Deepening' capital occurs when the capital–labour ratio is increased. If, for example, when there were 5 spades to 10 men, the men were given a further 5 spades, the capital–labour ratio would be raised to 1:1.

3. Technological Change

All we have done in our example so far has been to increase the stock of a given kind of capital equipment, spades. Over time, however, productivity can be raised much more significantly by technological improvements. Thus the 10 workers and their spades may be replaced by a single trench-digger and its driver. Because this does the job more quickly and efficiently the remaining 9 workers are released for other kinds of work. In practice, all three causes are usually operating at the same time to increase productivity (Figure 36.1). Thus, as the labour force or natural resources are expanded, new capital is required, and this allows for the introduction of new techniques.

The speed with which new capital and improvements are introduced also depends upon the price of capital equipment relative to the wages of the labour for which it can be substituted. Over time wages have tended to rise relative to the cost of capital equipment. This has been marked since the Second World War; the effect has been to increase the rate of technological change in such industries as agriculture, cargo handling, transport, shipbuilding and mining.

Other factors affecting growth are:

4. Fundamental Changes in the Composition of the National Output

As a country's standard of living improves, so spending switches from agricultural to manufactured goods and then towards services. Since the opportunities for employing more capital and technical improvement are greatest in manufacturing, the growth rate increases as countries industria-

FIGURE 36.1
Factors Leading to Growth

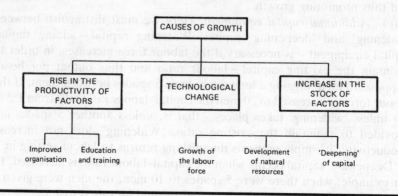

lise but then slows down as the relative demand for personal and government services increases.

5. A Sustained Improvement in the Terms of Trade (see pp.310–11)

Limitations to Growth

In practice, the UK has not succeeded in achieving the 3 per cent annual growth rate. Thus from 1960 to 1986 it averaged only 2.4 per cent. Why is this?

First, when full employment was buoyant, consumer demand left fewer resources available for investment.

Second, inflation proved inimical to investment. Government disinflationary measures undermine the confidence of entrepreneurs. Trade-union wage claims lead to industrial unrest and the dislocation of production. Furthermore, with wages rising faster than prices, profit margins are squeezed. Thus a low rate of return on capital together with a high rate of interest discouraged investment.

Third, 'stop' policies have been necessary, because, as the economy expands, inflationary problems arise (see p.356) and increasing imports produce balance-of-payments difficulties (see p.355).

Fourth, growth entails costs additional to the reduced current consumption necessary to accumulate capital. Growth usually requires change, and the more rapid the growth, the greater the change. Thus in the UK, even though the growth rate has been relatively low in recent years, coal-mines, cotton factories, shipyards and railway lines have been closed, while the electrical, plastics, aerospace, tele-communications and electronics industries have been developed. Such changes in the structure of the economy are, as we have seen, bound to lead to some unemployment, and if growth is to be achieved people must be willing to change jobs quite radically, three or four times in their working lives. This will entail retraining and probably moving around the country; and, as techniques change more rapidly, e.g. with the introduction of micro-chips, these processes will happen to a far greater extent than at present (see later).

Finally, growth is not achieved without environmental costs – pollution, noise, loss of natural beauty, destruction of wild-life habitat. And, as material wealth grows, people are inclined to question the full costs of growth with some consequent slowing down of the rate at which it can proceed.

Future Growth

Britain's rush for growth in the early 1970s soon came to an end when it ran into inflation and balance-of-payments difficulties.

But today (1987) earnings from North Sea oil have resulted in a much stronger balance-of-payments situation. Hence, with inflation under control and unemployment falling, the economy is growing at around 4 per cent a year.

36.2 Britain's Balance of Payments

Post-war Problems

Throughout the twentieth century Britain has been losing her share of international trade as other countries have industrialised and competed in world markets. But for a time net income from overseas investments which were accumulated during the prosperous nineteenth century covered the deficit on visible trade.

The two World Wars aggravated Britain's difficulties. Overseas investments were sold and external debts incurred to pay for essential imports. Furthermore, when peace came, Britain's industry, which had been geared to the war effort, needed time to readjust and re-equip.

To make matters worse, although sterling was still used by foreigners as a reserve currency, Britain's gold and foreign currency reserves were too small to provide an adequate cushion when confidence in sterling faltered through a balance-of-payments weakness. At first, in order to protect the reserves and the value of the £, deflationary measures – the 'stop-go' policy – had to be taken. Eventually in 1972 the £ was 'floated', its value now being determined by the day-to-day conditions of demand and supply on the foreign exchange market.

The rise in the world price of oil in 1973 added £900 million to the UK's annual import bill. Furthermore, since all oil-importing countries were in the same position, they, too, had less to spend on other goods. Only if the oil-producing countries had spent their increased revenues on goods from the rest of the world would incomes have been maintained. In practice, this 'recycling' was only partly successful; the oil-producing countries, with their small populations, could not spend anything like enough on imports to use up their vast revenues. With the world recession which followed, it became more difficult for Britain to increase exports. A persistent balance-of-payments deficit was covered by borrowing, chiefly from foreign governments and the IMF (see p.472).

The Effect of North Sea Oil

The discovery and successful extraction of North Sea oil transformed the situation. By 1980 the UK was not only self-sufficient in oil, but a net exporter. Surpluses on the balance of payments have been used to accumulate overseas assets, which rose from £5 bn in 1979 to £140 bn by 1987. Net returns on these assets are currently providing £8 bn a year of invisible earnings.

Nevertheless, the emergence of the £ sterling as a petro-currency was not without snags, for it meant that the sterling exchange rate became closely related to the price of oil. Thus when in 1984 the price of oil was above $30 a barrel, the £ appreciated to $2.50. This made it still more difficult for British exports to compete, and manufacturing industries in particular were forced to cut capacity. From 1983 trade in manufactured goods moved from surplus to deficit. Similarly, when in 1986 the price of oil fell to $10 a barrel, the exchange value of the £ fell to $1.50.

The Present Balance-of-Payments Position

But North Sea oil reserves are limited. By 1986 the oil trade balance was falling, partly through reduced production and partly through the fall in the price of oil. The result is that the balance-of-payments current account is now in deficit. Without the discovery of fresh reserves it is estimated that by 1990 net oil exports will be making no contribution to the balance-of-payments. Thus unless there is a major improvement in the non-oil trade account or in net invisible earnings, the balance-of-payments is likely to go still further into deficit. We could be back to what has been the recurrent restraint on growth – the balance-of-payments. As the economy expands, imports increase at a faster rate than exports. It has been estimated that Britain's income elasticity of demand for imports is 1.7, compared with a world elasticity of demand for British exports of 1.0.

It is essential, therefore, to achieve a major improvement in the competitiveness of British exports.

Some economists think this is best brought about by a depreciation of sterling and import controls. This would avoid severe deflation. But depreciation benefits all exporting firms, efficient and inefficient, alike. Efficient firms have tended to hold their own in world markets because they have modernised their methods and concentrated on the right products. Moreover, past devaluations have only provided a short-term benefit, since depreciation adds to inflationary pressures by raising the price of imported goods and of the import content of home-produced goods (e.g. raw materials, basic metals, manufactured components).

Nor do import controls, as advocated by other economists, appear to present a viable alternative. Not only do they offend the spirit of international economic co-operation which has been so laboriously fostered over the last 40 years, but, more important, they invite retaliation.

Two vital steps are necessary for a long-term solution: (*a*) controlling the rate of inflation below that of competitors; (*b*) restructuring British industry to provide a strong export base. It is to a consideration of these to which we now turn.

36.3 Inflation

Economic Policy to 1979

For the first twenty-five years after the war, successive governments managed to keep the rate of unemployment at less than 3 per cent by maintaining a high level of aggregate demand. This, however, resulted in periodic balance-of-payments crises as imports were sucked in by high incomes and exports became difficult to sell through rising prices. With fixed exchange rates under the Bretton Woods agreement, any strain on the balance of payments resulted in a fall in the gold and foreign currency reserves. Thus the 'stop–go' policy developed. To protect the reserves, the government had to take disinflationary measures.

The Abandonment of Fixed Exchange Rates

Although the rate of inflation was running at what was then a comparatively high figure of 8 per cent, the Heath government of 1970 decided to reflate the economy, relying on increased output to keep prices from rising. But the economy failed to respond in the way the government had hoped for – increased investment expenditure. Instead the extra spending power found its way largely into the consumer-durable goods markets, and prices rose.

By June 1972 Britain was again facing balance-of-payments difficulties. This time, however, instead of following the 'stop' policy of deflation to maintain the fixed exchange rate, the pound sterling was 'floated', with its value now being determined by the day-to-day conditions of demand and supply on the foreign exchange market.

The government had hoped that, in exchange for the promise of continued expansion, it could obtain a voluntary agreement to limit price and wage rises, but the unions rejected its proposals. Consequently a statutory freeze was imposed on most increases in prices, rents, pay and dividends.

The Continuing Problem of Inflation

Although the new Labour government of 1974 increased food and housing subsidies to keep down the cost of living, money wage rates leapt. In addition, the increase in the money supply of the previous two years was now pushing up prices. Above all, world inflation resulted from the 1973 rise in the price of oil, and the prices of British imports rose. By the end of 1974 inflation in Britain was running at the rate of 27 per cent.

To combat this, the Labour government placed the emphasis on the 'social contract'. On the one hand, trade unions limited their demand for wage increases; on the other, the government agreed to maintain as far as possible the level of employment and the real value of social benefits, and to pass legislation improving the conditions of employment.

However, the high level of *AD* led to a 1975 current balance-of-payments deficit of nearly £1700 million. The value of sterling fell, accentuated by the withdrawal of sterling balances. Not only did this raise the price of imports (thereby adding to inflation) but, to prevent the exchange rate falling still further, the Bank of England had to spend heavily from the reserves. By the end of 1976 Britain had to exercise her final borrowing facility with the IMF of £2350 million.

But this loan was advanced only on condition that Britain introduced acceptable economic measures. The size of the PSBR was giving cause for concern, for government spending had increased under the 'social contract'. In part it had been financed by increasing the money supply, and this was held to be a major cause of inflation. Britain therefore had to agree to cut the PSBR by at least £2500 million in each of the following two years and to an automatic decrease in the money supply should the balance-of-payments deficit increase. Government policy, although imposed by the IMF, was now reflecting the views of the monetarists.

Even the announcement of these measures eased pressure on the exchange rate, and the rate of inflation fell to 8 per cent. By 1978, however, the trade unions were in no mood to limit their wage demands and they achieved increases of almost 15 per cent. The rate of inflation moved once more into double figures.

Mrs Thatcher's government of 1979 considered that bringing inflation under control was necessary if other objectives, particularly a high level of employment were to be achieved. 'Fine-tuning' the economy by adjusting *AD* had failed. Instead it was replaced by naked monetarism, and its strategy followed that outlined in Chapter 27.

Strict control of the money supply was to follow a *Medium-Term Financial Strategy (MTFS)*. This sets targets for four years ahead for: (*a*) limitations to increases in M3; and (*b*) reductions in the PSBR as a percentage of GDP. Each year these projections are amended in the light of past experience.

The main weapon for *controlling M3* was the rate of interest, on the assumption that higher interest rates would reduce the demand for credit (reflected in M3). In practice M3 did not prove to be interest-elastic – indeed at times firms had to *increase* their borrowing when the rate of interest rose in order to tide them over the deflationary squeeze. Moreover, because of the increasing habit of credit-card buying, higher rates often had only a muted effect on borrowing. For their part the banks could still lend because the abolition of exchange control in 1979 and the development of the wholesale deposit markets enabled the banks to obtain funds at a price. Finally, the definition of M3 can produce difficulties, a switch in the sources of mortgages from building societies to banks, for instance, increases M3 since building society deposits are excluded from it.

While M0, which is virtually coins and notes, appears to be a more consistent aggregate, it simply *reflects* changes in GDP since cash is always made available on demand by the Bank of England; there is no *causal* connection between M0 and *AD* in the way that there is with M3.

The reality is that, because there is such a wide range of assets having some 'moneyness', there is no single aggregate which can be measured as representing the money supply. The result was that in March 1987 the Chancellor of the Exchequer announced that he would stop setting targets for £M3, but would retain M0 and also have regard to the wider aggregates when exercising his discretion as to the degree of monetary restraint required.

While £M3 consistently over-ran its target, the government has been more successful in *reducing the PSBR* both absolutely and as a percentage of GDP. Between 1950 and 1986 the PSBR fell from 5 to 1 per cent of GDP. This was achieved by: (*a*) a 27 per cent increase in tax receipts which more than offset the 11 per cent increase in government spending which resulted from the social security benefits paid to an extra two million unemployed persons; and (*b*) the sale of government assets (see p.96). The latter, however, is simply a one-off method, but by reducing the need to borrow it relieves the pressure of increases in the money supply and a higher rate of interest which bank and public borrowing could give rise to (see p.353). But the changed role of fiscal policy should be noted: instead of being the main weapon of Keynesian demand management, it is now merely a support to monetary policy in that it facilitates control of liquidity at a lower rate of interest than would otherwise be necessary.

Other Aspects of Thatcher Monetarism

A policy for wages was implicitly embodied in the MTFS: instead of playing an active role in wage settlements, the government leaves employers to negotiate terms with the trade unions. It was hoped that holding to a MTFS would convince the unions that wage-demands should be based on a *lower* expected rate of inflation. Alternatively, any inflationary wage increases which the unions did obtain would not be financed by an increase in the money supply. Instead firms' profits would fall, and unemployment follow. To limit the possibility of 'blood-letting' strikes and consequent damage to the economy, the government introduced legislation curtailing the powers of the unions.

The situation was somewhat different as regards labour in the public sector where output is not related to profits. Here, therefore, the government had to impose a wages policy, and its strategy of limiting public sector spending helped to influence the unions in their wage demands.

In addition to controlling the money supply, the Thatcher government took on board the politico-economic views of Friedman. He considers that the expansion the public sector in most Western economies has undermined the willingness to accept risk-bearing and thus the ability to increase wealth. This found expression in the privatisation policy. It is augmented by other measures to improve performance on the supply side – income and corporation tax reductions, start-up schemes and capital for expanding small businesses, training of the work-force for the requirements of modern industry and commerce (see p.373).

Assessment of Thatcher Monetarism

The abandonment of £M3 as a monitor of the money supply virtually represented the ending of an attempt to link the money supply to set targets – the core of monetarist policy. In its place, the Chancellor of the Exchequer has adopted a pragmatic approach which takes account of the wider aggregate as he exercises his discretion as to the degree of monetary restraint required. Moreover, the objective of varying the interest rate has shifted to maintaining the sterling exchange rate (at about 3.10 Deutschmarks). In short, an implicit commitment to monetary discipline has replaced an explicit target.

This should not imply that the Thatcher monetarist policy has failed. Instead the strategy must be regarded as a whole. The fall in the rate of inflation from 18 per cent in 1980 to 3.5 per cent in 1986 has provided a framework of stability within which the longer-term supply-side measures can more easily become effective.

But while monetarism provided the theoretical background for the government's policies, it is arguable whether it was the control of the money supply which actually produced the fall in the rate of inflation.

Until 1981 sterling appreciated, the result of the high price received for North Sea oil and the relatively high UK rate of interest. This reduced the cost of imported raw materials and components. Furthermore, as a result of the world recession 1980–2, the price of raw materials fell.

Nor must we overlook that the deflationary effect of reduced government spending has meant that the lower inflation rate has been achieved at a high cost in unemployment, which rose to $3\frac{1}{4}$ million in 1986. Some Keynesians claim that it was this weakening of labour's bargaining position rather than control of the money supply which was responsible for the fall in the rate of inflation. This leads to the question of what will happen when employment increases and the threat of redundancy fades. The best that can be hoped for is that the traumatic experience of unemployment over the past decade will have a long-term follow-through on the climate of wage negotiations so that supply-side policies can be sustained and developed.

World Inflation

One final point should be noted: the UK's price level cannot be isolated from general world inflation such as that which occurred following the large rise in oil prices of 1973 and 1979. We must therefore expect the UK's price level to continue to rise; what the authorities have to ensure is that it does not rise faster than that of foreign competitors in world markets.

36.4 Unemployment

In the post-war period up to 1974 (apart from 1971–2) Britain's unemployment rate was under 3 per cent. Fine-tuning the economy to adjust *AD* in accordance with Keynesian theory seemed to be working.

From 1974, however, unemployment began to rise, and it was accompanied by a worrying rate of inflation. Today (July 1987) persons unemployed number 2.9 million, 10.4 per cent of the working population.

Some economists have advocated reflation – an expansion of AD – with import controls being imposed if necessary to avoid a balance-of-payments deficit as the economy expands. But, as a long-term policy, reflation has serious defects. First, expanding AD may simply increase the rate of inflation. Second, it takes no account of the influence of foreign economies on the UK position. Third, in concentrating on AD, it overlooks measures which could be taken on the supply side. Fourth, it fails to recognise that much of the unemployment is structural. We will deal with each point in turn.

Unemployment and Inflation

In the past a policy of expanding AD to boost the economy had eventually led to inflation. The concept of a natural rate of unemployment forms the basis of a theoretical explanation (see Chapter 27). The balance-of-payments difficulties which inflation produced resulted in the pattern of 'stop-go' which was the feature of government policy until 1980.

North Sea oil has provided a temporary relief from the balance-of-payments constraint. Moreover, the rate of inflation has been reduced to 4 per cent (1987) though it must be noted that this is still higher than that of the UK's major competitors in export markets.

But North Sea oil is a dwindling asset and already by 1986 the non-oil deficit had given rise to an overall deficit on the current balance of payments. This is the problem that must be solved if a high level of employment is to be sustained. Policy must be directed to (*a*) preventing the UK costs of production from rising relative to those of foreign competitors; and (*b*) restructuring British industry so as to provide a strong export base (see below).

Unemployment and International Pressures

Expanding AD is not a solution to unemployment in the UK if this results from weaknesses in the economies of other countries, especially if these are significant importers of British goods. A striking example of this is the world economic depression which followed the ten-fold increase in the price of oil between 1973 and 1979. Because demand for oil is highly price-elastic, world spending on oil increased. Thus oil users had less to spend on other goods. Instead spending power was transferred to the oil producers, who were unable to increase their spending commensurately. Thus, in spite of the efforts made to 'recycle' the oil revenues by borrowing and re-investment, a shortfall was 'saved', i.e. lost to the circular flow of world income. This produced a recession in 1980–3 in the world economy with prices in general rising and the non-oil countries having an aggregate balance-of-payments deficit with the oil-producing countries.

These world recessions reduced international trade, reflected in the downturn in the demand for ships, steel, air transport, cars, etc. Thus all the major industrial countries have experienced a rise in unemployment.

Although the world economy has subsequently recovered the problem now (1987) presents itself to Britain in a modified form. Since 1985 the British annual average rate of growth of 3.5 per cent has exceeded that of other countries. Thus while Britain is likely to increase imports, increasing exports to pay for them becomes relatively more difficult.

Unemployment and Wage Rises

Until 1980 manufacturers were able to compensate for increased costs by raising prices. The Thatcher monetarist policy, by squeezing AD, prevents this. Instead employers, faced with a squeeze on profits, have had to show greater resistance to wage demands, reducing output and shedding labour in response to wage increases.

To a large extent the implications of this change in government policy have now been recognised by organised labour. Demands for wage increases have moderated. Moreover the elimination of over-manning produced increased productivity of some 4 per cent per annum, but the extent to which wage increases can be absorbed in this way in the future is limited. It is unlikely that improved labour productivity will be sufficient to sustain annual increases in real earnings in manufacturing of around 6.5 per cent, and since 1985 the increase in labour costs per unit has accelerated from 3.5 per cent to 5 per cent – higher than that of our competitors.

There is evidence that, in broad terms a 1 per cent change in the average level of real earnings will in time make a difference of 0.5 to 1.0 per cent in the level of employment in the UK. This means that if average earnings are kept in line with price rises (instead of rising by 3 per cent more), something like $1\frac{1}{2}$ million extra jobs would be created over three years, and these would be in addition to those created as the economy expands and supply-side measures bear fruit.

Unemployment and the Structure of British Industry

The danger of over-emphasising the effect of 'monetarism' on the level of unemployment is that it may divert attention from Britain's basic problem – the structural weaknesses of the industrial sector through low productivity, lack of growth and the decay of the old basic industries.

Growth in British industry is essential to raise living standards and employ the proportionately larger working population produced by increased female participation and the high birth rates of the late 1950s and early 1960s. Yet growth has been limited by lack of investment – the result of 'stop–go' policies, the diversion of resources to the public sector, the failure to develop export markets, and the reluctance to change the structure of British industry. It is the latter which is the long-term unemployment problem. Without such a change it has been estimated that unemployment could still be around 3 million in 1990.

Until the 1960s the older basic industries – coal, steel, shipbuilding, textiles, engineering and vehicles, on which Britain's nineteenth-century prosperity had been based – were fully employed in making good the shortages created by the war. But there emerged newly industrialised countries of the Third World (e.g. Brazil, South Korea and Taiwan), while others grew rapidly (e.g. Japan). These adopted new techniques, and Britain lost its early comparative advantages in production. Management was slow to revise the methods which had served so well in the past. Governments seeking a policy that would allow long-term industrial change without causing short-term political embarrassment, continued to support these industries with generous subsidies. As a result, resources were diverted from the new and expanding industries.

Britain's task is to identify and develop those industries which have a high income-elasticity of demand – especially those which can keep down import penetration, and at the same time, increase exports, e.g. chemicals, soap and detergents, industrial plant and electrical engineering, aerospace, electronics. It is noticeable that, even in the world economic recession of 1980–2, the last four more than held their own in export markets.

The income from North Sea oil allows this revitalisation of British industry to be accomplished without any serious lowering of living standards. Furthermore it seems that in recent years, workers and employers have adopted a more enlightened approach as regards wage claims. We can illustrate this by examining what is happening in the field of microtechnology.

Microelectronic Technology and Employment

Microelectronics is electronics made small, both in size and cost. For example, the first European computer marketed in 1950 filled a room and cost £1 million at current prices. Today the electronic circuits used in basic units can be provided on one or more microchips $\frac{1}{4}$ " square. As a result, a microcomputer 30 000 times smaller than the European original costs around £200. This represents a technological revolution having widespread social and economic implications. Here we concentrate on its impact on jobs.

Concern has been expressed that the adoption of microelectronic technology will result in increased unemployment. But for the following reasons this need not be so:

1. It should result in cost reductions in many existing goods through greater reliability (e.g. there are no moving parts, as with electro-mechanical controls), higher-quality products, better working conditions (e.g. through the elimination of many dull and repetitive jobs on the assembly line) and improved stock control. Lower prices can bring many such goods, e.g. programmed dish-washers, video recorders, telephones and fuel-saving cars, within the range of more purchasers both home and overseas.
2. New jobs will be created in the electronics industry, e.g. designers, and in associated software, e.g. computer programmers.
3. The earlier replacement of machines to incorporate microelectronics will create work in the capital-goods industries.
4. Microelectronics makes possible the production of entirely new products, e.g. word processors and medical-diagnosis machines.
5. Many applications, e.g. stock control and production control, tend to reduce capital rather than labour.
6. Increased wealth and shorter worker hours which are likely to result from the new technology should increase the demand for labour-intensive goods, e.g. arts and crafts and hotel and catering, and for services, e.g. hairdressing and entertainers.

Nevertheless there will be some job loss due to higher productivity or the outdating of existing products. In some cases this could be substantial and rapid. Yet it must not be overestimated. What is *feasible* can take time to become *economic reality*. While electronic components may be relatively cheap, the cost of the machinery which it controls can be very high, leading to a more gradual introduction. In practice, the balance between job creation and job displacement will depend on the extent to which industry invests in the new technology, the speed of change, the willingness of workers to acquire new skills and to change jobs, the extent of acceptance of a shorter working week and earlier retirement, and the intensity of overseas competition.

The latter is vital, for failure to exploit microtechnology would simply open the way to foreign competitors, thus providing a more serious threat to employment and the economy generally than the consequences of its adoption. The government can help by (*a*) promoting the retraining and education of workers in new skills; and (*b*) encouraging the application of the new techniques by providing technical advice and funding the cost of change, e.g. through its Microelectronics Industry Support Programme.

Index

481